Almost Heaven

by the Sea

CAROL COLEMAN

Order this book online at www.trafford.com
or email orders@trafford.com

Most Trafford titles are also available at major online book retailers.

Print information available on the last page.

ISBN: 978-1-4907-5490-1 (sc)
ISBN: 978-1-4907-5491-8 (hc)
ISBN: 978-1-4907-5492-5 (e)

Library of Congress Control Number: 2015901670

Trafford rev. 02/10/2015

www.trafford.com

North America & international
toll-free: 1 888 232 4444 (USA & Canada)
fax: 812 355 4082

Acknowledgements

I *wish to thank the following very special people,* as they have made writing this book possible: my husband Wally Coleman for his support through the three years that it took from concept to completion; Kathy Kali, Marcia Boettcher, and my daughter Glenda Peterson for their patience and skill in transcribing my very-challenging handwritten pages; my son Ronald Peterson for putting the pieces together so skillfully with his electronic genius; my son Patrick Yonally for his support; Ruth Miller, Ph. D., an author, futurist, new-thought minister for her support; Judy Ross Koral, for her willingness to share this creative journey.

A special thank you to my granddaughter Kayla McIguire, her friend Durham Allen, Tristra Trueheart, a special therapy dog, and Tristra's fortunate owner Sharon Watson for assisting me in the book cover photography.

The book's cover, ocean background art, by the author, and lighthouse art, by Wally Coleman, were skillfully woven together by my son Ron Peterson.

And a genuine thank you to many other supportive folks, too many to mention. It did take a village to write this book as well as the spiritual guidance gratefully received.

Prologue

I began these pages after spending several years with excuses as to why I couldn't. I was too busy. I wasn't a writer, couldn't use the computer, couldn't type, and had no idea as to what to write. Still, I strongly felt the persistent nudging to just sit down and write. So I did this with no conscious plot, outline, or characters, but facing just a blank piece of paper in a notepad.

Immediately the characters declared themselves. As I lost myself in this creative magic, the town emerged, and one of my favorite characters, Howdy, appeared. He took center stage as a brilliant example of unconditional love. He is a beautiful yellow Lab with a bit of Shepherd mix and a large supply of wisdom.

The town of Port Haven, Maine, a popular retreat for summer vacationers, began to be carved through defined patterns of living and a balance of work and human relationships. I observed the perfection of the inhabitants' smoothly ticking lives. This is a vibrant community that has thrived for at least eight generations. Their survival was dependent on a living philosophy based primarily on love. The foundation of this community was implemented in a cooperative, collaborative manner, resulting in a sustainable community model.

The primary character, Margaret Scott, is a thirty-three-year-old attractive librarian, poetess, and an active community member. She is a descendant of eight generations of Port Haven Scots. Her great-grandparents were world-traveled educators and historians. Her grandparents added to this background with a depth of knowledge in science, archeology, and philosophy. They were acquainted with the sorts of Kahlil Gibran, Albert Schweitzer, Mary Baker Eddy, and Baird T. Spalding, along with many others. From their relationships and connection with all of these great minds, the founders of the town were able to glean a powerful foundation for a community. Among the ideas they were exposed to and were able to utilize were a deep spiritual consciousness, a respect for human individuality based on a divine principle, consciousness of thought, health, honesty, love, and respect for one another. Port Haven has maintained basic values while also keeping up with the current trends and changes through the years.

The next character to evolve was Richard King, a strikingly handsome thirty-eight-year-old best-selling author. He arrived in this unique community for a three-day intensive, prearranged book-signing event at the library. This beautiful, old building is a major gathering place for residents of the community. The library also contains a book store and the Book Nook-coffee shop-bakery.

Richard, a widower, has recently discovered that he has a condition which will eventually lead to blindness. He decided that Port Haven would be a good place for him to stop, rest for a while, and perhaps rediscover himself. While arranging the book-signing responsibilities, he asked Margaret if she would be willing to assist him in finding a place to live, as he had decided to stay in the community for a while. And as fate would have it, Margaret had the perfect answer. She owned a guest-studio, which was quiet and had a magnificent ocean view. This turned out to be the perfect blend for the two of them.

Almost Heaven is a story of love, loss, and the ultimate discovery of paradise in this unique, creative haven in Maine.

"Good morning, Howdy. What a joy it is to awaken and see those amazing eyes quietly watching me with your paw on my pillow ever so gently. You are such a beautiful being. Yes, I know you want to eat and go for a walk. You know what? So do I. It's Saturday, our day of play. As if every day wasn't. Although one of us actually has to work. Oh my, what a look! I really did not forget that you are my assistant, and I also know that both of us love every minute of it.

"I do wish you would learn to make coffee, Howdy, my friend. Especially since you are always the first one to awaken. I do love our weekends. I have learned to rely on routine rituals and that kind of structure has been very necessary and predictable. However, Saturdays and Sundays are very special, and you, my friend, know very well that we do not get up at 6:00 a.m. on those days. Thank you for that.

"Howdy, let's walk into town, and I am going to have an exciting breakfast, maybe crepes with fruit and whipped cream or pancakes with our special maple syrup and Maine blueberries and ham and eggs. If I have all of that, we had better hike up to the lighthouse. As usual, you already have your leash and are waiting by the door. You silly creature, we never really use that leash. However, it certainly conveys a message. You are ready.

"What a perfect day in every way—great food, a beautiful autumn day, full of color, and, as always, that amazing mix of smells from the ocean. I am glad we decided to visit the lighthouse. I never tire of that and I know you don't. You always find new treasures to investigate. I love the way you chase the waves. However, I do get really cold on the way back. The fire feels so good. A great way to complete a perfect day."

*

Often Howdy goes to work with me. He is loved by everyone, especially the children. He has to be there during the children's story time. They take turns reading to him, and he always stays awake and often extends his paw to them when they finish. On those days, I take him for a walk at lunchtime. Everyone in town knows him so he would visit, while I sat in my favorite spot by the water.

I usually leave work by five, unless there is a special event planned, like on first Fridays the library stays open for evenings. Poetry night, with its poetry, art, music, wine, cheese, is very popular and always a lot of fun and not really like work at all. The other event, although not on a regular schedule, is where we host an author who does a book signing and sometimes have a discussion about the book. That was often a good time also. Although occasionally we would get one that we just wanted to get over with and get out; fortunately, that didn't happen often.

So after work, I go to the health center for a swim or an aerobic dance class, or Howdy and I take our favorite long walk to our special place. It is about a three-mile walk along the coastline up to the lighthouse. I don't know why, but there was seldom anyone there except during our summer tourist time. I always take a picnic for us while Howdy explored for the thousandth time. I could just get lost in my "daydreaming," currently called meditation. I never take any of my friends there. I love my quiet time—just the sound of the water and winds. The smells, ocean smells, wild flowers, smells from the village, were always a little different. Often there are thoughts about my parents, Chad, and the lovely memories. It is very special, and I love it.

Then I must have an action list. I check one thing off every day, for example, clean a drawer, vacuum, and so on. The list is part of my need for routine and order, but it works. Howdy and I have a few special TV shows. We watch very few. We usually listen to music or read; I always have a book. After all, it's my job.

*

It seemed he was always going to the next stop and never home because he didn't really have a home, and oh how he longed for that feeling again. He and Sylvia had such a great time finding that special place. Like so many other things, they both had the same dream home in mind. It was really a simple cottage, a quiet spot in a small village.

Enough space for both of them to have a studio, his for writing, hers for art, and then, of course, a small flower garden and an even smaller vegetable garden, large enough to be fun but small enough to enjoy.

As soon as they saw the cottage, after looking at so many places, they both instantly knew that this was home. There were so many wonderful memories, which were both a blessing and a curse. It truly was bittersweet. Everything could rush back in without a warning: a thing, a smell, a voice, a special floral arrangement, certain food, and teatime especially teatime. Every afternoon, we would both stop whatever we were doing and have tea, and some wonderful tea cookies, usually an English wafer. But the special and sweet part was the routine of sharing, taking time to really connect, and see each other and just listen.

What a gift we had: ten wonderful years of living life so fully and being loved so completely. We also shared a spiritual bond, both believing in a creator, the power of mind, choices, purpose of life, and the desire to fulfill our mission, which was pretty simple and covered by the ten commandments. As someone famous once said, all we need is love, and we had enough of that to go around.

Another thing we shared early in our relationship was a really big decision for both of us. We chose not to have children. There were many discussions. At times, either one of us would challenge the decision. We both loved children. We had nieces and nephews that we treasured and loved having them come and spend time with us, which they did every summer. After a few years of questioning ourselves, we were content with the decision and never regretted it.

Well, actually, after Sylvia's battle with cancer, I did question myself because I wanted a part of her to hang on to, and I mean literally hang on to. Because the *void* was so huge after her death that I didn't see how I could keep on breathing. Everything changed. The cottage was no longer home. The village became a strange place to be. I was a stranger wherever I went. Sylvia had been my best friend, my lover, my mentor, my everything. Oh, we had friends and were actually quite social, but the substance of my life was with Sylvia.

I eventually sold the cottage. It was like ripping out a part of my heart, but staying there was worse. I tried to have teatime. It was hell. I tried to visit friends. I had nothing to give. I tried going to our spiritual center, but I usually left early. I was truly a stranger in a strange land. I made this promise to Sylvia because it was so important to her and so hard for me. She wanted me to promise that I would find love again and live a full rich life. That is what she wanted for me, and I finally assured her that I would live for both of us. But I soon found out that I didn't know how to do that.

I was one of the walking dead. It was a year before I was able to think about writing. I don't remember much of that year. It was mostly filled with fog. I know I wandered, I drank too much, I felt so much anger—anger at myself for not spending more time with her, not realizing how very precious the moments were that we had and anger at her for leaving me, as irrational as that was and anger at couples that I would see that took each other for granted or envy for couples that were so engaged with each other and were oblivious to others.

Why me? Well, why the hell not me? You know, things happen. Eventually, I was able to start writing again, and then I became completely obsessed with writing. It wasn't the joy that it used to be, but I started having a lot of success. My first "best seller" was soon followed by another, and so forth. Then came the demand for me to travel and promote my best sellers. At first I thought why not? Then I found out "why not." It was a grueling, demanding life, especially when you really didn't want to smile and talk to stranger after stranger for hours. And then sometimes you got the opportunity to discuss your book with a group of people that you really would rather never see, much less listen to, as they discussed their version of your book. However, it kept my mind off my former real life, at least for a while. So I continued to write and promote and sometimes felt that strong emotion connected to my longing for home.

*

Margaret was preparing for a very special book-signing event. This author was pretty special. She had read all of his books, and he was her favorite author. There was something so passionate about his style of writing. She felt as though she knew him but not really. He was a very complex mystery, as were most of his books. She realized it was very silly of her to be so excited about a book signing. After all, it was a routine thing in her position. But yet, this was Richard King, and she was a fan.

Once she started reading one of his books, it was almost impossible to put it down. He had caused her many sleepless nights, and he would be right here in this very room next week. And, like it or not, she was excited as she also found his picture very intriguing. He was handsome, but there was so much more in those eyes. Yes, very silly. However, the emotions she was experiencing were disconcerting. She was used to everything being in control, and her mind was going in every direction and why? It was just another routine book signing, and she would prepare for it as she always did: get the newspaper article completed along with the picture she had just received with his press packet, post the flyers, send out the invitations, and prepare food for the reception. Just routine. But when she looked at that picture again, she could feel her pulse race and her face flush. She felt almost giddy. She had dated several people since Chad's death, but nothing serious ever, just friends, and certainly no racing pulse and flushed face. This could be embarrassing if not put into a professional perspective, which was exactly what she was going to do.

And then the telephone rang. It was after-hours, but she was there so she answered. This deep commanding yet gentle voice said, "Good evening, I'm so glad you are still there. This is Richard King."

Heart-pounding and voice shaking, I said, "Yes." And I just said "yes." He continued by asking for a favor. He intended to stay in Port Haven for a while and would need to find a studio. *Could I possibly give him some information about local accommodations?*

Fortunately my voice returned, and I was able to respond in what I hope was a reasonable tone. "Of course, I would be very happy to make some inquiries, and I do know of some possibilities." He gave me his phone number and thanked me very genuinely. He said how much he was looking forward to the book signing and his stay in our village. I, on the other hand, as I recall, had very little I was capable of saying: hopefully something appropriate. *Richard King is going to be living here in our town. I really must get myself under control. This is very silly.*

*

That certainly was an interesting phone call to the bookshop. I'm not exactly sure what was so different, but I do expect the Seascape to be somewhat unique according to all of the information I have gathered about the shop and the town. The library is not a run-of-the-mill library.

It sounds so warm and welcoming. Apparently, they do have a proper library where one may check out books. Then there is also a bookstore, where, of course, books can be purchased. And along with the coffee, tea, and pastry shop all combined as one, I find that quite appealing. And the descriptions I have of the town itself are actually intriguing. I haven't been interested in anything for so long. These feelings are actually quite strange but welcome. The voice on the phone, I believe, said her name was Margaret. She sounded so fresh and real. I certainly expect her to be pleasant to work with, and I am looking forward to her call about accommodations.

I was just beginning to feel alive again. Visiting my sister, niece and nephew, I actually had fun. Spent some time back in my hometown, and then the first time, I walked by our cottage, everything came back. I expected Sylvia to be waiting for me inside. The smells were familiar, and the flower garden was mature and beautiful. I could see Sylvia out there laughing, happy. It was probably only minutes that I stood there, frozen in time, but it felt like so much more. Finally, I walked on, and as I walked away from the cottage, I actually felt a sense of peace. I could feel that I was healing.

I visited with our friends, my sister and brother-in-law, and my almost grown-up niece and nephew. We had a big backyard barbeque like we used to, and I really enjoyed all of it: the people, the food, and the love and support. I'm sure it was always there, but I wouldn't be. Most of the folks were a part of the group from our spiritual center, which I had completely cut out of my life and replaced the love that Sylvia and I had shared with the anger I felt as I cared for and watched my brave beautiful wife literally wither away until there was a mere shell of what she had been. The one thing that never changed through her pain, the loss of her hair, her independence: she had never lost her spirit. She was complete love throughout the long transition from life to death. I can remember that now. What a relief. I can remember Sylvia with love, not clouded by anger or guilt.

Shortly after my visit, I noticed my vision was fine sometimes and other times I had to really focus to see clearly. I assumed it was one of those things that came with aging, and I may need to have glasses. Surely, I didn't look forward to that, but if so, best to get it over with. I was able to get in for a routine exam very quickly. After the exam, my doctor said there were some changes that he wasn't comfortable with, and he referred me to a specialist. He called before I left the office and arranged an appointment for the following week. I had a really busy schedule and was getting ready to do another book tour, so I was actually glad he was in such a hurry to have this visit. I thought he was doing it because he knew my schedule and was accommodating. I really didn't feel a sense of urgency myself. I went to the specialist fully expecting, if anything, perhaps a small adjustment—some eye drops or something like that. After all, I was physically very healthy, and I was emotionally healthier than I had been for the past three years or so.

After the exam was the consultation when this very pleasant physician told me I was losing my sight, and there really wasn't anything they could do about it. Wow! What a shock! He said the good news was that it was a very slow process. "No one knows exactly because it is rather unique, and varies with the individual, and of course perhaps something will become available." I remembered "research" and "hope" and "acceptance": scattered words, but what I heard clearly was that I was becoming blind.

Come on, God! This isn't funny. I'm finally beginning to be grateful for being alive, and actually feeling and seeing things again, like sunsets, and the wind, hearing the birds, being with people, even beginning to see the difference between women and men again and knowing that was healthy. The possibility of having a real relationship had recently entered my thoughts. And now this.

∗

Well, I am feeling very silly. I have so much to do, and I also remember promising Mr. King, which is what I have decided to call him and I think of him that way. I believe keeping my routines and professionalism will allow me to establish rapport and a realistic friendship. I have so much room in my home.

When my mother and father bought this house, it was with the expectation of having a large family, but as it turned out, it was only I, and usually half of the community. Both of my parents were activists, involved in politics, community events, charity balls, and our home was the center of the universe. After their deaths, I decided to accept the position of library director, which had been my mother's position, and it was also my dream to be one. My mother always wanted me to work with her. We were actually best friends, and I knew I could learn so much.

People loved to volunteer because she was such an inspiration and truly respected. She valued everyone, and in turn, she was a magnet for good. It was a very good thing that I have never tried to step into her shoes. She never expected me to either. She encouraged me to be my own person and so did my dad. They were the perfect couple. Oh, they had discussions; they were both intelligent and passionate. I think that was what made it work. They became better people together than they were individually and yet kept their very definite opinions and personalities. I am such a fortunate person to have had them for as long as I did.

They were so proud of Chad and me. At our graduation, they spent several days in town, and we really showed them the town. They were interested in everything: the museum, concerts, walking trails, and, of course, the excellent food. Chad and I originally expected to return home with them and start planning our wedding. But by then Chad had decided he really needed to do a military tour. I understood but certainly didn't like the idea. We decided to rent a car and take a road trip before he had to report for duty. Mom and Dad were planning to do some sightseeing on the way back home. So we went our separate ways after many hugs and kisses and happy trails talk. It was our second night on the road when I got the phone call that my parents had both been killed in a car accident. Just like that. The driver in the other car had gone to sleep, and it was a head-on collision. The doctor that talked to me said it was instant for both of them.

My life had changed completely. I thank God for the numbness and the out-of-body experience. Howdy stayed by my side. He was patient with me, but after a week or so of me staying in bed, he began to gently nudge me until I was on the edge of the bed, and he actually nudged me out of bed a couple of times. Then he would get his leash and bring it to me. He helped me get into a routine. I knew I made decisions: I fed Howdy, took him for walks, went through the days, and developed routines. Grief is, I'm sure, experienced in individual ways. Fortunately, I don't remember the days, weeks, even months after my parents died. Chad was there with me, thank God, for three months, so together we created routines, which I guess I have pretty much followed ever since. At first, the house and gardens were completely overwhelming. My parents always made sure everything was taken care of. Oh, I had responsibilities, but comparably speaking, they were nothing.

Before Chad left, he found a young man, Sam who was in high school. He needed the work and was capable of doing it. So by the time Chad left, the young man was well-trained and what a blessing that was. The library board met, and after a month or so, they called me for a meeting. I assumed it had something to do with my mother, but it actually did. They wanted me to take over the director's position. At first I said, I couldn't possibly. I had not been trained. They reminded me that I had volunteered there for years and that my mother cut me no slack. I actually had done everything in all departments, and of course, my degree was based on my desire to do just what they were offering. I expressed my gratitude for the offer, but I needed some time to think about it, which they graciously granted. It was exactly what I had planned to do. But my mother would have mentored me. Dare I do this? It was like my mother's strong voice saying, "Dare you *not!*" Yes was my answer, and I have never looked back.

*

I love my home, my Howdy, my job, my community, and my spiritual center. What more could I possibly want, and yet there was a void. I knew I wanted something like my parents had—love, that special love, the kind that Chad and I had for such a short time. I have many friends and a wonderful community. I am so thankful to my ancestors and their friends for leaving such a legacy as this community.

Oh well, every day is rich and full. I am a very grateful person, as well I should be. Oh yes, Mr. King. I really need to check out some accommodation options for him today. I know he expects my call. I do also have that studio that hasn't been used for anything really. It was my mother's getaway place, but mostly it was for guests, and they loved it. The view is spectacular. It is complete, very quiet and comfortable. I think realistically I should at least let him know it is one of the options. That is, if Howdy agrees. He is a very loving dog, but he responds differently to individuals, and I can tell immediately what his opinion is. So Mr. King will first be screened by Mr. Howdy before I mention the cottage.

*

My mother had started an effort to make sure that every pet had a loving family. There was a lady that lived in town that had the perfect spot to accommodate the plan and quickly agreed to be the interim host for animals in transition. So the Kiwanis club built kennels in her backyard and also a beautiful dog run. The 4-H club youth assumed the role of feeding, cleaning, and loving the animals. The Rotary Club assumed financial responsibility for expenses and the town veterinarian devoted his services. There were never many animals at one time and often there were none. My mother's philosophy was that pets were here as teachers to humans. They were the epitome of unconditional love and that is the greatest gift of all. As I watched the community come together for this project and how the children responded to the animals, everyone, including me, understood what she meant. We had never had a pet. We were a very busy family. But the first Xmas Eve I was home from college, my mother and father said we were going to add another member to the family. My God! I thought my mother was pregnant. So great was my relief when they laughingly explained we were going to get a rescue dog. There were several at the animal hotel. And my mother's goal was that all of them would find a home by Xmas. So we went to the hotel, and there were several beautiful dogs: a couple of pups, and one older dog, and several semi-adult ones. My mom and dad were running around talking to all of them. This one young golden Lab had been looking at me very intently. I went over to him (I swear it looked like he was grinning), and as I knelt down, he raised his paw to shake. So the name "Howdy." Mom and Dad saw what was happening, and we had our dog, or he had us, I have never been sure. He was just instantly a part of the family. It was a great Xmas, and thank God, he was there to help me though my darkest days.

I find myself waiting for the phone to ring. I really expect Margaret to call me back, although actually it's only been twenty-four hours since I talked to her, and I really do have a lot to do before arriving at Seascape. I love that name and all of the images that I have created surrounding it. I have no idea why I feel this strong compelling drive to spend time there. The brochures have been very informative, the pictures are perfect, and I'm sure the information that I get from Margaret will be fantastic, but it's more than that. I am a driven man. I could blame it on my condition. I don't know what else to call it but condition. Fortunately there hasn't been anyone that I needed to discuss it with. And strangely enough, I am either in deep shock, or I am managing quite well with the reality of impending blindness. I practice from time to time, just closing my eyes and using my other senses, and it is quite interesting. My mind becomes very alert. I can identify many odors that I really wouldn't ever have noticed before. I can hear the wind and leaves and people walking and dogs barking. I can tell what kind of bark it is: happy, sounding an alarm, curious, greeting. I have never even thought about a dog barking. It was just noise. I feel the sun and smell the rain. Blindness is certainly not something I am looking forward to, but I am not depressed, or fearful. I'm sure I have a little anger and frustration; there's still so much I want to do. I would love to have a partner and travel and most of all have a home. I can actually say that I mean it. I still love my Sylvia completely and treasure what we had, and that is a key word: what we "had." It is time for me to live fully again, and I just refuse to let the idea of blindness blind me from experiencing life and all that there is to discover.

I have a deep feeling of faith in my future which is very reassuring. I am excited about this book tour, not just because it may be my last one but because I sense it is the beginning of a fresh new chapter in my life and I so welcome it. I find myself being grateful most of the time for something or anything or everything. I really don't think I have ever felt life in the moment before. I treasure the moments.

I am so glad I decided to keep my car. Initially, I thought I would sell it and fly to Port Haven, but fortunately, I realized I was over-reacting. My vision is fine right now, and may be for many years. I want to pass through all of the little towns, see the countryside, stop at quaint shops, and follow the smells to bakeries, fish and chips, coffee shops, everything. However, since I am driving, and expect to do it rather slowly, I will have to leave this week. I don't think I told Margaret that I was on a rather tight schedule. If she hasn't called back by tomorrow I will need to call her. I wish she had a shorter name than Margaret. Somehow that seems so formal, and she just doesn't sound like a Margaret. Now that's rather presumptuous of me, never having met the lady. I know nothing about her, and I'm analyzing her name. Sorry, Margaret. I have a real strong sense of what I am looking for in the way of accommodations. I probably should just wait and see, but I have this vision of a cottage, very cozy. The most important part to me is the view: lots of windows, close to town but not crowded. I really do not want a room in someone else's house. I know I did not share a lot of this information with Margaret. So it is really important that I call her in the morning. It's not fair to have her wasting time, gathering information for me without knowing that I do have some specific ideas about my home.

*

I have made several inquires regarding Mr. King's request, and of course, the town is buzzing. It was exciting having him here for a reception, book signing and discussion. Now that the word is out that Richard King is going to be staying in town, excitement reigns, and options of accommodations are coming from every direction, literally. Although most of them I think I can screen out quickly, like Mary Dobbs a great lady but very lonely, loves to talk given the opportunity. She is a great volunteer here. She comes in at least an hour before we open and starts baking, and by the time the doors open people are waiting to see what Mary has created: the smells of the coffee and apple raisin bread (her family recipe) and all of the other special cookies, breads, and pastries. It was "Mary's Kitchen," and that is its name. When Mary is baking, she is completely focused on what she is doing and is very content.

She has a garage apartment, nice enough but right in town, and I doubt that Mr. King needs mothering. So I'll mark that one off.

Betty Jo Morton's offer is a possibility. Betty Jo is a very reserved lady. She has been a volunteer here at the library for a very long time. When I was in high school and volunteering here, she was my mentor-trainer and very good at her job. She checks books in and out and puts them back on the proper shelves and has a system for everything and is extremely efficient. She has a studio that is attached to her home by a breezeway with a nice backyard flower garden, and she is a very quiet person. However, there is a school almost next door and that could definitely be a distraction. So I guess I will screen her out, and all of the many people who want to rent him very special accommodations, such as a very large bedroom in their house. The more I sift through these options the more I am sure that my cottage is right for him (if Howdy agrees). Although I really want him to have more than one option, this is taking more time than I anticipated, and I'm sure he is wondering why I haven't called him back.

I do have one possibility, a Mrs. Florence Newberg. She is rather new in town. I have met her, but I really don't know her. The information she left looks pretty good: a studio, quiet, comfortable, good view, and about a mile from town. It actually sounds a lot like mine. As I recall, she is a widow, a rather striking lady, reserved, probably a no-nonsense person. She hasn't made efforts to be a part of the community yet. She has no interest in volunteering or joining any organizations. She has stopped by several times to have coffee and delicate pastries, and she purchased several books. She is always alone and appears to prefer it that way. Yes, I definitely will add her to the list, which at this point, is a list of mine and hers. I do wish I could find at least one more. I don't want him to think I am expecting him to accept the cottage. Why am I being so silly about this? I am a sensible, responsible person. My cottage is available and is just one of the options for him to choose from. It's really very simple, and it is his choice. So there. I have put that in perspective. Now I really do want one more choice and then I can call him.

Silly me, of course there is another choice, and it may be the perfect one for him. Mr. and Mrs. Jessup's caretaker's cottage: they don't use it anymore. They have a gardener that comes in to work two to three times a week. The cottage is quaint and comfortable, and the gardens are beautiful. It's a short distance to town, and the Jessups are delightful people. Finally, the task is done. I can let that go and move on to the many other things to do on my list. First is to call Mr. King and let him know that there are three options, and he can decide when he arrives. I do not choose to tell him one of them is mine. He will have to be screened by Howdy before I make that decision. And now the call. Why do I feel so out of control? I want to call, and yet I don't trust myself to be what? Perfect? Professional? This is something I have done many times—making arrangements for authors. It's part of the job.

Well, I called, and was both pleased and disappointed that I had to leave a message. Mr. King was not available. At least he has the information now.

So my responsibility is over. We'll see what happens. But first things first. Back to the check-off list. Things to do for the big event: Mr. Richard King, best-selling author, we will be ready for you.

*

A telephone message from Margaret, and now her line is busy. Of course, I go out for a run which turned out to be a brisk walk. Really out of shape. That's something I am looking forward to. A bit of a routine. I have been traveling for so long. I have forgotten what free time and familiarity feel like. I have very ambitious expectations: exploring the town and the many cluster towns that are close by. I am actually having dreams about the beauty of the coastline, the fishing villages, and the people I have yet to meet. Sometimes I'm not sure if I'm awake or asleep. It's one of the maladies of a writer, at least this writer. Well, I'm certainly not going to leave the house again until I have been able to reach Margaret. I have a long list of to-do things, but they can wait. My next priority is to have a cup of tea and calm my brain. It's working overtime and not very productive. It is nice to have tea without the sharp stab of pain that comes with memory of another life. Fortunately, that is turning into a very pleasant feeling, comforting and familiar. I can remember Sylvia's smile and genuinely smile back with a feeling of gratitude and not pain. I have seen a young man with a dog several times on my walks. They seemed to be having a great time together. Maybe I should be thinking about getting a dog. Realistically someday, I will need one. Something to think about after I get my new home and my new life. Maybe I should tell Margaret about the possibility of a dog. That may make a difference in choices. No. I think my mind is moving too fast. Better slow down and take a breath. One step at a time.

The telephone is calling me. Now who could that be?

"Hello, Margaret. I'm so sorry I missed your call earlier. So pleased to hear your voice, and I assume you have good news. Three choices? I think I was hoping for one! Just kidding. I think that is wonderful, and I'm sure I will be delighted with any of them. I really appreciate your kindness. I know you are a very busy person, and this is above and beyond the call of duty. Perhaps I can take you out for dinner some evening. You can introduce me to your favorite restaurant, and I will again be grateful. I do hope you will have the time to take me or at least guide me to the cottages. I have reservations at the Haven House Hotel for three nights. That will allow time for the business part to finish. I'm sure I can extend my time at the hotel if that would be helpful. I certainly don't expect you to overextend yourself. I am sure your schedule is already quite full. The good news is that I'm not going anywhere, and my time will be well-spend just soaking up the newness. There is so much that I want to see and do. By the way, do you happen to have a dog?"

"That's fantastic. I'm looking forward to meeting him. Perhaps he could show me around! Just joking. I would definitely prefer to have you do that. My goodness! I have taken up so much of your time, and you are so gracious, and I am so grateful for your help. I will keep in touch. By the way, I am driving, and I do want to enjoy the sights along the way, so I don't expect to arrive until the night before the first scheduled event. But I will be there bright and early and ready to be charming. As long as it's in short sessions, I can manage. Again thank you, and I'm looking forward to actually meeting you and your town and, of course, your dog and my new lease on life. Until then, good-bye, Margaret."

My goodness, I didn't even give her a chance to really answer anything. I just couldn't keep from talking, and generally, I am a good listener. Writers need to be good listeners. I really blew that. She probably thinks I'm a madman, and perhaps she is right. No, I'm really not a madman, at least not anymore. I am a very happy man, and she sounds like the kind of person who can understand that. I can't believe I asked her if she had a dog. What kind of question is that? Certainly not one I have ever asked before. But the young man and dog this morning definitely made an impression on me. Now it's time to get back to the list.

What an interesting, and different, conversation. Mr. King was actually exuberant. I have never had a conversation like that with any author I have worked with. They have generally been rather reserved and all business, at least on the phone, but certainly not Mr. King. He seems to say what he is thinking without a pause. I am more curious than ever to meet him. It really does feel like I know him. He is so excited about our town.

I am remembering why I have always known this is exactly where I want to be. When I was in college, most of my friends were so excited about getting away from home and leaving their hometowns, and I, on the other hand, was so smug in my satisfaction of returning to my real life, home, and hometown. Even after my folks' death, I never considered leaving my home, and I have never had a regret. I love to travel, but I am always so happy to get home. I have always loved to tell people where I am from. When I say Maine, there is such a feeling of pride, and then I go off on this endless discussion of picturesque New England towns with whale-watching, fishing villages, snug harbors, and its wide Atlantic beaches, historic towns, which mine is, of course. The striking seascapes inspired my mother and her committee to name our cozy library-coffeehouse 'Seascape'. These quaint villages have probably the most photographed lighthouses anywhere. The seafood is indescribable. Everyone knows about our Lobster. But not everyone knows about our equally famous blueberries Maine produces tons of them, and they are another of my favorite foods. Mr. King just reminded me of all this and more. He will experience it for the first time. What a joy to be reminded of why my life is so full and to experience that fresh feeling of gratitude that I sometimes forget to express.

Yes, indeed I am looking forward to next week and sharing the experience of rediscovering my town and perhaps extending the boundaries to include some very interesting neighboring towns. I am certainly taking a lot for granted. The man just asked for some suggestions regarding living accommodations, and here I am acting like a silly girl with a crush on a movie star. I am certainly not a silly girl, and Mr. King is not a movie star. He does sound like a very nice man, and I have seen his pictures. Unless they are greatly enhanced, he is drop-dead handsome. I wonder what his story is. He is thirty-eight years old and not married. So the obvious question would be "what is wrong with him?" Well now, isn't that interesting. He's thirty-eight and not married. I am thirty-three and not married, so what the hell is wrong with me? Why must something be wrong with someone just because they're not married? There are as many reasons as there are people, just like everything in life. Why do we insist on labeling everything? I am going to reserve judgment.

After all, the bottom line is Howdy. I can totally rely upon his judgment, primarily because he doesn't prejudge people. He takes them as they come and responds to the moment. Sounds so simple. At least I can give it a try. Very interesting that Mr. King asked if I had a dog. I did visit Mrs. Newberg's cottage. What an experience! I am aware that she chooses to keep her distance and is definitely not interested in socializing. But when she answered the door, I swear I could feel the cold air circulating around me. She was cordial, and she knew why I was there, and we had a proper appointment. After opening the door, there was an awkward silence, as I stood outside, and she stayed inside. I mean, after you say hello, what can you follow that with. We had a telephone conversation, clarifying interest in the cottage and my role in that, and a time was agreed on, and here I was, standing outside, just waiting. It seemed like a very long time, but probably only minutes, when she finally said, "The cottage is around to the right side of the house. I have left it open for your inspection," and then closed the door. I'm not even sure she actually ever said hello. I am intrigued. I have never met anyone like her.

Our community is pretty open and friendly, and we get quite a variety of summer visitors, but they are usually very happy to be here, and we are happy to have them. We never call them tourists. They are always warmly welcomed as friends. Our town knows that the summer folks help to keep our village healthy and well. But this lady must have some very deep pain to deal with. I am not sure what I can do about it, but I wish her well and make an extra effort to smile at her when she comes to the shop. The cottage is nice, actually very pleasant—a little larger than mine and the view is great. I believe it definitely meets the criteria for Mr. King. But I really don't think it is right for him. It feels cold. However, that will be his decision, not mine. I probably should bring Howdy out here to check it out. That was not a kind thought. I know Mrs. Newberg is allergic to animal hair. She has informed me, quite clearly, that Howdy should not be in the library. She is the only one that has ever complained; 99 percent vote for Howdy and they show it. So I have a little prejudice that I need to work on. I guess I'm not perfect. God, I guess you're not through with me yet. Enough of this. Time to get to the list.

*

Countdown time. I am really excited about this trip. I have read every travel magazine about the entire State of Maine. Salivated while reading the famous seafood recipes and about the fabulous chefs. Want to visit and photograph every lighthouse, especially the Nibble Lighthouse in York and the Lindy Harbor, maybe even go deep-sea fishing. I've never done that. I've written about it, but like so many things I've written about, it's primarily based on research armchair travel. This time, I want to freely see, smell, and touch. Oh my God! A flash of Margaret just passed through my mind. I am probably going crazy. Maybe there is a tumor in my brain, and they just didn't find it. I am definitely experiencing a life change. I like it.

Back to my fantasies about Maine. I had a preconceived idea that folks were tight-lipped, reserved, unfriendly, and, in general, thought if you weren't a generational New Englander, you weren't worth their time. As I read about and talked to folks that have lived there, or do live there, my opinion is quickly changing. However, I do not want my expectations to get too unrealistic. I want to just be open and ready to be there and accept things as I find them. That is a goal; I may or may not reach it. My excitement is running high. Tomorrow is the big day, a life-changing day. I am looking forward to the book signing: the discussion and, of course, selling books. And more than that, I am looking forward to meeting Margaret and seeing the town through her eyes: meeting people and finding my new home. I am really looking forward to that. I am ready for a daily dose of ocean fun and visiting the tranquil scenes at the Rachel Carson Wildlife Refuge, going antique-looking, and seeking blueberry things—pies, cakes, pancakes, muffins. Then I also plan on going to Summer Theater.

Things, so many things, but first just basking in the sunshine, smelling the flowers, and not writing, not thinking about deadlines or book tours, or "Will I capture that next chapter?" I am very tired, that bone-tired feeling. Going too long on fumes. Not eating right, very little exercise, very little fun. I haven't even seen my sister and her husband and my niece and nephew. They often spent the summers with Sylvia and me. It seems so long ago, and now they are becoming teenagers. I really love that beautiful family. I don't keep in touch too often. I get cards and messages and most of the time, I forget to even reply. But no more. I will have time, and my priorities are becoming very clear, and they are right up there. I will call my sister in the morning and share the good news with her. I know they thought I would go into a deep dark funk about my eyesight, understandably. I definitely will keep in touch, maybe even learn to Skype. Maybe. I do want them to know I am doing well. I know my life is a gift, and I intend to live it as such every day. I am ready to leave in the morning. I probably should go ahead and leave now because I may not sleep very much.

✳

Three days to go, and task list was looking good. I have never been so obsessed with a book signing before, also never so excited. But then again, so is the entire town. I would be concerned for Mr. King's privacy, but we are used to celebrities, politicians, VIPs from everywhere, and life continues as usual with friendly recognition and respect. Once in a while, other visitors can be a little rude, but we maintain a safe place for people to visit and privacy is respected. The three-day event is always a flurry of activity and an appropriate time and place for folks to get their book autographed and curiosity appeased. After that, Richard has agreed to do a special reading program for the children. I forgot, for a moment, I meant to say Mr. King. Also we have the big reception. I expect the town, visitors, and all to turn out, especially because word has traveled throughout the community that this famous, young, attractive best-selling author has chosen our town in which to spend an indefinite period of time.

Mary is in charge of the catering, so I really don't need to worry about that. She will have all of the best cooks in town assigned appropriately according to their specialties. Everyone contributes when we have a special event. Generally, we have a cookie contest. This time it will be a little different. We are hosting an informal open-house reception from 6:00 to 10:00 p.m., that is an hour longer than usual in order to accommodate the numbers expected, somewhere around a thousand folks. We will need at least that much time. Mary and I had better meet later today. I want to review her progress and make sure the cheese and crackers and fruit plates are on track. I know the punch and coffee and tea are fine. But this is a rather large event, even for a pro like Mary. I have ordered all the chairs available through the rental shop. Unfortunately, there are several weddings on the very same day. We actually couldn't have used many more anyhow. I am not a magician. This place is large, utilizing all three spaces. But I can't create a room stretcher so we will obviously have to manage with what we have.

The book signings usually go well. People are very patient and use the time to visit and read. We have never had complaints regarding book-signing events. The book discussion event was by first-come reservation, and that list is complete. Everyone knows by now whether or not they are on the list. So that should flow rather gently. I am so glad I scheduled the reception first, especially since Richard is arriving late the night before, or perhaps not until that day. I'm a little nervous about the timing and him driving without a real schedule. Oh well, he has been around the world, so I'm sure a few thousand miles shouldn't be a challenge. I have enough to keep myself busy. I don't need to think about his journey. I will have everything ready. The rest is up to him.

Oh, Howdy looks neglected, and why not. We have not been on our routine for several days. Now I realize just how wrapped up I am in all of this. Howdy and I need to clear our heads and get a little ocean spray. Beach sand on our feet, warm sun, and a walk up to the lighthouse will get us right back on track. It always does. I really need that quiet time to reenergize, clear my mind, and make sure I have a soundly based perspective before Richard arrives. I must remember to make an appointment tomorrow to get my nails done. Maybe I should get a facial. I haven't had one, but from what I've overheard, they are addictive. I really do need to get to my quiet spot and let all of this go.

"Howdy, let's go have fun, take a picnic, and run away." Up to the lighthouse we go!

*

What a magnificent trip. I am so glad I followed my instincts and decided on a road trip. I have looked a lot and seen little. All the travels but how much I have missed. I arrived at the destination and missed the journey. How in the world have I become a best-selling author? I know the years I had with Sylvia were very stimulating and exciting, and they were comfortable. I was successful, writing magazine articles for a living. I really had little ambition to write a book. Even now, the beauty of those memories are intertwined with sadness. I wonder sometimes which memories will endure. I really don't dwell on the past, but I also know that I can't and don't want to erase that chapter of my life. The sadness and the joy—they are all a part of who I am.

And who I am right now is a very hungry man, ready to go make some inquiries about the very best specialty the town chefs have to offer. I am running out of time to explore each town and every restaurant and museum and sometimes just listening to the folklore. I really thought I was through writing, but this trip has been so full of stories, colorful people, history, grand hotels, charming inns—a complete change of pace for me. I feel so much more alive now. My energy levels are amazing. I love walking and exploring places I could never see by car. However, unfortunately, my walking has not been able to keep up with my eating. I just want to taste all of the bakery specials. When I get to Port Haven, I will really get a routine and at least a bit of discipline. Day after tomorrow, I will arrive at my new destination, and believe me, I have enjoyed this journey immensely. My new camera and I can never capture on film the spectacular scenes and people that I have in my mind. I find myself thinking about painting. I'm sure Margaret will know some patient art teachers.

Poor Margaret! I don't think she knows she is inheriting a major project. I am really being presumptuous, assuming she will have time to do more than guide me through my three-day commitment and then escort me to the cottages. Oh yes, and we do have a dinner date. At least I think she accepted my invitation. As I recall, I really dominated that conversation. I'm not sure I gave her an opportunity to respond. I don't usually share that kind of emotional information. For some reason, I don't feel as though I need to be on guard with her. Well, we'll see, and soon. If my calculations and my GPS, which I detest but humbly admit I need on occasion, are correct, I may arrive early evening on Thursday. My first event is on Friday evening, and I would like to settle in at the hotel and at least locate the Seascape. I wouldn't expect Margaret to be there, if not, I'm sure I can wait until Friday morning to see her and Howdy. I will need to keep the meeting short unfortunately because I am sure she will be very busy making sure the details are all under control. I can use the time to make sure I am prepared. Once we get going, it sounds like a full schedule, which I love. Then the time I am so excited about—finding my new home at last.

*

Finally, the time has come. The atmosphere is amazing. It's as though a major holiday is approaching. Anticipation is mounting. There is electricity in the air. I thought it was just me and my silly schoolgirl crush on a stranger. Although, to be very honest, Richard does not seem like a stranger. He seems more like someone returning after an absence, and *his* town is preparing to welcome him back. I have never allowed my thoughts to be so uncontrolled. It's probably because my routine has been so erratic for the past several weeks. Poor Howdy, he has been so neglected. I simply have been so distracted, not to mention my work schedule, which is also out of control, and, along with that, all of the preparation for what promises to be a three-day extravaganza. It is also inventory time for the library and the book shop. Our audit is next month, and I have to present my budget for next year. Fortunately,

I know we are in excellent financial condition. It's still a major report to prepare; the board was very concerned about expanding the book shop and adding the Book Nook which was very simple initially.

Mary volunteered to make coffee, tea, and filtered water. Just a few tables, a book or magazine rack, and then it was blueberry bonanza time. So, of course, she had to start baking. At first, it was just her delicious blueberry muffins, but the people couldn't get enough, which was exactly what she needed to hear. Soon, very soon, we were the place to get those wonderful fresh homemade bakery specials.

So the Book Nook has taken on a life of its own, and Mary has brought her granddaughter in to help. She says she wants to teach her how to bake and how to welcome folks so they will always want to come back. Neither of them are paid, but I intend to have pay for them included in this budget. That little shop is making a very good profit, and they will be given recognition for it. My mother would be so proud of the changes that have been made. I know she had a vision of progress and having a place that always had an atmosphere of warmth and love in it, and that is exactly what we have. Mary's baking aromas filled the air along with the mixture of coffee, and scones, or whatever, along with every volunteer's warm greetings. So, of course, we are successful. Love is the answer. I am really looking forward to preparing my annual report and budget proposal. Just not this week.

Richard will be arriving tonight. When he called to check in, he thought he was approximately three to four hours away. So I won't be seeing him tonight, and I am a bit surprised that I am so disappointed. Although I really shouldn't be, I am tired, dirty, and probably don't smell like a rose. So yes, I will just be grateful that I can have a fresh start in the morning. I just remembered the tea-bag trick for my eyes which I'm sure could use a nice tea bag soak. I remember my mother used to do that. Oh my God! I'm turning into my mother. Also the lavender bath. I remember that wonderful smell, and tonight, I will stop by the boutique and get some special resurrection items. I need a miracle. I feel like I am about a hundred years old. I must remind myself, thirty-three, I am a vibrant young thirty-three-year-old lady. We are, after all, only meeting for coffee in the morning at the Book Nook, and it is a professional meeting simply to review the contract and confirm agreements. However, I feel like it's my first prom, and I can't decide what to wear or how to fix my hair and what shade of lipstick should I wear. I don't remember ever having this kind of confusion or concern.

Usually I just get out of bed and have a quick shower and a nice walk with Howdy. A routine breakfast, yoga, fix my lunch, and off to work. Why is this so much different? I may be having a midlife crisis although I certainly hope that half of my life is not over.

"Well, Howdy, at least you're the same—full of love and happiness. Good old steadfast Howdy. I promise after three more days, I will be back on routine, and you and I will have our sane and safe life back. Tomorrow, you will be meeting Mr. Richard King, and I expect you to do a complete appraisal of him, and let me know exactly what you think. I know you are total love, but you also have a fine gentlemanly way of sensing people and responding accordingly. So I will be watching you. OK, I know you just want to get out of here and do something. Anything, right? You are so patient with me, and I love you so much. Let's go walk to the beach on the way home, and you can play with the waves while I think about tomorrow morning."

*

Finally, here I am in Port Haven. I am not disappointed. I was up early and had time to wander a bit. I can smell the ocean, and there is so much variety—unique little shops, bakeries, and a cannery. I see stunning views and palatial homes, as well as modest cottages, all of them expressing a historic era. This hotel that I am staying in has beautiful artwork everywhere: sculptures, genuine antique furnishings, but so comfortable, not like a museum. When I arrived late last night, all of the staff was so accommodating. No, more than that. It was thoughtful. My wonderful feather bed was turned down. There was a pitcher of ice water, and yes, a special chocolate on my pillow. What I enjoyed most was the attentiveness. I got an offer for room service at that late hour. I was given a fantastic variety of information about local events, places to visit, restaurants, and sailing lessons. That one really got my attention. I used to have a recurrent dream about this beautiful harbor and a sailing boat that this gorgeous lady and I seemed to know how to sail, and sail we did. I had forgotten about that until I saw the brochure, and I believe I really do want to learn how to sail. First, I will go, but as a quest. All of the brochures were presented in such a warm way, not touristy, but like they were inviting a friend to share some adventures. Well, it is finally a decent time to go to the Seascape. I am anxious and reluctant. What if I have created a major fantasy about this great adventure, and the excitement about meeting Margaret? I will soon know. At the very least, I will have completed my tour and can spend some time without a deadline pressure and have no excuse about painting or sailing or just being.

*

Here we are. The Seascape, what a wonderful building! It looks like a grand old mansion. I can see how it can be combined into a library, bookstore, and Book Nook. I have never had a book signing in such a fascinating place. Usually, they are all pretty straightforward and stark but not this one. It has a beautiful archway covered with jasmine, how nice. And what a massive front porch. It has columns. I love this place, and I haven't even been inside. I can hardly wait to see inside. It has a lot to live up to. Oh yes! And it does. What is that heavenly aroma? Coffee, for sure, homemade cinnamon rolls, maybe? The rooms are massive. Margaret said we would meet in the Book Nook Bakery. I know I can find my way there. I just need to follow the aroma. And there is Margaret, I am sure.

"Good morning, Mr. King. Welcome to our community."

When we shook hands, his fingers wrapped around mine like a familiar warm blanket. I found myself blushing and quickly looked away. You are acting like a silly schoolgirl. I reminded myself of why we were meeting. I looked up and saw that he had looked down as well. *Had he felt what I had?*

"Mr. King, would you like some coffee. Mary has made a cinnamon roll special, and I do hope you like blueberries because they are in almost everything."

"Yes, I love blueberries. That is the primary reason I chose Maine," he said with a bit of a mischievous grin.

I am relaxing. He has such a reassuring presence. As his warm brown eyes looked into mine, I felt a definite sensation that I had not felt for a very long time. As we sat outside in the garden sipping our coffee and sharing one of Mary's huge cinnamon rolls, I remembered that I had the information packet and terms of agreement forms, which was the reason for this meeting. As we reviewed the sequence of events, Richard, as he insisted I call him, was very animated about everything I had planned, especially the children's event. This was where he would answer questions, tell stories, and be very informal as it is generally with children. It was obvious that he was going to have fun.

"Margaret, I am so grateful to you for arranging all of this. You have absolutely gone above and beyond any expectations I could possibly have. How can I repay you? Oh yes, there is the dinner I promised. I do hope you will have time for that. I have really been looking forward to being able to spend some time together just talking, no business interference. I want us to take the time to get to know each other."

"I am looking forward to sharing my very own special restaurant with you, of course, a favorite of mine and about thirty other folks. It is a small, out-of-the way place, very casual. The food is unforgettable and so is the view, and that's all I will tell you about that now. Because I have a long list to check off before 5:00 p.m. If you wish, you would be welcome to come a little early and I can give you a brief tour. And tomorrow, we will have more time between events. By the way, I think you know the reception is open-house style from five to eight. What you may not know is we are expecting to have approximately two thousand folks come through during that time. So charge your batteries. You're going to need them. I will look forward to seeing you around four if that works for you."

"Margaret, you are everything I thought you would be. Yes, I will be here at four, and I will be looking forward to it from now until then. And by the way, when do I get to meet Howdy? I expected him to attend the meeting."

"Oh, Richard, you will meet Howdy. He will be the tour guide this afternoon."

*

What an enchanting lady Margaret is—beautiful and poised. I loved watching her respond earlier to the many folks asking questions or clarifying some task. She was always clear and gentle. I have absolute respect. Time flew by as we sipped our coffee, and chatted in a strangely familiar way, and still accomplished all of the paperwork that generally I detest doing.

I have developed a thing for coffee. My morning coffee is a private ritual, a peaceful little space of time that gives my day structure. The very aroma of fresh ground coffee carries with it a reassurance, warmth, comfort—a certain kind of intimacy. But I really enjoyed sharing coffee time with Margaret. We were actually also sharing thoughts, which happened so naturally.

I didn't spend any time analyzing what was going on, as is my habit. I know that often keeps me from being in the moment, which is one of the many things I am here to review. I am committed to increased awareness of life in the moment.

Sharing that indescribable cinnamon roll with the sweetest most robust blueberries was an experience itself, and Mary, that delightful lady that bakes with the main ingredient all the same and that is love, was obviously so happy to see the expression on my face. I couldn't help but be humbled by her gift. I think she was being very honest about no one ever expressing her baking as a gift. Every bite was like a celebration and certainly to be remembered. She will go in my daily diary. After Margaret, of course.

Is love at first sight possible? I don't even really know Margaret and yet when we met and I took her hand, it was like coming home. So exciting, and yet familiar. I guess safe or secure would best describe it. I'm sure it must have been only seconds, but time literally stood still. And yet I felt no awkwardness, and I sensed that she was experiencing a connection as well. I came away from our meeting feeling refreshed, feeling as though I had been understood, and even now, I feel very relaxed and eagerly looking forward to this evening and of course meeting my tour guide Howdy and seeing Margaret again and of course enjoying the reception although I am a little awed at the thought of an intimate reception of over two thousand folks. I have spoken to many more from a stage, but not on a one-on-one level. Oh well, as I think Margaret would say or perhaps really did say, it's only one at a time. And I am very confident if she sees me needing to be rescued, she will certainly know how to do that. So not to worry. I am very glad to have some time today to explore the town. I just want to walk slowly with no destination in mind, although I do remember seeing some information on a lighthouse. That sounds like a perfect place to be. I think I will pick up something to take with me, and perhaps after the walk, I will feel like having a picnic. Although I am sure the cinnamon roll will still dominate my taste buds.

I do need some time to let the morning emotions be mixed with perspective. I don't want to presume too much too soon, but what I do know is that I definitely want Margaret and me to be friends. I find myself wondering what she's doing right now. Whatever it is, I'm sure she is gently but surely directing and inspiring everyone to move in the same direction. How do I know that? What do I really know? What I really know is that a walk to the lighthouse is a good thing.

*

Mr. King has arrived, and even with my imagination running at top speed, I still could not have imagined how our first meeting would be, from the first look into the very soul of the man, to the warm comforting hand shake. It was not really a hand shake. It was like hands melting into each other. Oh, I am definitely not disappointed in Richard, and I really can't imagine calling him Mr. King again, although I will have many more opportunities the next few days with so many introductions. My coffee was so much more than a simple beverage. It was like the rich smell and warmth encouraging us to share thoughts. Our easy conversation was strung together with slow thoughtful sips.

I know I came away from that meeting feeling refreshed, knowing my thoughts were understood and valued. And now I am thinking poetic. "What a thing friendship is, world without end! How it gives the heart and soul a stir-up!" (Robert Browning) I have completely neglected my poetry. I used to spend so much time reading and got so much comfort from poetry, especially after my mother's and father's death and then Chad. I am so grateful that I had my love for poetry, which for me is very spiritual, and of course my constant companion Howdy. I have been so busy, or lazy, for a long time. Very complacent.

But today, my soul really got a stir-up. It's interesting how you can believe you understand something and even appreciate it until something happens and it's like an epiphany, when the meaning becomes so much more. Well, this is wonderful, but I do have a lot of things to do. And I will just have to get started and go down the list.

I know everyone has their assignments and generally follow through very well. But once in a while, there are a few missteps, and that's my job, setting them back on track. And this is the largest event we have had, and I have been pretty clear that we really want it to be a reception that the town can be proud of.

Thank God for Mary and her crew. I just went over her check-off list which is a very high priority. Sure enough, everything has been ordered, except of course her specialty surprise. She won't even tell me what it is. I know I don't have to be concerned about that.

For some reason, perhaps because there was a special potion in that coffee, I am very relaxed about the preparations. The flowers are lovely, the tables and chairs have arrived, and it looks like a small but orderly army is focused on tablecloths and decorations. Everything is checked and double checked, and we are ahead of schedule. I do believe I have time to run home and freshen up a bit before meeting Richard at four o'clock. I have managed to stay focused all day, and I'm sure the evening will be full of excitement, good food, wonderful people, and Richard will of course be the feature. Howdy and I will need to be aware of his time being monopolized, which I know can happen, and gently move him from place to place. That will be a challenge, but it's part of the job.

My mind keeps jumping back to this morning and our brief but powerful encounter and then ahead to our dinner date. I am already planning that, and we have two more events to complete. We may both be so tired by then that we will simply want to call for pizza delivery. Now that is just absurd. We will have a grand celebration—a quiet spot with only the ocean sounds and the best Maine Lobster in Maine and have time to get to know one another. Good friends and great coffee. It's an association worth celebrating. So, Mr. King, be prepared for an evening to remember.

*

What a day, actually what a life. I am still a little foggy about actually being here and spending time with Margaret. It was truly magical, becoming acquainted with the town, which is perfect. Actually looking forward to a huge reception normally I would not be excited about that. Just wanting to get it over with. I am truly in the moment and what a blessing comes with that. Everything is so much more—lying here right now, smelling the grass, feeling the sun, watching the clouds, and knowing that they are changing every second. They are never the same and neither am I. As I focus on breathing, I mean really breathing, experiencing the deep satisfaction, and connection to life or spirit or whatever . . . why do we get so hung up on words? That's somewhat ironic coming from a writer. But then again, perhaps a wordsmith is an appropriate one to make such an appraisal. I tend to admire and feel much more comfortable with folks who leave a little space between thoughts or questions and are comfortable with silence.

I remember my grandmother saying rather often, after a chatty neighbor had given a full report on her chosen target of the day, as my grandmother would quietly go about her tasks of canning or baking bread. After the lady had left, Grandmother would look me straight in the eyes, and say, "Richard, remember, folks that talk too much, often have very little to say." Then she would go about her tasks. She was an amazing woman, very wise, strong, and in her own way, very loving.

My sister and I were very lucky to have her. We had to work hard, and especially at school. She made it very clear when we were at school, that was our work, and we didn't dare to do any whining about working too hard. She was a fine example of all of the really important things in life—honesty, service to neighbors, us, or anyone in need. We had a garden, chickens, and a cow. We were pretty self-sufficient. I had the privilege of milking the cow. I still have very strong hands and very strong memories from what now seems like a pretty ideal childhood. Now where did that come from? One moment, I'm watching the clouds, intent on staying in the moment, and then this flood of childhood memories. I haven't thought about my childhood for a long time. Perhaps I haven't let my mind just wander freely.

I really enjoyed the walk up here to this fascinating lighthouse. Everything is perfect—the quiet, the sea breeze, and the view. I know this is going to be one of my favorite spots. I can imagine Margaret, Howdy, and I having a picnic, perhaps right here. There I go again, how can anyone ever stay in the moment? Obviously a worthy goal to pursue. "To have joy, one must share it. Happiness was born a twin." Lord Byron, I believe. I certainly will be sharing and very soon. My time here has gone by so quickly and peacefully. Now it is time to get back to my hotel and freshen up both my body and my mind. I do not want to lose a moment of this evening. Margaret said four o'clock, and I can hardly wait. Oh yes, and I will finally get to meet Mr. Howdy. I feel so excited and yet relaxed. Oh well, I am ready for the next chapter of this fascinating adventure.

$$*$$

It is 3:55 p.m., and here I am at this massive beautiful door, feeling like a schoolboy going to his first prom. Sweaty hands, rapid pulse—none of these are good signs. I know it's not because of the reception. I have never physically reacted to any of my professional events. I can't say that I have ever really had a feeling of anticipation, excitement, or adventure regarding a book event. When I think about the evening, it's not the crowds of folks coming to the reception that I'm looking forward to, although I am sure I will meet great folks I can learn a lot from and probably many of them will become friends as I become a part of the community. OK, open the door and walk right in and there she comes.

"Margaret, you look enchanting. I mean beautiful. I don't know what I mean. Forgive me, Margaret, but I will start over. Good evening, Margaret, what a pleasure it is to see you, and I might say you are quite stunning."

"Thank you, Richard. I love how well we complement each other. Our colors I mean. We are perfectly coordinated. People will probably think I arranged that also. I'm glad you're here Richard. This is going to be a gala event. So are you ready to meet your public?"

"Margaret, I think you are forgetting a very important promise you made. One that I am looking forward to and that is my tour guide Howdy. No one can forget Howdy, Richard. He is probably just coming in the back door. He has a stroll through town every day when he comes in to work with me. He usually goes out from about three to four. Everyone loves him, and he has his special visits to make. I'll show you the main reception area, and he should be back by then."

"Oh, Margaret, what a transformation, not that it was bad before, but this is formal and still very warm and comfortable. The flowers and napkins match, and everything is just right and perfect. You are a magician. I rather suspected that. Even the champagne fountain is brewing."

"Well, thank you, I think, Richard. I'm not sure if you think I'm a magician or a witch. But I'll take either one as a compliment. I have plenty of dry ice to keep the punch brewing. Margaret usually I really am a reasonable person, very self-contained and appropriate, but when I'm with you, I feel so many emotions. I get a little lost. Oh, I think I am saved by my guide. That has to be Howdy."

"Howdy, I want you to meet my friend Richard. Up comes the paw and a big grin from Howdy. (*Boy, Richard passed the Howdy test with an A plus.*) Now that you two have met, Howdy has been trained to lead tours. He has his own way of doing it, but I think you will find him to be quite thorough, and you will know where every bathroom is, the library, kitchen, bookstore, which is where you will be tomorrow, and, of course, the famous Book Nook which we have already explored. So you guys need to get along, so I can make sure my witch brew is brewing. Seriously, I'm sure some folks really do think I'm a witch, but they get over it. The doors actually will open at 4:45 p.m. so you two had better get a move on. See you back right here at that time."

I have that shivering tingly feeling again, like when he took my hand. I am so glad that I was able to keep my composure. I am attracted to him in a way that actually I can't remember when. With Chad, it was so different. We were young together and great friends. Love sort of grew as we did. It was so secure and planned. This is like a giant tornado that grabs me and just won't let go. I missed him this afternoon. How crazy is that? I don't even know him. I keep telling myself over and over, I don't know him. He is only a visitor, and I need to keep my distance. But then he walks in the room, and logic walks out. Oh well, I don't have time to stand here thinking about it now. The place will soon be full of excitement—nice background music, great food, and, of course, the main attraction Mr. Richard King. I will be able to stay detached though the evening, and between Howdy and me, we will keep him moving through the room, meeting as many folks as he can. I'm sure this book is going to be the best seller, at least in this town.

$$*$$

"Richard, there are about fifteen people in the reception area. This is perfect timing and a wonderful way to start the evening. This small group of folks is very interesting, and I happen to know they are among the first to order the next Richard King book, and they are so pleased that you are here. I am not sure if they know you intend to stay for a while.

I didn't tell anyone, but in a close community like this, I think as soon as I looked at the first studio for you, word started slowly flowing on the wind. I will introduce you, and between Howdy and me. That is what you meant, I presume?" we will keep you moving around the room. We have a system. If you feel Howdy moving around you, actually nudging you, that is your cue, and he knows to guide you to me. I expect the most challenging time will be between seven and eight. I really don't expect that we will have a break at all. If you need a minute, you will just need to excuse yourself. There's always the bathroom escape. Let's go meet some people and have some fun. Don't forget to at least taste some of the great food that Mary has begged, borrowed, and stolen. Actually, she knows everyone's specialty and how to flatter them into wanting to share their best creations but not their recipes. Best not to make the mistake of asking for a family recipe—that would be like asking them to give you a precious family heirloom. Just enjoy. That's all of the thanks they ever need. Here we are."

"Good evening, friends. It is my great pleasure to introduce someone who realistically doesn't need an introduction—Mr. Richard King."

It took all of at least fifteen seconds for the conversation to take on a life of its own. I was very busy greeting everyone, or trying to, and come in they did. Every time I checked on Richard, he was doing a very good job of floating through the crowd. At every opportunity, I would check in, and Howdy stayed on track as well. By seven or so, Jasmine, one of my assistants, gave me a count. She was in charge of the guest book. We were at one thousand and two hundred. Fortunately, I had chosen two very nice guest books, enough for two thousand signatures. I do have an old one in my office in case we need it. The food trays are being replenished very well. As a matter of fact, everything is wonderful. The few moments that Richard and I have had our brief encounters have been very special. It was maybe a quick eye contact, or several times, he has touched my arm, and for those fleeting seconds, nothing else existed. In the midst of all this, it was like, for those seconds, we were in the room alone. I know something very special is happening with us. I don't know what to do about it.

We are coming to the countdown. Fortunately the flow stayed manageable with folks coming, and fortunately going. I was a little concerned that the last count I got from Jasmine was at thousand and seven hundred, and we have slowed down quite a bit during this last thirty minutes. I have completely lost Richard and Howdy, but I'm sure they are fine, wherever they are. Only thirty minutes to go, and I have had a very good time. Everyone was in such a great mood, and every time, I saw Richard, he was either listening intently or laughing so it appears that he has held up quite well. The next two events will be much less demanding for all of us. I think I can genuinely say this evening has been a success. I think when the crowd leaves, Richard and I deserve a quiet cup of tea in our cozy Book Nook where we can put our feet up and just relax. Maybe sketch out tomorrow.

"Richard we did it. What a night! Howdy, you definitely deserve a treat, and Richard, I think you and I do too. What do you say to a cup of special blend lavender chamomile tea?"

"Margaret, I say yes, and I have not had a cup of tea in a very long time. It used to be a daily ritual. I'll tell you about it someday, but for now, let's just enjoy the moment.

"I do have a comment, Margaret, and questions, although I realize this is not the time for a long conversation. Perhaps something you can think about and we can discuss tomorrow evening. The people tonight, though as many as there were and, at times, the crowds were quite large, no one was impatient or pushy. They were gentle, kind, and really listening to the conversations. No one was dominating. Usually, after one of these events, I am exhausted mentally and physically drained. Not tonight. I am physically, a little tired, as I'm sure you are, but mentally, I am pleasantly stimulated. Is there a special secret to this town? I have felt this gentle genuine kindness from everyone, everywhere. I keep wondering, when I am going to wake up. So is my very active imagination making all of this up, including you, or is there something more substantial? By the way, this tea is absolutely wonderful. I hope I make it home safely. So what can you tell a crazy man, Margaret?"

"Richard, you were right about me needing some time to answer your questions. I will need to start at the beginning and that was in my great grandmother and grandfather's early days. There is quite a history to reflect upon, and I would love to share that with you later. Let me just tell you, yes, I do believe there is something very special about this town, which is the reason I would never want to live anywhere else. My years in college were challenging ones, not scholastically, but socially. So, yes, we can begin the discussion tomorrow evening. Oh no, I just remembered. The board, all of whom you met tonight, are hopeful that we could have dinner with them tomorrow, if you're free. What do you think?"

"I am intrigued with the town's history, and I also know that we will have many opportunities to share those conversations. Yes, Margaret, it would be my great pleasure to be your escort to dinner tomorrow night. That is what you meant, I presume?"

"Richard, I do enjoy being with you. You are fun and witty and yes that is exactly what I meant. I kind of told them I thought you were free, but I'll confirm in the morning. Dinner will be at seven, so we will have a little break after your book signing. I may need to feed you if your hands are cramped from writing. If so, I'll be gentle. We have finished the pot of tea, and I am looking forward to a good night's sleep. Howdy had a head start. He's actually snoring. I've never heard him do that. Oh, you heard your name, did you? Come on, boy, it's time to go. Richard, rest well. I am looking forward to another amazing day. Good night, my friend."

Our handshake turned into so much more. It always does. His hands are so gentle, yet firm and safe. I will sleep very well tonight or maybe not at all. So Richard wants to know about our town. Great!

✳

This has been a fantastic day. I actually feel like I am awakening from several years of sleepwalking. From the moment of my arrival in this town, I feel so alive. It was so amazing to be surrounded, and I do mean surrounded by so many people and not feel any tension or frustration, just like a really big family gathering. Every time, I looked at Margaret, which was rather often, she looked so serene. In the midst of what could be called chaos, she very clearly was among friends and at ease. She is an amazing woman. Howdy, bless his heart. He could herd an entire cattle ranch, I'm sure. He gently nudged me through the crowd in a very timely manner. He is already a great pal. I loved our teatime tonight. Not much time but great quality time and absolutely no negative feelings about tea. I had associated tea drinking with Sylvia, and before tonight, the thought was repulsive. I enjoyed the tea, conversation, relaxation, and I had no idea I was going to ask Margaret that question about the town. It just came out. I am so comfortable with her. I feel free to share my thoughts sometimes as I am thinking them, like tonight. I know I have felt at home here, totally accepted and safe. It's hard to describe even to myself, but basically, I think it's like people are genuinely happy and enjoy just being, and children are out playing. I haven't actually seen that for a long time and I guess I had just accepted it. But here there is so much laughter, and parents are talking to each other and their children with respect. I guess that's it. That's what I have felt here. I am accepted and respected. I see people in town, playing checkers, talking and laughing. I haven't heard one "fuck you" or any other derogatory word, no obnoxious boom boxes through town. It is just so pleasant. I don't know if anyone watches TV. I know there is one in my hotel room, but I certainly haven't had it on. I haven't seen one anywhere else, and people are always doing things. As a matter of fact, I am a bit of a news junkie, and I haven't even read a paper or thought about the news. I certainly don't miss it. The conversations are very different—more philosophical or discussions regarding book recommendations and concerts which seem to occur frequently. There are apparently several theatre groups in town. There is so much life. Something happening every moment, somewhat like the ocean. There is always a rhythm.

I was quite surprised when I asked Margaret about the town. I certainly never planned to say that. It just came out. I was even more surprised that she accepted the question. As matter of fact, I am really looking forward to that conversation. But first things first, and tomorrow will be another fun-filled day—book signing, which Margaret has organized so well, and then the children's circle. I haven't done that before, and I have absolutely no anxiety about it. Just play time. Let them ask the questions, and if I can't answer, I have two wonderful backup plans: Howdy and Margaret. I think we will all have a great time, then dinner with some more wonderful new friends and, of course, being Margaret's escort. I actually prefer a date. Do I take her flowers? Or corsage? Wine? I don't know. I'm sure anything or nothing is fine, but I really do want to do something special because she is such a very special and lovely lady. I know I felt compelled to come here, and I do feel so at home.

I also want to know more about that beautiful historic building I went by today. The sign that was beautifully carved and looked as old as the house said it was "The Community Center for Conscious Living," and then under that was inscribed "Welcome, I love you, my brothers and sisters, whoever you are. You and I are all children of one faith, for the diverse paths of religion are fingers of the loving hand of one Supreme Being, a hand extended to all offering completeness of spirit to all." I believe that is a quote from Kahlil Gibran, another one of my heroes. I had to write it down. It was such a compelling moment. The building seemed to vibrate with great energy. People came and went, greeting each other with great pleasure, and it really smelled like Mary must be in there baking. I would love to know more about it. Unfortunately, I was out of time today. I think I'd rather visit when Margaret can go with me. I have a feeling she is very familiar with the "house." It seems as though there is no end of treasures to be found in this town. My town. After I had that second cup of tea, I was so pleasantly relaxed. I could have gone to sleep right there. Now I have stirred the pot, and my brain is boiling, not in a bad way, just anticipation, as I remember anticipation at Xmas as a young child. The world is full of awe and wonder, at least this town is, and so is Margaret. We are becoming fast friends or quickly becoming friends. Something is definitely going on, and whatever it is, I love it and I am ready.

What a change a day or two can make. I feel like a flash of lightning has struck. It was beautiful, powerful, and left a bit of a shock in its wake. I also feel a bit like I must be sleeping and just can't quite awaken. Yet my senses are sharp. Wow! Mr. Richard King. You have indeed arrived and nothing is quite the same and yet not really different, although I am talking to myself. I do realize I am talking in riddles. Just an hour ago, I was so pleasantly tired and relaxed as I am every night when I drink my tea, and now I am wide awake and not really tired, although when I reflect on the day, I have been very busy. The reception was a bit demanding and yet it flowed so easily. I really did have a good time. Poor Howdy is not having any second thoughts. He is sleeping and has been since we got home. He is such a love. He always seems to know just what to do and very quietly goes about doing it. I think that's how I learned a very good lesson and that time does not hurry us. We hurry ourselves. I need to remind myself of that on days like today. Thank you, Mr. Howdy. After the reception was the most rewarding time. I think I had been looking forward to Richard and I having a good time together, just relaxing and reflecting on the day. It was a good thing. We are so comfortable together and have been from the beginning. I can't imagine now that I had such reservations. Everything has flowed so naturally. I am ready for tomorrow's event; as a matter of fact, I am looking forward to it. The book-signing schedule is hectic, but I know Richard can handle it and still make everyone feel special. It seems to be a part of his personality. I know it works for me. I am especially looking forward to the children's event. I think we will have quite a large circle. Howdy definitely will have to work with Richard on that one. I think I may be needed also. To be very honest with myself, I want to be there and be part of the process because I want to see how Richard responds to children, and they to him. I have a hunch he will know how to keep their attention and not have them running amuck. The kids are really fun to be with, but they can take control if not managed well. And after all of that, we are going to dinner. Oh my! What a full life I am having! My safe and secure routine schedule has been abandoned for the past several days.

Tomorrow morning, I am going back to my structure, and yes, I will get a late start and that's fine. I know all the volunteers know what to do and will be so far ahead of me anyhow, and I'll certainly have time for myself and Howdy. By missing my routine, I realize how grateful I am for every part of my life. I have had such wonderful teachers and opportunities. I love yoga and all of the wonderful people I have had the good fortune to learn from and how it helps me to remember to greet the day with joy, knowing that I will experience only the highest and best of everything. It reinforces my intention to start my day with gratitude, for each breath reminds me that in this moment all is well. I am fully present right now.

My life is very good, and I am very content, and yet, I am aware, especially right now, that something is missing. I think I have known it before, but that was not the right time to think about it. A quote from W. Somerset Maugham comes to mind. "Do you know that conversation is one of the greatest pleasures in life?" I believe that to be true. I'm glad I have some time to think about how to share the history of this town. Most of the tourists never ask a question, they just know they love to spend their summers here and they return and their children return, and so forth. Occasionally someone will relocate here. A few have sensed a feeling of belonging and have gradually become a part of what we like to think of as the family, but more often the stay is short and many have moved on.

My great-grandfather always said to only give answers when questions are asked, and few seem to have time to ask the questions, but Richard has asked rather specifically, and with what I sense is a very sincere openness to receiving answers. It will be quite a challenge for me to explain the founding principles and structure of our community and how we have managed to keep the basic integrity. It seems so simple yet it has not necessarily always been easy. I am so glad I have already planned a time off from work because to share the creation of the principles that we share in this community and have shared for so many years I need some contemplation time and clarity. My meditation skills will be very helpful to get me centered in the truth and history of our very special community. I do believe Richard very sincerely wants to know the entire story. He has asked the question! Now it is time for me to be able to answer the questions. I am looking forward to our conversations and tea, of course. I do believe it will be best to share the information over a period of time, several days at least. Only one moment at a time, no need to rush. Just enjoy the moments of shared conversation and now "to sleep perchance to dream," although I'm not totally sure that I'm not dreaming now.

*

"Well, good morning, Richard. I have only just arrived myself. I am a bit late, and you are a bit early. Our timing is perfect."

"Margaret, I hope I am not in your way. I promise I will busy myself, unless of course there is some way I can be helpful to you. I just awakened so early, and rested. I have been to the mountaintop this morning. You know, I mean, the lighthouse, I think."

"Yes, Richard, as crazy as it may seem, I did think you meant the lighthouse, and that is exactly how I think of it. It is my mountaintop. I do a lot of mediation there. Howdy and I have spent a lot of time there. Someday perhaps, we will all go together, but today, we have another kind of mountaintop to climb. I know you have seen the book-signing schedule, but I do want to actually review it with you and get your take on it. Perhaps there is a better way to manage it. I am very glad that you came early. I'm just getting ready to make some coffee, would you like to join me?"

"Margaret, I love coffee! Yes, I would love to share both coffee and conversation with you. I have a love affair with coffee, and while you are about the brewing I will share some background of coffee. Stop me anytime you wish. I can become a bit of a bore when I get started on coffee. Historians have tried to tie coffee to the writings of the ancient world. After all, how could ancient people have survived without coffee? The very idea is hard to imagine, and that's why some have claimed that Homer mentions coffee. They insist that the nepenthe that Helen of Troy brought with her from Egypt, sort of her hostess gift, must have actually been our favorite brew, and there is so much more. Even in the Bible and the Arab world, obviously. I could go on and on and probably will, given another opportunity. Truly there is much more to be said."

"I believe you, Richard, and I am convinced that we shall resume this topic at another time, and I am looking forward to it. I love your passion, and of course the information. I will just add one of my favorite coffee sayings and then we will enjoy. 'Good coffee is black as sin, pure as the angels, strong as death, and sweet as love.' It is a Creole saying."

"That is beautiful, Margaret. I am once again in awe of us. We are truly sharing coffee and conversation. Certainly two things worthy of time well spent."

"This coffee is strong, bold, and confident. Thank you for everything."

"Richard, you are most welcome."

"Shall we review the book-signing schedules? I believe I reviewed the pricing with you, although everything has happened so quickly, I'm not really sure how clear I have been."

"Quite frankly, Margaret, I have been and still am so grateful that you have everything so well-organized that I have not given any thought to the whys and hows. I realize that's not really fair to you. So I am very happy to be involved at any level. As I recall, you said you had signed folks up in advance. I believe every ten to fifteen minutes, is that correct?"

"Richard, you have done this many times. Do you think it's realistic? I wasn't sure. I know each person would love to talk with you for hours, and I also know that is not possible. So at this point, I have the schedule for every ten minutes. However, I did put a couple of extras in each hour. Is that too much time? Not enough? I am really thinking now that I should have talked with you more about this, but that ship has sailed. We could make minor adjustments. What do you think?"

"Margaret, I think it's perfect. Fifty-five or sixty folks to meet and sign their book. I am looking forward to this. It is rewarding, and I am so humbled by this community. I would love to spend more time with everyone and be here for ten to twelve hours. But that is not realistic. So I think the schedule you have is perfect. Am I correct in remembering that we decided to do two days of signings, and I believe you have, what, eighty to hundred books presold for me to sign for folks that will not be here?"

"Your memory is right on. That is the plan. We extended today and tomorrow from nine to four with a couple of breaks and lunch, a quick but special lunch that Mary has prepared for us. And tomorrow, the children's circle will be from 4:30 p.m. to 5:30 p.m. Richard, that was so gracious of you to not only read to the children but to also give each one their own signed copy. They will never forget this day. And then tonight is our dinner at 7:00 p.m. Poor Richard, I am so sorry that I have created such a marathon for you. Actually, for us. I don't really know what happened."

"Margaret, I am so grateful to you. I am loving every minute of every day that I am here. I have from the first moment I arrived, and it's only getting better. This day will fly by, and then tonight will be a celebration time with friends. What could be better? And I have another day tomorrow to look forward to. So I had better get busy signing books, and please let Howdy know he is welcome to join me, as often as he'd like. He really is a great helper. I love having him with me, and of course everyone else does too. I doubt that we will have much time to talk today, but I am so looking forward to our teatime after four today. Is that a possibility?"

"Yes, Richard, and I have already chosen the tea. Ginger and lemongrass, unless of course you would prefer something different. That was a bit presumptuous of me, assuming we would meet for tea and have Mary's special tea biscuits."

"No, Margaret, it wasn't presumptuous. I love ginger tea, and anything Mary bakes is worth waiting for, and so are you. So off I go to meet and greet my new neighbors. Stop by anytime you get a chance, Margaret."

*

Well, I am definitely intrigued with Mr. Richard King. I cannot find a flaw anywhere, and why should I? All of my life I have been shown how to see and know the basic good in people and to believe in kindness and caring. That's what our community philosophy is based on. It is basically the Ten Commandments, a little Buddhism, and so-called New Thought beliefs, and ideas drawn from some pretty powerful people. It's going to be so much fun sharing that process of community-building from a historic perspective. I think it will be very good for me. It's so easy to take things, and people, for granted. I really want to review our fundamental structure from the beginning. I haven't done that since childhood. But I am certainly getting out of the moment. I need to focus on what's happening right now. Time to get out and about. I am supposed to be the major support person, and of course, the cheerleader, as if Richard would ever need a cheerleader. Wherever he is, they are there—his adoring fans. Now I really know why. He sees every one of them, and at least for that moment, nothing else exists. I just may be projecting that, but I don't think so. He is so sincere and interested in everyone and seemingly everything. There actually seems to be a higher vibration in the room, especially when he has a discussion point and there is like one breath that the crowd is breathing. I want to make this day and evening last forever. As a matter of fact it very well may seem like it. Now focus, and get to work, Margaret.

"Well, at last, do I get that special ginger tea I've been promised? I really do smell it, or I have a great imagination."

"Oh yes, Richard, we shall have our moment of respite from the frenzy. Not really frenzy, from wherever I was, it appeared to be a major success. Everyone left very happy, and I heard so much laughter from the children. I must have you read that story to me. I did read most of it, and it is a very good children's book. Not to put the book down, but the reader was obviously having such a good time that the children just had to join in. If I'm out of line by asking, please feel free to tell me. As I understand it, you do not have children. Is that correct, Richard?"

"Yes, Margaret, that is correct, and no, you are not out of line by asking, and I do want to share that part of my life with you but not crammed into a schedule like we have today. We have about an hour to refresh ourselves for our dinner date, and you look as fresh as a breath of spring. I, on the other hand, really need a shower and change of clothes. I am so looking forward to dining and conversation with our friends."

"Richard, you are right. I tend to forget time as it really is. I also need to take Howdy for a quick walk and freshen up a bit myself. And thank you for the compliment, but if you were a little closer, you may find me a bit wilted, and in need of spring showers."

"Margaret, I am closer now, and you still have eyes like violets, cheeks like the pinkest rose, skin like porcelain, lips of lavender, and your hair, your beautiful hair, that I can hardly wait to see loose and flowing freely in the breeze. Smells like jasmine, and if that's not a spring package, I don't know what is."

"Well, maybe early summer."

"Seriously, Margaret, I love being with you and thinking about you. I want to know so much, and I want to share so much with you. I cannot believe it's been only days since we actually met. Do you believe in soul mates, Margaret?"

"Yes, I do, Richard. Now go away but hurry back. I will meet you here at 6:50 p.m. which is only an hour and fifteen minutes for both of us to do what we must do. Go away now."

*

What a day! What a life! I can only begin to understand what this library means to the community. I know I continue to be surprised at the excitement and buzz I have felt from my first step inside the door, and I can see it on the faces of the volunteers. Actually, it's is on every one's face. And the children, what a joy! I have been to many libraries in my life, but never anything like this. I expect books, DVDs, CDs, digital services, a few programs, and events. This library is so much more—a community center, a place where minds meet and conversations begin, a shared space with the children's art museum, youth activities, family game night, with programs taking place every day. It's hard to imagine they could do anymore, but it's still growing. The K-9 reading buddy program brings such vitality, combining therapy dogs with beginning readers. The children are encouraged to share a story with a furry reading buddy, and Howdy is, of course, right in the lead. And the special programs on the schedule are amazing—everything from recycling to artistic adventures. Those events are free and feature poetry and local talent. Some both write and recite the poetry and short stories. I think what I like best is the conversation and projects that continue all year long to encourage public dialogue about topics relevant to the community, primarily facilitated by university leaders and apparently centering around controversial ideas or themes in our society and maintaining civil engagements and conversations. I know there is so much more that I have yet to discover about actually everything—the library, under Margaret's leadership, and of course Margaret herself. Which reminds me, I do have a date, and it's time to make a move.

✳

"Well, Richard, you are right on time and looking amazingly refreshed and ready for our evening of great food, wonderful friends, and stimulating conversation."

"Margaret, you are an amazing woman, in case I haven't told you that yet. You never fail to surprise me with your vitality and genuine love of life. When I am with you, I feel rejuvenated. So let's go to this intriguing dinner house where we can eat, drink, and be merry. And yes, we can sleep in tomorrow, right?"

"Yes, we certainly can, at least until 8:00 a.m. That is what you meant, right? Remember, we have another full day tomorrow. So we may save some of the drink until another time. However, I am definitely going to have a ginger martini. It is a house specialty, and I have never had one like it anywhere else, and believe me, I have tried it. I know you like ginger tea, so I think you should give yourself a treat, Richard, and try one. Just make it last and savor every drop. And I guarantee you, you will never forget it."

"Well, that was a short walk. We have arrived, and so has everyone else. What an aroma! I love it. Every time I come here, it still excites me."

"Good evening, folks. I believe everyone has met Richard, and you all know me perhaps too well. What a wonderful table you have arranged! And, Richard, as the guest of honor, it looks like you get the perfect place to sit, to enjoy the full view of the ocean, lighthouse, and what a beautiful sunset. A feast for the eyes and soul, and you have already ordered my favorite appetizers. They are called Angelinos (angels on horseback), and they are luscious—oysters marinated with a hint of lemon juice, Worcestershire sauce, anchovy paste, and wrapped in lean crisp bacon, and broiled. They are ready, so please take the first one, Richard, and we will begin the feast. It's very difficult for me to recommend any one thing on the menu because I love it all, and I know I am in the mood tonight for stuffed flounder."

The conversations were as satisfying as the food. The ginger martinis (I had to have two) and the dessert which everyone had, Postre Borracho (drunken cake), was really quite simple but oh so good. I enjoyed every minute of the evening, and again it felt as though we had all known one another forever. There were no pretenses, or expectations, just friends having a very good time, enjoying one another's company. The atmosphere, the incredible food, and conversation were great. And perhaps the most interesting part was when one person talked, everyone listened. No one dominated the conversation. It just flowed gently and clearly. There was a mutual unspoken agreement to respect one another. I don't know if I have ever had that experience before. Usually the tone just gets louder and less is actually said, and by the end of the evening, conversation generally has diminished to trivia, and I'm glad when it's time to leave. But this evening, I felt like we could have continued forever, and I would still be curious about the next topic. At least my mind said that. My body was saying something quite different, and I noticed that Margaret was getting a bit of a glaze, so we thanked everyone and excused ourselves. I did manage to walk Margaret home, and I think I kissed her forehead. I was so tired I barely remember finding my way home, but apparently I did. What an evening!

✳

"Good morning, Howdy. You are very energetic this morning. Ready for a quick walk? I think I can manage that, and then I really do want to have at least a short session of yoga. I do miss our routine, Howdy, and I know you do. But I am having such a wonderful time. I'm so glad you like Richard. I remember thinking that you would need to give me approval, which you did of course, but I knew from the first moment that my life had changed. It has been so right. We were even finishing each other's sentences last night, not in a rude way but very comfortable. Oh my, you are a good listener, Howdy, and I love you very much. I slept so soundly last night, and I feel almost as energetic as you are. Almost. We have another full day today. I hope Richard gets by in time to share a cup of coffee. It is so much better shared. 'When friends meet, hearts warm.' Yes, I am a bit giddy, and we had better get a move on. You, my friend, are going to be working this afternoon for the children's circle time. The K-9 therapy dogs will be there also, and I think they depend upon your leadership a lot. I know I do. You are such a wise one. I think dogs are here to teach us how to love unconditionally. I am learning from you all of the time and always have. Well, here we are, Howdy, and as usual, the crew is already here, and Mary's kitchen aromas are already drifting outside, welcoming us in. What an incredible place this is. I love it, and they pay me! See you later, Howdy, go do your rounds, and I'll catch up soon."

"Richard, you are already here! Good morning. You look refreshed, and ready for another full day."

"Yes, I am, Margaret. I slept very well last night. I barely remember getting back to my hotel. It was not the martinis, by the way. You were right. They are memorable, as was everything, actually, and now, may I pour you a cup of coffee? Mary has a special treat for us, and it should arrive any moment. I am aware that once again we have only moments before the action begins, but for this moment, we are here and sharing our perfect blend of coffee, of course. I am very happy to see you, Margaret. 'Where our work is, there let our joy be.' It is very obvious that your work is your joy and it is very contagious. I could hardly wait to get here this morning. Mary made my favorite chocolate swirl coffee cake. She knows I keep saying my favorite, because my favorite is always the one I have at the moment. Thank you so much, Mary. Well, I haven't had the pleasure of tasting it before, but the aroma is so rich. I love chocolate—anything made with chocolate. The deeper the richness of the chocolate, the better. I know it's supposed to be a woman thing, but I am a chocoholic, or at least I'm sure I could be. Thank you, Mary. You are a lifesaver. I skipped breakfast this morning, and now I am so glad I did. Will you please save a small piece for us for break time? Then I will be sure to take a quick break. Margaret, would you mind if we have another cup of coffee for our break? I love our teatime, but chocolate just loves coffee."

"Richard, I totally agree, and I am also a chocoholic. I do ration myself most of the time, so maybe just a wannabeaholic! I think I will stick with the tea.

"Good idea, Margaret."

∗

We will have time for tea after the children's circle or maybe before. We'll see how the day goes. The time flies by so quickly, and trying to embrace the moment, when so much is happening is a real challenge, but

45

it is so worth the effort. Everything is so much more. When I am able to just take everything in, to take a deep breath and focus on right now, there is such clarity, color, and joy.

"Go get to work or play or whatever it is you do, and I will see you soon, if I can peer through the crowd. Margaret, I will know you are there even if I don't' see you. Your presence is so powerful and peaceful. I know when you are in the room, and I love it. See you later, love."

Oh my goodness! He said the four-letter word, "Love." I know he said it lightly, but there was such an awakening in me. It's certainly not a new word, especially in this community, and it is shown in so many ways by almost everyone, and yet coming from Richard evoked such a strong response in me. This is the last day of what has been a major event, in more ways than one. I do need to see that everything is in order before I take my vacation. I am so glad I followed my intuition and scheduled vacation time. I only have to attend the board meeting. My report is prepared, and I will review the volunteers' schedule, which is always so easy. If someone can't show up for their shift, they always arrange for someone else to fill in. So I am really just a formality, which is great. This was the last book-signing event until spring. The summer people have left, or are leaving, so we will slow the pace down a bit. And then the holidays start, and we go into high gear again, and I love it. I'd better at least mingle a bit and see how things are going.

"It appears as though Richard is almost out of books. We'd better take a short break and see what the game plan is. Ten-minute break, folks. Richard will be right back. There are refreshments on the back table. Please help yourself."

"Richard, are you out of books?"

"No, love. I have another box in the closet with the children's books. But I do need a breather and a moment to go get the books, so your timing was perfect. I bet I'm going to have to settle for a glass of lemon water for now right and tea later."

"Richard, have you had anything to eat? I got so involved in proofing my annual report that I completely lost time. I have realistically never found time, as I think you are beginning to realize."

"Thank you, Margaret, but I had a wonderful and healthy protein bar and some dried fruit that I have been able to eat between signings. How about you?"

"I pretty much did the same, Richard. Are you ready to go to the closet, and no, you can't stay there. Can I help in any way?"

"Just by being concerned and caring, Margaret. That means a lot. Thank you. So it's still children's circle from 4:30 p.m. to 5:30 p.m. and then a tea break?"

"Yes, and I will be there for the children's circle. I need some of their wonderful energy, and I want to hear the story. Sorry to say, I haven't read it yet. And yes, then tea outside in the garden where it's very quiet, and we can catch our breath. Oh yes, I do have another surprise to tell you about. I do hope you don't have any plans for this evening, or I am in big trouble."

"You wicked woman, how unfair to tease me with this and then send me away. On the other hand, how exciting is that? To have yet another surprise which I know will be wonderful. See you at the circle, and yes, I am free this evening."

*

I am so glad I got here in time for the beginning. The children are completely captivated by him. As a matter of fact, so am I. Every child and their K-9 pals look so happy. And my Howdy looks quite content with Richard. Richard is like a magician, somehow managing to bring each child into the story as an active participant and still not losing anyone else. He is indeed a master storyteller. I am really curious about why he has only one children's book, and it was written a long time ago. He obviously is enjoying this event a great deal and not one child has lost interest for a moment. I have seen some wonderful storytellers but never one this good. The hour is over and no one wants it to be. Now is the perfect time for Richard to give them their very own autographed copy of his book. I am so glad I had admission by reservations only. I know all the children, so that's something I can finally do to help.

"Well, Richard, that was fascinating. I loved the story, and the children were mesmerized. Next week, we will finally have time for me to answer some of your questions and for you to answer some of mine. Yes, I know after you have found your new home. For now, let's go out to the garden and have a cup of tea and take a nice deep breath. The silence is golden. I am just enjoying the moment, smelling the different flowers, feeling the evening breeze, and the delightful taste of jasmine tea. I haven't even had time to show you the real garden. This part with the tables and umbrellas among the herbs and flowers and bordered by the trees. This is part of Mary's kitchen, and right around the corner of the building is almost an acre of garden space. It's a community garden. It was started by the Master Garden Group and quickly expanded to include 4-H children, parents, and gradually pretty much the entire community. The herb garden is my favorite. I come in to work an hour early one day a week and primarily work in the herb garden. When everyone gets involved, no one has to do more than they enjoy doing. We have abundant crops.

"Margaret, just when I think I have seen the library, there is another part added to the puzzle."

"Oh yes, Richard, just wait until you see our Community Center for Conscious Living. There are so many moving parts. It is constantly evolving. Well, time has gotten me again. What I neglected to tell you about tonight actually was a surprise to me also if that's any consolation. After all I'm supposed to be 'in charge.' The volunteers, as we speak, are setting up the great room for a grand buffet in your honor. They do not do this for every author. I think they like you, and I think this may be their way of welcoming you to the community, and of course Mary's crew had a lot to do with it. So my friend, we have no time to freshen up. They will take us like we are."

"Margaret, I keep thinking I am going to awaken, and this entire community and everything in it, including you is just going to disappear. I would ask you to pinch me, but I really don't want to awaken yet. I am having such a wonderful time. So when you are ready, just lead me to the grand buffet. Will there be champagne?"

"Actually, Richard, I saw them setting up the champagne fountain. So yes, I think there is champagne, and I know Mary ordered the chocolate fountain as well. So we both may be in the same dream."

*

"That was without a doubt the best food I have ever eaten. Margaret, what is the secret?"

"No secret, and yes, we do hear similar comments from out-of-town folks all the time. Although I must say they really did take an over-the-top effort tonight. I think the secret weapon here is probably love. Our town food is grown and cared for with respect and prepared with love. It is a self-sustained community. You may have noticed, if you'd had time, we only have local markets, restaurants, and shops. We even have our own shoe shop where they repair and make new shoes. We raise our chickens, pork, beef, vegetables, fruits, and of course, we have the ocean for seafood. I realize it is really late, and we are very tired, but I really will give you more information later. The shorter version for now is yes, I agree we do have a secret weapon, and it's called conscious living, and until another time when I am more coherent, that will just have to do. The food was great, the company was fantastic, and the background music was a real treat. Overall, it was a first-class offering. I don't mind saying that we deserved every bit of it. Well, at least you did, Richard. You have been a real trooper throughout this marathon."

"Thank you, Margaret. I wouldn't have done it without you and Howdy, of course. So what's my agenda for tomorrow?"

"You have no agenda tomorrow. I suggest you sleep until you awaken, have a nice walk before breakfast, check on the ocean and make sure it is still there, have some quiet time, and really relax. I am going to have a quiet day, get caught up on some things on my list, attend a board meeting in the afternoon, and just enjoy being in the moment. So, my friend, we will not see one another until day after tomorrow. First appointment is at 11:00 a.m. to see one of the three choices for your new home. Then I thought we would have lunch together. You pick the place and then we will see the second choice at 2:00 p.m. And if you're up to it, we'll see the last, but hopefully not the least desirable. Really, Richard, if you think that's too much for one day, we can revise the plan. You tell me how you want to do it."

"Oh yes, Margaret. All three sound great. I am so excited about finding my home. You have no idea what this means to me. I'm not entirely sure if I know exactly what it means, but I do know I am ready for the adventure. I do hope the cottages have some furniture, at least a bed. I don't think I asked you one way or the other, and it's really OK either way."

"All the three are furnished, Richard, somewhat sparsely but comfortably. You may want to add a few of your own choices as you settle in. And by the way, you are not committed to anything. If you don't feel at home in these three, we are going to see other choices, but I do know you are ready to check them out. Sorry, it can't be tomorrow. But the day off will probably do us both good."

"Margaret, you may be right, but I will tell you that just the thought of not seeing you tomorrow leaves me feeling a bit lonely. I know it is crazy, but it just doesn't seem right for us not to have coffee or tea and no conversation. I get bored talking to myself. At least, I will now, after having had such meaningful conversations."

"Thank you, Richard. That is very sweet, and honestly, I know what you mean. I think it may be because we have been in such an intense time challenge and we have had such great experiences, and now that we are in real time, we'll see how things are for us. I am looking forward to day after tomorrow, and I know I will miss you tomorrow, and yes, my world is a bit topsy-turvy, and that's all right. For the moment, Richard, I am very happy to be here with you and feel the warmth of your presence and the joy of life. Now I am going to go home and get some well-deserved sleep, and I will see you day after tomorrow at Mary's place. Shall we say 10:00 a.m. for our perfect blend of coffee and conversation? Our appointment is only ten minutes away."

"I would like to push for nine o'clock, but I won't. I must have some discipline surely, so yes, Margaret, 10:00 a.m. Mary's place. I will miss you, and I am already looking forward to our date. If you change your mind and just can't wait until then, you know where I am. Just call and I'll be there. Just joking, sort of. Until then, love."

✳

"Good morning, Mr. Howdy. I guess you are thinking it is time for me to get up. Actually, I was awake but still kind of dreaming. You and I must have a talk about Richard. But not today. Today is 'recovering my center' day, before I do anything else. Time for yoga, and you can do that with me, if you'd like, and then my special morning drink before you and I go for a nice brisk walk. I love our routine, Howdy. It's so energizing, in a simple, quiet way. Off we go to sniff the flowers, feel the wind, and ocean mist, and just be so grateful for this moment. You lead today. I need to watch you, as you rediscover the world as new which you do so naturally all the time. Your natural curiosity and joy is such a pleasure to be a part of. When I am with you like this, I can live fully aware of the beauty we are always surrounded by. Thank you, my friend. You are a forever young spirit. I completely forget how many years you have been with us, and still you always have that look of eager anticipation. It seems so easy for you to live in the moment. That's who you are."

I do feel completely refreshed and ready to deliver my PowerPoint presentation to the board. I am quite sure they will be very surprised when I get to the point of my presentation, regarding another expansion. Fortunately, our financial status and projected budget is very positive. We have consistently been financially solvent through every expansion which has actually been about every three years, and the community has totally supported every change we have made. We never even really have to have special fund-raising events. Our activities are offered by donation. Our memberships come in consistently. Between the Center for Conscious Living and this library, the foundation is very firm for a healthy, happy community. And the number of endowments to the library enables to continue serving and expanding as the needs increase. A special youth space is what we need to focus on for our next expansion. I have researched and, hopefully, have the answers prepared before the questions are asked. I am really looking forward to the meeting and even after the past few days' activities and emotions, I feel very confident, refreshed, and sure that this is a very important issue. One real advantage is that basically we all have a common goal regarding the quality of life for our children. So I do believe my plan for projected expansion will be supported, after a lot of questions, and discussion, and that's a healthy process. I am glad that the board members are very responsible people, always there when I need them. Most of them are volunteers as well, so they really know what goes on here and frequently make very constructive recommendations and I value that. So just time for a cup of tea in the garden and maybe a sample of Mary's "special of the day." And only a few minutes to think about Richard, and yes, I do miss him, he has become very important to me, in such a short period of time, although it really does feel like I've known him forever.

*

Is love at first sight truly possible? I have turned that question inside and out and I still come back to the question. What I do know is that I feel completely safe, comfortable, and yet very excited when Margaret and I are together. And when we are not together, I feel like a part of me is missing. This relationship is about so much more than sex, although I have certainly given that some thoughts also. I miss everything about her: her smile, energy, her sense of humor, quick wit, wisdom, and her beauty. I want to know all about her. What she did as a child? Did she like school? I know nothing about her family. I guess in all reality, I know nothing about Margaret, and yet I feel this deep intense trust, and I would like to have a fast-forward button to press and just have all of the information processed, and we could just get on with our life. I have never been more sure of anything than the fact that I want to spend the rest of my life with Margaret, and of course Howdy. And we have never even kissed. But we have such intimacy. Even our short coffee breaks and teatimes are so special. I haven't been here for a week yet and everywhere I go I feel so welcome in this community. No, more than welcome. A sense of belonging, that's what is so special about this community. It's a lot like Margaret or vice versa. People are really glad to see each other and take time to share their thoughts and feelings, and listen to each other; there is such respect. As a matter of fact, I wonder if they have a police department. I haven't seen a policeman or a police car, and I have walked from one end of town to the other, and then some. I haven't heard profanity or even see tattoos, and there are a lot of young people in this town. Sidewalks are really for walking on. No bicycles or skateboards on the sidewalks. I do see a lot of bicycles. People of all ages ride them, but on the bike lane or trail. I just thought of that, and how pleasant it is to not have to dodge the skateboards and bicycles and even the groups of teens taking the entire sidewalk. Apparently, that is not OK here.

I have been to many, as a matter of fact, towns and in most of them, I have had many close calls, and I am pretty agile. Too bad for folks that aren't. I was tempted to go to the Community Center for Conscious Living today. I saw the daily activity list; something for everyone—tots, teens, adults, and also special family times. There was a meditation group meeting this morning and art classes. I really want to check that out. There is a potluck lunch outside, and for the early riser, working in the garden. They call the program "Reap the Harvest." I went by on my walk this morning, and again there was the smell of coffee and a mix of aromas and laughter. It was quite challenging not to go inside. But I know it's special, and I really want to go there with Margaret. Somehow that seems very important. But of course, I also want to be with Margaret on my walk, drinking coffee, seeing special clouds in the sky, sitting quietly, and just enjoying the moment.

✱

I need to switch channels: think about seeing my new home tomorrow morning. I know one of them will be just right, and I am so ready to settle in and feel at home again. I haven't felt that for so long. That's not exactly true. I have had that feeling since I first arrived and met Margaret. My channel didn't stay switched for very long. I keep reminding myself that I am a reasonable person and have been for most of my life, except for the years just after Sylvia died. Those are truly almost like lost time. I was lost. But that aside, I am a responsible, reliable, disciplined person, who just simply has lost his mind. The very best part of it is, although I am feeling a little schizophrenic, I am very sure that Margaret and I will be together in this lifetime sooner than later. As a matter of fact, in a few short hours, finally. I am very proud of myself. I made it through the day and didn't call her. It was a real struggle. I know she had that important board meeting, and I am very interested in how her day went. But I get the distinct feeling that she really wanted the day for quiet time. I actually really do understand that. So for the coffee time in the morning, I will surely be there and ready for an adventure.

✱

"Good morning, Margaret. Mary and I have a treat for you. We are of course sure that we are celebrating a very successful board meeting yesterday. So we have baked a new special, never-tasted-before item this very morning called the 'Morning Glory Muffins', full of walnuts, raisins, cranberries, spices, and, of course, all of the other stuff."

"Good morning, Richard, and a very good morning to you, Mary, and the taste cannot be better than the smell, or I'm not sure I can stand it. No kidding, this is a treasure. After I get my coffee and we go out into the garden where we can all appreciate the beauty and the feast, I will share a short scenario of the board meeting. Mary, does this wonderful gem of a muffin have apples in it also?"

53

"Yes, indeed, it does. Mr. King was so anxious to do something that I put him to work in the kitchen, after he scrubbed his hands and put a proper apron on. I was so hoping you would come in while he was chopping, slicing, and dicing like a professional and humming a catchy little tune and singing along with his culinary skills."

"I am so sorry I missed that. Richard, I must insist on a repeat performance in the near future, and I'll just bet that you can't come up with anything better than this."

"Bet's on, Margaret. Mary, you and I have been challenged. I guess you know what this means, and I have a secret arrival. I researched cookbooks back to the 1800s. I think I can find a jewel or two that you could improve on, and so, game on."

"Now, Margaret, you have your coffee and the best muffin in the world. We have been patient long enough, so give us a replay. OK, but this needs to be kept quiet please. The board will make an announcement after I return from my vacation. So promise me, Mary, Richard, not a word."

"Absolutely," they said in unison.

"My proposal was conceptually very simple—expanding our children's and youth program is a natural process of growth. I knew we were all of one mind about our commitment to children and share an awareness that there is no greater opportunity than having the ability to help raise the next generation. This community has always done that, and we know how successful it is. So primarily I knew I needed to clarify the difference between our role and the Community Center for Conscious Living's role. The center provides physical activities—a gym, swimming pool, tennis courts, and so forth. We offer opportunities for expanded learning through our mentoring program, and how to utilize technology responsibly, and that's one of the reasons for expansion. Most of the children in the community don't have computers. If we didn't provide them with an opportunity to explore and learn the skills necessary to navigate in the world, we would not be providing the leadership necessary for them to be adult models. Richard, the reason most homes don't have computers is by conscious choice. We don't believe technology itself is bad. However, it needs to be managed and channeled in a healthy direction, similar to television, and life in general. I'll catch you up on all of that later, as I promised, but the short version is, yes, there was a unanimous vote, and I might add, an enthusiastic one, to have me prepare a model including space, activities, growth potential, and, of course, cost. It's a bit overwhelming, so as always, I will proceed with a bite at a time. So there you are. Now, Richard, as I recall we are going to go on an adventure, and I think you have been extremely patient under the circumstances that this is your day actually. I apologize. I know how important this is to you, finding your new home. So we shall get about it."

"Margaret, I love hearing about your plans and the energy you have as you're sharing. It's very contagious in a good way. So thank you. And now, yes, I am so ready to get started. What's the game plan?"

"The first cottage is an easy walk from here. The lady's name is Mrs. Florence Newbury. She is not a local resident, at least has not been for very long. She came for summer visits for several years but always stayed pretty isolated. I was really quite surprised when she decided to stay permanently. Most folks that make that transition become immersed in the community. She is quite reserved, so I'm sure the cottage would be quiet, and the gardens are beautiful. She has a very good groundskeeper and the cottage itself is in excellent condition. Just don't be surprised if she doesn't give much information. I think you had better be prepared to ask about anything you want to know. "So if you're ready, we'll be on our way. I wore my walking shoes, as usual. Mary, we're off on an adventure. Thank you so much for that delightful muffin, and I love the name 'Morning Glory.' Well, Richard my friend, off we go to see the first cottage. This is the street that the cottage is on, Serene Street."

"It really does appear to be the right name, Margaret. The trees along the side of the street provide shade and protection. It's very quiet. There are flower gardens in every yard. This place never ceases to amaze me. What address are we looking for?"

"It's in the next block, Richard. 768. The main house is a bluish-grey shade with white shutters, and of course a large wraparound porch, which almost everyone has. Most folks actually spend a lot of time on their porches, but not true with Mrs. Newbury. I don't know, perhaps she is sensitive to sunlight, and . . . here we are. What do you think so far?"

"The house is charming, the neighborhood is seemingly without flaws, so let's go for it."

"Mrs. Newberg is expecting us. I called her and confirmed the time. However, the last time I was here, she was somewhat preoccupied.

"Good morning, Mrs. Newberg, I believe you have met Mr. King. Thank you for attending the reception."

"Yes, I was there, and it was very nice. I do read your books, Mr. King. If you want to see the cottage, she knows where it is. She also has the pertinent information. As you remember, I'm sure you'll just follow the walkway around the house. The cottage is in the back. Very private. I like my privacy." She closed the door.

"Yes, Margaret, I do see what you mean. She is probably a very lonely lady. Well, this is a very nice garden and a lovely setting. Oh yes, there are many things I like about this cottage. It's large enough to not be claustrophobic. I do have just a touch or at least the potential for that. The view is wonderful. But it's just not a happy place. I know that may sound silly, but I am absolutely sure that this is not the place for me. Shall we go tell her right away?"

"No, Richard, I think she would prefer that I call her, which I will do later."

∗

"Well, one down. Two to go. I do appreciate the effort you made to line these plans up for me, and this is really lovely, but it's just not right. Are you disappointed, Margaret?"

"Not in the least, Richard. I was very serious when I told you there were other options as well as the three we will see today. I just want you to know it's right for you. I know finding a home base is very important to you, and I'm sure you will know it when you feel it. Our next appointment is a little further out, and not until two o'clock, so we have time to have lunch, and then you will meet two very special people, Mr. and Mrs. Jessup. They are both third-generation families and are very generous people. They are active in the community center and volunteer at the library. The cottage is vintage, but spacious, clean, and sits almost in the middle of a flower garden. And yes, there are flowers everywhere in this community. Richard, I know I asked you to find a place for us to have lunch, but would you be disappointed if I made a suggestion?"

"Margaret, I would be relieved, because honestly, I was kind of daydreaming, or perhaps we can call it meditating, yesterday, and I completely forgot to fulfill my duty. So what is your suggestion?"

"It may be a place you haven't discovered yet, Richard. It's disguised as a pharmacy, so if you don't know it's secret or need medication, it's easy to miss. It has a soda fountain, and not just a soda fountain. The fountain and actually the building are well over hundred years old. The wood is beautiful, and it has the original huge engraved mirror behind the fountain, and the food is excellent. They have a special soup of the day and a special sandwich of the day. They get their bread from Mary, and everything is fresh and freshly made. If you ever want a milk shake, that is the place to get it."

"They make the shake in these large stainless-steel mixer things and it's thick and creamy and so much. They pour what they can in a glass and the rest is left in the mixer thing and you get that too."

"Margaret, I would love to go to the pharmacy. Nothing could keep me away from it. Are we almost there?"

"Yes, we are, Richard. It's about two blocks further, and fortunately we are late enough to miss the major lunch crowd. I guess I did get a little carried away about the pharmacy, but it is so special. The same family has owned the building. Actually, they had the building built. It is like a living museum, and of course, it was one of my favorite spots as a child, and it still holds a bit of magic for me, and I want to share that with you."

"Margaret, you are the only person I know or have known that can make a milkshake sound exciting. You make life exciting, Margaret. Thank you."

"Oh, Richard, we are here, and we have missed the crowd. This is perfect, and thank you. I think you are pretty special too. Now to decide, and you really can't go wrong. I know what I'm going to have, but take your time, and look at the menu. After you do decide what you want, turn the menu over, there is a wonderful story about the history of this building and business. You see you get lunch and a history lesson, and by the way, lunch is on me today. I believe you said that dinner you owe me is tonight. Or had you forgotten about that too?"

"No, ma'am, I have not forgotten. I have the reservation made. No, I'm not going to tell you where. We will be driving, and dinner is at 7:00 p.m. tonight. So everything else will just have to work around that."

"It sounds like another adventure, Richard. I think you already know how much I love adventures, and by then, you may have found your dream home cottage. Things are moving rather quickly. Such is life."

*

"Margaret, that was truly an experience. Everything—the food, the ambiance, and the people. You do know everyone in town, don't you?

And they know you, both young and old. It doesn't matter. The energy is the same. Thank you. That was a real treat. Now I'm ready for the second treat, the next cottage."

"Yes, I just confirmed with the Jessups that we are on our way. If I know them as well as I think I do, they will have the tea ready and will be looking forward to us having at least a short visit. These folks really use their front and back porch. My hunch is we'll be on the back porch this afternoon. They have a lovely herb garden, as well as the inevitable flower garden, and the smells are delicious. Her specialty to serve with tea is a family recipe—anise cookies, very delicate and quite good. If we weren't on a schedule, I would suggest we walk, while we still can, but I guess that will have to wait."

"Margaret, in this town, there's beauty everywhere. Where is the other side of the track, so to speak?"

"We are so fortunate. There is no other side of the track. Of course, we have many of these large Victorian homes which truly do look rather storybook style. We also have many modest homes, some rather large and many quite small, much like the cottages you're seeing today, but the respect for one another creates a blindness to differences, and everyone takes pride in themselves, their homes, and their community. So the result is harmony, and I know I'm just scratching the surface again, but I promise before my vacation is over, you will have so much information about this town. You will probably yell, 'Uncle' because it is a story I haven't been asked to tell for a very long time, so I may have forgotten the shortcuts. We will see. And here we are."

"Margaret, before we go in, just let me say, I really don't want you to take any shortcuts. I want to travel every pathway."

"OK, Richard, remember you asked for it. Now to the next cottage, with tea of course. Mr. and Mrs. Jessup, how nice to see you. I know you must have met Richard. I noticed you having what seemingly was a very energetic discussion."

"Oh yes, Mr. King, how very nice to see you. We are honored to have you as our guest, and of course, our own sweet Margaret."

"You look stunning, my dear, as usual. Welcome, have a seat. Those two rocking chairs were just waiting for you two young things. Please call us Carl and Melba. My parents were Mr. and Mrs. Jessup."

"Well, Carl and Melba, this is a spectacular view that you have from this spot, or actually I think from anywhere. How long have you folks lived here?"

"Well, let's see. Melba, how long have you been here? I was born here, and Melba and I have been married for a great, and I do mean that quite literally, part of our life. You know, we might as well tell you, we really don't even have a calendar. We know when the seasons change, and when the major holidays come around, our children make sure we know about them. Other than that, we just get up every morning, grateful for the day and all of the many blessings we know it will bring. Do what we can to make someone's life a little better and then of course we know ours will be. Is that about it, Melba?"

"Yes, my darling, that's about it. I think it's time for tea and cookies, and I'll just bet these folks have places to go and things to do, so we mustn't take too much of their time. Mr. King, I understand you are going to become a part of our family, I mean, the community family."

"Please, call me Richard. Yes, I am, Melba, and I can honestly tell you I find this community fascinating. I have been here for such a short period of time, and yet it's kind of like I've thrown my calendar away. Time has become very different for me here, and that's a good thing. I am looking forward to seeing the cottage that you have available. I can't imagine having better neighbors, and I love your cookies, Melba."

"Carl, do you have a wood shop? I thought I noticed one on the way in."

"Very good eye, my boy. Yes, I do have. I don't really use it very much anymore. I used to make custom-order furniture. I loved every piece I made. My dad and I worked together for a long time. I was his apprentice, and he was his dad's apprentice. My son has the skill but not the connection to the wood, at least not now. He may come back to it. We'll see. But now my grandson has his own shop and is continuing the line. If you ever have the need for furniture, he's the one to see. He doesn't ever pay me to say that. The door to the cottage is open. Take your time. If we're not around when you leave, just shut the door. We never lock anything. Wouldn't even know how to unlock it, and if it's not the right place for you, you'll know that. Please don't be a stranger. We will look forward to next time."

"Melba, Carl, it is a pleasure to meet you, and I certainly will see you folks again either way. Thank you so much."

"Margaret, don't you be a stranger either. You get a little busy sometimes, I think. At least you're doing what you love. Thank you for bringing this nice young man our way. It's great to have another friend."

"Margaret, they are everything you said they would be, and if possible, even more. I really like them. Now to go inside the cottage. This is absolutely incredible. Every piece of furniture is a work of art and comfortable. The view from every window is both stimulating and restful. Margaret, have you been in this cottage before?"

"The only time, Richard, is when I was here to see if I thought it may be of interest to you, and it appears as if you are."

"I definitely am, but, and here's that darn but again, there's just something holding me back. I love the cottage—the furniture, the setting, the people. There's nothing really that I don't like about it. Yes, there is something, and it may be totally unrealistic, but I want to start painting. I just don't see the space that I'm looking for here. I really want a porch, one that if it is not enclosed perhaps I could do something with it. I'm rambling I know, the words are just coming out, and I don't even know where they are coming from. And this may indeed be the perfect place. I'm probably just being silly."

"Richard, if you're not sure, you don't need to make a commitment now. Respect your intuition. Don't be afraid of it. I know you want this next step to be completed. However it is a very important one to you, and deserves thinking about."

"You're right, Margaret. Thank you. I know I will know when the time is right, and this might be the right decision, but I am certainly and literally going to sleep on it. So what do you think? Do we have time for the next one today, or shall we start fresh tomorrow?"

"I'll leave that decision up to you, Richard. It is almost five o'clock already, and while I'm sure Mary's granddaughter has kept Howdy company, I'm also sure that he is ready to go home. I don't like to think about it, but he has had a lot of birthdays, and he deserves to have some special consideration. So I'm thinking my vote is for us to resume the hunt tomorrow and give ourselves a little time to relax and enjoy the evening and not focus on my job or your home search or anything except good food, excellent conversations, and perhaps a ginger martini. "Oh no, you said we were driving. Sorry, I guess you'll just have to watch me enjoying mine."

"And, Margaret, I will enjoy it. I'm serious. I look forward to seeing you the next time from the last time I've seen you. Now I'm talking like I have already had a martini."

"Obviously I agree, and now let's be on our way. May I pick you up about 6:45 p.m., or I could call and change the reservation for later?"

"No, Richard, 6:45 p.m. is fine. There's really not very much that I have to do. Howdy has had his frolic on the beach, and he is going to be ready for his own quiet time. So 6:45 p.m. is perfect. By then, I will be very ready to eat. I will already be in town, so I'll meet you at your hotel, OK?"

"Whatever works best, as long as I am able to fulfill my commitment to take you to dinner, which, I must add quickly, I am looking forward to. I will count the minutes until I see you."

Well that was close. I really don't want Richard to come to my house until after he has seen the cottage. He has been here once just after he arrived, and it was dark. I think if I take him by way of the back road, we get to the cottage first. I just want him to see the cottage for what it is. If it's right, he will know it, and I will feel so much better about it. If he doesn't know I would be his landlady. That sounds so silly. I am being so silly. Why can't I just be clear about the whole thing and just let it be? I think it is very important to me to have Richard love the cottage, and be very comfortable, maybe even excited.

"Oh Howdy, I feel like a crazy lady. Poor old guy. You are tired tonight. I bet you're glad I'm going out, so you can really have some quiet time. You had a very busy week. You deserve your rest time. I can't believe it's only been a week since my life changed. I am so glad that I have ten days to just be. I love my job, my routines, and yet I do have a strong desire to just have no schedule, no routine, nothing except whatever happens from moment to another. Oh my! I am going to be late again."

"Richard, I am so sorry. I just got lost in my thoughts, and I actually have no excuse."

"Margaret, you are here now, and this is when time begins for me. You are lovely, you smell good, and your shoes are awesome. I assume you are not planning on a hike tonight. In which case, you would be correct.

Let's go, love. I did call and change our reservation to 7:15 p.m., so you are right on time."

"Richard, are you for real? You seem to know me so well, and I love it. Yes, let's go to dinner. I am so ready to relax and be taken care of. That was part of the bargain, right? You'll order for me, get me a ginger martini, laugh at my jokes, even if they're not funny, and dare I ask, will there be music?"

"Just wait and see, my dear girl. Remember your job is to relax and just be."

"Well, here we are."

"Oh my goodness! Richard, did I doze. I am so sorry."

"Margaret, no sorries!"

"Right. I'm awake now. Oh, this place is wonderful! Flowers everywhere, and this view of the ocean is like a painting, and I'm not even inside yet, but I am definitely awake. The aromas remind me that I am famished. What a nice table and view. Richard, is this an Italian restaurant?"

"Yes, Margaret, and the best. You are going to have chicken piccata, with garlic, mushrooms, and lemon sauce, and so am I. The chicken will literally melt in your mouth. You will hardly have to chew."

"Richard, I love it, and the hostess was so happy to see you. You have been here before?"

"Well, not really, but yes. I was just walking around as I have done every day, and I smelled this place, so I had to come in, although they were not open. The hostess is one of the owners. She and her family were cooking and drinking wine. The kitchen is immaculate. So I had a glass of wine, complimentary. I knew I had to bring you here. Oh yes, I did have one little taste of chicken piccata, that's all. We'll start out with minestrone soup, family-style, then a delicious salad with an old family recipe Italian dressing. You, of course, will have a glass of warm red wine, which I will have to taste to be sure it is perfect, and here we are. It has begun. Your wine, my lady. I have ordered two tasters so you do have to choose either one of those, or something else."

"Richard, they are both wonderful, but I'll have this one. The soup is so good. Are you sure the chicken is better than this?"

"In its own way, Margaret. Everything in its own time."

"There is music, Richard. I hear violins."

"Yes, my dear, and they will soon be asking you what you would like for them to play."

"I think I must be daydreaming again, but don't pinch me, Richard. I don't want to wake up quite yet."

✳

What an enchanting evening; we simply enjoyed good food, no, great food, music, and one another. I do believe in soul mates, I have no doubt that Margaret is my soul mate. We finish each other's sentences sometimes in a comfortable way. I am at home with her. I have been looking for a place, when really I know now, wherever I am I will be at home. Even, heaven forbid, if Margaret and I are not together, I feel whole again.

I have found myself in this little community that's so full of love and beauty. Everywhere I go, I am so warmly welcomed. I am ready to hear the history, and story of this community. It's like a safe haven. I have never experienced a town like this. I love it. Margaret and I are meeting for lunch and then on to the next cottage. I almost hate to see the search end. The adventures, as Margaret calls them, are so much fun. However, I am ready to settle in and build my nest. So we shall see what the day has to offer. Margaret has ten days of vacation. I do hope she hasn't made plans to leave town; that would be a real disappointment, unless of course she would like company. There are several places in this area that I would like to explore. I am really getting ahead of myself. Slow down. Take a deep breath. A shower may help.

✳

What a memorable night. I didn't get home until after midnight, but I feel surprisingly refreshed.

"So, Howdy, my friend, after I have my special morning drink and we do our yoga routine, we will be off for a nice walk. I think the lighthouse special will be perfect for this morning. I need to clear my head. Yoga will get me ready for some decision-making. So off we go, fellow. You lead the way. I will follow your pace or at least try to."

That food last night, every bite, my taste buds were orgasmic. Now that's an interesting analogy! But true. The mood was festive. Everyone

63

was having such a good time. And the music, so romantic, and when Richard and I danced, it was so easy. He knew how to lead, and I could just relax and follow the music, and our bodies seemed to be as one. I have danced with a lot of people, but in retrospect, it was more mechanical. With Chad, we were so young and what we did, which was called dancing at the time, was fast, loud, and fun. Last night was fun but on a much different level. Time passed so quickly. When I realized we were the last couple there, being the sharp lady that I am, I realized it must be closing time. Richard didn't seem to be any more aware of time than I was. The family, don't remember their names, just the family, were all wonderful. They seemed to be so happy to have us there, and they obviously have adopted Richard. It's amazing that I didn't know this restaurant. It is so close, just twenty miles away, but certainly tucked away. I haven't been exploring much outside of our little community, but what a rich jewel. I'm sure we will return and perhaps not stay quite so late.

"Howdy, you are really keeping a nice pace. I think your rest last night was very good for you."

Today is the day Richard sees the cottage, and silly me, I have cleaned and picked flowers for the table. I love the porch swing, always have. That's where I would spend a lot of time, when my mother would be about her writing, reading, artwork, and research. She had such a curiosity about everything, along with a great sense of humor. I do miss both of them a lot. But I also feel their presence and guidance often. I haven't spent much time at the cottage, but I do truly love it, and if Richard decides it is right for him, I am sure I will spend more time there.

I can really see him living there. I have not wanted to think about it very much because, more than anything, I want him to find the right place for him. I just happen to think the cottage is that place. We will very soon know. Because we have to go back now, Howdy. I have a few things to do before I meet Richard for lunch. I am so glad he suggested 1:30 p.m. He seems to sense what I need before I know I need it. I would probably have said noon and been rushed and late. This way, I will possibly only be late. My first day of vacation, I do have some plans, and after Richard settles in, I think there are some special little towns that I know I want to visit, and I'm pretty sure he would find them of interest also. It is apple time, and there is this very special orchard that I am very familiar with, and they will be having this special pie-baking contest this next Saturday. It's an all weekend event for Apple Harvest Days. I can hardly wait to tell Richard all about it. First things first. Remember, he is in the moment. Right.

Speaking of the moment, it's getting close to time to meet Richard, and maybe I'm just procrastinating about him seeing the cottage. I really still think it would be better to have him see it in the late evening, and I do have a plan. I know an ideal place on the beach for a picnic and a walk, and we're not meeting until 1:30 p.m. He doesn't know about the picnic, especially since I just thought about it. So it would be almost sunset, and the beach spot is a natural for taking the back road to the cottage. So that's what we'll do. It even feels like a picnic day.

"And, Howdy, you can have the afternoon off. You're on vacation also."

"Richard, I am on time! Thank you for a lovely evening, and that sounds trite even as I say it. Really, I enjoyed every minute and morsel, and I have a surprise for you. A picnic on the beach. I hope you like picnics on the beach."

"Hello to you, my dear one. I had a magnificent evening. There was one problem! The time passed too quickly. And yes, I love picnics, especially at the beach. What is our schedule for the cottage?"

"Oh, that's very flexible. The owner of the cottage has given us an open time frame. Totally at our leisure. So we can take our time, although I do understand you are a little anxious, and perhaps ready, to go see it right now."

"Oh no, Margaret. I am ready to go on a picnic with a very interesting person who has, I am sure, brought lots of good food and drink, and of course conversation that brightens the universe. Well, just for that, I will also drive today, and you just relax and enjoy."

"Well, here we are, our own little cove. I have been here many times, and seldom is there anyone else here. Don't get me wrong. I love people, but there are times, like this, when I am very pleased to have this ideal place to share with only you. So do you want to eat right away or walk on the beach, or just be?"

"I am so ready to eat, Margaret that I can't think of anything else. If you would be willing to bring the basket, I will choose the place, and spread the cloth.

"There we are. We have a natural rock table and chairs. Margaret, they are perfect. Are they really natural?"

"Yes, Richard, they are real rocks."

"Yes, I know that."

"But I know what you mean, Richard. They are perfect, and yes, nature is the master carver."

"Thank you again, my dear. The food was so good and what were those drinks?"

"Richard, another one of our marvelous gifts from nature are apple orchards. We are blessed with orchards that are over one hundred years old. One that we will talk about later is over two hundred years old. The drinks are from one of those orchards."

"Yes, it is so good."

"I feel like taking a walk, Richard. Would you like to join me, or do you want to just relax?"

"I want very much to join you, Margaret. I think there was more than apple juice in those drinks. I am feeling very energetic. Margaret, what are you feeling right now? You look absolutely radiant."

"Oh, Richard, this is such a special time for me. I love the ocean as the waves wash in and out. I feel the flow of life. As I breathe in and out, I feel the energy of divine love flow in and through me. This energy is what sustains me and this community. And yes we are in human form, and we have challenges, but we come together in times of need. Like the energy from the ocean, through love for one another, we live as though we are one. Richard, I will always be honest with you. If you ask me a question, I will answer it as simply, but as clearly as I can. I know you are interested in knowing more about our town, and there is a lot to know. I will just tell you that we are a community that has up to eighth generation families. A very solid foundation was created by our ancestors, and I have learned that it is very special, and that's all I will share for now. Pretend it's one of your mystery novels. One evening soon we will begin the process of history sharing, until or unless you get bored, and we can stop when you say 'uncle'."

"Margaret. I can't imagine ever wanting you to stop. I love watching you as you talk. You are so intense and yet so radiantly serene. But OK. I can wait. And thank you for sharing what you were feeling. And now, is it time to go to the cottage?"

"Yes, Richard, you have been very patient. It's only a short drive from here."

"Margaret, this is a beautiful countryside, and I love this old road. Every time we turn another corner, the ocean view just keeps getting better. If this is an indication of what the cottage has to offer, I love it already."

"Well, here we are, Richard, the Westwind Cottage."

"Is that a swing on the porch?"

"Yes, it is, Richard."

"Oh, I love it."

"You haven't even been inside yet."

"I know, but I know that I feel so good about this one. Yes, let's to inside. I am excited. Oh, Margaret, a reading nook and shelves for books and a great desk. Windows with views of the ocean, the brilliant colors of the trees, and oh my goodness, this is it! I feel like only goodness has lived here. It's hard to explain, but this is a happy house, and that's what I'm going to call it—Happy Home. So needless to say, Margaret, yes, this is it. So how soon can I see the owners and move in?"

"Richard, you are looking at her, and you may move in right now. That is if you don't mind having a landlady that intends to have visitation rights. May we put that in the contract?"

"Margaret! This is your cottage?"

"Yes, Richard. I didn't mean to withhold information, but I really didn't want to influence you in any way. Perhaps I couldn't have anyhow, but I felt better, perhaps somewhat selfishly, by having you discover it yourself and you certainly did."

"Margaret, I am ecstatic, and your house is close by, I assume."

"Actually just beyond the hedge in the back. I will honor your privacy, Richard."

"We can certainly work that out. Margaret, I have no concerns, only joy. This cottage feels so good. Who has lived here before?"

"No one has actually lived here, but it has been a very busy little house. My parents and their parents traveled a lot, and they had fiends from all over the world. Writers, poets, philosophers, anthropologists— you get the idea. This became a haven for many of them. Also, it was primarily my mother's hideaway. Our house was, is, certainly large enough to accommodate everyone. They also entertained often, but Mom liked the quiet, the view, and the cottage itself. She did a lot of her writing here. She did a lot of technical writing, but it was done so well with very colorful, descriptive language that it often felt like reading poetry to me. She had a very unique style and did a lot of research. She would bring me down here often. I love the porch swing and the reading nook. I used that more often than she did. She was also quite spontaneous. She would appear to be completely engrossed and suddenly say, 'Margaret, my darling girl, let's go climb a hill or go play in the sand on the beach.' And away we'd go. So, yes, Richard, this has always been a very happy house, and I am so glad you are going to be in it. I think it's been somewhat neglected."

"Not any more, Margaret. After tomorrow, it will have tender loving care, and when I say tomorrow, I mean in the morning. I am so anxious to be here, and I really don't have very much to move in, so I'll just pack my suitcase, buy a few groceries, and settle into my nest. When shall we do the paperwork and make an honest man out of me?"

"Richard, being on vacation allows me a great deal of flexibility. Howdy and I have our routines, but they're flexible also. So I'm thinking anytime after 11:00 a.m. I will be available. So your call or we can just leave it open, and you get here whenever you want. If I'm not home I will be soon, and we're not that far away now, you know. So no problem with time frames."

"That sounds great, Margaret. I definitely owe you another dinner, and oh yes, the rent money."

"Well, the rent money is negotiable, but I already have a plan for the dinner. Actually, if you're free on Saturday, I have a whole day and evening planned. See how I am. 'Give an inch, take a mile.' Saturday is a date, for sure. I don't know or care what you have planned. I do know it will be another memorable time. Oh yes, Richard, there is just one other part to it. On Friday we have to drive around the area, maybe to several apple orchards and fine the ugliest apples possible, because we need to bake an ugly apple pie for the pie contest on Saturday, and that's all I will say about that for now and very soon we will start the historic perspective of this community. You have been very patient. I know you have mentioned several times your continued interest and I haven't forgotten. It will take some time, and now that you're here, it will be easy to have more spontaneity about coordinating time. Now, my dear, I have some errands that I must do, and you have a new home to prepare for, so I will take you back to your hotel and look forward to seeing you tomorrow, and Richard, welcome to Happy Home."

"Margaret, it has been a long journey for me to get home. I'll tell you about that some day soon. Also, we always have so much to talk about and so little time to do it. I may have to be around here for a very long time."

*

I find this incredible. I read about this rather small (I thought) library in a small (I thought) community in a town with a beguiling name, Port Haven, Maine. A place where I kind of thought I would retreat and contemplate the process of going blind. Instead, I have acquired insight about myself, life, love, and I do believe I have only scratched the surface. Margaret is the most unusual person I have ever met. She has an inner glow and serenity about her, and yet she is very human, humorous, witty, extremely intelligent, and attractive. Everything is like it has been scripted—Margaret, the town, the cottage, and my sense of peace and pleasure.

I do feel at ease and complete with Margaret. I can at last be comfortable, thinking about Sylvia and not holding on and no guilt. I know what she meant when she made me promise that I would fall in love again. She wanted me to live for both of us and, of course, there will always be a part of Sylvia with me but certainly not in a negative way. I am a stronger and better person for having had her in my life, and I am ready to move on and I have no doubt that Margaret is the one for me, and after finding the cottage today, which was like finding another part of me, I know I am home. However, home has a different meaning now.

I have been looking for a place, and instead, I realize it's me. I can be content anywhere as long as I am comfortable with myself and I am. Although I also realize there are still some pieces to my puzzle that I am seeking and I'm pretty sure the next few weeks are going to be an adventure, I have so much that I want to know and so much that I want to say to Margaret and yet I don't want to rush anything. Very confusing. I find every day absolutely full and running over, and it's all good. I don't feel overextended or frustrated, and I am beginning to be in the moment more often, and I love it when I do. But it really does take a lot of discipline and motivation. It is so easy to slip ahead or behind, but the outcome is so worth it. I will continue enjoying the moments I can. I am sure they will grow. I think it may be like a garden. You just keep pulling the weeds. I think I will keep that image. When a negative thought comes, I will think of it as a weed and pull it up. Some weeds are more invasive than others so those thoughts, or weeds, may take a little longer. When a garden is tended, it produces abundantly, and I think perhaps our minds are a bit like that.

This time tomorrow night, I will be at my Happy Home, and I am really looking forward to this whole new chapter in my life and what in the world is this "ugly apple thing"? We are going to forage for the most ugly apples? I've always looked for the prettiest ones, the ones that had a regular apple shape and no spots or blemishes of any kind. I'm sure it will make sense, but right now it's just a bit confusing. So I will just go with the flow and enjoy the hunt. It's been a long time since I've done any baking, but I can follow directions and we will all have a good time. I do love apple pies, and the apple harvest festival sounds like a lot fun. I have no idea what it is, but I'm sure I will find out.

$$*$$

What a wonderful response to the cottage. I really did expect him to like it, and in my heart of hearts, I was so sure it was the right thing at the right time. It was a perfect connection, and his response to us being neighbors was great.

"Howdy, you have a new playmate, not exactly new to you, but certainly at a different level. I love Richard and that's that. And furthermore, I think he loves me. And I know he loves you, so the recipe is perfect, a successful outcome."

"He is always so receptive to everything and sincere. Certainly not doing anything to appease me. I would know that. He is just awakening to so many things, and I suppose I am also in my own way. I've been pretty set in my routines, which I do love. However, I'm beginning to remember what a beautiful and full life my parents had. They loved their routines and rituals, but they also loved to travel and entertain. When I was talking to Richard about the cottage, I remembered so vividly how exciting and alive the very atmosphere would be when guests were at the cottage. They had their privacy, but we also had such wonderful conversations and exploration walks and games. My mother especially loved to play board games, as do I, and I was never treated any differently than anyone else. They would ask my opinion often and frequently said that was exactly what they were looking for—a fresh perspective. It didn't seem unusual to me to be an accepted part of adult conversation. My parents had always respected my opinion. However, they also made sure I knew boundaries and expected me to respect them, as I did for the most part. They were so much fun to be with, and yet there was no doubt they were my parents and provided structure and guidance to me, and I am so very grateful for the time I had with them. My grandparents were such good storytellers and, most of the time, the stories that I thought were made up were actually true, as I found out later. I am so blessed to have the good fortune or destiny to be a part of the roots of this community and all that it means to me. I am so looking forward to sharing all of that with Richard or as much as he is receptive to. I know he is seriously seeking real information. I just want to share so much so fast because I am excited to have the opportunity especially with this very special man. We have blended so well.

Obviously, the next thing on the agenda is our "ugly apple pie." This event has been going on in some form for at least a century, and my family has been involved in it since the beginning, and now apples have become a major obsession through out Maine so that will be chapter one for Richard, along with an introduction to meditation. He may already have his own style. If so, we can share with each other. There is no right or wrong way, whatever works. This weekend is something I look forward to and actually planned my vacation around the festival because it is a gathering time, a time for us to remember we are family and renew who we are and how our ancestors created such a legacy for us. Not necessarily in a formal way, but just by being together, eating, dancing, music, storytelling—overall joy just to be together. Richard will learn a lot just being a part of the celebration and, of course, the pie-making contest.

I'm thinking I'd better check in with Margaret and find out more about this apple event. She seemed pretty excited when she was talking to me about it. But then again, she is just pretty exciting to be with anytime.

*

"Good morning, Richard. Did you rest well in your new home?"

"Oh my dear, yes I did. So well I've only been up a short while. Yes, Margaret, I love my home, and I love that you are only minutes away. So what is this apple thing you started to tell me about?"

"I just made some coffee, Richard, would you like some?"

"I thought I could smell coffee when I opened my door. But since I had forgotten to buy it, I thought it must be my imagination. Yes, Margaret, to answer your question, there is no beverage which I hold in higher esteem, especially in the morning. Which it still is, just barely. This tastes as good as it smells, and that is a treasure."

"Thank you. Well, we might as well get comfortable since this will be story hour. I will try to give you the short version and still have it be meaningful. This is a very special time for me."

"Every year, I take vacation time so I can become fully immersed in the spirit of the festival. I have been going I guess since I was born. It is tradition and I love it. Today, we will scour the countryside, choosing our apples. My grandmother would look out in her yard and say, 'That tree is for that dish.' She always had five or six varieties, and neighbors had other varieties. My special morning drink also comes from my grandmother. The story goes that citizens and army legionnaires in ancient Rome would drink a daily tonic of posca, a mixture of apple cider vinegar and hot water sweetened with a bit of honey. My parents carried the tradition, and so have I. My apple cider vinegar is made from fresh apple cider. I feel very grateful for the variety of orchards in this area and how well folks take care of them. The Apple Harvest Festival is like a celebration of having so many self-sufficient homesteads that had multiple trees—a time for sharing secrets and recipes, food, dance.

"I'll tell you about the pie contest. Each pie must use the same crust recipe. Then choosing the apples is the secret to success. I think you will be very surprised. I know I still am when I am tasting the pies. Well, first never count out an apple's ability to surprise you. Sometimes the worst-looking apples turn into the best-tasting pies. Therefore, the legend of the ugly apple pie quest. So today we will scour the countryside for ugly apples. We will need enough for three pies: One for the contest, one for us, and one for a neighbor. And of course, I will need to get enough for apple cider also. I have a picnic already proposed. I'm good with the picnic thing. So, Richard, shall I continue and give you a general overview of Saturday's activities? And by the way, you probably won't get to sleep late on Saturday morning because it is a full day."

"Yes, Margaret, I am intrigued. I'm also going to have another cup of coffee. Please continue."

"We will start out with breakfast, about 9:30 or 10:00 in the morning. We have plenty of choices. My favorite is a decadent French toast with apples of course and real maple syrup. There are vendors and music. We'll take blankets and chairs. Howdy absolutely loves the day. He knows everyone, and of course, the other dogs. There are games and, in general, just a lot of happy people. One of the big events is dinner. All of the food is from the local farms. I think it's currently called Fork to Farm or Farm to Fork, something like that, but we have been eating like this forever. We just call it 'Come to Dinner.' And yes, there is a big dinner bell, and we eat out under the apple trees and the host at our table. There are about twenty-two people per table. And everything is family-style because that's really what we are. Anyhow, the host will do a tribute to our ancestors and to the Native Americans and to our creator. Then the feast begins and what a feast. Of course, there is plenty of apple cider.

"After the dinner, that's about two hours because there is as much talking as eating. After dinner, yes, Richard, there is more. There is the Harvest Moon Hoedown, a barn dance. So that's a thumbnail sketch of Friday and Saturday. Sunday events start later. There is a brunch with every apple thing you can think of. It is wonderful. Then we kind of get in a circle, a very large circle, and mostly talk about the things we are grateful for and the coming winter season and find out if anyone needs wood or supplies of any kind. No one thinks of this as charity. It's always been a custom, actually, an honor, to be a good neighbor. We also talk about filling the storehouse for the winter. It's kind of like bartering. Someone has apples, someone else has honey, and so forth. It's all on the honor system. In this community, a person's word is honored, and we thank our ancestors for that as well. So Sunday is a very special day. After the circle, there are more games and music. People kind of drift off as they choose, and the festival is over. I know that must sound pretty overwhelming, but when we take it a moment at a time, it really flows very well."

"Margaret, I love watching you talk. Yes, I did listen, but no, I'm not feeling overwhelmed at all. I'm going to learn so much and meet so many wonderful people and eat the food. We will have a very good time. So I'm thinking we had better get started on this ugly apple search. It kind of reminds me of an Easter egg hunt."

"Yes, Richard, here are the bags for the apples and the picnic basket, and we'll start the party with fresh apple cider to drink. I have a map of the orchards and the priorities. We are certainly not the only seekers today, but I do know of some pretty hard-to-find places, so we will be walking a bit. Richard, we will be doing this again next week. We glean apples from trees throughout the county and bring them in to the community center where some are boiled down to molasses and for applesauce, and some will be fermented into vinegar or hard cider. So I guess really it is still an apple harvest event. There will be music and people peeling apples and doing the variety of things there are to do with cooking, spies. Oh and we also have a giant drying thing. The peelings are dried as well as slices of apples. Only the good peelings are kept. Some of them make it to the compost pile, after doing all of this. I still love apples, maybe because of this, actually. I can't imagine just going to a market and buying an apple, although I did when I was in college and they did not taste like an apple. As a matter of fact, as I recall, they often didn't have any discernible taste at all. Trust me, Richard, you will taste these apples."

*

"Margaret, what a day! We should be totally exhausted, but I'm not, and you don't seem to be. We covered a lot of territory, beautiful country, and the apples are so good. You were right. I could not only taste these apples, but I could taste the difference in the texture and the taste. You can climb those trees like a monkey. I couldn't believe it. I was struggling to climb my first tree, and you were already on your third."

"Oh yes, Richard, but you caught on really fast. Remember, I've done this for my entire life. When did you last climb a tree?"

"You know, honestly, I'm not sure. I do remember climbing trees as a very young boy but certainly never as an adult. I am so glad you had that mini ladder. It really came in handy. You do know your apples, my lady. And Howdy seemed to be grinning a lot, especially at me. I need to have a shower and change clothes before we start the pie baking, so I will be back shortly."

"Take your time, Richard. Really, the pie baking is fast and easy. Wear comfortable loose clothing. We'll do a simple yoga meditation perhaps while the pies are baking, if that's all right with you. I know it's what I want to do. You can watch if you'd rather."

"Margaret, I'm letting go of the person I used to be, at least that's what it feels like and becoming the person I am. I don't know if that makes any sense. I'm not even sure if I totally understand it. But I am very content, and I would love to join you, and it may be kind of like me climbing a tree. It took a few trips, but I got it, and I really enjoyed it."

"So I will be back shortly. Oh, by the way, Richard, I have a stew prepared. All I have to do is warm it. It is full of vegetables, chicken, and lots of good spices."

"Margaret, that sounds fantastic. I didn't realize I was hungry until you said that, and now I am famished. See you in about thirty minutes, love."

We did have a wonderful time. I have often done this by myself, and yes with you, Howdy, and I have always enjoyed it. But not like today. This was special. I remembered something my mother used to say, "Two are better than one. If one person falls, the other can reach out and help. But people who are alone when they fall are in real trouble." I think it is from Ecclesiastes. She didn't quote the Bible often but that obviously was very meaningful to her. I probably remembered because I almost fell. I just got distracted for a moment. I thought I was going down, and in that moment, I thought, "Oh how silly," and then, "I am so glad Richard is here." Well, now it is time to focus—make the biscuits, put the stew on low, have a quick shower, and we'll be ready to eat and relax with a cup of tea before the pie-making event. It will be so nice to have both of us working in the kitchen.

"Margaret, am I early?"

"Perfect timing, Richard. The biscuits are ready to come out of the oven, the stew is ready, and so am I. Let's do it. I always have a moment of silence before eating, Richard. Just to express gratitude for the many blessings in my life. And there, I just did it. This is a very simple dinner but it's also one of my favorites, so I hope you like it."

"Margaret, I could just smell it and be filled with satisfaction. However since it's right here in front of me, I am ready to eat. Oh my God, Margaret, this is delicious, and the biscuits just melt in my mouth. You are a magician. I just know it. I love your magic potions. I am under your spell, and I don't want the spell to be broken."

"Thank you, Richard. Things do seem better when they are shared."

"Would you like a cup of chamomile and mint tea, Richard? I'm going to have a cup."

"Yes, I would love it. It's very nice to just sit here with you, Margaret. I love having you close. I don't know how to explain it, but your glow is very soothing."

"Thank you, Richard. I feel very comfortable with you. I enjoy just being together, whatever we're doing, and if we're not doing anything and speaking of doing nothing, this is a time for Howdy and I to share our yoga routine. Please do as much or as little as you wish. A brief introduction quote, 'Do not pursue the past. Do not lose yourself in the future.' The past no longer is. The future has not yet come. Looking deeply at life as it is, in the very here and now, the practitioner dwells in stability and freedom. We must be diligent today. 'To wait till tomorrow is too late.' This is by the Buddha.

"First, get in a very comfortable position. There is no right or wrong position. Howdy lies down. I sit up. Find a focus point. That helps me to quiet my mind. I'm going to suggest you focus on one word, either silent or spoken. It can be any word. I suggest 'love'. If you haven't been practicing this consistently, don't be surprised or discouraged if thoughts keep crowding in. We are only going to start with ten minutes, unless you have been doing this or a similar exercise."

"No, Margaret, I have been totally inconsistent and discouraged. The times I have tried have been in a group setting for at least an hour. And honestly, my mind went everywhere. It was totally a wild thing, but I do want to learn, and I believe the time is right. So about ten minutes it is."

"You don't think about the time or anything but that one word, 'love'. And are you familiar with deep breathing?"

"Yes, I used to put a book on my abdomen and watch it as I learned to breathe. However, again, I have not been conscious of the practice for a while, but I do think it will come back."

"OK, so we are going to concentrate on breathing in 'love' and out 'love', and if your mind wanders, just gently bring it back."

"Margaret, that was wonderful, and the time just wasn't even there. I never thought about time or if I was doing it right. I can do this."

"Of course you can, Richard. We'll do it together. Now it's time to get busy. Would you be willing to peel the apples and I will make the pie crust while you do that?

"Yes, my dear. I would love to peel the apples and then what do I do with them?"

"After peeling them and coring them, put about ten at a time in this pot of cold water with lemon juice. Only leave them in the water for five to ten minutes and then out on this rack until they are all peeled, and then we can slice them, and I will have the secret ingredients ready, and we'll get them in the oven for about fifty minutes. Then we can actually lie down in the living room and listen to music and have a glass of wine if you'd like. You don't have to drive home now. What an incentive for me to get these apples peeled."

"Let me get to work, woman. You're in my space."

"Oh I see how you are taking over the kitchen, and I love it."

"The aroma coming from the kitchen is intoxicating, or is it the wine?"

"Well, Richard, if it's the wine, you'd better not have anymore. You do live three minutes away, you know."

"Oh yes, I do know and I love it. Margaret, this is the first time I have had my arms around you, and it feels very good to be right here, right now. I can smell your hair. I remember the first time I saw you. I also smelled you. Now that didn't sound like I meant it to."

"I know what you mean, Richard, and yes, it feels very good just being here, lying close, and enjoying this moment very much. I am so glad that my vacation time was planned so well. Maybe I am a magician, and I must wave my wand and break the spell. It's time for the pies to come out of the oven. Oh they are perfect, Richard. I can tell by the smell of the crusts that everything is perfect except for having to throw you out of my house."

"We do have a full day tomorrow. So until then, good night my magic lady."

Thank God for the pies. I was much too comfortable, and when Richard kissed the top of my head, I'm sure he could feel my body vibrating. I was shivering from head to toe, and then the timer went off. What if it hadn't?

∗

Another day in paradise. It does feel like that. I feel so alive. I guess that's a good thing, since I am. This harvest festival sounds like a lot of fun. I am quite sure that I will meet a lot of people today and wonder if they are like the ones I have already met. What a day! I just bet that

Margaret will have coffee made, and everything ready to go. She is really something. Last night when we were snuggling, I really didn't want to move because I wanted it to last forever, and she was very responsive. Then it was almost like an alarm clock went off, and said, "Wake up. You've been sleeping." Probably a good thing that the timer kind of awakened us. I'm not sure it was a good thing. I love Margaret, and I don't think we have to wait any decent amount of time to share that, but I do want it to be the right time and place, and that certainly isn't this weekend. But next week, I have a plan. Now I'd better go get that wonderful aromatic cup of coffee. I don't know what she does to it, but it's certainly not something I know how to do.

"Good morning, Richard. I do have the coffee ready, and Howdy and I have just finished our exercises and meditation, and I have had my special morning drink, which I will treat you to some morning in the near future. Now don't make a face like that. I think you are going to love it."

"Well, actually, Margaret, you have been right so far so whenever you are ready to offer. I am ready to give it a try. And I am really ready for this day. I hope I haven't gotten your expectations too high, although honestly I don't think I could. It's that special, at least for me it is. Let's go."

"Margaret, did I tell you that I had my car serviced a few days ago by a young man. I think his name was Edward."

"No, you didn't tell me, but I am sure your car got the servicing of its life."

"Absolutely, he is quite a guy. He obviously loves what he does. He treated me and my car with great respect. He actually recorded a history of when it's had what. It was very obvious that this was not a ten-minute-In-and-out operation."

"Yes, Edward loves what he does. The shop was his father's, and before that his grandfather's. Edward loved being in the garage with his dad who also loved cars. His older brother Marshal never wanted anything to do with grease or cars. He avoided the garage as much as he could. He chose to become a dentist."

"Is he a local dentist?"

"No. After becoming a dentist, he relocated in Boston, and he met a girl in college, who was from Boston, and so that's where he is now. They come in for holidays, and obviously Marshal misses family and being here. What I have seen happen often is after children come into the family, it's not unusual for them to return because they want to raise their children here. Occasionally, it's a challenging transition for the spouse. Turn right at the next intersection. We are getting closer."

"Yes, I have been seeing the signs. Actually how could anyone miss them? A huge scarecrow holding an APPLE HARVEST FESTIVAL sign. I love it."

"Well, looks like we have arrived. Howdy is really excited. He's been a little quiet lately. It's good to see him perk up."

"Well, Richard, shall we?"

"Let's go for it. I am ready for that fantastic breakfast you talked about, but you had better lead the way."

"Oh, Richard, the smells are so delicious. I can smell caramel apples and apple fritters, and oh I just love it. Martha, George, Betty and John, and their children are saving a place for us.

"Thank you, folks. How nice it is to see all of you. I want you to meet my special friend Richard. We are ready to eat. We'll be right back with some food, and then I swear, I will be more civilized.

"Come on Richard, I'm having a hunger fit."

"Well, those folks were fun. Are all of your friends like that?"

"Every year, I think it can't really be this good, and every year, it's even better. After breakfast, we'll just walk a bit, while I still can. We can talk to people, spread our blankets, and put up our chairs, and then Howdy will know where home base is, and he can visit with his friends."

"Margaret, none of the dogs are on a leash. How can that be? We have never had a leash habit nor have we ever had a needed to even consider it. As a matter of fact, just as an example of the value of not having to use leashes, last year a little girl fell off the dock at the lake. She panicked and was drowning. Howdy took off like a rocket, jumped in, and brought her to shore, before most of us knew what was happening. And there are many stories like that. Our dogs are companions, heroes, and sometimes even guide dogs. So no, we don't need to do leashes, and I'm so glad. We don't even use leashes for our children."

"Well, I can understand about the dogs, but children, now, that's just bad. Here's my special place for the blankets and chairs and stuff. Of course, under an apple tree, but I guess that would be almost anywhere. This is an apple orchard. Yes, it is, Richard, well over hundred years old, and still in the same family."

"Margaret, I have been to festivals but never one like this. All of the vendors are really artisans, like those beautiful quilts, and the ladies were actually making a quilt and telling stories and obviously having a great time."

"Oh yes, Richard, you get a real taste of what life is like in this country. I get my soap here. Something I don't like to do is make soap. But I love the way Margie makes soap. We can watch for a while if you like. My favorite is one that's made with real lavender. Yes, I love lavender tea, soap, to cook with. It's so soothing. And then Robert, her husband makes fudge, and he uses lavender for some of the fudge, and yes I hope to have some of that also. I didn't bring anything with me this time to barter with. I usually bring some scarfs to swap, but I didn't get them ready this time."

"Margaret, what are the prices? I don't see any price tags or signs. Oh, there are no prices. You pay what you can or you pay what it's worth to you. Really! That's incredible and that works? For over a hundred years, yes, Richard. We wouldn't have it any other way. So if there's anything you need or want, this is the time and place to get it."

"Well, I know right now that I want one of those quilts, but I wouldn't begin to know how to be fair about paying for it. Can you help me? I'm sure they must have worked for many hours, days, maybe even months. I don't know. Well, Richard, things that folks have made, they make because they love doing it, and part of the enjoyment is knowing that someone appreciates the work, and that's the greatest part of the pay. So let's think about replacing the material and stuff to make the quilt primarily. What's it worth to you, Richard?"

"More than I could ever pay, Margaret."

"Wow, that's a good answer, because you see, none of these folks are materialistic. I think a fair amount would be $50.00. Yes, I know in other places it would be $500 but not here."

"Well, I love this quilt, and it will have a good home, and I respect your skill in creating such a masterpiece. Thank you so much, Richard. I am so glad that you are part of our community, and it looks to me like you may not need the quilt to keep you warm. You two really have that glow. So enjoy, and I'm sure I'll be seeing you later."

"Margaret, I just bought my first quilt, in my whole life, and I love it, and yes indeed you do have a glow. If I glow half as much as you, we will not need the flashlight tonight."

"I'm happy for you, Richard. Everyone should have their own special quilt. And there is so much more. Margaret, I am so grateful that you brought these blankets and chairs. I am having so much fun. You do know everyone, don't you?"

"Well, Richard, my roots run deep in this community. Many of us go back for several generations. So I guess we're like an extended family, not from interbreeding, but from a sense of belonging. We have been fortunate to be able to keep our values. We are connected through our sharing philosophy, respecting one another's skills, and differences. Everyone finds pleasure in serving. I have traveled. I do have awareness of what's going on in the world. I am a librarian. My parents and grandparents and actually great grandparents traveled the world, spent time in India, China, Germany, and goodness knows where else. Their friends were scientists, philosophers, archaeologists, and people like Kahlil Gibran, Albert Schweitzer, Ernest Holmes, Mary Baker Eddy, and so forth. This place was first called Port Refuge. It was a place to escape to, and the result is that Port Haven is a result of some of the greatest minds leaving a legacy, which we value immensely. We live here by conscious choice. Oh my, I did not intend to lecture today, but this festival just reminds me of how much I have to be grateful for. Thank you for being such a good listener, Richard."

"My dear Margaret, I am totally enchanted by this day, and all of the genuinely wonderful people I have met, the incredible food I have eaten, both physically and mentally. I think I could listen to you for the rest of my life and never tire of the sound of your beautiful voice and the joy you express, even when speaking of concrete matters. I did beat you at checkers, not just once but two out of three times. Am I gloating, you say? Yes, I am. It was a lot of fun to watch your beautiful face express surprise. I'll just bet you haven't lost many games of checkers. Now have you?"

"Not for a long time. My father used to win an occasional game, but you know what? That is just what it is, a game, and I enjoy the sport of it. So we will have a rematch, my friend. Probably several. This is a good day, isn't it?"

"Richard, I am so glad that you are enjoying this experience, and of course there is so much more to come. I think it was a great place to rest, and actually, I think we both dozed a bit, even in the midst of everything that is going on. The dinner bell will probably ring in a short while. Just to kind of prepare you, and I think I sort of did already, but this dinner is really kind of like a traditional Thanksgiving Day dinner, without the focus being on the turkey. Although there may indeed be turkey, this is a celebration day of gratitude. And there's the bell. I love that sound. And here's Howdy. He always stays close to the table during dinner."

"Margaret, this entire table is full of food. I don't even know what half of it is, but it is beautiful—the colors and smells and everything. Instead of Haven, I think it must be heaven."

"Richard, Mr. Mitchell is the host of our table. He will give a very short but meaningful talk. He's a very good friend."

"Good evening, friends. We are once again blessed to be together on this special evening. I will try to keep this short. I can see, and smell, the abundant pleasures before us. But as most of you know, we do not live by bread alone. So go into the fields and countryside, where you will see farmers and gardeners busy sewing seed in prepared soil. If you were to ask them what they expected to produce from their labors, they may regard the question as frivolous, and tell you that they do not 'expect' at all, that they know exactly what will be produced, and that it will be whatever they have sown. Every fact and process in nature contains a lesson for the wise ones. There is a process of seed sowing in the mind and life, a spiritual sowing which leads to a harvest according to the kind of seed sown. Thoughts, words, and acts are seeds sown, and by the law of things, they produce after their kind. In other words, 'that which ye sow, ye reap'. See yonder fields. So you who would be blessed, scatter blessings. We can certainly witness great blessings in this abundance that has been produced by all of us. So please eat, spiritually and physically. I am grateful to our creator for each and every one of you, my friends. Enjoy."

"Enjoy we shall. I want one bite of everything, Margaret, but that may be impossible."

"Nothing is impossible, Richard. It just takes a little longer. That's why I told you that we would be at this table for at least two hours. It will go so quickly, like the blink of an eye."

"Margaret, I am very familiar with the 'reap what you sow' quote, and it makes sense. But it also seemed as though there was so much more to it. What do you think?"

"Well, Richard, by scattering blessings, as an example, I believe in life we get by giving. We grow rich by scattering. For example, a person who says they are in possession of knowledge which they cannot give out because the world is incapable of receiving it, either does not possess such knowledge, or if he does, he will soon be deprived of it. To hoard is to lose. Even the person who would increase material wealth must be willing to part with (invest) what little capital there is and then wait for the increase. As long as one retains a hold on money, one is essentially poor, but if wisely lets it go, like the farmer, he scatters his seeds of gold, and then one can reasonably expect the increase. So very simply, we are encouraged to stay conscious of 'what mental seeds have I been sowing?', 'what have I done for others?', 'what is my attitude toward others?' Let us learn from the farmer the simple truths of wisdom. This festival is a time for reflection, resolution, and gratitude, and, of course, for joyful revelry. I just don't seem to be able to give you a one-liner answer to anything, Richard."

"I am so glad you don't, Margaret. That's not what I'm looking for. Another bell ringing."

"I hope you have left room for the pie-tasting event because that's next."

"Well, fortunately, I was talking as much as I was eating. So I think, no I know I can manage. Let's do it. Oh my God, Margaret, this is incredible. This is the one we baked, isn't it?"

"Yes, I put the little star crusts on ours, and I haven't seen another one with that design. We take a sample cup for as many as we can and vote for one, two, and three, and put our votes in the water bucket."

"Margaret, I can't decide. They are all number one."

"I know what you mean, Richard. It is really challenging. Oh well, fortunately, we all know we are winners, and it's all for fun. Mrs. McAllister will win this year, I'm sure. She is the one that has entered this contest for seventy-plus years, and she has the best apples in the county. Her husband and her father did some fancy grafting of their apples trees, and there is no doubt that whatever they did, they did it right."

"Taste this one, Richard. This is the one. I am sure of it. It is perfection, the texture, the spices, and the incredible taste. What do you think?"

"I think this one is number one for my vote, and besides I can't eat another bite of anything."

"Neither can I, Richard. I hear the music."

"The barn dance is starting. Then we'll start with something slow."

"Fortunately, they always do that because none of us can move right now. But we will soon."

"Margaret, these people can really play."

"I know. It's magic. The music awakens the spirit, and soon we'll be dancing like the wind. Just let the music be your guide."

"Margaret, I am really not a dancer, but you're right. It is effortless, and you are like a feather in my arms, and after all that food, how can it be? I feel intoxicated. Was that just apple cider?"

"Yes, my dear, just apple cider. I think the intoxication is from the magic of the moment."

*

"Poor Howdy, you are so tired, but you really had a good time yesterday."

What an event! I have loved the festival forever, but this time it's different. Actually, I'm different. The spark that has been ignited between Richard and me since our first contact continues to grow. Last night, when Richard walked me to my door, I laid my head on his chest. I felt the electricity between us immediately. Then when he put his hand over mine, I looked up instinctively. As our eyes met, the heat intensified. Then Howdy came to the rescue. I had forgotten to let him in, so he gently reminded me with a nudge. So the spell was broken, at least for the moment. But the intensity of the emotions have been unsettling. Richard has awakened sensuous feelings that have been dormant for years. We are a great blend, and I am excited, just thinking about seeing him soon. One more part left of the festival: Richard has fit in to everything as though he's been a part of the community forever. That's kind of the way I feel about him also, like he's been a part of my life forever. I can't even imagine him not being.

Oh, Margaret, slow down a bit. There's no need to rush anything. Take a breath, literally. It is time for meditation and very deep breathing. I can always depend on that to clear my mind and bring me back into the moment. Conscious mindfulness always helps me to concentrate, focus better, with increased awareness—an awareness into everyday life. I do absolutely always feel body vibrations while meditating, and there is a sense of energy along with such a calm clear focus. Well, this is Sunday. Last day of the festival. I do hope Richard is not exhausted by all of this. He certainly doesn't seem to be overwhelmed at all. I am so glad. Definitely coffee-brewing time.

"Howdy, you are not your usual perky self. I could tell you wanted to go for a walk, but we didn't get very far, did we? Maybe you need to take the day off and rest today. I will miss you a lot, but you had a great day yesterday, and last night. So if you would rather rest today, that's fine with me."

*

"Richard, good morning. I swear you know when the coffee is ready. How do you do that?"

"Good morning, darling I just used your crystal ball, and it tells me all things that I need to know."

"Oh great! Now I suppose you know all of my secrets. No, my dear, just the ones you want me to know, and when you want me to know them."

"Well, that's a relief. Did you rest well?"

"Well, Margaret, to be quite honest, I suppose I did. I'm not sure exactly when I was asleep and dreaming or when I was just dreaming. Now that is not exactly a riddle. You kept running through my mind. However, I am refreshed, energized, and ready for the day. Where's Howdy? He's usually right here by my chair by now."

"Richard, I'm concerned about Howdy. He is really beginning to tire easily."

"How old is Howdy, Margaret? I don't remember exactly. I'm thirty-three, and we got him when I was home for Xmas from college. So probably about thirteen or fourteen years old, I suppose, but he has always been so full of energy and adventure. I am going to take him to visit John, his vet, tomorrow. It's time for a checkup anyhow. And I will feel better."

"Shall we stay home today, Margaret?"

"Oh no, Howdy would not want us to do that. He may just need some peace and quiet."

"No, my dear, you don't get out of this that easy. Margaret, I am so ready for the brunch although I didn't think I would ever want to eat another bite or see another apple. That was yesterday. Today, I want to smell the cinnamon and nutmeg and all of the wonderful aromas that will be there, and I am really looking forward to the circle. What do you call it?"

"You know something, Richard. I don't think we've ever called it anything. It's just something we do. So I guess we would just call it a tradition. So let's do it.

"Howdy, you take care of things here, and we'll be back soon. I will miss you, buddy.

"I will really miss him, Richard. He has just always been there for me.

"I can see that, Margaret. You and Howdy have a special connection. That's very obvious. He is an amazing companion. He'll probably be running circles around us tomorrow. I would love that, Richard. By the way, I realized last night that I have kind of just thrown you into this weekend. I've been a part of this tradition all of my life, and I'm sure it could be a bit overwhelming to someone that just dropped in. However, also let me say you have adapted very well. Margaret, I feel like this experience, and you especially, are like finding missing puzzle pieces of my life. Every day, the puzzle comes together, and as it does, my life has direction and meaning. I look forward to finding the next piece."

"I am so happy to hear you say that, Richard. I'm glad you're having as much fun as you appear to be having. So I'll give you a briefing about the day. I know I told you that after the amazing brunch, which is not an eating contest but may seem like it, we will take it slow and easy. The circle time is usually about one hour or so, it's actually when folks start wandering, after the brunch. And the time seems right. We have our chairs. Everyone brings them, and the circle gets quite large, very large. However we have always been able to hear each other. We hold hands, and someone makes a short statement about setting our intentions.

"For me it's so powerful to be clear about my priorities of growth and making a clear shared commitment because I know everyone there will be supporting me. And the energy, actually, I can feel it. My body tingles usually for the entire time, and I always feel so peaceful and yet completely revitalized. Sorry, I got a little bit ahead of myself. After the opening, each person says from one to three words. That's it. No comments. I know what I will say, and I do have three and have been in meditation in preparation for this transition. I feel this will be a time for many transitions in my life. Gratitude. The more grateful I am for the changes, the more I will receive in growth. Love is my pillar, the foundation for my life. Oh poor Richard, I haven't done this well. Have I? You look bewildered. You don't have to say anything in the circle Richard. No one judges or has expectations, but I do believe you will feel the energy, and I will love having you there beside me."

"Darling, I may be a little bewildered, but I am ready to immerse myself in this experience. I am not only ready. Three words just come to me, and they make me feel like I am in the right direction. The first is 'compassion'. I have witnessed that in you and many others. You seem to know what people need and respond so naturally. For the past few years, I have not been me. I have been angry, arrogant at times, and in general, not a happy person. I want to understand humility, which I think necessary for compassion. Second is 'transition'. Definitely, I know change is constant, but I want to be conscious of the process, and of course the third one is 'love', which I am understanding more each day. I like what you said about love as life's foundation. I am grateful for this moment, Margaret. Just being here with you is almost heaven."

"Thank you, Richard. We have a very special relationship, and I value your friendship very much."

The moment of silence was so intense between them; it was such a powerful feeling.

"Another saved by the bell, Richard. Will there be a time when I am going to make sure there are no bells, my dear. I will look forward to that, Richard. Now let's get our chairs and circle up."

"The circles are growing by the moment. This is huge. Do you think the entire community is here?"

"Most of the time, the majority of the community is here, and the energy is amazing. I love the way the energy flows as the circles turn into circles, inside of circles, but we never lose contact with each other because someone from each circle connects with the next circle."

"How does that work, Margaret? Is this all planned by someone?"

"Well, Richard, that depends on what you mean. We believe everything is through divine guidance, but no, not in my generation. Perhaps initially it was. It just works. The one that speaks first will sit in the middle of the circles first and then join in the first circle as we focus our intentions. There she is. She is one of our eldest and known as the wise one. She is a great teacher of our youth. They love and respect her and she them."

"Margaret, there is a sudden silence. Is this the way we start?"

"Yes, Richard, about five minutes of silence. It's a great centering time."

"Welcome, my friends. We are gathered here in the great circle, of circles of love once again, as has been our custom for well over a century. We honor all those who have gone on before us—the way-showers Legacy. We are grateful to our creator for 'love' which is the foundation of our lives. Planet earth is repairing itself. We have been careless caretakers. This is not retribution, merely a necessity, the natural way of repair. To cleanse, such as our glorious rain does. To create a balance in nature and this includes humankind. Repair through natural tools, which include earthquakes, tsunamis, disease, and other events to come.

"We have an opportunity to learn and listen to our spirit self and grow stronger and better, growing in respect and restoring ourselves and our planet to true beauty and peace through our journey based on 'love' which is the foundation this community has built on for at least the past eight generations. We are grateful to be a part of this tradition. Let us begin. We will first raise the group vibration by quietly repeating the word 'Om', taking a deep breath between sounds. There is nothing special about the word, except through this process we become one energy. Then each person that wishes to speak will. We will start with this: those that wish to set their intentions quietly will do so. The energies will raise vibrations either way."

"My word is love," and circle by circle the power became almost tangible.

"Richard, you are so quiet, darling. Are you all right?"

"Margaret, I have never experienced anything like this is in my life. I have been to many churches, actually used to go often, and enjoyed it very much. But this, it was like time stopped. I don't really have any idea of what time it is and certainly don't care. I only now that I felt transported as I felt the energy of the group. And honestly, it was like we were one. I know I'm not saying it well because I don't really know how to express what I mean. I could hear each person speak, but it was more like feeling what I heard. And yes, the connection was also indescribable. I have never felt like this before. I think I am repeating myself to answer your question, Margaret. I am so all right. Thank you for sharing this incredible experience with me. How are you going to top this? Wait, no, I don't even want to know yet. Because somehow I believe you will, and that's incomprehensible to me right now."

"Richard, thank you for sharing that with me. For me, this never gets old. As you know, I look forward to this event with great anticipation. I receive so much sheer joy through sharing, and it was even more powerful this year, perhaps because you are here with me. Are you ready to go home now, Richard?"

"Yes, I am, and I love that word 'home'."

"I missed having Howdy there. He has always sat in the middle of the first circle. I trust he is all right."

"Margaret, I think we know Howdy is absolutely fine, whatever the situation may be. He is unconditional love. I know I have already learned so much from him, and expect to learn much more. That song, or chant, that we ended with: I wasn't familiar with it. At least, I didn't think I was, but I joined in, and the words just seemed to flow, 'circles of love forming circles of love, building circles everywhere, then the world will be filled with love'. I know there was more to it, but the energy generated was enough to light up the world."

"Richard, I was holding your hand, and yes, I agree the sparks were there. Will it bother you if I lay my hand on your shoulder while you are driving?"

"Oh yes, my darling, it will bother me a lot! But in a very good way. Please do, Margaret. I can't think of anything I would enjoy more right now."

"Margaret, we are home. I could carry you in."

"Maybe, but you would awaken me either way, so I might as well wake up now. I slept all the way home! I didn't even realize I was sleepy. I was just so content and happy. Oh yes, let's go in, and see how Mr. Howdy is.

"Hi, buddy, right here to greet us. Oh, Howdy, I missed you so much tonight. You look much better. I am so glad. We'll just take it easy tomorrow.

"So what are you plans tomorrow, Richard? And would you like a cup of tea?"

"No thanks to the tea, Margaret. I think you and Howdy could use some quiet time together. I will be picking my car up tomorrow and will do some errands. I will probably be through by four or five. How about you?"

"I am planning on a routine day, Richard, and of course, depending on how Mr. Howdy is, we may have a pretty slow pace tomorrow, which is fine with me. If you don't have plans for dinner, Richard, I would love to prepare dinner for us."

"Are you sure, Margaret? I thought maybe it was my turn to do something for you."

"You can do something for me. Bring the wine, your choice, but red would probably be best. Would 6:30 work for you, Richard?"

"You mean I won't see you until 6:30 tomorrow night? I don't know if I have that much self-control, but yes, I will be here at 6:30 p.m. tomorrow night. Good night, my darling. I had another indescribably delicious day. I trust you and Howdy will have a perfect day tomorrow.

"Howdy, that's the first time you've snuggled up to me. You are something, pal, and a good night to you. But if you don't mind, I won't kiss you good night.

"Not you, Margaret. I definitely want to kiss you good night. Well, the sparks are there, and there's only the three of us. I guess where two or more are gathered . . . Until tomorrow at 6:25 p.m. Good night, my darling Margaret. Sleep well."

✳

"Oh, Howdy, what a day we have had. I am so sure that Richard and I are soul mates, and yet, the rational part of my mind says, 'Wait a minute. You really don't know anything about him. You haven't known him long enough.' And then my heart, my spirit part which is really what I trust, says, 'Living in the moment means now! Whatever was, is in the past, and whatever will be, does not exist.' You are looking straight into my heart, Howdy. You always have. I just completely calm down when you do that. Thank you. Come here, buddy. Let's cozy up and enjoy the fire and just breathe. I know everything will evolve just exactly the way it's meant to."

I have only been away from Margaret for minutes, and it is just not right. It's not exactly like a need, it's more like she is the piece of the puzzle of my life, that I have found, and I am just more complete with her than without. Could I live without her? Yes, of course I could. However, the quality would definitely not be the same. So why would I? I think it's just silly to pretend that we need to wait. For what? I love her. I know it. I want to be with her for the rest of my life. I love this community. It already feels like I have been here forever. Howdy and I are already great friends. Why would we wait? Well, maybe from her perspective, she doesn't really know anything about me, at least not much. I've been pretty sketchy with details, but that will be easy, no major complications there. Except I had completely forgotten about my vision, or the potential lack of, now that's something Margaret needs to know. The rest—my childhood, college years, marriage to Sylvia, all of that is past, and just information.

However, my sister and her family are a definite plus. I know Margaret will love them. Actually, I am fine with talking to Margaret about my vision and potential blindness. I know it is not a problem for us, primarily because it is no longer a problem for me. I really don't think I will be blind, but if that should be one of my challenges, I am ready to accept the gifts that will come with it. There. Now I've gone through all of that, and I'm back at the same place. I love Margaret, and I want to marry her. And I definitely will ask her soon. I just want it to be perfect. I would like to locate a special spot and have the ring designed. The jeweler in town knows Margaret very well, and together we can do a pretty good job of getting it right. Perhaps, I am assuming too much too soon, but I don't think so. I am listening to my spirit self, and I know this is right and good.

*

What a wonderful day, and routine is not that bad really. I have seven more days of vacation, and I intend to enjoy every minute of them. That's kind of a strange statement, because I enjoy every day anyhow. It's just different.

"Howdy, does my life feel different? Yes. Do you feel up to a little autumn walk? The colors are so brilliant, and I love the smell. I'm not sure exactly what it is, but it definitely is a special smell that happens every autumn. There is so much going on during this season. It really is a season of abundance, all of the fruits, vegetables, and stocking the storehouse. I also love preparing for the winter season. Each season has its beauty and bounty. Let's just sit for a few minutes, and soak up the sun. It feels so good, and it's so easy to quiet my mind here. There's just enough of a breeze to help the trees loosen their leaves.

"Oh my, I really quieted my mind. I have no idea how long we have been here, but I do have a feeling that it has been a while. You look very content lying there, Howdy. You really needed a day off. You are usually smelling everything and running around. Maybe a slower pace is what you need for now, and that's OK. You seem very content. However, we do need to head back. I have a few things to do, and of course dinner to prepare. Just thinking about it, I can feel my pulse racing. I will pick up some pumpkins from the garden. I want to make pumpkin bread pudding. Take a little break from the apples for tonight, and Mom's recipe for white bean and kale stew. I haven't had that for a long time. But I have many wonderful memories of sharing that stew with so many of Mom and Dad's friends. There was always such lively conversation. I am a very lucky lady, Howdy."

Well, everything's ready, and it's 6:15 p.m. Pretty good timing, and it was so much fun. I just realized how long it's been since I have been really excited about preparing dinner. I am going to put the biscuits in the oven now, so when Richard gets here they will be ready to come out of the oven. I love the smell of bread baking.

"Good evening, Richard, my, you do look handsome, and of course, it's because you are."

"Thank you, my darling. I'm glad you think I'm handsome. This has been a productive, but also a very long day. It seems like days since I last saw you, Margaret, my love. I missed you. And Howdy I missed you too, my friend. I wasn't even hungry until you opened the door and the smell of bread, and unknown pleasures, have overcome me. Now I am famished."

"How can I help?"

"Oh yes, I did bring the wine, and Stan said it was your favorite."

"No, you don't have any secrets, and why should you?"

"Everything is ready, Richard."

"Margaret, what a lovely table: candles, the centerpiece of leaves, and baby pumpkins and squash. Everything is perfect. Shall I pour the wine, Margaret?"

"Oh yes, but, Richard, you should be kissing me!"

"I absolutely should be, and I absolutely shall. Margaret, what was that bell?"

"I kind of set you up for that, Richard. The biscuits are ready."

"Will we be having bells ringing every time I start to kiss you tonight?"

"Nope that was it for the bells. You are on your own."

"What is in this stew?"

"Don't you like it, Richard?"

"Like it? I love it. I've just never tasted anything like it."

"It is one of my mother's favorite recipes, and it has wonderful memories associated with it. It's really very simple. I think the spices make the difference. It has white beans, onions, garlic, carrots, celery, tomatoes, small red potatoes, spices, and herbs. Everything is from the garden. Oh yes, and kale, and freshly grated parmesan cheese."

"Oh yes, it is delicious, and the biscuits are as good as they smelled."

"I think everything is better when it's seasoned with love, Richard."

"I think you are absolutely right."

"I'm so glad you enjoyed the day. So did Howdy and I, although while meditating lying in a nice big bunch of freshly fallen leaves, I guess I kind of dozed off. So did Howdy. I was enjoying the sun, autumn smells, and watching the breeze loosen the leaves. I remember seeing the leaves dancing in the wind, and then I didn't know anything else for over an hour. It was very refreshing. I love all of the seasons transitioning. I assume you got your car?"

"Yes, I did, and not only did he replace the part, he also served it, washed it, and charged less than half of what it would have been anywhere else. I don't know how he can do that."

"You will find that's true for everything, Richard. People do what they love doing, and our needs are few. Together we grow, and raise our food. There is one thing the men do that most women don't. Generally, it's the young men that cut and deliver wood to everyone. I still have a lot from last year, but I'll be getting a delivery to fill my wood shed soon. Most of us have our own wells and septic systems. We are pretty self-sufficient. If the school or anything actually needs repair, it's a community project. My goodness, Richard, this is not the conversation I have been fantasizing about all day."

"Margaret, I love hearing you talk about our community. There is so much I want to know."

"Thank you."

"However, you are right. That is not what I have been fantasizing about either. Right now, I smell coffee and something spicy and mysterious. Yes, it is time for coffee and pumpkin bread pudding with gingered crème anglaise. It's decadent. Why don't you and Howdy go in the living room by the fireplace, and I will be your servant."

"Somehow that sounds sexy, especially the servant part. Come on, Howdy, let's go. I know how to do what I'm told, especially when I am told by such a persuasive lady. This is perfection. I don't just mean the dinner, the dessert, coffee, but you, and Howdy, and this warm fire. Perfection."

*

Howdy was lying on the rug in front of the fireplace. Richard was sitting in a chair with Margaret across from him. Howdy got up, put his paw on Richard's lap, and looked at Margaret. Then he went to Margaret, put his paw on her lap, and looked at Richard.

"Richard, he wants us to be closer."

"Once again, Margaret, he has read my mind."

They met in the middle in what was becoming their special place—on the big cozy rug with lots of comfortable pillows. For a while, they just watched the fire and enjoyed being together. Then Richard took her in his arms. He spoke tenderly, and provocatively of his admiration, desire, and love for her so clearly, and he was saying exactly what she was feeling. Her body melted into his. As he smiled at her, Margaret traced his lips with her fingers. He drew her closer, and when their lips met, the last bit of her reservation dissolved. She felt as though they were one.

"Margaret, it's the chemistry inside, the spirit, whatever. I have never been more sure of anything in my life. I love you, Margaret. Will you marry me? Wait! Don't answer. I was going to do this so differently. You know what, I still am. You still have a formal proposal coming, my darling. I'll keep the where and when a mystery. I know you love adventures, as long as we keep the same destination."

"Richard, I love you. I also have no doubts or reservations, and I will wait somewhat patiently for a proper proposal."

Then they lay together silently for a long time, and their breathing was as one.

"Richard, does this mean you are not going to spend the night with me?"

"My darling Margaret, there is nothing I would rather do. Right now, however, I want our first night together to be something we both have time to think about, and after we are properly engaged, and that will be very, very soon. I want champagne, strawberries, and you know, all of the romantic novel stuff. After all, I am a best-selling novelist. Surely, I can create a memorable occasion for a lifetime."

"As a matter of fact, in all honesty, this evening is one of many to come, absolutely memorable. We are both starting a new chapter in our lives, Richard. I am so grateful for each new page. So if you're not going to spend the night with me, you probably had better go home because it is already midnight."

"I love you, Margaret. I will see you tomorrow, and we will make some plans together."

"Good night, Richard. I expect to be around the house most of the day. Come over whenever you are ready."

Their kiss good night was again full of passion and promise.

"Well, Howdy, I'm glad you're able to sleep. I think my adrenaline is pumping out high octane.

"Yes, Richard, my love, this evening is definitely memorable. I have very mixed emotions, not about us, but because I really wanted him to spend the night. What I really wanted was for us to have sex. However, I am also glad that we didn't. I want the candles, music, champagne, and dark chocolate-dipped strawberries, and I want to buy a really sexy gown with black lace."

"Oh, thank you, Richard, for being such a wise man. You knew what I wanted before I did. So the hormones are racing. That's OK. As a matter of fact, I am very happy that I am in the race. It's been a long, long time. Tonight will be a test for meditation, if I can clear my head and body enough to focus, and I know I can. I am so glad that I have always had support and love in my life. I understand it is a true treasure."

Richard, are you crazy or what? You left that desirable, adorable lady that you are in love with. You just walked out when every fiber of your being wanted to be there with her completely. You say wait? On the other hand, I do think I did what was best for both of us. This is one of if not the most important event in my life, in our lives, and the occasion deserves to be honored, and I am glad that I was able to catch myself in time to gain some self-control, actually, a lot of self-control. My emotions were twisted like a pretzel. I'm glad I didn't say that, but I do kind of still feel conflicted. No, I really don't. I made the best decision, and I am glad that we were able to talk about it. It felt so great to hear Margaret say that she had no reservations. I am feeling better by the moment. This has really been a magical evening. This deep breathing exercise really works. My pulse is regular. I think I can actually go to sleep.

✳

"Margaret, would you like to have a cup of tea and biscuits? I got them from Mary yesterday, and I forgot to tell you. Everyone is missing you at the library."

"Richard, your timing is perfect. Howdy and I have just returned from doing some errands, and I would love to have a cup of tea. Ten minutes be all right?"

"Absolutely. I'm hoping we will have some time to just be. That sounds wonderful. I'll see you in a few minutes.

"Margaret, I'm so happy to see you. I have missed you these twelve hours or so that we have been apart."

"I actually am serious you know, Richard. I love it when you hold me so close. I've missed you too, and I'm ready for my tea to be served, sir, and Mary's tea biscuits. What a treat. You know something, Richard? I haven't thought about the library since I left it. Don't get me wrong. I love it. And when I'm there, I'm 100 percent there, but when I'm not, it's just not something I think about."

"I think that's very healthy, Margaret. I'm really focusing on living in the moment, and you are such a great example. Now let's sit on this side of the table so we can both enjoy this magnificent view, and we will be close also. Margaret, there are some things I'd like to share with you about my past. I know I want to know everything about you because you are such an interesting person and you are an integral part of this unique community. My story will not be nearly as fascinating as yours, but then, that's not the point. I want to cover a few of the major highlights today. Then it can be like chapters as we go along."

"That sounds wonderful, Richard, I would love to hear as much as you choose to share."

"Well, I'll just jump in. I was married for ten years to a vivacious, beautiful person. Her name was Sylvia. We met when we were quite young. She was in college. I had just graduated with a degree in communication and journalism. I was freelancing for a few magazines. She became an art teacher at the high school. Gradually, I had a column for a newspaper and a few more magazine contracts. We were very much in love. Our life was quite simple, really. We had some really good friends, enjoyed our small community and our community church. We found our dream cottage, which had enough space for my writing and her artwork. She loved to work in the garden. We kept changing our minds about having children. One time she would want to, and I wasn't sure, and then I would decide yes, and she wouldn't be sure. We finally agreed that we didn't want to have a family. We had my family. My sister and brother-in-law had two adorable children. They had sort of adopted us. It was almost like co-parenting, which worked well for us and for my sister.

"Sylvia became ill quite suddenly, at least as far as I know. She never complained about anything. When she went to the doctor, and they did a lot of tests. They found out she had cancer, and it was terminal."

"Oh, Richard, I am so sorry."

"It was a very challenging time. She went through several series of treatments, which were devastating. It was so hard to watch her just gradually fade away, physically, but she kept her spirit. She was so practical and strong. I was falling apart inside, but I tried so hard to be there for her. She made me promise her that I would love again, marry, and that I should be very, very happy and live for both of us. I was scared, hurting, and angry at the thought of losing her, but I finally was able to promise her I would, although at the time, I thought it was impossible.

"After her death, or transition, I was a mess. I didn't feel like I belonged anywhere. I wasn't a very nice person. I started doing travel pieces just to fill up my time. I also started drinking and everything that goes with that. After a few years, thank God, I got through that. I sold our cottage and started writing seriously. That consumed all my time. Are you OK, Margaret?"

"Thank you, Richard, for trusting me enough to share that part of your life with me. I think you are a very strong man, and now that I know more about why you are who you are, I love you even more."

"Thank you, Margaret. There is much more that I will share, but I think that's enough for Chapter One. Do you have questions, or do you want to just digest it, and questions can come anytime?"

"No questions now, Richard. I just want to go out to the porch swing and sit with you for a while and just enjoy being with you."

"Margaret, I love you."

"I know you do, Richard."

"How is Howdy? I was surprised he didn't come with you."

"He's not eating well, and our walks are getting shorter, but his spirit is strong. He is alert and happy. I took him to see Dr. Brown today. He talked to me about the aging process. He doesn't really think Howdy is ill, but he is at least fourteen years old. You know I never think about, or really understand aging, probably because I have never understood time, and they are relative. So we'll do what we always do, live in the moment, and every moment is precious. Just like this moment is with you right now."

"Margaret, how do you feel about taking a little road trip, just overnight? I have a special place I would love to share with you. Howdy is invited also, if you think he would like to go."

"When are you planning to go on this little adventure?"

"Would tomorrow work for you? Or the next day? Your call."

"Actually, tomorrow would be perfect. The next event we have planned is on Friday. That's the big day at the community kitchen. Remember, the apple thing—canning, drying, juicing, making apple cider, and apple vinegar, and so on."

"Oh yes, I do remember. I get to peel and dry apples, and I am looking forward to it. So tomorrow works for you?"

"Absolutely. Howdy loves to stay with Mary, and he hasn't done that for a while. As a matter of fact, I think he really misses the children fand all of his friends at the library. So I will call her this evening and see if she'd like a houseguest, and my hunch is yes. I think that would be a treat for both of us and him. I love spontaneity, Richard, and as you know, adventures, and you're not going to tell me where we are going?"

"No, at least not now. But I can tell you that we will see some spectacular scenery. Autumn is in full color. I know I will take some pictures which I may attempt to paint."

"Richard, shall I bring a picnic lunch?"

"I love our picnics, Margaret. I think that would be great, if you don't mind, and I'm sure you don't as you wouldn't have suggested it. Margaret, I call that kind of thinking, pulling weeds. You see, I truly do know that you don't suggest doing something unless you really mean it. So there really is no 'if you don't mind', so as soon as I catch myself doing or saying something I want to change, I imagine that I'm pulling weeds. Of course, they, negative thoughts, are stubborn and often grow right back. However, I am finding this visualization very helpful. I replace the weed with a positive thought, and it's working. So thank you, Margaret. I love the picnic idea, and the weather is still good enough to do it."

"What time would you like to leave, Richard?"

"Whatever works for you, darling. We are not going to be on a schedule. How about ten-ish?"

"That's wonderful, and Richard, we have stew left, and the pumpkin bread pudding. If you would like, we can have dinner at about 6:00 p.m."

"Yes, my darling, I would love to have dinner at 6:00 p.m."

"Richard, I may challenge you to a game of chess or checkers, and I probably had better prepare you: I am very good."

"That does sound like a challenge, and I believe I am up to it."

"So that sounds fun. I will see you, actually in just a couple of hours. I had no idea it was so late, but then, I really never do. I definitely am time-challenged, but it seems to work. I am really excited about our adventure tomorrow, Richard."

"So am I, darling. I'll see you about six. I love you."

So Richard was happily married. I am so glad we are beginning to share our stories. It just helps to put the pieces together. I am so glad that he had that chapter in his life, but I know how hard it was when Chad was killed, especially when I was still grieving for my parents. And I also know there were so many gifts I received through the process, although I certainly didn't realize that at the time. I have learned so much about this gift of life and living intentionally. I believe Richard has also. He is a very strong person and so eager to learn, and he is a very good listener. I am so glad that both of us have healed, and are ready to embrace the next chapter of our lives together.

"Howdy, how would you like to spend a couple of days with Mary? I know she feeds you things that I don't, and that's OK. You will get to go to the library and see the children and visit all of your friends in town. Your tail is going to wag off if you're not careful. I think you are bored, just being here with me. Just joking, I know you love me. But your heart is so big and so many need your love, so you do have quite a mission, and friend, you fulfill it so well. OK. I will call Mary, and see if she's ready for company."

"Hi, Mary. Yes, it is good to talk to you. Yes, Richard did share the tea biscuits and your greeting. Thank you so much. Oh yes, we are getting along quite well, and you don't have to keep it a secret. As a matter of fact, that's what I'm calling about. We are going on a little road trip adventure, and I think Howdy would much prefer to stay with you, if that's all right. Yes, I know you always look forward to time with Howdy. That's great. Mary, he hasn't been eating as much and napping a little more. He's fine, but I just wanted you to know, so you wouldn't worry. Yes, he is getting on in years. Aren't we all. Thank goodness. So I will see you at about 8:30 in the morning, and I'll call you as soon as we return, and of course, you can call me anytime. If I don't answer immediately, I will call back. Thank you, Mary. You know I love you. See you in the morning.

"Well, Howdy, you are all set for a couple of days back to work. I guess you're not quite ready to retire yet. Let's do our yoga practice, and then I'll fix dinner."

"Hello, Richard, you are certainly looking chipper. Welcome."

"Good evening, my dear one, and how's Mr. Howdy? My, he looks pretty chipper himself. You know, I think he really misses the library, well, actually, all of the stimulation he has there."

"He really perked up after I talked to Mary. Actually, I'm feeling pretty perky too. I warned you this was leftover night, and that's exactly what you get, a repeat performance of last night. Well, maybe not completely."

"Margaret, this is even better tonight. I didn't think it could be. Thank you, Richard. I am really looking forward to our road trip. I'm already packed and ready to go."

"So am I. It only took me about ten minutes. I do have a couple of errands in the morning, but I think I'll be ready to leave about 10:00, if that still works for you?"

"Absolutely, I'm taking Howdy to Mary's at 8:30 in the morning, and if I know Mary, and I do, she will have enough food ready for us for a week. So I'm not going to get the picnic prepared until after I get back, and then I'm pretty sure that base will be covered.

"I love this community, Richard. We are always there for each other and never have any expectations of return. We are very fortunate to have each other and this haven of happiness to live in."

"I know, Margaret. I still wonder occasionally when I am going to wake up. But the dream goes on. Now I suggest we play a game of checkers, as a warm up to a real game of chess. What do you say?"

"I say game on. If you'd be willing to set up the game, I'll get us a cup of lavender and chamomile tea."

"I see how it is. You think you can drug me, and while I'm groggy, you will make a wily move, eh?"

"No, Richard, of course not. This is just to help us relax, so we can think more clearly. Even playing field."

"OK, Margaret, I give. You have two out of three, so I will concede for now. And we will have a rematch soon. I love you, even if you are smart, sassy, and beautiful."

"I love you too, Richard, and I'm sure you will catch on to the game soon."

"Ouch, the barbs. Yes, but they are lined with velvet."

"Richard, I'm not sure if that was a good night kiss or a hello kiss. Maybe a little bit of both."

"I'll see you in the morning, love. Good night."

"Wow! Howdy, I am a very happy person. And you know what? I was already a happy person, so now I must be beyond happy, whatever that is, and it is good. Howdy, I will miss you, but it's only for two nights, and I know you are looking forward to it, and actually so am I. So let's just have our adventures and then I'll tell you all about mine and you can listen. You always have, Howdy."

"Good morning, Mary. I came in the back door. I didn't mean to startle you, but I just don't have time to talk to everyone."

"Good morning my dear, and Mr. Howdy. How very glad I am to see you. Margaret, you are missed, but this one, the children especially miss him. They say the library is just too quiet."

"Yes, Howdy, go on, check everything out, and make your rounds. I'll see you in a couple of days. I love you. Look at that tail wag. Thank you, Mary. I really appreciate what you are doing for me."

"You know that I am looking forward to having that sweetheart around, and by the way, I have a picnic prepared for you and Richard. I know how you both love to eat, especially Richard."

"Mary, thank you, and yes we do have a picnic in the plan, and this is a real treat, so thank you again. Now I'm going to go before you unlock the door and let the crowd in. As usual, this place smells so good. Love you, Mary. See you soon."

Well, I am ready to go, and ready for this adventure. I have a feeling it's going to be a very special time in our lives, and certainly a memorable one.

"Good morning, Richard. I am ready. Any clues yet as to where I am going?"

"Morning, darling. I will give you a few clues about things we will see and do, and general clues. All of that after we are on our way."

"Great, let's do it."

"Clues: The destination for tonight is an elegant Victorian hotel, actually sort of a bed-and-breakfast. It has six suites, all with magnificent views. There are several historical points of interest. The quaint town is easily toured by walking, driving, or bicycling. Do you like to ride a bicycle, Margaret?"

"Oh my goodness, it's been a long time, but yes, I do. That's the only transportation I had in college, and I loved it. Except in the winter, then I tolerated it. I would love to ride a bicycle, Richard. And you?"

"Absolutely in theory. I haven't ridden one for a very long time, but yes, I do remember the freedom and actual joy of riding."

"Another clue: this town is actually an artist colony. So there are dozens of art galleries, antique shops, bakeries, and great places to eat. Any guesses yet?"

"No, I really don't have, and I don't think I want to know. I am loving the mystery. It sounds delightful. Do you have a clue as to where we will have our picnic lunch? And by the way, Mary did have a huge basket of food for us, as I knew she would. I brought the drinks. We are really going to need those bicycles, and hiking, after lunch."

"Oh yes, my dear. I am sure we will be very physically active. Margaret, you are blushing."

"Oh no, I'm just a little warm in this sweater."

"Sure, you are. Anyhow, I plan to stop at what is described as a must experience. It's a state park, and there are several nature trails and private nooks for picnickers. It's about thirty miles, forty-five minutes from here. I am purposefully choosing scenic routes, understanding that there may be, just a possibility, that we could be temporarily lost from time to time.

I don't read maps very well, Margaret. But I always manage to get where I'm going."

"Well, that's reassuring, Richard, and since I have no idea of our destination, I'll probably never even know if we are lost. That is, unless we end up spending the night here in the car."

"Funny lady, that's not going to happen. There's the sign for our first stop: the Acadia National Park."

"This scenery is beautiful, Richard. Thank you for being you."

"Margaret, I love you so much. Shall we go on one of the nature trails first and then find out what treasures Mary has packed for us?"

"Sounds good to me, Richard."

"Let's take this one. The colors of the trees are so bright and the trees still look so full and yet the ground is covered with leaves. I know and I love the sound of walking on leaves and the smell of autumn in the air. I am so glad you can smell it too, Richard. I love it."

"Well, that was perfect, of course. What a variety—pine trees and chickadees, the pond, the breeze rustling the leaves, and two miles before lunch was just right. Let's get the basket and have a well-deserved lunch."

"Richard, this picnic spot is so private, and yet we have a perfect view. I am so content, but hungry. Let's see what we have here. The sandwiches are in an insulated packet, so let's see. Turkey, Havarti cheese, and Mary's special cranberry sauce on sourdough bread—my favorite sandwich, of course."

"I can really see why this is delicious. What is this exotic drink that you brought, Margaret? I have never tasted anything like it."

"OK, another long answer to a short question, but I can't help it that you asked. Before the soft drink technology existed, nonalcoholic beverages were brewed at home, directly from herbs, roots, spices, and fruits and then aged like wine and prized not only for their taste but also for their tonic, health-giving properties."

"So are you saying you made this?"

"Yes, I am, and yes, I did. Home brewing is quite an art. So I suppose I am an artist. After soft drinks took over worldwide, home brewing almost became a lost art, but fortunately not for us. This delightful drink is cherry ginger ale. I am so glad you like it because there is plenty more where this came from. We have sarsaparilla, and of course apple, cherry, and pear. I think that's about it for now. We have a huge storage building in the community, and I have a smaller version in one of the buildings by our house just for the home-brewing process and storage area. I don't do wine or beer. You may want to add those later. There's a lot of room."

"Margaret, every time you give me a little bit more of the amazing story of the community, I am in awe. You do realize how unique and precious our community is?"

"Yes, I do, Richard. I realize how fortunate I am. Now for the dessert. I can smell it, and it's wonderful, of course—carrot cake with apples, raisins, and her secret spices, and walnuts with a special frosting like I'll bet you have never tasted before. She won't even tell me how she does it."

"What do you think?"

"I think I'm going to have a challenge for dinner tonight. By then, Richard, we will be in another world, although it is hard to imagine now. We will be ready for the next course."

"So let's be on our way to the next bend in the road. This is great fun, Richard. I feel like a kid again. We are, Richard! Actually, we have a new body every five years, so maybe this is our birthday. I don't know about you, but my body is not old."

"Ouch, I think the lady doth protest too much."

"You just wait, mister, we'll see about that."

"I can hardly wait, Margaret. Let's be off."

"Do you have another clue for me?"

"We will be staying at the River House Inn, which just happens to be on the river, in historic old town. That was a major set of clues."

"Tell me what you think it will look like?"

"It will be very old, but elegant. Beautiful architecture. Our suite has a breathtaking view, I'm sure, so we will be upstairs. It will be furnished with authentic antiques. How am I doing?"

"Remarkably well. We'll leave a few things for discovery."

"I also have reservations made for dinner. We can always change our minds, or should I say, you can easily change my mind. I will give you a hint about what they feature. It's called 'Port and Starboard.'"

"What else can you tell me about it?"

"What appealed to me most I think is the forty-eight-year family-owned part. Also fresh local seafood, handmade pies, and desserts, and then the most important part: award-winning clam chowder. I researched that claim and read customers' comments, which were of the highest praises. So enough clues, my lady?"

"Oh yes, I am enjoying every minute, Richard—the trees, all of the colors, even the cows look happy."

"Of course, they always do. There is a sign. It said there was a scenic loop one mile ahead."

"Do we have time to do it? Or should we get to our quaint artistic town? What do you think, Margaret? I want to see our River House Inn, and besides this route is all scenic."

"How much further?"

"Approximately an hour, if my calculations are right. If you see any place that you me to want to stop, just let me know.

*

"Margaret, you rested your eyes for a few minutes, but we're coming into town, and I know you don't want to miss it. I am glad the speed limit is 20 mph. I'll have a chance to look. There is no traffic. I like that."

"Oh, Richard, this is quaint. I love the bicycle racks on the streets, murals on every building, and they tell a story. Oh, what fun this will be tomorrow. I may want to get up very early."

"We'll see, Margaret. You know we can always come back again if we don't get to do everything this time. So we can just do as you are always telling me, one moment at a time. Live fully in this moment, and take a deep breath."

"Oh, Richard, you are just like Howdy. Only he just looks at me, and I know what he's thinking. However, you are so right, my darling. Thank you. But I do love this place, and I can tell it is a good place to be. Thank you, for finding it and making all of the wonderful arrangements you have made, and for being you."

"I love your enthusiasm, Margaret, and well, actually, everything about you. There's our sign to the historic part of town—River Road."

"There it is, Richard, that beautiful Victorian mansion. It's even the color of blue that I thought it would be. Let's go explore. Then we can get our luggage. You know, it is more beautiful than it looked on the Internet."

"Good afternoon. Welcome to River House Inn. I am James, and this is my wife Betty. Would you like a short tour before seeing your suite?"

"Oh yes."

"Both of you said that at the same time. So I guess, a tour it is. This is the most popular gathering place, other than for brunch."

"Oh my goodness, Richard, look at that fireplace. We are very proud of our home, and that we have been able to restore everything to its original beauty. The fireplace is the focal point of the room, and it's very functional. The bookshelves have many original classics, and you are encouraged to treat this as your home—the books and the game tables. There's a coffee, tea, and hot chocolate cart over there in the corner, and Betty always keeps something special there as well. And let me tell you, after twenty-five years together, I know everything that comes out of her oven is special. This is a great place to mingle, or if you choose, to just relax, and enjoy the lounge in front of the fireplace. Folks tend to respect each other's choices."

"This is truly a perfect room, James. I love the artwork, the rug, the warmth of the room, and I don't just mean the fireplace. Everything. It's very authentic."

"Betty and I had so much fun on our antique treasure hunts. We scoured the countryside, actually several country sides, to piece together every part of our dream, and we still love antiquing although we are actually running out of space. Betty had a much clearer vision than I. I suppose what I did best, was to trust her judgment. The dining room is just down the hallway, and is always of interest. You will probably awaken to some wonderful smells of things baking in the morning."

"Oh, Richard, look at that dining table. It is massive and marvelous."

"That was one of our most exciting treasures to find and the most challenging to have delivered. We found it near Boston, from a family estate. It has quite a history. Perhaps we'll have time later to discuss it, if you'd like. This is where we serve brunch from 8:00 to 10:30 in the morning. Of course, if you'd prefer we can do room service, but you will have to let me know tonight if that's what you'd prefer.

"Now the suite. I understand this is a very special time for you folks, and we think you have the best room in the house. Of course, actually there's not a bad one. This house was designed to accommodate the beauty of nature outside and comfort inside. So here you are. If you need anything, other than what you have already requested, please just ask. You are honored guests in our home, and we want your stay with us to be remembered as a special time. I'm sure we will see you later."

"What do you think, Margaret?"

"Think? I am beyond thinking. I know I'm dreaming—this canopy bed, the fireplace, French doors that open out onto the terrace. We can hear the river and see the trees and flower gardens. As late as it is in fall, there are still flowers. I would ask you to pinch me, but I'm not sure I want to wake up. Oh, Richard, this is almost heaven. I love it!"

"My darling Margaret, you are so delightful. I love having you as my best friend, my mentor, and companion in life, and well, we'll leave it at that for now. I'm so glad that we are sharing our first road trip. It is so very special. Now shall I go get our luggage, and we can settle in? We will have a few hours to explore or enjoy the family room. You choose, my lady.

"Well, you do travel light, Margaret, only one small bag."

"Actually, what I do is pack efficiently. You will be surprised at what all comes out of that bag. You're kind of a lightweight yourself. And you, my dear, may also be surprised at how well I can pack. It is definitely a skill."

"Richard, come, look at this bathroom. It is a very large room. The wallpaper is beautiful, the tub is huge, and very old, but it has jets, and candles, and flowers, and a huge window. We'll be able to see the moon, which, by the way, is full tonight."

"Margaret, did you see the cozy robes and house shoes?"

"Oh, Richard, they are perfect. Everything is. Well, we're settled in, and I could be very happy just staying right here. However, I do remember you said something about a dinner arrangement, as I recall."

"Yes, indeed I did. If you'd like we could go a little early and walk through town a bit. The Dinner House is downtown."

"Oh yes, let's do that. Just give me a minute, and I'll be good to go."

"You look radiant, darling."

"Thank you, Richard."

"Our walking tour begins, bicycles tomorrow. I am so glad that we can walk. I don't want to miss anything, like these spectacular tree-lined streets."

"And look, Richard, there are covered game tables everywhere, and the streetlights are right by them. It is so wonderful to see folks of all ages, playing and laughing together, obviously enjoying each other. Richard, one night is just not enough, I want to see so much more, and I want to really absorb it, not just a quick glance and move on."

"Margaret, before we left, actually, when I went down for the luggage, I reserved tomorrow night, just in case! I knew at least we would not want to just get up, pack, and leave. I wasn't sure of your schedule, so we won't have to hurry tomorrow, and if you can stay another night, I would love it. I am enchanted and inspired. I want to take pictures everywhere."

"I know, Richard, and yes, yes, I can stay another night, and I am feeling inspired to write poetry, which I haven't done for a long time. This truly is a magical place. How did you ever find it?"

"Well, I let my fingers do the work. I looked for historic towns or art colonies or romantic locations within hundred miles or less in any direction from our town, and when I found this, there was that 'Aha' moment. I just knew it was our place. However, I didn't know if you had been here before. So I think we hit the jackpot, and we haven't even had dinner yet."

"Oh yes, Richard, I feel so nourished just by being here and with you."

"Does that mean we should skip dinner?"

"Oh no, you don't get off that easy. Dinner is part of the deal."

"Well, that's good because here we are."

"What a spectacular building, like a grand mansion in the middle of the town."

"Well, not exactly in the middle of town, but yes a grand building it is."

"Richard, I find the outside so interesting. I'm sure the inside must also be very special."

"Good evening, welcome to the Port and Starboard."

"Richard, party of two."

"Oh yes, sir, we have you seated upstairs, as you requested. Your table is ready."

"Oh my goodness, this is a historical building, isn't it?"

"Yes, darling. It was built in 1892. What a beautiful staircase, perfectly curved. What craftsmanship!"

"Here is your table. Your waiter will be Henry. He has been a part of our family for thirty years, so if you have any questions about the menu or our town, I'm sure he will be very happy and prepared to answer them. Thank you for choosing us. Enjoy your evening."

"Richard, we have a full view of everything. The murals on the walls are beautiful, the chandeliers are everywhere, and yet the lighting is subdued. You really did a lot of preparation for this trip, and I thought it was a spur of the moment, 'land where we may' kind of road trip. Don't misunderstand me. I love it, and I am very pleased that you have created such an ideal adventure."

"Thank you. And here comes Henry."

"Good evening, I am your waiter. My name is Henry, and it is my pleasure to serve you this evening. Everything we serve here is special. However, we do have two chef's choice specials of the evening as well. Everything we serve is grown locally, and we have the very best quality. We serve an excellent choice of wines as well. Our first 'special of the evening' is consommé Bellevue, a mixture of chicken and clam broths served with dollops of whipped cream. Chicken with ham slices in a sherried cream sauce follows, and a puree of broccoli, flavored with ground nutmeg and garnished with chopped egg. Buttermilk biscuits and white wine accompany the main course. The 'next choice' is fruit-filled cantaloupe, choice of potato, soup, or clam chowder, Lobster Thermidore, sautéed potato balls, hearts of lettuce salad with Port Salut cheese, and white wine. Then of course we do have other choices on the menu, and if you prefer a vegetarian choice, our chef can provide you with some recommendations. I will bring your hors d'oeuvres. Is there anything else you would like?"

"Thank you, Henry. We will need a few minutes to consider our choices."

"Richard, I can't even consider the menu. Those two specials sound so appealing. Why don't I order one of them, and you the other? I'm not sure how they will mix and match, but at least our curiosity would be satisfied."

"That sounds like a great idea. The music is so right for here. It truly is background, mellow and rich. Margaret, it sounds like you are describing coffee, which is obviously on my mind, and I just may have some with dessert."

"I love this place, Richard. I think I told you, it is so storybook. Which reminds me, have you started on your next book yet?"

"No, my darling, for the time being, you are my book. I am living instead of writing about living. I will write again, but it's not a priority at this time in my life. I am very serious about us, Margaret, and our life together. Right now you, us, is my priority. There is so much more I want to learn about my new community, myself, and how I can contribute. Here comes Henry with our first course."

"Henry, we have chosen, and we are ready to order. We would like one of each of the specials. We really could not resist either choice."

"That happens often, and seems to work out very well. Would you like your wine now or later?"

"I would like mine now. How about you, Margaret?"

"Yes, I would also. Thank you."

"Richard, I am so glad that you are so sure about us and all of the lifestyle changes that will mean. It has appeared to me from the first day that you were very comfortable being in town. All your meet-and-greet affairs went so smoothly. You just immediately fit in, and I have felt that way about you, us as well. Even when I talked with you on the telephone, there was a real connection. I just didn't know how to respond to my emotions, and when I first met you, that electricity in our handshake was jolting. I felt it and saw in your eyes that you did also. So I guess we started off with a bang, and you have never felt like a stranger, just someone I was wanting to meet. I am so happy that we have met, Richard. I do love you so much."

We have the next course arriving. Oh my, that does smell good. I feel like the Belle of the Ball, or Cinderella, or something like that. Everything is total perfection. Every course served elegantly and the food was perfection in every way: presentation, taste, texture, and fortunately the portions were also. And now Henry tells us that we have a dessert tray to be served with Locust Blossom wine. The desserts are described as being a sample size of apple Jonathan, peach custard, and strawberry Flummery.

"Richard, you are so quiet. Are you all right?"

"My darling Margaret, I don't see how I could be any better. This has been a day I would never be able to capture with words, and I am a wordsmith. I must ask Henry about this Locust Blossom wine. I am sure it will be perfect also, but my curiosity will not be denied."

"Well, Richard it is arriving so your opportunity is now."

"Henry, you have so graciously answered all of our many questions about everything. I think I may have only one more. What can you tell us about the wine?"

"It is a specialty wine that has been a family tradition for a very long time, and fortunately, for us, that family lives here. I can tell you that it takes a year until fermentation ceases. It is made from Locust Blossoms. I am really not sure where they come from—sugar, lemon, orange, yeast, and egg whites. I understand it is a labor of love, and not sold to the general public. We get a limited quantity each year. I trust you will enjoy it."

"Thank you, Henry. You have given us superb service, and you are an amazing storehouse of information. This will absolutely be a night for us to remember."

"Thank you, sir. That is exactly why I have been here these many years. It is very rewarding to be a small part of dream making. If there is anything I can do for you wonderful young folks, I will be most happy to do so."

"Actually, Henry, we are ready for our bill anytime. We certainly are not going to rush through this part of the experience. I am quite sure we will not be needing anything else this evening. Everything has been perfection."

"Richard, this wine is so good, very different and perfect with dessert of course."

"Margaret, this is almost as sweet and exotic as you. Almost!"

"Richard, I'm not exotic, but thank you."

"Darling, to me you are mystery, intrigue, excitement, beauty, comfort, trust, and much more. You certainly know how to answer a question. A toast to us. May we always give thanks for our abundantly fulfilled life. As Gandhi said, 'Happiness is when what you think, what you say, and what you do in harmony'."

"And, Richard, I love you."

"And I you, my darling Margaret."

"Let's go home, shall we? You don't mean go home, do you, Margaret?"

"Oh, Richard, I mean to our beautiful romantic home for the next two nights. Oh of course, you do."

"Yes, let's go home, love."

When they return to the suite, the fireplace is glowing, soft romantic music fills the air, and candles and roses are everywhere. There is a bucket with champagne in it and a tray with dark chocolate-dipped strawberries.

"Richard, am I awake or dreaming? How did you create this masterpiece? We've been together all evening, and this room certainly wasn't like this when we left."

"Are you pleased, my darling?"

"Yes, oh yes, just a little mystified."

"There's no real mystery. When I booked our reservations, I included this request. James and Betty were thrilled to oblige. Shall we get comfortable and enjoy our fire, champagne, and, most of all, each other? Oh Margaret, you are absolutely right. I had no idea what you had in your overnight bag: black lace, silk, and you. You are so beautiful."

"Thank you, Richard, you are quite handsome in your silk pajamas. They are not black, but very seductive. Come, lie beside me, darling. I have our pillows and cozy comforter ready for us. I see you have opened the champagne as well. I thought I heard that infamous pop."

"Margaret, 'to everything there is a season and a time for every matter under heaven' according to Ecclesiastes 3:1, and this is the time for me to ask you, Margaret, to be my wife. Will you accept this ring as a token of my love?"

"Oh, Richard, it is perfect. I love the design. I love you. Did you even arrange to have the moon right there behind you? Oh yes, Richard, I will marry you. I am receiving this ring with gratitude and joy."

"Margaret, I did plan one other thing. There are no bells, or chimes, or interruptions tonight. This night belongs to us."

"Oh yes, Richard, every cell in my body is a center of energy. This energy is an expression of the power of love shared in joy."

As they kissed, that magic tingle, more like an electric shock, consumed their bodies as they became one.

They awakened still wrapped in each other's arms, to the morning light, birds singing, especially the chickadees. A very gentle morning. A very gentle love.

"Good morning, Richard."

"I love hearing you say that, Margaret. Our first night together, and we have that big beautiful cozy canopy bed, and we sleep on the floor."

"My darling Richard, I slept so well and so warm. However, tonight I suggest we try the bed."

"Margaret, is that a family name, or do you know why you are a Margaret? I'll confess when I was talking to you about arrangements for the town, and then later my living arrangement, I felt a very warm connection with you, but I thought the name Margaret was a bit formal. Don't misunderstand. I love your name because it is you. It's just that I want to know so much about you."

"Well, Richard, here goes the story-telling again. Remember you asked. During the first revolutionary war, in 1775, the Colonials captured the British sloop Margaretta off Machias on the Maine coast. Of course, it wasn't really Maine then. At one time Maine was a part of Massachusetts. It became its own state in 1820, the twenty-third state. Both my parents and grandparents were historians by hobby and professions. So while many girls were named after glamorous movie stars or famous people. I was named after a captured British sloop. Fortunately they rearranged the name a bit from Margaretta to Margaret, and I have always been Margaret. No cutesy nicknames, just Margaret. My parents always talked to me with respect, and I was around adults a lot during my childhood. I never remember being treated any differently because I was a child. I was encouraged to be a part of the conversation at the dinner table, and my questions were always answered to my satisfaction. I did have a reasonably early bedtime, that's when I'd often read or write poetry, or just enjoy the quiet. Well, that's enough of that. How about you? How did you get to be a Richard?"

"I have a short story: I was named after my paternal grandfather. I had so much teasing about my name. Just imagine what kids could do to a Richard King. I was Dick and Dickey with many rhyming chants, and King wasn't much better. In high school and even college, it was 'King Dick,' and so forth. I resisted it for a while, a few fights, a lot of verbal exchanges, and then I finally wised up and joined them, laughed with them, and said thank you guys. Once I did that, it was over, a great lesson. So I became a Richard. Occasionally, someone will call me Dick. It doesn't bother me at all. Once I knew who I was, the rest didn't matter."

"I love sharing like this, Richard, and I am content, cozy, and beginning to smell something wonderful from Betty's kitchen. Whatever it is, it is awakening my appetite. I swear after that dinner last night, I didn't think I could ever be hungry again, but I am. Shall I shower first?"

"We could shower together, Margaret. Save water, time, maybe?"

"That actually sounds like a great idea, and we may not get to go to brunch at all. You know you are right. You get the bathroom first, Margaret, this time."

"Good morning, Margaret and Richard. You two look like you are ready for anything this morning. You are absolutely glowing."

"Good morning, Betty. I was perfectly content to sleep all day until all of these tantalizing smells awakened more than my taste buds. So here we are following our noses.

"Good," Betty said with a smile. "Were you comfortable last night? Coffee is freshly made. It's on the tea cart. Help yourself. I won't attempt to name all of the teas in the tea basket. However, I can tell you that they are all excellent. Our specialty teas are sold in at least forty states. It has become a source of employment for all of our local youth during the summer and several folks year round. Everything we prepare comes from our valley. As you can tell I have a slight bias regarding our tea."

"It sounds like you have every right to be very proud of a marvelous accomplishment.

"Richard, did you smell that tea? Pumpkin spice. We definitely appreciate both tea, and coffee."

"I am going to have coffee this morning, and I am sure we will be taking some of the teas home with us. Oh yes, ma'am, we certainly will. What a treasure you have here, Betty."

"I believe I heard something about you folks being hungry. We have several choices. You may have whatever you'd like or try them all if you wish. Honey wheat pancakes with cranberries and bananas, triple berry French toast. We do offer real maple syrup, whipped cream, or butter as you like, also sun omelet. I keep that as a surprise, but I've never had a complaint, and always eggs to order, country ham, and our orange juice is freshly squeezed. What is your pleasure?"

"Richard, how are we ever going to decide? I know I can't eat everything. What are you going to do? I am going to have a two-egg sun omelet, half a slice of country ham, and one pancake to start with. Now you, my love, decision time."

"I would like two pancakes, one basted egg, and the other half slice of ham to start. Richard, will you give me a bite of your sun omelet?"

"I am sure we can negotiate, love."

"I will have that ready for you in a few minutes. Margaret, I don't remember seeing that beautiful ring on your finger yesterday. Is it new?"

"Actually, yes it is."

"James, come in here. We have something to show you."

"Yes, love, what is it?"

"I think Margaret and Richard may have something to tell us. Just look at that beautiful new ring on her finger. Oh, Margaret, it is beautiful, and so are you my dear. Well, Richard, shall we make our first announcement?"

"James, Betty, first, thank you for all of the many things you have done to make this trip one that we will treasure for the rest of our lives. Everything was perfectly arranged last night, and she said yes! We are engaged, and you folks are the first to know."

"Well, this is a celebration. Do we have the champagne open yet, Betty?"

"No darling, you take care of that while I do my magic tricks in the kitchen. I will be back shortly."

"Well, Richard, we are now formally engaged. I mean, publicly. Exciting, isn't it?"

"I love you, Margaret. I know that we will love and support one another for the rest of our lives."

"Richard, I have no doubt. Well, I have the champagne, glasses, and right on cue, as usual my beautiful wife! Now a toast to the happy couple: Our wish for you is for you to enter your lives together based on a very simple, solid concept. This has worked so well for us, we wish it for you. Just remember, 'As you give, so shall you receive.' We have not been able to outgive each other, as we continue to experience happiness, health, and peace in our lives. Here's to a long and joyful adventure together. Now you folks better be ready to eat."

"James, would you be willing to help me serve these special guests of ours?" "I would be delighted."

*

"Richard, they are so special. I love this place. I love them! Oh, I know, Margaret, you just love everyone. Question is, are you going to love that bicycle today?"

"Oh my, I had forgotten, temporarily. But yes, I am really looking forward to all of the pleasures of the day."

"How about the pleasures of the night, Margaret? Saved by the food."

"What a beautiful presentation, Betty."

"Thank you both so much. When we say it is our pleasure, we do indeed mean it. If there is anything else we can do to make your stay better, please let us know.

"By the way, I don't know what your plans for today are. I just want to make sure you know about the Fall Harvest Festival of Art and History. I know you have the bicycles reserved for the day, and the weather is going to cooperate."

"Where is the festival, Betty?"

"It's actually in Hollowelle. The riverfront bike trail is perfect. The trees are spectacular. You just stay on the trail which is paved and very bike-friendly. It's about four miles. Hollowelle is celebrating its 250th anniversary. I have a paper that will give you a program for today."

"What do you think, Richard? Four miles?"

"She did say it was an easy ride, and we can stop along the way if we need to, so I'm game if you are."

"Well, I haven't been on a bicycle for so long, but I loved it. Yes, I think it will be perfect. Art and history are two of my favorite things."

"Here's the program. It sure looks good to me. James and I may sneak away for a while. Remember, if you need anything, let us know. You folks have a fun day, as I am sure you will. See you later."

"Let's go in the family room and look this program over. I really want to at least sit on that comfy-looking sofa."

"Great, let's do it."

"Well, it got me with the first line. 'All day free coffee and cookies at Slates Bakery,' in fine print, for anyone wearing a Fall Festival Historic shirt."

"Oh absolutely, Richard. I do want a shirt. We'll have our first matching set of something."

"There is a giant potluck supper, celebrity chefs, art exhibit, antiques and local crafts, live music, and a farmer's market. Sounds like everything we planned to see all in one spot. Perfect. Admission to the potluck supper is one dish to share, created with local ingredients."

"Oh, Richard, I am sure we could get something from the farmer's market. They always have great things prepared."

"Does that mean you're interested?"

"Oh yes. Do the bicycles have lights? Because, at 7:30 p.m., there is a community bonfire and spectacular Taiko drumming performance, following by an old-fashioned sing-a-long."

"Margaret, what is taiko drumming?"

"I don't have a clue, but it sounds intriguing. What a perfect time to be here. Now I know you are good, Richard, but this is a 250th Anniversary, so I'm thinking you didn't arrange this, right?"

"Right, Margaret, I didn't arrange this, but I absolutely agree it sounds like the thing to do. Do you have some warm clothing?"

"Yes, I do have. I have everything in that bag I brought. It's like my magic bag of tricks."

"I love you, Margaret. Did I tell you that yet?"

"You'll never tell me too often, Richard."

As their lips met, electricity filled the room.

"Oh my, if we are going, we had better go, before we both change our minds. Right?"

"Right, my lady. Let's go upstairs and become bikers."

*

"Our bicycles have lights and safety stripes. It looks like they have been out at night before. So let's get down to the trail. James gave me detailed directions although it's only a few blocks away. I confessed that although I am a male, I do not do directions well."

"So we are all checked off and checked out, Richard."

"Yes, we are on our way. I don't know about you, but I am as excited as a kid on Christmas Eve."

"That is pretty excited, Richard, but so am I."

"This trail is amazing. The trees are every shade of yellow, orange, crimson, burnt amber, green, and I love the way the leaves fall. It really is like a symphony. They fall like notes of a melody. Shall we sing?"

"Margaret, that is something we may want to wait on. Best that I blend in with a big crowd."

"Richard, I think maybe you have not really listened to yourself. You have a very strong speaking voice, and yet when you were reading to the children, it was musical. So you really were listening to me."

"Oh yes, I was. I don't understand it, and I don't need to, but from our first telephone conversations, I have felt strong vibrations between us."

"So have I, Margaret. That's why I even surprised myself when we first met, and when I took your hand, there was an undeniable electrical sensation."

"Yes, I know. I was sure you must have felt it, but I was trying to be very professional, and you were my darling."

"Well, we have made very good time. We turn right here, and then I do believe we can follow the signs. I can see them already. The first signs have directions to the harvest festival building. I'll just bet that's where we get our shirts, and then coffee and cookies at the bakery. After all, we have just traveled cross-country on bicycles. We need sustenance."

"Yeah, really four miles maybe, but you're right, the bakery will be next."

"Oh my goodness this has everything. This building is huge. There's antique alley, art exhibit, craft fair, and food samples everywhere. I can smell them. And then the arrows to the next building show the grower's market. I hear the music coming from that building. Oh yes, Richard, let's do get our shirts, find the Bakery, and let me settle down a bit. I want to do everything all at once."

"Margaret, remember to take a deep breath, focus, right here, right now, living in the moment."

"Richard, you are an excellent student. Thank you for your soothing presence."

"I am much calmer already. I love these shirts. Just think, a 250th year birthday celebration. That's pretty special."

"Yes, it is, my love. The bakery is down the street just past the building where the market is. We can listen to the music while we drink our coffee. We actually have time to do what we want and enjoy it as we go."

"Again, Richard, you are right. Here we are. I can smell it before I see it. That's a very good sign."

*

"The coffee, cookies, and conversations were all equally wonderful. But now let's go back to the harvest festival and enjoy ourselves. I can't believe we have seen so much, talked to so many wonderful people. It's like time slowed down, when I did. We have learned so much about this community. The historical display was so complete and entertaining. The people who came here to begin a new life were determined to make it more than a place to live. Their dream was to build a commercial and cultural center, and they certainly did. I want to take this idea back to our community council. Our town can do this, only in late spring."

"Absolutely, Margaret, and I'll be glad to help in any way I can. But it is almost five o'clock, probably time to get over to the next building and decide what we want to take to the potluck."

"Oh yes, I had almost forgotten we have a mission. My mind is still on the art exhibit. My parents knew the Wyeth family. It had slipped my mind until I saw the Andrew Wyeth exhibit. It seemed so familiar. That was fun, and so is this. What a market! It's everything a market should be—people sitting on straw bales and food, food, everywhere. I don't think we'll have any problem finding our potluck dish."

"Well, Margaret, maybe a little problem, so many choices and so little time."

"Oh so, now it's my turn to say breathe, Richard."

"OK, you got me. We're good."

"I'm really pleased with our choices. I chose the savory chicken pie that smells heavenly, and you chose the blueberry pie. I think our admission is secured. Perhaps we should go and see if we can secure a place to sit. I wonder how they will manage with so many people. Perfect arrangement, tables for twenty, family style, and they put a mixture of salads, main dishes, desserts, pitchers of water and lemonade, and homemade rolls with butter and lots of jam and honey. This is so good. Thank you, Richard. Thank you for finding this place, for finding me, for loving me, and everything."

"Margaret, you are absolutely adorable. I love every minute of our time together. And this food is fit for a King. That's me, you know."

"Yes, I do know, and yes, you are."

*

"What a day! We are going to the taiko drumming ceremony and bonfire, aren't we?"

"You bet we are, and it's time to do that. I think it's at the end of this street. We don't have chairs."

"That's fine, Richard. We have each other. I can sit on your lap, can't I?"

"Well! Oh good, hay bales, and we got here in time to sit on one."

"Those are the largest drums I have ever seen."

"Me too. This is intriguing. How are they going to play those things? They're huge."

"Richard, that ceremonial tribute was enchanting. I loved the elaborate costumes and angelic voices. I could never have imagined such a performance associated with drumming. This has been simply one of the best days of my life."

"Margaret, every day, hour, minute, is the best time of my life with you. Mahatma Gandhi said it far better 'Happiness is when what you think, whatever you say, and what you do are in harmony.' And so it is."

"I didn't notice before. Of course we had the bonfire and torchlights, but now I know it is cold out here."

"Yes, my darling, you are right. I'm glad we're well protected, because I just felt a couple of raindrops, and we have four miles of bicycling to do."

"I know, Richard, and here's our trail already."

"Yeah! It is well lit. I know we have lights, but having the trail so well lit is a definite plus. So off we go, back to our little paradise."

"That was refreshing."

"Yes, and we are soaked. That was a good ride, and I am grateful that it didn't really start raining until we were almost home."

"Richard, I do hope we can start a fire in our suite tonight."

"That would feel so good."

"I'm sure I can figure that out. Remember I'm the magician."

"Of course you are, so let's go do it."

"Oh my goodness! They did it again. The fire is blazing, and the bed is turned down."

"Margaret, I am as surprised as you. I didn't even request this. And a really big bonus—a pot of hot chocolate and some great little delicacies."

"Richard, we must be doing something right because we are getting so much in return."

"Yes, like these wonderful robes. I am already warm, comfortable, and feel completely at home. How about you, Margaret?"

"Oh yes, the fire and its magic, hot chocolate, warm robe, and you. I am content. Actually, Richard, I'm not sure content is correct. With your arms around me and your lips so close to mine, my body is beginning to tingle, and it is not from the cold. This amazing electrical charge we have together seems to have a life of its own. Richard, the bed is turned down and looks so inviting. Suddenly, I'm not tired, cold, or sleepy but very stimulated."

"And, Margaret, let me add, stimulating. You are beautiful beyond words and so right about this energy that so naturally consumes us. Oh my darling Margaret, I love you."

"Richard, are you sleeping?"

"No, I'm just completely content holding you, watching the fire create wonderful stories, kind of hoping this night would never end, and yet knowing that tomorrow will be another day of miracles for us."

"Uh huh. I love you. Good night."

∗

"I love awakening with you in my arms, Margaret."

"Me too."

"You are so comfortable."

"Well, that sounds a bit like a pair of comfy house shoes."

"Oh, I love it when you get that mischievous twinkle in your eyes. Let's get up and get down to brunch, I do believe they pipe those smells into the rooms. What a wake-up call. Also, Margaret, I found a note from James and Betty that said, 'We trust you had a great day and evening. We thought you might enjoy a little warm fire and hot chocolate when you returned. And we do not have this suite reserved for tomorrow. So take your time checking out, unless of course you decide to stay another night, which would be fine with us. Looking forward to seeing you for brunch,' James and Betty."

"Richard, they are so thoughtful, and I feel like I've known them forever. We will come back here again, don't you think?"

"I do think we will, darling. This is a special place that I know I will never forget. Nor shall I. So let's go eat, shall we?"

"Another sensory banquet. I want coffee and tea. How do I work that out?"

"Choices, Richard, sometimes you just have to make the tough ones."

"Right. Coffee it is. Good morning, Betty. Thank you so much. We were so cold and wet when we got home, and that warm fire and the hot chocolate was absolutely perfect. You and James have spoiled us, and we love it."

"I'm so glad, Margaret, that's our reward. Did you two enjoy the festival?"

"Oh my, yes. The bicycle trail was wonderful. The festival was perfect, and the taiko drumming ceremony was indescribable in its beauty."

"I'm so sorry that James and I had to miss it but so glad you folks enjoyed it. I have never had a complaint yet."

"You mean for the whole 250 years, Betty?"

"Sure, Richard. Flattery will get you actually, breakfast. What is your fancy this morning, my friends? Warm blueberry muffins, eggs benedict, assorted fruits, yogurt, oatmeal with cranberries, chopped almonds, and raisins, and of course fresh orange juice, coffee, and assorted teas. I think that's about it."

"Betty, the more you talked, the hungrier I became. Well, I know I want a muffin and jam. I can smell them, and I am imagining I can taste them. I can't resist the oatmeal. How about you, Richard?"

"Are you going to eat breakfast? Am I? Oh yes. I am hungry. I think we worked up an appetite last night."

"Oh you did, did you?"

"Margaret, you must be too close to the oven, your face is flushed."

"Oh, the bicycling was quite vigorous!"

"Yes, of course it was."

"James, good morning, how nice it is to see you, and thank you for your thoughtfulness last night."

"You are so welcome. We love doing little surprises for our guests. We keep getting back so much more than we can give. It's a wonderful life, don't you think?"

"Yes," they answered in unison.

"So, Richard, what are you having for breakfast? Eggs benedict, fruit compote, and then we'll go from there. Fair enough, help yourself to the orange juice and fruit. We'll have the rest out shortly. By the way, are you folks staying over another night?"

"We really want to, but we have some commitments. We would appreciate a late checkout, if the offer is still open."

"Absolutely, no rush at all."

*

"Well, darling, are you ready to leave our paradise?"

"Richard, you know, we won't ever lose what we have. Wherever we go, whatever we do, we will share this synergy. But yes, I am a little sad to leave our perfect paradise—our first home, but not our last."

"Margaret, this place will remain in my heart forever. We will definitely return often."

"Before we leave I want to buy a few things from Betty's gift shop."

"Good idea, Margaret. I know I want some tea. Yes, and jam, although you know that's really pretty silly. We have so much jam and jelly in our community center."

"Tea it is, and we can tell Betty and James good-bye."

"We are on our way, and now that we are, I am excited to be going home. I called Mary this morning, and told her I would see her tomorrow. Howdy has been enjoying his vacation also, especially with the children. She has noticed that he is resting more and has only made his town tour one time. However, he seems content. She frets a lot about his appetite, or lack of it. Her mission is to make sure everyone, and everything, eats very well."

"Did you tell her about our engagement?"

"No, I want to wait a few days, and just savor the time before our community becomes involved. Believe me, Richard, we have a very large family, and that's exactly what our community is."

"Again, darling, I think you have made a very good decision. I want everyone to know, and yet I really want it to be just ours for a while. Are we doing back a different way? I don't remember this part of the trip."

"Yes, we are going back on a different route. I thought we might as well see some different scenery. I really checked on the directions. It's no further going this way, and if my calculations are right, we will get to Steveson's Apple Farm at the right time for dinner, and we'll only be an hour and a half-ish from home. How does that sound?"

"As always, intriguing. I am familiar with the Farm House Restaurant. I know its maintained traditions, and the last I heard, it was still producing some of the best apples around. Some of the trees are very old and still producing quite well. But you have never been there?"

"No, I've intended to. I think I was waiting to go with someone very special."

"Flattery will get you anything you want, my love."

"Richard, stop. I want to take a picture of that covered bridge."

"So do I. I am so glad you saw that. What a beauty. This I may try to paint. You paint it, and I'll write a poem about it. Perfect."

"What a magnificent farmhouse. I love the porch and those huge red barns. It is very picturesque. Shall we go in? Since we're here I suppose we might as well."

"Oh, Richard, when you opened that door, the mixture of odors was like an aphrodisiac. Perhaps we should see if we can order to go? Silly man, you know what I mean. Uh huh."

"Good evening, folks. Do you have reservations?"

"Yes, we do. Actually, I called about an hour ago. And the very nice person I talked to said there was a cancellation, so we got lucky."

"Very good, sir. Your name please?"

"Richard King."

"Oh yes, Mr. King, welcome to Steveson's Farm House. We are running just a little behind. If you folks would like to wait in the parlor, I'll bring you a glass of our special warm apple cider. My name is Stanley."

"Thank you, Stanley."

"This place is so interesting. Everything in here is authentic—the fixtures, furniture, artwork, and that beautiful fireplace. This continues to be such an adventure. I am so grateful for this trip, Richard. It's like a dream. Everything has been so perfect."

"Just like you, Margaret. Oh, I am so happy and hungry."

"Oh me too."

"Here you are, madam, sir. We have had no complaints about our warm spiced fresh apple cider. Are you familiar with our history?"

"I read a bit about it, enough to be intrigued and wanting to know more. We have a family scrapbook on the table. It really is very informative and mostly pictures with short captions. From the beginning of the orchards, building the house and barns, to the restaurant transition. Many of our recipes are still the same ones the family used. I really suggest you order the green rice casserole as one of your side dishes. It has herbs, cheese, and well, we can't say very much about it, except once a person has ordered it, they always order it. There are assorted cheeses and herbed crackers also. Also, your table will be ready shortly."

"Magic again, Richard. This book is wonderful and so is the cider and cheese. I agree. Look at these pictures and the story they tell. What a happy family picture. These are quite old, but they are so lively. Not like the usual posed pictures. There is so much activity. Yes, they did well preserving the historical review."

"Your table is ready. How many dining rooms do you have, Stanley?"

"All of the downstairs rooms have been converted to dining rooms, except for the parlor where you folks were. We have five rooms, and each room seats twenty to thirty guests comfortably. The owners still maintain residency upstairs. The family has always lived here at Orchards. This is your table, and your waiter will be right with you. George will be your server tonight. Enjoy."

"What a perfect way to end our lovely journey."

"Only the first chapter, Margaret. We have so many more. As a matter of fact, another one begins tomorrow."

"Yes, and tonight, right now, I am really enjoying this apple cider. This menu is lovely."

"Yes, and the food choices aren't bad either."

"Yes, silly, I am ready to order."

"So fast, Margaret. I'm surprised."

"Well, I know they raise excellent pork, right her at the farm, so I am having the ham dinner."

"Well, I'm going to have the same. I saw them serve the table behind you a few minutes ago, and they had ham, and from their expressions at the first bite, I'm betting that it is very good."

"Good Evening. It is my pleasure to be your waiter for the evening. My name is George."

"Good evening, George. Your timing is perfect. We have both decided to have your ham dinner special."

"Excellent choice. Also, we would like to have one side order of the green rice special dish. I see you have already heard about how special that dish really is."

"Yes, we have. I would like a pot of tea, and for the lady?"

"That's what I would like as well. Thank you."

"What are you thinking about, Margaret? You have that look about you."

"Richard, have you thought about when we get home tonight?"

"Interesting that you asked. I was just thinking about that, and I definitely think there are no wrong decisions. We will be fine whatever we decide."

"I absolutely agree, Richard. We can explore options. I think our lives will just flow. You can continue living in the studio, if you wish, and we can focus on the transition of merging our lives."

"Margaret, I know I am absolutely committed to our life together, and I am also somewhat patient about the process. Have you thought about when you would like to have our wedding? I don't want to rush you, darling. If you need more time to think about it, that's fine."

"Richard, I have, and I do, yes, New Year's Eve."

"Well, you have indeed. That's wonderful!"

"Here is George with our celebratory tea. Great timing. Thank you."

"Your first course will be served shortly, sir."

"You were saying, Margaret?"

"Yes, it just seems so right to me for us to start the New Year together, and of course, I think you know the entire community will attend, and we should spend New Year's Eve together at the Center of Conscious Living. Am I going too fast, Richard? I want you to be involved in the planning also, and if that's too soon, we can wait."

"Oh no, my darling, I love everything you have said. I am ready today, so it certainly won't be too soon. I am also excited about having some time to just enjoy the adventure, which it certainly is. New Year's Eve just seems actually so simple. Everyone will be expecting to have a celebration together. We could have the wedding and reception right there at the center. Everyone would be a part of the celebration. Every year we have a potluck and champagne. We'll just add the wedding cake. Mary and her crew will have a great time creating it. Doesn't that sound fun and easy?"

"Oh yes, Margaret. Everything is easy with you. I'm glad we've worked up an appetite because that tray is very full."

"Oh yes, and it looks and smells fantastic."

∗

"Are you all right to drive, Richard?"

"Oh yes, Margaret, why do you ask?"

"Probably because I am so content, relaxed, and maybe a little sleepy."

"You just relax and sleep if you like, darling, I am fine. Actually, my adrenalin is probably pumping a bit because I am so excited about everything."

"I'm glad, Richard because our routine starts tomorrow. Well, maybe day after tomorrow. Tomorrow I will get Howdy and spend a little time at the library. I hope you understand. I will not wear my ring tomorrow, until I get home."

"Good idea, Margaret. So what happens day after tomorrow?"

"Well, we start with meditation and then our special start-up morning drink. You'll love it and then yoga. You and Howdy can do the beginning stretches, our walking routine, and then breakfast. That's enough to know for now."

"I can see you are going to whip me into shape, and goodness knows I need it. I'm ready. Bring it on."

"Richard, I love you."

"Darling, we're home. You had a little nap."

"Again! I'm sorry, I wanted to keep you company while you were driving."

"You did, my love, you did. I'll take your things inside, and make sure everything is all right, and then I'll go to the studio."

"Richard, would you just spend this night here? I'm not quite ready for you to go. It's late and kind of cold tonight."

"I was thinking the same thing, love. It only makes sense. I'm so glad you thought of it, and the answer is, oh yes."

"Good morning, Richard. Have you been awake for a while?"

"Just a few minutes, darling. I love waking up with your nice warm body beside me, but I guess Howdy will have to suffice for a while. Is there room for me, you, and Howdy in this bed?"

"I was just joking, Richard. Howdy sleeps on the big shaggy rug beside me on the floor. Although he has been known to nudge me out of bed on occasion, and speaking of Howdy, I am really looking forward to seeing him this morning. So therefore, I will beat you to the shower, although there is another one downstairs if you want."

"No, thank you. I am content to just lie here and revel in my memories of the past few days and nights, and then I promise I will come right back to conscious living practice. So go to your shower while I fantasize."

"I'm on my way."

"Richard, you are sleeping."

"Oh no, only dozing a bit. There's a difference."

"Oh sure. I'll go down and fix our wake-up drink and coffee while you're showering, and then we'll see what we have to prepare breakfast. It seems like I haven't been here for weeks. I know there is a time warp. Maybe we are getting younger."

"Well, don't get too much younger before you get downstairs, I'm grinding the coffee."

"I took a cold shower, Margaret, so I would be ready for that special cider vinegar, lemon, honey, hot water, whatever else special drink we're having. It's really good, Richard. I'm really sixty years old and only look half that age. This drink is the fountain of youth."

"Well, I'm going to need it to keep up with you, woman. It does have a bit of a zing to it, not bad. It does have a wake-up flavor to it."

"Great. Enjoy."

"That coffee smells really good. Where's the honey?"

"Right in the honey jar, darling, by your cup."

"Oh yes, thank you. This is so much fun. I love being with you. You really wake me up. Literally."

"I know what you mean, Richard, exactly."

"While you were showering, I made breakfast. Oats with blueberries, ground flaxseed, raisins and nuts. Sound OK to you?"

"It sounds almost like heaven, Margaret. I am going to miss you today, you know."

"Yes, I do know, so will I. It will be a sweet miss."

"Yeah, I guess you're right. We both have very full lives. It's just that I know now how much more rich my life is since I met you."

"Yes, darling, I am very grateful for that meeting."

"It is time for me to get to the library, so I will see you this evening?"

"I am already looking forward to it. Tell everyone I said hello, and I'll see them later."

"Well, that was more like a hello kiss than good-bye."

"I know, but it really is. See you later, love."

It seems like a long time ago since I left the library, and yet it also feels so familiar. I do love this place. My life feels so full, sort of bubbling over. I really want to see Howdy. He is such a dear friend. Well, here I go. Thank goodness all of these folks care so much for me, and I know they would love to hear all about my trip, and I also know that they will never be intrusive. We respect one another so much. They will be very pleased to have me share whatever I chose to, with no pressure to discuss it further.

"Oh, Howdy, you knew it was me at the door. You beautiful, warm and happy friend, I have missed you so much. Yes, let's just sit here for a few quiet minutes by ourselves. You know I don't feel like I have to really tell you anything, Howdy. You just seem to always know everything I'm thinking, and in your own way help me to understand myself better, just by being together. You are my special angel, Howdy. I love you. Now I think we should see people.

"I have a little present for everyone. Yours is at home. Let's sneak into the Nook first and see Mary. Maybe she'll have time for a cup of tea."

"Good morning, Mary."

"Oh my darling girl, it is so good to have you back. I am so glad you had a holiday, but we really missed you. Welcome home. And Mr. Howdy has been a perfect gentleman, as always, but I know he missed you too. My daughter is helping out today. So do you have time for tea and a chat?"

"Just what I was hoping to hear, Mary. This tea is so good. I don't know what you do to it, but whatever it is, just keep doing it."

"I think it's not necessarily the tea itself but the joy of sharing, Margaret."

"I do believe you're right, as usual, Mary. So what is new and exciting?"

"Well, the first thing I want to tell you about, I can tell you everyone that knows about it is excited. I'm willing to bet you will be. You know Brady, our resident sculptor? He is doing a beautiful bronze piece which will have a very special place in our community. It's to recognize our longtime honorary mayor, and, Margaret, it brings tears to my eyes, it's so lifelike. I can hardly wait for you to see it."

"Mary, it sounds mysteriously exciting but we call Howdy our honorary mayor."

"Yes, Margaret, that's what I mean, for Howdy's birthday, which the town has celebrated for at least the past ten years on the first Saturday of December."

"Well, Brady expects to have the piece back in time to unveil it for Howdy's birthday celebration. I took a picture of it. I'll show you tomorrow. We've been keeping this secret for a long time. He didn't want to disappoint you if it wasn't good enough, but it certainly is. This town loves Howdy. He brings so much joy to so many people, and we are all so grateful that you have shared him with us so freely. So it really is a tribute to you as well, Margaret."

"Mary, I am overwhelmed, I really am. I don't even know what to say, except I am so grateful, and humbled by this outstanding gesture. I think it will take a while for me to grasp it."

"Yes, I'm sure it will. I know you are going to be very pleased with the piece. He captured the spirit of Howdy. It is such a great piece of art, and only a few of us have seen it or know anything about it. Brady wants you to decide about how to do the presentation to the community. But not today, darling. Our timing was perfect. I hear the sound of excited people finding their way back here. I think Howdy rounded them up. He's good at that."

"Mary, thank you for everything. I have a lot to tell you soon, all good. I had a wonderful holiday."

"I'll just bet you did. You are absolutely glowing. I can hardly wait to hear all about it. But I was just busting at the seams to tell you about Howdy's piece, as you know it's really hard for me to not share everything with everyone, but I did it."

A chorus of, "Margaret, you look absolutely stunning. We are so glad to see you, and obviously you are having a great vacation."

"Yes, I am. I have six more days of total self-indulgence, which I plan to enjoy every minute of. I do have a little momento for each of you. We really had a life-enhancing journey, Richard and I. I will share more later, but for now, let's just enjoy the moment together, and then I know you all have to get back to work."

"Yes, Margaret. We really do miss you."

"Howdy, I'm not going to be here very long. I just wanted to say hi and most importantly to pick you up. I drove the car because we have several errands to do, such as groceries, mail, and then we'll see, oh yes we will stop by the center. Our big food preparation day is day after tomorrow. I did volunteer to be responsible for all of the spices so I'm thinking we had better go there first, and of course you always get a special treat there. Of course, you always say thank you, which means you will definitely get one the next time you are a sly one, my friend. Howdy, do you have any idea of how much joy you bring to everyone? I am so excited about your birthday celebration. We'll share that with Richard tonight. I'm going to my office to pick up a few things and then we'll be on our way."

*

"Hi, Laura, I see you're busy as usual. How's it going?"

"Hi, Margaret, welcome. Where's Howdy?"

"He's out back with William. They had something important to do."

"Well, I'll have his treat ready for him. We haven't seen him around the past several days. Is he all right?"

"He's been staying with Mary this week. I've been on holiday for the past three to four days, and also he is not making his rounds in the community as frequently, Laura."

"Oh, he's all right, but you know he is having another birthday, and well, he's just slowing down a bit."

"I certainly know about that, Margaret, that's why I'm here today instead of tomorrow. I can still get everything done. It just takes a little bit longer."

"Laura, do you need more help?"

"Oh no, Margaret, I am doing just exactly what I want to do. I love this time of year where we get to see the results of the harvest and all come together with one purpose. The joy is so powerful. I can tell you I don't want to have anything to do with that new flash-freezing part. I am very happy with canning. I love seeing those jars sitting on the shelves (ready for the winter). Vegetables and fruits, jams and jellies, and especially the apples, sliced, sauced, juiced, whatever. Yes, there is a deep satisfaction and appreciation of nature and oneness, and of course food for all winter."

"I can see you have your territory staked out. Do you have your crew all confirmed?"

"Yes, ma'am. We also have two new young ladies to train this year."

"That's wonderful, Laura. Well, I'd better check the spice cabinets. I will bring everything we need tomorrow, and make sure we're ready to go. This will be Richard's first year. He is really excited about learning. He is going to be mentored by Jack. He will start out with the apple preparation process. I'll let Richard and Jack work that out. I'm sure he will have fun at whatever he's doing. Don't we all."

"Darling, does Richard know that we have music going, people singing, and bodies moving like fine machinery?"

"I've told him a little bit, he'll find out the rest. He winced just a little when I told him we started at 6:00 a.m. and went until we finished."

"Well, he's a fine, strong young man, and he will have a great time."

"Thank you, Laura. You have taught me so much, and I still have a lot more to learn."

"There's my Howdy. It is so good to see you. I'll ring your treat right out."

"Laura, I would say you spoil him, but I know that's not possible. Thank you, and we'll see you tomorrow, and then of course early Friday morning."

"Be sure, and tell Richard we're glad he's part of the team. I have a feeling he's going to be here for a long time."

"Laura, I think you're right, and I will tell him. Come on, Howdy, we still have errands to run. Bye, everyone, see you later."

"We have had a very full day, Howdy, and I think we are very tired. Your tail is dragging instead of wagging, and I'm a bit droopy myself. A very productive day. I had such a good time on my trip with Richard. Everything was perfect, and you know something, Howdy, everything is perfect here today. I wonder what Richard did today. I guess we'll very soon find out. It is so good to be home."

✳

"Good evening, my sweet Maggie, and gentle giant Howdy. Oh yes, I am glad to see you too Howdy. He seems to have some energy in reserve."

"We were both pretty drowsy a few minutes ago. Hello to you, Richard, it is so good to be in your arms. I can use some of that wonderful energy this evening."

"Thank you."

"I have so much to tell you, Richard, and I am so anxious to hear all of it, but not now."

"I have the fire going in the living room. I have a pot of tea ready, and Howdy has already found his spot right in the middle of the rug. We'll just have to nudge him over."

"This is nice, Richard. You always seem to know what I need, often before I know it myself. Quiet moments can be very restorative."

"Turn around, Margaret, and I will massage your neck and shoulders. They are a little tight."

"Thank you so much, Richard. That was wonderful. It was a pleasure for me, and I tried a new but old recipe, Margaret. I hope you like it. It's basically a chicken pot pie. I kind of put a lot of stuff in it. I even experimented with some spices."

"Richard, it smells so good, and it is so nice to have dinner prepared. You are a magic man, I love you so much."

"Thank you, Margaret. The pleasure really is mine. I missed you today, but I did get a lot done, as I'm sure you did. The timer went off, and I wasn't even kissing you. I'm out of step, I guess."

"Well, the wonderful smells from the kitchen have awakened my taste buds, and you already have the table set. My goodness, Richard, your talents continue to pleasantly surprise me. Oh this is very good, where did you find the recipe?"

"Well, I kind of made it up. My grandmother used to make this dish a lot, and I guess I remembered more than I thought I knew because it really does taste a lot like hers did."

"Did you spend a lot of time with your grandmother, Richard?"

"Yes, I did. She raised my sister and me since the time I was five and my sister was three."

"Do you want to tell me about it, Richard?"

"Yes, I do, Margaret. I want to share everything with you. I will let that be your bedtime story. We can lie by the fire after I clean the kitchen, and you can bathe if you want or just get comfortable and snuggle with Howdy for a while. I need to run down to the cottage and work on a little project I started. It won't take long. Do we have an early start morning tomorrow?"

"No, we don't. It's going to be a pretty routine day."

"Good."

"I see you have the hot chocolate ready. That's a very good thing. It is pretty cold out there, and that makes it even better to be in here with you and Howdy. Although Howdy certainly did not wait for my story time. He is actually snoring."

"Yes, he is. I think I kept him a little too busy today, but he had a good time, and later, I want to tell you about another community custom having to do with celebrating Howdy's birthday. But that's later. Now I am ready for your story."

*

"My father was a global journalist, and my mother was his mentor, editor, and soul mate. My father traveled often. Before I was born, my mother always traveled with him. After I was born and then my sister two years later, my mother stayed home with us most of the time. My mother's mother and father lived close by, and the family was very close. When my mother traveled occasionally, we would stay with our grandmother and grandfather, if he was there. He also traveled often. He was a wildlife photographer and was often on assignments. I remember him talking about retirement. When he was home, my grandmother was a very happy person. She obviously missed him very much, but she did not like to travel. She was a self-described homebody. When I was five and my sister three, my parents and my grandfather, were on an assignment together. They were all very excited. I don't know what the specifics were, but I do remember, my mother was concerned about leaving us. But also she really wanted to be involved in the project. It was the first time they had all been on an assignment together, and we were always very happy to be with grandmother.

"They were in a small plane going to a remote village when the plane crashed. There were no survivors."

"Oh, Richard, I'm so sorry." "I never saw my grandmother cry, and after that, I seldom saw her really laugh. I know now that she had to be strong for us and for herself. However, she was never the same after it happened. There was never a question about where we would live. My grandmother raised us. We had an uncle that lived close, but not close enough to be with us a lot. But he was my pal. I tried to take care of my little sister, until in her early teens she declared her independence. I was a little over-protective, I'm sure. We basically had a good childhood, but there were hollow spots. The house was very quiet. My grandmother made her transition a few years after my sister and I had finished college. She came to our graduations and was very proud of us. She was a very special lady. I do miss her. But a part of her went down with that airplane. It was kind of like she went through life sleepwalking. My sister and I have always been so grateful that she was able to give us a home, and we knew that in her way she loved us, but we really missed our mom, dad, and grandfather.

"I remembered them more than she did. So I used to tell her bedtime stories about them. I'm sure I embellished them, but I enjoyed telling the stories and she loved hearing about them. My grandmother was uncomfortable when I did that, which is why it was always a bedtime story. And that's enough of the bedtime story for now, my darling. It is late."

"Richard, thank you for sharing that with me. I do have some questions, especially about your sister. I must ask at least one question, OK?"

"Yes, love, ask away. Are you and your sister close now?"

"Yes, we are. After my wife died, I withdrew from everything and everyone, so I haven't physically been close to my sister, and her lovely family, for the past few years. I reestablished phone contact earlier this year, but it's been very erratic. That's going to change right away."

"OK. I won't ask any more for now, but I will be looking forward to more chapters of your life, and I my dear one, am looking forward to hearing a chapter of your life."

"We have so much to share, Margaret, and I am so glad."

"I love you, my darling, and I will see you tomorrow, when you are ready for me, just whistle, or send Howdy down."

"Good night, and again, thank you, Richard."

"Good night, love."

"Oh, I almost forgot. I saw Laura at the center today, and she asked me to say hello and remind you that we start at 6:00 a.m., day after tomorrow."

"Oh yes, I remember, and I am really looking forward to it; honestly, even the 6:00 a.m. part. Night, love."

*

"Good morning, Mr. Howdy, so you are the messenger? I am ready to go. You look vigorous this morning. You were really snoring when I left last night, and I probably was about five minutes later. So let's be on our way."

"Good morning, darling. This woolly creature led me to you, and I came very willingly. Did you rest well?

"Yes, I did Richard, and you, like the familiar log, whatever that really means."

"Well, my dear, I am at your mercy. I am like malleable clay ready to be molded into a masterpiece."

"You are goofy. That's what you are. OK. First is meditation. We have done this before. First, just start becoming aware of your breathing. Take deeper and slower breaths as you continue to focus on one word. I am focusing on gratitude, just letting myself go into a state of being at-one-ment. I use the lotus position to start. You and Howdy find a comfortable position. I usually do this for about twenty-five minutes. If you need to do some stretching, please do. It will not bother me at all. Well, step one completed. Now I just do basic stretching. Next is our power drink."

"Margaret, I love this routine. I realize it's new, but it feels so right, and you are also right about this drink. It's good. What's next in the routine day? Now we go for a short, brisk walk."

"Even when it's snowing?"

"Yes, unless it's a blizzard, then we just slow our pace for a few days."

"Obviously, Howdy know the routine. He's already at the door."

"Yes, he certainly does. Actually, Richard, our brisk walk has slowed down a bit recently. I let Howdy set the pace. That is probably good news for me. Let's go after my consciousness of gratitude time. When I get out here, I can't help but be deeply grateful for all I see, hear, smell, and touch. It's kind of my wake up and 'know the joy of life' feeling."

"This place is so beautiful, Margaret, and so are you."

"Well, Richard, that was a good-morning kiss for sure. Now I'm all tingling, and I love it."

"Margaret, I think Howdy is ready to go back. He has really slowed down."

"You're right, Richard. I wasn't watching."

"There are two of us now. You don't have to do things alone anymore."

"Thank you, Richard."

"Howdy, let's go home, boy."

＊

"I smell coffee. Is it my imagination? I set the coffee to brew before we left, and it is ready. If you would be willing to squeeze the orange juice? I will do a quick but amazing omelet, and we will be ready to eat."

"Yes, my dear, we are ready to eat."

"I shouldn't mislead you, Richard. When I am working, I make oats with berries, apples, nuts, whatever I have handy. Saturday is my off routine. It's just unstructured. Sunday often I go to the griddle downtown, or I fix a decadent breakfast, read the paper, listen to music, and then go to the center. We gather at about 1:00 p.m. for spiritual fellowship, and then a potluck. I love Sundays. They are just cozy."

"Margaret, I am loving your routine. It doesn't even sound like a schedule. It sounds like life in its highest form."

"Do you realize Thanksgiving is next week, Richard? And then it will soon be Xmas and then New Year's Eve."

"I am marking the days off on my calendar, Margaret."

"Are you going to invite your sister and family, Richard? They could use the cottage, or they could stay here, wherever they would be most comfortable."

"That is a great idea, Margaret. I am really looking forward to seeing them. I know they will love you, and this community. They may even consider moving here."

"Richard, you could be going a little fast. We may want to start with an introduction first."

"Yes, Margaret. I did get a little over the top. But it still could work out that way."

"Yes, it could."

"So let's call them this evening."

"We can if you wish, but you may want to call your sister yourself, get caught up a bit on the family, and then tell her about me. Then we could talk on Saturday, give her a little time to process it, and get the family all together."

"Margaret I never get tired of saying you are right. Thank you, darling."

"You are welcome. You are also a very good dishwasher."

✳

"So what are you about this afternoon?"

"I have dried and ground a lot of herbs for the food preparation tomorrow. I still have to put them in containers."

"Do you want some help with that?"

"I thought you'd never ask. Yes. I would really appreciate it. I had to buy some of the spices at the market yesterday. I think I have everything now."

"When do you want to start, Margaret?"

"I think we could do it in a couple of hours, so how about two o'clock? That's great. I am finishing a project at the cottage. I should be through by then, so I will see you about 2:30 p.m., darling."

"Well, Howdy, we have a quiet day. Busy but quiet. I love the smells and textures of the herbs and spices. Just think these are the same ones that I planted and cared for in our spot behind the library. This is my fifth year of providing the herbs and spices, and this year, I have a special gift for all of the women, a special lavender blend. I don't know of anyone that has been sensitive to lavender. I know I love it for bathing, sachets, tea blends, cooking, aromatherapy. It's such a delicate odor, yet very definitive. We enjoy each other's company very much, don't we? You watch everything I do, and I can feel your love. I am so excited about your birthday celebration, Howdy."

*

"So here you are. I couldn't find you anywhere. I searched your house thoroughly. I thought you guys may be out walking, and then I remembered this wonderful building."

"I'm sorry, Richard. I had no idea of the time and no bell ringing to remind me."

"Well, that was nice. Will you kiss me every time I say, 'Bell ringing'?"

"I just may do that. I may be conditioned already. So what's happening?"

"Actually, we haven't been out here very long. I got kind of caught up in the wonders of herbs and spices, and what a contribution they make to food preparation. So actually I don't have anything done. I was just mentally preparing for the process. I see, and how is that working for you?"

"Now that you are here, it's working very well because I have a plan."

"Margaret, you always have a plan. So what do I do?"

"I have the containers lined up and will label them in alphabetical order. I think Basil is first. I do have the full list prepared. So while I'm finishing this lavender project, if you would be willing to label all the containers and line them up, by then I should be through and ready to help with the next phase. Oh also, Richard, would you use the black fine point marker on the labels? They need to be easy to see. Thank you, darling, I am so glad you're here. I forget each year how long it really takes to do this."

"The time will fly, Margaret. With you, me, and Howdy, as a team, this project will be accomplished in short order. I love the way it smells in here. Every time Howdy moves, you will get a fresh smell of mint. That's his favorite. So I save some especially for him. He reminds me of a cat with catnip. He kind of rolls around in it and acts goofy."

"Maybe we should try that, Margaret. What do you think?"

"I think we had better get to work or no tea break for us."

"That would be cruel, woman. I am working for my tea break."

"Good, then go to work."

"Slave driver, that's what you are, and a lovely one at that. OK, I'm working."

"I love it that you whistle while you work. It's much better than the tea kettle."

"Well, thank you, I think. By the way, doesn't the law say that I get a break every three or four hours?"

"And what law might that be?"

"The law of human kindness."

"Oh you are good. As a matter of fact, I was thinking the same thing. I'll go put the tea kettle on. You and Howdy come on over in about ten to fifteen minutes. I have a special mellow blend I want to try. One of the ingredients is lavender."

"Sounds great. I am thinking we may be working a few more hours, Margaret, what do you think?"

"I'm afraid I think you're right. I underestimated time once again. Sorry about that. Oh we'll be fine, although after tea, I think a little stretching will feel very good."

"Oh yes, I agree. After our break, we'll work for a couple of hours and then have dinner. I really think we can finish by dinnertime."

"I'm quite sure we can if we push dinner out a ways, say seven or eight."

"You're probably right, Richard. If you hadn't been here to help me, I would probably have been up most of the night. Thank you again. I really do appreciate you. I'll see you in a few minutes. I do have some pumpkin spice bread and cream cheese to go with the tea."

"That sounds wonderful."

"Perfect timing. The tea is ready, and so is the pumpkin bread."

"I'm not sure which smells best, Margaret, the tea, bread, or you. You do smell really good, kind of lavender-ish."

"Yeah, I wonder why. I'm really glad you like that smell, Richard, because I use it a lot. Howdy found his place by the fireside. Shall we join him? We will need sweaters for the rest of the time we're working. The heat system is not really effective in the store room, but we won't be out there much longer."

"No, actually, I think another hour, maybe two, and we will be ready to load up, clean up, and be through."

"I hope you're right, Richard, especially since we start so early in the morning."

"Yeah, I know we leave here at 5:45 a.m."

"Yep, that's the plan."

"I'll be ready."

"I do believe we both went to sleep. Actually, all three, and Howdy is still sleeping. We just dozed a bit. Now back to the spice rack."

"Richard, if you don't mind, you could get started, and I'll put something in the oven for dinner and then be right out."

"Sounds like a plan. I may even be finished by the time you get there."

"No, it won't be that long. We are going to have a very simple dinner, but what I'm not sure."

"Sounds great, darling."

"Whatever, see you in a few."

"Well, Howdy, you decided to wake up, did you? I know you heard kitchen noises, and you just had to see what was going on. We're not through working yet, you know, and tomorrow is the big day. It always amazes me, how so many people can do so much in one day, and have so much fun doing it.

"We practically prepare enough food for the community to enjoy throughout the entire winter. The teamwork is a thing of beauty. We work so hard, but it still seems like a celebration. We have a great life, Howdy, always have had. How could we not be grateful? I'm really grateful for Richard, and I think we had better get out there and do our part."

"We made it, Richard. How are you doing?"

"I really like that music."

"Good. I'm glad you do."

"It's really powerful, and I forgot that I'm actually working. It's so energetic."

"So are you, my darling. You have just about completed the project. Thank you so much."

"Everything is fun with you, Margaret. The only flaw I have found is that time goes so fast. I used to be keenly aware of time. Recently I am only aware that there's never enough time to do everything I want to do. That's when I know I've stepped out of the flow."

"What do you mean, Richard?"

"When life seems to be going too fast—opportunities arising on all sides, meeting new people, learning new things, and making new discoveries about myself, I tend to feel like my energies are flowing in a dozen directions at once. It seems like being on the edge of chaos and then I realize that out of this chaos, something wonderful is emerging. Creative energy is flowing, a new wholeness, a new life, actually is taking shape, a life where I am at peace with myself and my world, where abundance thrives, and I don't have to figure everything out. I can breathe a little easier, and yes, a little deeper. I feel so light, Margaret, and I don't have to understand it. I know I am finding myself in a new and better place. I am so happy, Margaret, and I love you so very much. Thank you for sharing your life with me."

"Richard, I think we are all taking the same journey, and there are many roads that lead to the same place. I know I am always exploring possibilities. Sometimes it seems as though I'm wandering aimlessly, but most of the time, I know I am striding forward with great energy, and then I will realize that I've come a long way from where I began. Problems that seemed so large no longer exist. It's wonderful to know that powerful creative energies are at work. I don't need to understand how it works, only trust that it is working. I certainly trust that it is working for us, Richard. And I am so grateful.

"We have completed the project. Everything is organized and ready to go. Yeah for us! Now let's go eat, Richard. When I said simple, that's what I meant. We are having baked potatoes with a variety of stuff to stuff in them: sour cream, cheeses, broccoli, and we have baked apples for dessert."

"Margaret, that sounds like a feast."

"Actually, it's sounds like a party. I love baked potatoes."

"Let's go party! Margaret, this is great."

"It's amazing what you can do with a baked potato."

"I agree. I love all of the choices. It is like building a great ice-cream sundae, except it's a potato."

"That's great, Richard. I had never thought of it just like that, but you're right. It is a party. Thank you again, Richard. This has been a very productive day."

"Margaret, I am loving the joys and rewards of hard work and simple pleasures. I have even been doing some writing in my spare time, and it is different. It's a more relaxed style of writing and a lot faster flow. We'll see where it goes. I am not driven, and that is wonderful."

"Richard, I am so glad. I had no idea. Whenever do you have the time? It seems as though I have dominated your time pretty much recently."

"Not dominated, inspired, Margaret."

"Thank you, Richard. I know if you need time and space, you will let me know, right?"

"Yes, ma'am. We both know how to do that, and it's a good thing."

"Well, I don't know about you, Richard, but this is one of those times. I am ready for a lavender-scented bath and relaxation, actually, sleep."

"Yes, my dear one, that sounds great. And Howdy is showing us how that looks. He is so contented! But he does snore."

"Yes, he does, just a little, and he actually quits snoring after he is really sleeping well."

"Good night, darling. I will see you at about 5:30 a.m., right?"

"Afraid so. I am actually really looking forward to it. I will learn so much and meet so many wonderful new friends, and I am sure from previous gatherings that the food will be bountiful and so good."

"You are right, Richard. It will be a day to remember."

"Sleep well, my love. Good night."

*

"Good morning, Richard. I swear you look energetic and ready to go."

"That I am, darling. I slept like a baby, or perhaps better."

"So did I."

"So let's be off. I'm sure we will not be the first ones there. I have never been sure who the first ones were, certainly not me, and I'm OK with that. I love going in with everyone bustling around and ovens ready to go. Usually the first thing I hear is Laura's laughter, and we will certainly hear a lot of that today. How about you, Richard? Any anxiety?"

"Nope. I am open and ready for the day. I expect to be like a willow tree. I will just move with the wind, do one thing at a time, be watchful, open, and flexible."

"Oh my Richard, all of that at the same time?"

"Absolutely. If I do get in trouble I'll have Howdy right there, at least some of the time, to help me out.

"Right, buddy?"

"Well, here we are, Richard, ready to jump in and get going."

"Good morning, Laura. My goodness this place smells good already. That's probably the coffee and cinnamon rolls. They are right over there. I just took the rolls out of the oven, so be careful. I thought this would hold us until breakfast time, which will probably be about 9:30 or so."

"Good morning, Richard and Mr. Howdy."

"Good morning, Laura."

"This cinnamon roll is delicious. Thank you so much."

"You are most welcome, my dear, and trust me, you will earn every bite of it."

"I'm ready, Laura. Steve said I would start by learning about the machinery, so I guess I'd better go do that. I'll see you lovely ladies later."

"This is a good time to take a break and have breakfast. We have accomplished a lot already. What a crew. Laura, I'll go alert the rest of the folks that we will have breakfast in about twenty minutes. I just put the biscuits in the oven, and everyone knows what they're doing to prepare breakfast."

"Thank you, Margaret. You are a first-class organizer. And believe me, I know one when I see one."

"Laura, I really appreciate that, coming from you, that is quite a compliment. Be right back."

*

"Hi, Richard. You look like you know what you are doing."

"What I am doing is having a very good time."

"Hi, Steve."

"Margaret, Richard is a natural. He certainly know how to focus, and have fun.

"I really believe you know how to use all of this equipment, Richard, what do you think?"

"I think if I am vigilant and watchful of my behavior, I am safe enough. I'm certainly ready to give it a go. This is a perfect time to tell you folks that biscuits are in the oven, and breakfast is in ten minutes."

"That is good news, Margaret. I know I'm ready for that."

"Yeah, aren't we all?"

"What is your first task, Richard? My first task is to enjoy this wonderful breakfast, and then I'm going to start with the hand-turned mill. That is a beautiful piece of equipment. I love cast-iron stuff. I'm going to start with the bushels of corn for livestock. I believe there are five of us doing that, and then we will start milling fine flour. Those grinders will virtually grind anything."

"Sounds like you're pretty well set for the day."

"We've already got a very good start on the livestock corn. We'll probably start on the fine flour soon. So I just may get to learn how to use the steam juicers. I understand the juice can be stored for up to five years."

"Yes, I've heard that also. However we've never, at least to my knowledge, stored it more than two years. Everything is dated and rotated. It moves quickly. There's a lot of us, and it's very good. Have you learned about the composting yet?"

"No, I suppose that's later. The youth and children usually do that, Richard. Everyone gets to do something."

"Speaking of that, break time is over. Back to the grind, in your case, that's quite literal."

"Yes, it is, and I love it, and I love you. See you later."

"Laura, you've finished canning the green beans, cherries, and peaches. It takes the whole team to keep up with you."

"Margaret, these new pressure canners are miracles. No more gaskets to worry about. They're simple, safe, and I can thirty-two pints, or nineteen quarts, in one canner. I know, we have made some very good investments in equipment and what a difference! With six of us canning, and about that many doing prep, clean up, and labeling, it is so much quicker. I hear the men have started the music. I think it's time for us to do the same. We are already in the rhythm so we must be ready."

"Margaret, did you assign a team to fix the lunch trays?"

"Sure did, Laura, and they will deliver them. Guess what we're drinking, besides water?"

"Could it be apple juice?"

"Right on the first guess."

"Margaret, I love doing this."

"I do too, Laura. When all of the shelves are full, and we join in our gratitude circle and bless the bountiful supply we have and the pleasure and health, we will all have from those tiny seeds we planted, the fruit trees some of which our forefathers planted, it is so powerful, and I am never really tired when I leave here."

"I don't think anyone is, Margaret. Although it is sometimes a fourteen-hour day. Although this year, I think we're going to have time to actually gather for dinner and still finish before midnight. What do you think?"

"With all of this new equipment, every team is functioning as one. I'm thinking by 10:30 p.m. or 11:00 p.m."

"I love your optimism, Margaret. I'll go with your hunch, but not unless we pay attention to what we're doing."

"Laura, it's during times like this I miss my parents so much. I could always hear Dad's big hearty laugh and Mom was like a little fairy, everywhere all at once, singing, working, and laughing. I feel their presence often, but there are these moments, and they are good ones, so I linger a while."

"So do I, Margaret. After all these years, I love those moments when I get a flash of how it was when we were all together. And I feel that warmth of pure love. We are very lucky people, Margaret. Our ancestors had a purpose, and they fulfilled it. The legacy they left this community is healthy and vibrant. The community is a pioneer in establishing a progressive, beautiful place to live. Our summer visitors are so surprised at the natural and artistic beauty of the town and the people."

"I know I am blessed to be in the hub of activity. Our downtown sculpture exhibits are so beautiful. We have the old and new so well balanced, so nothing ever feels too quaint. I knew when I went to college I could have gone anywhere, and I did explore several places. Chad and I talked about moving, but what we always ended up wanting was everything we have right here. Well, I am glad that I can talk and work at the same time, just like my mother used to do."

"How are you doing, Laura?"

"I am having such a good time, Margaret. This is my kind of project. I love my quilting and gardening, but this is a bonding experience. Seeing all of my friends and the young people learning so much. We are passing it on, Margaret."

"That we are, Laura. And you know what, I just heard Richard's loud hearty laugh. He is quite a guy."

"Yes, Margaret, I think he is. You two are a couple that fit together like a hand and glove."

"Well, thank you, Laura. I think I better check on dinner. We have several young ones learning to cook in large quantities. I'll see if their mentors need a break."

"We are doing really well. I think we'll be practically through by dinnertime, except for some cleaning up and labeling. So I'm still betting on 10:30 p.m. completion."

"You know what, Margaret? I think you're right. This will be a first."

"I think I'll tell Richard it's because he worked so hard."

"Well, Margaret, you know that's somewhat true. Everyone makes a difference."

"You are absolutely right, Laura, as always. I love you a bunch. I'll be back shortly and give you an update on everyone else's progress.

"Laura, a great report—everyone is on the same time frame. We'll have dinner at seven, have a little music, and relax a bit. Let the men brag a bit about their new equipment, which I am so glad we decided to invest in. Today, we have all been able to see what a great decision that was."

"Yes, but I'm still not sure about that flash-freezing part."

"Well, Laura, all I know is the food tastes very good, but it will never replace canning, not to worry."

"Margaret, you are a born peacemaker."

"You're probably right, Laura. I come from a long line of them. Whenever we have a gathering like today, I can hear my mother singing, 'Love wasn't put in your heart to stay. Love isn't love until you give it away.' I heard myself singing that today, Laura."

"Well, my darling girl, that is surely what you do, and you do it very well."

"Shall we let Betsy and Melanie ring the dinner bell, Laura? This is their first year to help prepare dinner."

"Oh yes, I think they will like that. And they certainly have done well today. They are both sharp as a tack. They never missed a beat. They want to start coming to the quilting parties this summer."

"Laura, that is wonderful. I know you are very happy that quilting is finally being seen as an art. I know we were a little concerned for a while that there was so little interest but not anymore. I'll go tell them as soon as dinner is ready to ring the dinner bell. I'll be right back.

"I was right. They are excited to have the honor of ringing the bell. We probably have about fifteen minutes. I'm going to check on Howdy. I haven't seen him for a while."

"I'll bet he's out there with Richard, Margaret. If I were you, I'd go there first."

"Yes, Laura, that is where I'm going. I can't hide anything from you. It's just a good thing that I've never wanted to. I'll be right back."

∗

"Richard, you are a mess."

"Yes, I'll bet I am—a little mixture of apples, grapes, cherries, and various other shades of fruits. I think I am a work of art."

"Yes, you really are, you silly goose. I love you. And there's Howdy. Laura said he would probably be here with you. He followed the children to the compost for a while and then it was nap time, so he came up here, found a cozy spot under the tree, and took a nap while we were slaving away."

"Yes, and singing and telling jokes, I'm sure. I heard your laughter a lot, and I loved it."

"Margaret, my dear, have you looked at yourself lately?"

"No. I haven't had time to look at myself. Why?"

"You are quite a piece of art yourself—flour and spice, and I'm sure everything nice, but you are a mess."

"Then we fit in very well, Richard, because that is the test, I think. If there was anyone who didn't look like us, they probably still have a lot to learn. The dinner bell will be ringing in just a few minutes. So save me a seat please. I'm going to help with the first five tables, but I'll join you soon."

"Margaret, I have had an amazing day, I love you so much."

"Me too, Richard. See you in a few. Howdy, you look nice and rested. I'm glad. I'll get your dinner first. Be right back."

"Laura, you were right. Howdy was with Richard. I'm going to take his dinner out to him and then I'll be ready to serve, and I want to serve your table, since it is one of the honored ones' tables. You will be served first. I love it that we honor the wisdom of aging. Most cultures do honor their elders. I wish our culture would. I think anyplace that doesn't is losing a great opportunity. So there, honored elder. You need to be ready to sit, my dear."

"Oh my, whose giving orders now? OK, Margaret, I'll sit."

"I know how Howdy feels now, Laura!"

"What I mean, Margaret, is how loved he feels. This time, I'm not kidding. You really do make me feel loved, Margaret. Your mother's song was right, you know."

✳

"What a day. It always amazes me how so much can get accomplished when everyone has a common purpose and love."

"Me too, Margaret. Of course, I'm experiencing it for the first time, and you have practically lived in this environment your entire life."

"Yes, I have, Richard, and I am still humbled and grateful for this extended family community. I am blessed to have all these wonderful people, teaching, always by example, all of them, and now including you to travel with me on this amazing, adventurous, and joyous journey called life."

"Margaret, I never think it's possible, but every day, my love for you grows deeper. I am exhilarated by the opportunity to explore new options, to walk a new path, to continue pulling the weeds out as they show up in my life, and then sowing seeds of kindness, love, and watching the new thoughts grow and thrive and produce an abundance of life's gifts. And now I think one of those gifts is very tired and wants to go home to his bed by the fireplace."

"Yes, Howdy, you have had a very long stimulating day. I'm glad you took a few naps. I know the children wanted so much from you, and you always give that wonderful gift of unconditional love you have. So we are finished here, Richard. Our work is done. Larry and Barb are going to check everything before they leave. They will lock up."

"So let's go home, darling. I believe all three of us will sleep very well."

"Good night, my angel. I will see you tomorrow. Call me or send the messenger dog. We'll talk about my sister and family coming out for our wedding."

"Oh, Richard, I am so looking forward to meeting them."

"And what? Excited about the wedding?"

"Oh yes, I am so ready for that event. Well, not ready, ready, you know what I mean."

"Yes, I do. And I also know that we are ready for bed and sleep. Good night, darling."

*

"Good morning, Howdy. Yes, it is good to see you too. I think we will have a quiet day. Yesterday was a marathon. I feel like I ran it and I won the ribbon, but today, I want a little quiet time. How about you, buddy? Yeah, Howdy, you are actually shaking your head. I think you know everything. I mean everything. Let's go see, Margaret."

"Good morning, my darling girl."

"Good morning, Richard. Did you rest well?"

"I totally passed out, and I had just finished dressing when Howdy came. Have you had breakfast yet?"

"No, I haven't. Good because I just baked a ham, cheese, and potato dish, and the coffee is ready, so if you would be willing to squeeze the oranges, we'll be ready to eat. I would be very happy to do so, as soon as I pour my coffee. It smells so good. Or is that you, from yesterday?"

"Funny man. I had a nice soaking lavender bath last night, so it must be the coffee."

"This is so nice, Margaret, the food, you, and Howdy, this wonderful cozy home, and everything. I am so happy."

"I am too, Richard. I really miss you when we're apart. The house seems so empty, and that was not true before I knew you. Howdy and I filled the place up, no voids. Now if you're not here, it's just not right. I love you."

"Well, we are going to fix that very soon, right?"

"Right. Have you told your sister about us?"

"Yes, sort of."

"Now what does that mean? Sort of?"

"Well, before we went on our holiday, I told her about you and Howdy and the guest house and a little bit about the community. Then after our holiday, I called her and told her what an adventure we had, and she asked if this was a serious relationship, and I said yes. But I haven't told her we were getting married."

"Do you know why you haven't told her, Richard?"

"Oh yes, I wanted us to be together when I told her. She hasn't really talked to you yet. So today will be perfect."

"Do you really think they will come to the wedding?"

"Absolutely. We are both so happy that I am out of the fog and back on planet earth, and the kids are real excited to explore Maine and see us, of course."

"When do you want to call, Richard?"

"Well, Kevin gets home about 5:00 p.m., and dinner is usually ready, so I think a little after six would be good. Will that work for you?"

"Absolutely. It will be hard to wait, but yes, and we can have dinner before or after. What do you think?"

"I think pizza and beer would be a great plan for dinner. I'm going to town to pick up a few things, so I will bring the pizza back about five, if that works for you."

"That works so well for me. Howdy and I are literally going to take the day off and just be very lazy."

"Good. I'm glad. You know I am going to have an adjustment time when your vacation is over. I am lining up projects though, so I will definitely be busy."

"I'm sure you will, Richard. You have a lot of very good energy, well-directed to purpose."

"Thank you, Margaret. Well, I'm going to be off after I do the dishes. And is there anything else you'd like me to do before I leave?"

"Yes, kiss me good-bye."

"I will never forget to do that, Margaret. And that's a promise."

*

"Oh, Howdy, I am so happy. I have always been happy, but this is a very special happy. We are tired, aren't we? I have a pretty full schedule, it seems. I think going back to work will be like a vacation. No, I don't mean that. I am really having a very good time. I just get to consciously practice my living in the moment, full of gratitude process, along with deep breathing. Now all is well. That works every time, Howdy. Everything just slows down and goes into perspective. And now it's certainly time for us to slow down and relax.

"What a beautiful morning and you look rested, Howdy. Let's just have a regular routine day, but in slow motion. Yes, we will go to the lighthouse. We'll just take our time doing it. But first, a shower, my power drink, and oh yes, your breakfast. You're actually wanting to eat. That's a good thing.

"That shower was great. Now for a cup of coffee, and then we'll go to the lighthouse, as far as you want to go. I'll take a little picnic, although it may be too cold to linger. We'll see. One thing at a time. Let's go. Yes, it is brisk, but no rain or snow. It's actually a beautiful day. Howdy, let's take a break. We're about halfway up the hill. We have a beautiful view of the lighthouse and the ocean. This place is so beautiful. We don't need to go to the top of the hill. You're a little tired, and this is our rest day.

"We've spent so many days, months, and actually years at this spot, and I have never tired of it. How could one? I am so glad I have you to snuggle with today, Howdy. It's pretty cold up here. After we rest a bit, we'll head back home, and we will really enjoy that wonderful fireplace.

"It is good to be home, and I think a cup of tea, some crackers and cheese, a book, the fireplace, and you, my friend, is just about perfection. Yes, I miss Richard a little. OK, a lot. However, I really think we will probably both take a little nap. I just can't think of any reason why not."

✱

"Oh, Richard, where did you come from?"

"I beg your pardon."

"What time is it? It's about five o'clock."

"My goodness! I said I was going to be lazy today. But I never expected to sleep the afternoon away."

"Margaret, relax. I have been enjoying watching the two of you sleeping so peacefully and quietly. Howdy wasn't even snoring, and you never do. I was really curious about your dream. You were making little soft sounds and smiling a lot. But of course, you always do anyhow."

"Actually, Richard, I think that's why I was so startled to see you because I was dreaming about you, and then, when I saw you for a moment, I wasn't sure if I was awake or asleep."

"Well, I am so glad that you were making very pleasant sounds and faces in your dream, since I was there with you. I really missed you today, Margaret. I was able to get a lot done, but you were never far from me."

"I know, Richard. Me too. Howdy and I went for a walk. We started up the hill to the lighthouse, but it was too much for him. We made it about halfway up and then just sat together, very close. It was really quite cold, but the view was beautiful, and we enjoyed the day. I will be more mindful of his needs as they continue changing, and you certainly have my permission to help me remember, I would appreciate it. I think you have more objectively than I do. I probably have a little denial which might cloud my reasoning."

"I will do my best, darling. I do see that changes are occurring rather quickly now, and I know that has to be very challenging for you. Howdy is definitely a special gift. When will his special celebration and unveiling be?"

"Actually I got a call today. The bronze piece arrived today, and the time is my decision. I'm thinking about the first of December. That's when we typically celebrate his birthday. We turn on the town lights and have downtown decorated by the first weekend in December. Howdy loves it that the children are there and Santa. It's a lovely time. What do you think? Do you think it would be too much for him?"

"Honestly, Margaret. I think he's the kind of fellow that wants to live every moment as fully as possible and would not want to be protected, so, I think, yes, go for it. If he needs to change his behavior, he will, but I think he will relish every moment of the adoration he so deserves."

"Thank you, Richard. I know you are right, and it helps so much just hearing you say, what I already feel. I appreciate you so much. Oh, Richard, that electric tingle I get every time you kiss me is so . . . I don't know what to compare it with. There just isn't anything."

"Why don't I try it once more just to test it?"

"Oh yes, it only gets more tingly, and so we had better save the next one for later, and we can start dinner. What do you think?"

"I think dinner can wait, darling. I think I don't really care if I ever eat again. At least that's what I think for now."

"Sounds good to me, Richard."

"I love to tingle. I love you. Come here, darling."

*

"Richard, I went to sleep again! Honestly, I never sleep in the daytime."

"Yes, my dear, you do, and I love watching you do it."

"Well, I'm awake now, and I am starving."

"As a matter of fact, so am I."

"Let's go play in the kitchen."

"You do mean cooking, right?"

"Yes, I do mean cooking or something like that. Fortunately I did remember the pizza so that will be pretty easy."

"We do work well together, Richard. It feels like we have been together forever, in a good way."

"Yes, I know, I feel like that too. So now that our appetites are satisfied, what's happening with your sister and family?"

"Well, why don't we just call them and find out."

"Good. This is exciting. The Great Richard King has a mortal sibling."

"Well, if I were you, I wouldn't refer to me as the 'great' anything. She always had a way to see through any charade I may be attempting, and call me on it, every time. Although she was younger, I think she actually helped my grandmother raise me. I love her very much and her family, our family. I know I have missed out on a lot, recently, but that's over. We will definitely be together more now. So here we go."

"Hi, Sis. Yeah, that was your first clue as to who this is. You only have one brother, and you remember that lovely lady librarian, the one who has provided shelter for your poor homeless brother?"

"Yes, Margaret. I am at her home right now, and we have wonderful news to share with you folks. We have set the date for our wedding, which is on New Year's Eve. And we have wonderful accommodations for all of you. As a matter of fact, you will have some choices about that, but now that you have had what! A second to digest all of that. Would you like to talk to, Margaret?"

"Hello, Mary Beth. It is so nice to have an opportunity to talk to you. Yes, Richard has filled me in a bit about you, your husband, and his niece and nephew. He loves you all very much, and I'm absolutely sure that I do also. We are very happy together. I am so glad you are all planning to come. I do hope you can arrive as soon after Xmas as possible. I understand you not wanting to leave until after Xmas, but I do so want family time with all of you. Let us know as soon as you've made final arrangements. Yes, I will call often, and you do the same. We will keep in touch, and here's Richard. I know he wants to talk to all of you."

"Hi again, Sis. Ditto everything she said. Yes, I am so happy that we are creating a beautiful life, Sis. I can hardly wait for you guys to be here, and see this wonderful community. It is truly an extended family. The town itself is beautiful, quaint, friendly, and I love it here. And yes, I love Margaret. She is everything."

"Margaret, that was wonderful. It was a little strange talking to the kids. I think I'd better quit thinking of them as children. They sounded so grown up. I have missed a lot. But we will be fine. We basically have a great foundation, and I asked Sis to send me some pictures right away. I think that will help me put this in perspective."

"Richard, this is beginning to feel very real and very soon."

"Are you feeling too rushed, Margaret?"

"No, darling. It's just, you know, how I am about time. It just slips by, and I don't know. Sometimes it seems like there are time warps in my life, but no, I'm not having any problem with our choices. I think the more successful I am living in the moment, the less I am concerned about time. It's like time is only in that moment, and it is a little challenging once in a while. What I know in this moment is only love."

"Margaret, I feel complete oneness with you. I love it when we are like this, so close and our breathing becomes as one. I truly feel like we are."

"So do I, Richard, and it's in a good way. Kind of like being a part of the ocean and yet being individuals, and if we're not careful, I'm going to sleep again."

"You know what, Margaret, it's actually time to go to sleep now, and Howdy knows it. I'm going to be off now. Send Howdy tomorrow whenever you wish. I'm going to be working around the house, so whenever. Until then, sleep well, my darling."

"Good night, Richard. I'm sure I shall."

"Good morning, Howdy. I'll bet you're hungry. You just have the look, and it's wonderful. I don't see that often. We really rested yesterday, and I'm sure we both needed it. OK, I'm getting up. No wonder you're hungry. It's almost ten o'clock. I am really off schedule. Oh well, that's the way it is on vacation. No clock. I love it. Our lifestyle is changing, Howdy. I have decided that I am going to work part-time. I haven't worked it out completely, but I'm thinking to start the transition I will work Tuesday, Wednesday, and Thursday, and then gradually as Lizzie . . . no, I'd better start calling her Elizabeth. She is the right one to job share with me. I've been training her already. She's the one that is covering for me now. She's a natural choice, and this morning my decision is clear and firm. I know it's right. I have no ambivalence, only clarity. That's a good thing, and all of this before I have my coffee. Life is good. So is this coffee and egg scramble. I wish Richard was here to squeeze my orange juice. Actually, I just wish Richard was here. Period. The house just doesn't seem right anymore without him. That's so strange. We shared this house for so long, and it seemed so full. The wonderful memories, work, and always upgrading something. I never felt this void, like I do now when Richard is not around. I think that's the way it should be. It's just different."

*

"Good morning, Howdy. Come on in. I will be ready in a few minutes. I'm just finishing up here. OK, fellow, lead the way. I'm ready."

"Richard, I didn't realize Howdy had gone down to greet you."

"I assumed when he came down, you had sent him."

"Well, I did tell him I missed you, and I wished you were here."

"That sounds like a mission to me. Good morning, darling. I missed you too."

"You feel so good, Richard. You smell good too."

"Thank you. I know you like my shaving lotion, so I just use it to drive you mad, and you have, and you do."

"I slept until ten o'clock this morning. I never do that, see? I'm completely mad."

"You don't look mad, Margaret. You look beautiful, serene, and happy."

"OK, Richard, thank you. You arrived just in time for yoga, meditation, and your assignment for tonight is to familiarize yourself with the parts of your brain and their function. Mindfulness meditation is to anchor your mind in the present and eventually train it to the present, not to the past or future. I'm suggesting three minutes for four or five times a day. Get your body and brain used to the down time, like brain breaks. You can then choose to extend the time as you need or want. Sometimes, I just really lose all consciousness of time. I know I do anyhow, but this is different. I always feel clarity, direction, and rested. I know the deep breathing is very helpful. So get comfortable and I will be mindful of the time for now."

*

"Margaret, thank you. I have been aware of increased focus and relaxation with meditation. I have been practicing at night before I go to bed. I really like the way I feel, and I love it when we are together. I can tune in to your breathing, and it's so relaxing. Now is the part Howdy likes, the stretching. I never know if he's making fun of me or if that grin is my imagination. I think he just likes stretching. I have a light snack ready to go. You are ready for our walk right?"

"Right. I thought you'd never ask. Except, Howdy standing there by the door with his leash in his mouth is a very strong hint. I don't know why he gets that leash. We never use it."

"I think it works for him, Margaret. He lets you know what he wants."

"That he does. We are kind of creatures of habit, I guess."

"So let's go. My! It is brisk out here. I forget when I'm so cozy inside, just how cold it is out here. It's exhilarating. I am so ready for the first snow storm. When does it usually snow, Margaret?"

"Any time now. Occasionally in November. Almost always by the first week in December."

"Well, we should be seeing some very soon. I bought some new snow boots yesterday. So I'm ready."

"We'll see, Richard. When is Howdy's big celebration? I did confirm it will be the first weekend in December, and that's when we have our Xmas lights, caroling, of course, food at the center, and Santa is there sitting by the fireplace. The children always come prepared with their list, which is usually two gifts for them, and then a longer list for family and friends. We'll probably have Howdy's bronze unveiling just before the Xmas lights are turned on. He always sits by Santa, so I don't want to interfere with that. Richard, have you noticed that the last couple of days, he seems to have a little more energy."

"Yes, I have. I think he's had time to rest a bit, and I know he loves being at home with you."

"Yes, we really do enjoy being together and with you, of course."

"I was beginning to get jealous. Not really. There's enough love to go around to everyone, and yes, I am finding that the more you give, the more you get. It's wonderful. Speaking of love, are we going to have wedding invitations?"

"Well, I create a special Xmas card newsletter every year. This year, which actually is now, I thought we could design our invitations, which would go in the newsletter. What do you think?"

"I love it. Let's do it. We could have a few special ones to send to relatives. Maybe we can work on that tonight."

"Would you like to have spaghetti for dinner? I make my own sauce, and it is quite good. I've been told, and I agree."

"That sounds wonderful."

"I'll toss a salad, and I have French bread."

"Now I'm hungry. How about you?"

"Yes, let's have that snack, and Howdy is ready for a rest I think. Sure Howdy is. How about you, Richard?"

"I guess I'm busted."

"This is delicious, Margaret. This can't just be hot chocolate. What else is in this?"

"Just a hint of hazelnut and nutmeg."

"It is really good. Thank you. The crackers and cheese taste pretty good too, just enough. My darling girl, I do love you so much."

"Me too, Richard. Yes, Howdy, you too. Come here, baby. Oh, you are so warm."

"Obviously it's time to go home. Howdy has started back down the hill. I've been letting him set the pace."

"Actually, I'm very glad he is going back. I am cold. I must get winterized."

"I have very comfortable and warm clothing. I just need to get them out of the storage box, and I am now very motivated to do that. Richard, you may see your snow any time now."

"Do you like the winters, Margaret?"

"I do, very much. I love to watch the snow falling, especially early evening, and I love to be out in the snow. I just need to have my winter gear and then I'm good. Do you ski, Richard?"

"Maybe, yes, at least I have, but not for a long time. It kind of seems like another lifetime ago. But as I recall, I did like it very much. How about you?"

"Kind of the same situation. I used to ski frequently. My parents loved to ski. We had many wonderful ski trips, and I do say had, because I haven't skied for probably ten years or so. I don't know why, I just quit doing it."

"Well, it sounds like we are going to do some skiing. Do you still have your equipment?"

"I'm sure I do have, although we'll have to check it out. How about you?"

"Not one thing. So it will be easy, I will just go in and say I need everything, and I will do that tomorrow. Suddenly skiing sounds so much fun. I can hardly wait. Margaret, stick your tongue out."

"What in the world for?"

"Just do it."

"Here we are with our tongues sticking out. I know why Howdy does it, but oh yes, Richard, now I know why. There are a few very large wet snowflakes falling. It's beautiful. What a perfect day! Howdy is ready to go inside. He's right by the door. So am I, Richard, how about you?"

"Yes, I'll bring some more firewood in. I think we're going to need it. OK, Howdy, I'm coming. I know you're cold."

"Here you go, yes, straight to the fireplace. You really love that rug, and fire, don't you? I do too."

"Come here, and let me warm my hands. Thank you, my friend. Now I can really enjoy watching those big beautiful snowflakes fall."

"Richard, you really got your wish. I did, didn't I?"

"Although the flakes are large, they are gone before they hit the ground. I think this is going to be a little preview of coming attractions. It's probably a good idea for me to winterize. I'll cover the outside faucets tomorrow, Margaret, as a matter of fact, make a list, and we'll take care of everything tomorrow."

"I'm so glad you like lists, Richard. I personally find a great joy in marking things off. I love the feeling of accomplishment.

✳

"I'll call the center tomorrow also to see how many people are on the list for winter assistance. I know Jesse recently fractured his arm, so he will need some help. I'm sure there are several, and there are so many ready to help. None of us have to do very much."

"I really want to be on the list of helpers, Margaret. I am absolutely sure the helpers get back much more than they give."

"I know I have found that to be true, Richard. I can never outgive the return. Gratitude is contagious."

"And for now, my dear, I would be very grateful for spaghetti, and I'll get the materials out for beginning the process of creating our wedding invitations. Every time I say that, Richard, I get that tingling sensation, and you're not even touching me."

"Yes, I think I am, Margaret, at least in my mind."

"Do you have to go to the cottage tonight, Richard?"

"No, I don't, and if that is an invitation, it's accepted."

"Great. I really do want you to stay. I mean with the snow and all."

"We need no excuses, Margaret. I want to be with you forever, and we have a lot to do tonight, so let's get to it, shall we?"

"On my way, Richard. I can practically smell your spaghetti sauce already."

"While you have been creating this amazing aroma in the kitchen, I have retrieved my winter clothing box and started writing a few thoughts that come to mind about our announcement and invitation."

"Care to share what you have?"

"Always at the closing of a year, I am grateful for the memories and lessons of the past, as the New Year begins this year especially. I realize we have an opportunity to joyfully co-create circumstances. Transformation is at our fingertips. That sounds like a great start to me, Margaret. Last year on New Year's Eve, I did a symbolic burning of the past, not in anger, but in gratitude. And for the New Year, I lit a torch, again a symbol of light, hope, and love finding my way."

"That's beautiful, Richard. I want to release my thinking to imagine all the possibilities the year might hold, and yet I know I couldn't begin to fully embrace that much stimulation. I do know that we have a rich supply of divine ideas, understanding, wisdom, and strength. These gifts we already have, and I know together the more we access and use our gifts the more they will grow. However, I do think I got a little off the subject. I want us to be able to be clear, somewhat concise, and to convey how much we wish to share this very special ceremony and celebration with everyone."

"That sounds good to me, Margaret."

"Thank you, Richard, but it doesn't sound, I don't know, maybe not elegant enough."

"I have a suggestion. Let's have a cup of hot chocolate and a mini brownie and then meditate before we start brainstorming."

"Richard, of course. I do believe the student will soon be teaching the teacher."

"Well, that's co-creating, don't you think?"

"Yes, I do. And by the way, dinner was delicious. You are a very good cook. And I love it that we so easily take turns doing kitchen stuff. It is fun, Margaret, and these brownies you made are a perfect touch of completion, for dinner I mean."

"Yes, darling, I know what you mean."

"I'm not sure how much work we're going to get done tonight. I am enjoying holding you close to me, watching the fire, and listening to Howdy's sleeping sounds. Really, I'm serious. I know all I need for a full and complete life is right here, right now. I feel complete."

"So do I, Richard. I'm so glad you stayed."

"I think it was a very natural choice, Margaret. How do you feel about my sister, and family visiting us?"

"Last night I realized I haven't really talked to you about it. I know it will be a very busy time for you. They can stay in the cottage, if that would be helpful. Richard, I can't tell you how much I have missed family. This house used to be full of laughter, wonderful conversations, and games, a lot of happy people doing a variety of things, but somehow being together. It has always been a happy house. Although the past few years I have spent more time at work and the center than having friends come here, so it's been rather quiet. I guess what I'm trying to say is I really am hopeful that they will want to stay here. There's plenty of room, and I certainly have room for them in my heart. I know I love them right now. Not to worry, Richard, I will give them whatever time they need to get to know me."

"I know my family, darling, and I am pretty sure that they are looking forward to seeing us as much as we are them. Our home is going to be that happy, busy, yet serene place where everyone will feel better for having been here."

"Richard, I am so grateful that you chose Port Haven for your resting spot."

"Me too, darling, instead it became my Haven forever."

"Richard, after mediation, I want to write some thoughts about my part of our ceremony."

"I will too, Margaret. Then we can merge them or let them go until another time. How are you doing, darling?"

"I have some thoughts to share. How about you?"

"Likewise."

"Ladies first. We are familiar with endings and beginnings every day of our lives, in large ways and in small. As spiritual beings making footprints on the grounds of earth, we are a vital part of that cycle. I choose to trust life, as I trust you, Richard. We are moving together to another beginning, and another. This union will unfold intimately and intuitively within each of us. My experience must necessarily be different from yours which provides us with an opportunity to shake off harsh judgments and negative comparisons and simply enjoy the presence of one another and the power of love as we experience it. I have gifts to bring. I have the love of God to share. I have a mind willing to receive the joys and woes of our community. I am a part of it also. With trust and ease I welcome you in to my life as my soul mate and husband."

"Margaret, my darling girl, I am so touched by you. I love every word you said and the depth of your love."

"Thank you, Richard. You were so right about the meditation and clarity. Are you ready to share?"

"We read, we dream, we imagine, and we let senses and images come to us. A fearless thinker doesn't worry about fantastic ideas that may come to mind. Each new day is sprinkled with new awareness. We only need to make the invitation. My innermost longings are rewarded with new inspiration and colorful images. One of these rewards is you, my darling Margaret. It is through the receptive feeling nature that we can change the facts of our lives. Sometimes faith and trust seem diminished for a while. They may ebb and flow and move a bit through our awareness until, once more, they course through us with strength and light. They resurge in us once more as treasured companions, such as you, my darling, are my treasured companion. The Bible says that when we love, we are like God. That is, when we love, we use the divine energies in the most constructive ways. Love heals, love reveals. No person, place, nor thing need be exempt from our love. Whatever lies ahead, it is our road, it is salutary, and it is good. I am so proud to have you as my wife, Margaret."

"Richard, that is beautiful. I don't think we need to change or add anything. I think it is done."

"So do I, darling. Let's do the invitations later, OK?"

"Absolutely, Richard. I have enough to work with, and they will be simple and sweet."

"Just like you, my dear."

*

"I'm like Howdy, now, Richard. I want to lie in front of the fire, and just be."

"Me too, darling. We went to sleep again. This fireplace must be hypnotic. I know it is for me, Margaret. I notice our breathing, and when you're in my arms, I can feel our heartbeat, and our breathing becomes synchronized. I feel such a surge of gratitude and love."

"Me too, Richard. And the pure joy and them is just a total release of tension and a feeling of oneness."

"Well, now that we have slept, shall we go to bed?"

"Oh yes, I am so glad you stayed, Richard."

"So am I. Being here with you is so right."

*

"Good morning, Howdy. It seems as though you are the first face I see every time I am here. Do you think I'm going to jump up and be at your beck and call? Well, you are absolutely right."

"Good morning, darling. Stay right there. Howdy and I have some things to do, and then I will prepare your breakfast and bring it right up here to you. We'll mix up the routine just a little bit, if that's OK with you."

"Uh huh. Take your time. I'm fine right here. Do you know Howdy's routine?"

"Yes, darling. We're good."

"Yes, you certainly are. Morning, Howdy. You are in good hands. See you guys later."

"You are a lazybones. Still asleep?"

"No, not really. Just very relaxed and happy, except . . ."

"Except what?"

"I'm ready for coffee. That's probably because you smell it. I have your orange juice and coffee right here. So if you are ready to sit up, I have the tray ready for you."

"Oh, Richard, am I really awake?"

"Not quite, but you're getting there."

"This is so special. I feel like a princess."

"You are, Margaret. And you always will be."

"That was a wake-up kiss, Richard. Now I'm really hungry. OK, back to the kitchen. Enjoy your juice and coffee and the morning paper if you'd like."

"Thank you, darling."

"That was a very special breakfast. Thank you so much. I feel so good."

"Me too. Truly a labor of love. Actually there was very little labor, mostly love."

"Where's Howdy?"

"He and I went for a morning stroll. He had breakfast and is back in front of the fireplace napping."

"How did he do on the walk?"

"I let him lead and return as he was ready. We had a short walk, Margaret, but watching him enjoying every smell, the birds, he doesn't miss anything, and he obviously loves every minute. You can see it in his body."

"Yes, I have seen and felt so much more through my time with him. I'm so blessed he is complete love, nothing else. He is a wonderful companion."

"I haven't known him long, but kind of like with you, it seems as though we've always been together. We will truly treasure the time we have left."

"Yes, we will."

"Speaking of time, it is time for me to get up and fully embrace the day."

"I may be gone when you come downstairs, darling. I'm going to do the dishes and then get down to the cottage to work on my project."

"Are you ready to tell me what that project is, Richard?"

"No, not yet. Actually, I have two projects going, and they are both very exciting for me. And hopefully will be for you. Soon, darling, I will be ready to reveal my secrets."

"Sounds intriguing. I am of course curious, and I love surprises, so mixed emotions. Is it all right if I come down to the cottage? I just realized I haven't been down there for a long time."

"Well, it is your cottage."

"Our cottage, Richard."

"I would appreciate it if you didn't come down just yet."

"Enough said. I will send Howdy or call you if I need to. Enjoy yourself. I love you, and now to the shower for me."

"Well, Howdy, that was a short nap. My secret is still safe. I wonder if I should have shared the changes that I'm making to the cottage with Margaret? No, I trust my instincts, and they say this is a good thing, and Margaret does like surprises. The other project has been a real surprise to me. As you know I'm writing another book, and it is so different than anything I've written before. I really like it, and it is flowing like a river, effortlessly and powerfully. I'd better get down there and put this energy to good purpose. See you later, buddy. You are a very good listener. I am learning from you what a gift that is. Thank you, Howdy. I really love it when you give me your paw. It's like an agreement, or something like that."

✳

"Yes, Howdy, I am finally up and about. I suppose you and Richard already did your meditation and yoga routines. You can watch me if you want but no grinning. I only have four more days of vacation in the weekend. There I go slipping and sliding, out of the moment. A few deep breaths and I'll be back.

"The snow is gone. It was very pretty, and it will return. I'm making a big pot of chicken soup with lots of vegetables. We will take some over to the center. I'm sure there are several folks that can use a little chicken soup for the soul. And Richard will enjoy some tonight, I'm sure, after working all day on his projects. Yes, I am very curious, and a little excited, it sounds so intriguing. Oh well, whatever it is, all in good time. After we stop by the center, we'll go downtown. I have several things to check on, and it is story time for the children at the library this afternoon. They will be very happy to see you. Actually it will be very nice to see everyone."

"Soup's ready, Howdy. Let's be on our way. I'm glad Richard winterized everything, including the snow tires. There are still a few tricky spots. We used to walk to town most of the time, Howdy. I'm glad we didn't today. I'll just bet you are too. Sure the center is buzzing today. This is apple cobbler day, and our timing is perfect. Here we are."

✳

My, what a wonderful mix of smells: cinnamon, and spices, bread baking. Wow. We timed this right.

"Margaret and Howdy, what a treat! We haven't been seeing you two as often, since your vacation. What are you up to?"

"Hello, everyone. I made a lot of chicken soup, so I thought I would check in and see if there was anyone on the list today who could use some soup and cornbread."

"As a matter of fact, Margaret, the Blackwell family have the flu. I was going to go check on them later, but it would really help me out, if you wouldn't mind, and I know how you love those kids. I am sure they would welcome you and your special chicken soup, and of course, when the children see Howdy, they will probably get well."

"Howdy and I would love to do that, Elizabeth. You do at least want some cobbler and coffee before you go, don't you, Margaret?"

"Absolutely. I smelled it as soon as I opened the car door. I love the smell of this place. There's always something on the stove, or in the oven, and there's always folks here to find out what's happening, and there is always something happening."

"There's going to be a new card game after lunch if you'd like to come back."

"It sounds like fun, Elizabeth, but Howdy and I have some things to do this afternoon. So another time. Thanks for the cobbler and coffee. It was great. I'll tell the Blackwells you're thinking about them, and if there's anything else they need, I'll let you know."

"Thank you, Margaret. You are an angel."

✳

I am making good progress on this project and very pleased with the way it's turning out. I had a pretty clear picture of what I wanted and by sharing that vision with John and Thomas, we have really created more than what I had initially considered and so fast. It's amazing how much fun it is to work with folks that love what they're doing, and fortunately for me, they know what they're doing. It is definitely a labor of love for all of us. When I first saw this cottage, I fell in love with it. The view is perfect. I immediately imagined a glass enclosed addition, and then when I went inside, I knew I was right. The position of the cottage is perfect to catch the sun and light, so solar is a natural. I can imagine Margaret and me sitting in our special tea room, enjoying nature surrounding us, very cozy and comfortable winter or summer. I love the way we've designed so many built-ins. I'm so grateful that Thomas is a carpenter. We will have our tea table, desk, easel, game table, and they can all be used at the same time, or separately, and in the summer the glass will have sliders. We can have screens, or not.

Margaret and Howdy will love this. I know we will hear the laughter, and conversation of many friends and family, as Margaret fondly remembers from her youth, as I am looking forward to in our life together. Now it's time to spend a couple of hours writing. What a joy it is to be in the flow of life. We are ready to go with the project in a major way, as soon as Margaret goes back to work. Everyone has arranged their schedule, and it will be complete within a week. What a community. It truly is an extended family. I love it.

"Howdy, you seemed to approve of your special bronze likeness. It is absolutely wonderful. What a gift Brady has. I especially love the expression shown through the eyes. Nothing could ever capture your spirit, Howdy, but he did a fantastic job on this piece, and I am so grateful that he is donating this piece to the community for Christmas, which is quickly approaching. I am so glad you will have Richard when I go back to work on Monday. Of course, you will still come to the children's activities whenever you want, and I have submitted my proposal to the board to increase my assistant's hours and responsibilities and to revise my contract to three days a week. I know it will be fine, and I am so excited about the transition. Everything is as it should be. We have had a full day, and I can see that you are a very tired, Howdy. We're on our way home, and you can snuggle up by the fireplace. Richard has the fire going and dinner ready. We are very lucky, Howdy."

*

"Anybody home? There you are, Richard, in the kitchen. I love your apron, darling. Now that was a welcome-home kiss. I love you so much."

"And I missed you, guys. No Margaret. No Howdy. However, I am so glad you found something to do, like finding dinner, which by the way smells intoxicating."

"Interesting that you say that, Margaret, because I used a lot of wine to prepare my special chicken dish, which will be ready in a few minutes." Howdy is already in dreamland."

"Yes, I think I overestimated his stamina again. He tries so hard to keep going, and I really forget. I promised myself today that I will be more aware of activities with Howdy. I love him so much and I also tend to take him for granted. He's just always been there. Well, enough of that. He's in his perfect spot, and we did have a very good day, Richard. We saw the Howdy Bronze today, and it is magnificent. You must see it soon."

"Actually, Margaret, everyone will be seeing it soon. Do you realize the festivities and unveiling are only a week away?"

"Richard, time is so strange. Sometimes, I wish I understood it better, but I don't and that's OK. But right now, in this moment in time, which I do understand, I am loving you and ready to eat."

"How can I help?"

"You may pour the wine, and I will get the salad, and we will begin our culinary adventure."

✳

"Richard, that was an amazing dinner. I am impressed. I know you are an excellent cook, but this was above and beyond expectations."

"Thank you, darling. It was nothing. I only slaved over a hot stove all afternoon. Really, Margaret, it was a joy to prepare. I think love is the secret ingredient."

"I think you're right, Richard. I'll clean up, you go sit by the fire and relax if you'd like."

"Oh no, my darling. I made this mess, and I'm cleaning it up, and that's all there is to that. Then I'll fix our tea and we'll soak up the warmth of the fireplace. We may need to nudge Howdy over a bit, but I don't think he will mind."

"You may be spoiling me, darling, and if you are, I love it, and I love you. I'm going to go get into my comfy robe while you're finishing the kitchen. Thank you for a perfect evening."

"But, Margaret, it has barely begun."

*

"I love our quiet times by the fireplace, Richard. Howdy and I took some soup to the Blackwell family today. They are all ill. I wanted to do more for them, but I had a lot of commitments, and fortunately, her sister was there. I don't think you have met them yet, but the Blackwell family has been our primary poultry raising resource for as long as I can remember. They have trained many young people. Some of them have continued, and others have moved on to other things. They have continually expanded and recruited new poultry growers successfully through the years. Charles, Mr. Blackwell, and his brother Herbert are the core operators, but it is a huge responsibility. All of the children are involved, and of course, many other community members. They have approximately 125,000 birds on an average."

"Margaret, that is a lot of chickens!"

"Yes, it is a major operation. They have kept up with technology, so the feed, water, and heaters and all computerized, and they have alarm systems in place for proper management. But they still check each house every six hours. I know they have a lot of folks to help out, but would you like to check on them tomorrow and see if they are all right? I have several deadlines that I really need to manage tomorrow."

"Well, obviously I know how to cook a chicken, and I certainly enjoy eating them. I can't say that I really know much more than that."

"No, that's not true. My grandmother had a few chickens, and my sister and I used to feed them. It was more like play than work, though. Do they process on site, or how does that work?"

"Yes, it is a full scale operation. We use what we need for the community. Many families raise their own because they enjoy it. The company is also a major distributor, primarily within the state. Our chickens are almost as popular as our blueberries."

"Margaret, I would love to visit the Blackwells, although I don't think I will take chicken soup. I definitely would love to know more about the operation and help out anyway I can."

"Thank you, Richard."

"Another adventure, Margaret."

"Somehow I think that's going to be the story of our life, and what a life it is! Speaking of adventures, we have more family joining us for the holidays and, of course, our wedding. I got a pleasant surprise telephone call from my Aunt Elizabeth, my mother's sister. By the way she prefers to be called Betsy or Betts. Well, that is a surprise. I don't believe I've heard anything about her, have I? No, darling, you haven't. There are probably many other skeletons to climb out of my closets. Not that Aunt Betts is a skeleton. She's a very hardy soul, absolutely delightful, a world traveler. She's an artist, always fiercely independent, with a highly developed sense of humor. She is a gifted pianist, vocalist, composer, and anthropologist. She and my mother were very close and had such fun together. I think it was hard for her to spend much time here after Mom and Dad's accident. She kept in touch for a long time and then gradually, the past few years, we've talked less often. She always has a project going somewhere in the world. Today, I could tell she really wanted to come visit for the holidays, and, of course, after I told her about you, and our wedding, it was quickly settled that she will be here."

"That's wonderful, Margaret. I'm so happy she's coming. We are going to fill this old house with happiness, aren't we?"

"You know, Richard, with only Howdy and I living here for so long, I forgot what a lovely large home it really is."

"This will be the first time in many years that it will finally really awaken. We'll actually use the dining room which hasn't been used for a long time and is such a lovely room. I love this house, Richard. It is full of happy memories."

"I love it too, Margaret. I could never imagine us living anywhere else."

"I am so happy to hear you say that. I think I knew it, but we've never really talked about it. I never want to take you for granted."

"I know, Margaret, and I know we will not do that. We will probably always have to catch up occasionally. Because that's how we are but that's OK."

"I am so ready for bed, darling."

"So am I. Let's do it. Howdy hasn't moved a whisker. I overestimated his stamina again, Richard."

"Maybe not, darling, as long as he is doing what he loves, and I'm sure he was. Let's let him do whatever he can."

"Yes, that feels right. You are wonderful, Richard. I love you."

"Good night, darling. Sleep well."

*

"Good morning, sleepyhead. I'm usually the sleeping beauty, but I awakened early, and I am ready to go. Breakfast will be ready in a few minutes, Margaret, my sweet love."

"Do I smell coffee, and is it in that lovely pot you have?"

"Yes, you get your own pot of coffee this morning, and I think you're going to need it. Remember the poultry promise?"

"Oh yes, I do, now that you mention it. I'll have my coffee and be down to breakfast in a jiffy."

"I don't know what we're having but it smells fantastic, and I am ready to eat, and run. I am a bit awed about the poultry promise but very excited also. I have found every adventure in this community to be so rewarding. I respect everyone so much, and they have all welcomed me into their lives. I still don't completely understand how everything works, but I can see that it does."

"Richard, it's really kind of like, you've always been here, only just away for a while. I know that doesn't really make any sense, but some things just don't have to be logical. Such as, I really like you in those jeans. You are a very sexy chicken tender, no pun intended."

"Well, thank you, lady. I'll just have to wear them often. However, when I get back this evening, you may think differently, especially if they need help with bagging the fertilizer."

"Oh, Richard, you did just change the picture. So go and have a great learning experience. Howdy and I have a very busy day planned. Thank you for helping out. I do hope everyone is feeling better, and please tell them Howdy and I send our love."

"I will, darling, and I'll do whatever I can to help out. See you this evening."

"Howdy, you get some time off today. You can rest by the fireplace if you'd like, and later if you are up to it, we'll go for a short walk. I have several projects to finish today. One is to do my check-off list, between going back to work, your special event day, Xmas preparations, company coming, and our wedding, if I don't get my action lists prepared so I can start checking them off, I just may begin to feel overwhelmed. Who am

I kidding? I am feeling a little anxious. And yet I know I will have all of the help I need, as soon as I am clear about what needs to be done. It will all come together as it always does. I am blessed to have such an extended community family. There, now. I have relaxed and released. Deep breathing and meditation creates miracles. I am totally focused and clear about what needs to happen and how.

"Howdy you look as refreshed as I feel. I have my plans completed, and I am ready for a bit of a stretch, how about you? Do you feel up to a short walk before lunch? Oh yes, you do. Leash in your mouth by the door. You silly goose, you know we never use that leash, but it does the job. Let's go.

"I really had a productive day. Every project organized, newsletter laid out, house preparation and decorating plan complete. I am so excited about meeting Richard's family, and Aunt Betts is great energy to have around. She always knows exactly what to do and how to have fun doing it. She also reminds me so much of my mother, and that's a special treat. Well, enough daydreaming. I'd better check on dinner. I'll bet Richard will be glad that I didn't fix chicken. It might be a little much for one day. You heard him before I did, Howdy. Your hearing, or whatever sense it is that you have, seems to be working very well."

"Hello, darling. I missed you today. It's good to be home, and it smells like dinner is ready, and so am I. How was your day?"

"Margaret, I had a wonderful time. What a family! By the way, they are all much better, and they're sure it was your chicken soup and Howdy's love that did the trick. When I got there, the home teacher was there, and all of the kids were very busy. They looked pretty good. Everyone was very glad I was there.

"I had a very good orientation. What an operation! I'm sure I didn't get to see everything, but I certainly stayed busy. I'm going back tomorrow, and then we'll see how things are going. I'm going to go wash up a bit and change clothes. I did wear coveralls over my clothes, but I will feel better, and maybe smell better if I change."

"Please do, Richard. I agree. Even Howdy is in agreement. Dinner is ready when you are. I'll put the rolls in to bake now.

"Oh that is much better, Richard, I mean the odor. I'm glad everyone is feeling better. They are a hardy bunch."

"This is delicious, Margaret. We do eat well, don't we?"

"I think we do everything well, Richard, really. I had such a great day. I have all of the projects ready for us to review if you feel up to it. I am hoping we can do that tonight. I really want your feedback. It's so nice to have someone else to share ideas with, and I know you will be very helpful in seeing things that I have missed."

"I would love to see what you have and contribute what I can. And, Margaret, thank you for inviting me to help the Blackwells. It was a really special day. I met some wonderful new friends and learned so much. My life is so full. I feel so alive, and I am so grateful."

"I do know what you mean, Richard. We just can't outgive, can we?"

"I think if I'm going to be any help at all tonight, we had better get to it. I'm really looking forward to seeing what you have. But I am beginning to have a bit of brain fog. You know what I mean?"

"Yes, I do. Let's just do some deep breathing and quiet meditation for a few minutes. It always helps me."

"That was exactly what I needed, Margaret. I'm fully here now. Let's see what we have."

*

"I am impressed, darling. You have very clearly laid out every step. I can see the full picture of activities what, when, where, how, everything. It seems so simple when it is outlined in a sequence. You were a very busy lady today, that's very obvious, and I honestly don't have any suggestions, at least not now."

"Thank you, Richard. We will revisit and revise as necessary. But I feel so much better having my check-off list."

"I can see why. It's almost like having things already accomplished, and I love everything you have planned, Margaret. Thank you for doing this."

"You are welcome, my darling. I am glad you enjoyed your experience today."

"I really did. By the way, how does this home-teaching program work? I was really surprised that a teacher was actually there with the family."

"The home-support program is not just for children if they're ill. It's also a family-coaching program if a child is having a learning challenge. The teacher comes to the home and a full-support approach is implemented. The older children, if there are any, become like tutors and the entire family becomes mentors. It is a very successful model. Our children can get into any university they choose. Generally speaking, they have the highest academic scores consistently in the national percentile, averaging.

"Our schools are all family-centered, and the children are encouraged to help each other succeed. The classroom work is usually team-oriented, and the older ones work with the younger ones."

"That sounds wonderful. So children actually like going to school?"

"The short answer is yes. As a community, we have always considered education to be a privilege and are grateful for the opportunity to learn. It is a value that has been sustained."

"So, Margaret, what is the dropout rate?"

"There is no drop-out rate, darling. Occasionally, there will be a choice made regarding a family vocation, that is, horseshoeing, then, that will become part of the high school vocational curricula. Not everyone wants to or should go to college. The point of education is to become a thinking, productive member of the society. What kind of discipline is used?"

"In school?"

"Yes."

"Let me think about that, Richard. I am a relief substitute teacher. Only in an urgent situation that fortunately hasn't happened often. I enjoy it, but I'm pretty busy with the library. I really don't remember reading a policy regarding discipline as such. What I have experienced is what I would call peer modeling. Teachers are there to teach and children are there to learn. There is always mutual respect and trust. Ground rules are very clear and consistent, and if a student is rude or disruptive, the other students quickly let them know that is not acceptable. I have never known of a situation which ever got out of control. Of course there must be conflict resolution, that's a normal part of life and learning. Folks don't always agree, and that's OK. But most of the children have learned a lot about that process at home, so the skills just have to be fine-tuned."

"That really makes sense, Margaret. Are you aware of how the educational model has changed in most of our school systems?"

"Oh yes, Richard. That's why I am grateful to be part of a community that nurtures and supports one another and remembers what and why our ancestors created this haven of safety. We are very protective of our town. We know it is a treasure and could be lost if we were not willing to maintain the stability we have."

"Thank you, Margaret. I know we've discussed this somewhat several times, but I hear it at a different level each time."

"I appreciate your patience, Richard. I love sharing this with you. I know you are sincerely interested, and you need to know. However, now I think we both need to get some rest. We have a lot to do tomorrow. You and your poultry project and me and my checklist. I go back to work day after tomorrow you know."

"Yes, I do know. I'm glad I have a lot on my list as well. I will miss you like crazy, you know."

"You know what I think, Richard? I believe we are both very adaptable people, and we will be just fine, and yes, of course, I will miss you or I should say, I will think of you, although we have much to do, my darling. We will always still have room for one another. Good night, Richard."

"I love you, Margaret."

"Me too."

"Good night, Howdy."

*

"Good morning, Howdy. You look bright-eyed this morning. I hear Richard is up and about, and I smell breakfast. I'm awake now."

"Good morning, darling. I never know when you sneak out of bed. I've noticed that you are a very good sleeper."

"Well, thank you, and you are a very good breakfast maker. How long have you been up?"

"About an hour or so. Howdy and I went for a very short stroll. It is very cold out there, but the sun is warming things up quickly. It is indeed a glorious day, brisk, sharp, and clear."

"Richard, you make the best coffee in the world. What's your secret?"

"The only thing I've done differently is something you told me a while back. I put a pinch of cinnamon in the pot."

"Good job."

"I will clean the kitchen, Richard. I know you are ready to get over to the Blackwell's farm, and I have a lovely scheduled day. So be off with you. Have a good time, and learn lots of stuff."

"Thank you, Margaret. I'll see you guys later. Love you. Do you have your work gloves and everything?"

"Oh yes. Charles made sure I had the right stuff for whatever I was doing. Later."

"Well, Howdy, I am glad you have already been outside. I don't mind letting the sun do its magic for a while longer. Everything is pretty frosty out there. I know it's winter. I'm acclimating. And I do love the seasonal changes, even this one, maybe especially this one really—all of the wonderful holidays, celebrations, feasting, singing, yes, winter sparkles. There now, I've made my peace with winter. I can really enjoy it. You are a very good listener, Howdy. I know you know that, and it is a very special gift that you give to everyone. I'm off to the shower, and then we'll get to our routines."

*

"What a wonderful day we've had, Howdy. I must say you have been very relaxed today and quite content to nap and watch me go through my closets like a crazy woman. What a relief! I feel so good about my decisions. Anything I hadn't worn for a year went to the clothing barn. There were some really nice things. It is time to pass them on, and my closets can really be organized now. I think Richard is going to be very surprised at how much room he has. This transition is going so well, and I know you really like being with Richard. By the way, I am going back to work tomorrow. If Richard doesn't need to help the Blackwell's tomorrow, I know he wants to work on his projects at the cottage. It may be a good thing for you to stay with him tomorrow. I know I will be pretty busy, and it's not children's day, so we'll see.

"I just heard his car, and so did you. I hope I haven't burned the dinner. I got so involved with closet planning. Well, let's go, greet the master."

"Hi, darling, welcome home. You do smell funny!"

"I'm glad you think it's funny. I'm not kidding, I did help out today by bagging fertilizer, which I understand is the best on the market. By the way, the family is up and about. They are all much better. Charles was back to work most of the day, and the rest of the crew will be back tomorrow."

"So you won't be needed tomorrow?"

"Right. Now I'm going to the shower, and then I'll put my clothes in the washing machine. Then I will definitely be ready for dinner. It's not chicken, is it, darling?"

"No, we're having Mexican food, beer, and flan for dessert."

"Margaret, that sounds perfect. I'll be right back."

"Oh, Richard, one of my projects today was our closets, and I have an organizational plan for us to review later. Just didn't want you to be surprised. Thanks for the heads up."

"Margaret, what did you do with all of your stuff? Those closets are huge now. I did what I have been procrastinating about for ten years or so. If I hadn't used or worn it for at least a year I took it to the Clothes Barn. There were a few exceptions, but not many, and I feel so good about it."

"Quite an accomplishment, and these fish tacos, rice, and beans are so good. If I could have chosen anything to eat tonight, this would be it."

"It is good, isn't it?"

"And the beers not bad either."

"So maybe we shouldn't talk about your day at least not while we're having dinner."

"Oh, it really wasn't that bad at all. Once I got used to the smell, it was actually fun. There is a rhythm to it. Everyone is singing. It really was more like a party, but we got those bags in the boxes and on the trucks. What an operation! I really did have a good time. They offered me a job, so I guess I did OK."

"I am sure you did, Richard. So did you take it?"

"What? The job?"

"Yes."

"No, Margaret! I'll be glad to help out when necessary only!"

"So are you ready to resume your projects at the cottage, whatever they may be?"

"I am, Miss Margaret, and no, I'm not ready to share with you about what they are right now, but soon."

"OK, Richard. I am patient but very curious."

"So, are we ready for flan and Mexican hot chocolate?"

"Yes, we are. Move over, Howdy, we're going to join you in our favorite spot."

"Howdy may want to spend some time with you tomorrow, Richard. I don't think it would be good for him to be at the library. There's always a lot going on the first day back."

"That's right, Margaret. Your vacation is over. Sure, I would love to have Howdy with me tomorrow, as long as he promises not to reveal my secrets. Oh, I'm sure he'll never tell."

✳

"You are back on schedule. I see, early to rise and ready to go."

"Yes, I am looking forward to seeing everyone, and, of course, actually getting back to work. And again, thank you for breakfast. I have noticed that you are joining me in my special drink routine. It's really good after you get used to it, Richard. I made a mixed bean soup yesterday and corn bread so all we'll need to do tonight is a salad, and I have a surprise for dessert."

"Oh really, that sounds seductive."

"Well, it does include red wine and dark chocolate, so who knows where it may go from there. See you tonight.

"Howdy, you take care of Richard today. Tomorrow is children's day at the library. They will be so glad to see you. So rest up for the big day tomorrow. Love you, guys. Have fun today."

"Howdy, let's get down to the cottage. The guys will be there in about an hour. If it gets too noisy for you, you can come back up here. I'm glad I have so much help with this project. They say we can have everything done in seven days. Boy, we are cutting it close. Especially since Margaret's only working three days a week which is wonderful! Just means a little tighter schedule. Also, I need to remember to call my sis tonight. This is a very special time in my life, Howdy. I am a very lucky and grateful man. Let's go to work. Well, actually, you can supervise."

"Good morning, everyone. It looks like I must be late. Sorry."

"No, Richard, you're not late. We just got here a little early, but before Margaret left. Morning, Howdy. I see you brought a helper."

"Howdy is our new supervisor. Good job. I'm glad someone knows what we're doing."

"Hey, guys, let's don't even joke about that. I know I'm on shaky ground here, but I trust you guys. As well you may note, I brought the plans for us to review, and we're ready to go."

"This looks perfect."

"Exactly as I see it in my mind. I shared my vision with Margaret shortly after I moved in here, and she said she had thought about doing something similar several times but was just never motivated enough to follow through. I know I am taking a risk here, but it really feels right and she has certainly encouraged me to follow my instincts, so here we go."

"Let's do it."

∗

The closer I get to the Library, the more excited I am. I can already smell Mary's bakery special of the day, the coffee, and even Mary's smell. She always smells like spices, warm and sweet. I realize that I have really missed her. Actually everyone, but Mary is more like a mother. I know I can share anything with her, and although she loves to talk and does to everyone, she also know when not to, and if I share something, that's just for us. I know that's a safe thing to do. She also senses my unasked questions often. Sometimes before I know the question, she has answers. She is a very special lady.

Well, here I am, right on time. It somehow always amazes me.

"Good morning, Mary, you look bright and cheery on this fine chilly morning."

"Margaret, I am so glad to see you. You always wake this place up. Oh everything has been fine. I didn't mean that. It's just that you bring a special spark with you."

"Thank you, Mary. I really wanted to come in here and have a cup of coffee and whatever you just took out of the oven and talk to you for a few minutes, if you have time."

"Oh yes. I have my daughter and granddaughter in. We have a big anniversary order to fill today. So yes, let's catch up a bit. How is Howdy?"

"It's really hard to watch him change so much Mary. He is just getting very tired. He still has a bright spark, from time to time. He's sleeping more, and his walks are getting shorter. Mary, thank you for knowing that I really needed to share that with you. Richard understands, and that's wonderful, but you have known Howdy for as long as I have, and you know how much he helped me after Mom and Dad's accident."

"Yes, I do, Margaret, and of course Howdy is going to leave a big void, but more importantly, he is going to leave all of us better people for having him in our lives. Just think, this entire community is so proud to honor him. All I've heard for the past weeks is about 'Howdy's Day'."

"I saw the bronze piece last week. What a magnificent piece of art. He captured Howdy's spirit in that piece."

"Margaret, we have all been blessed by having Howdy, and all of us have learned a little bit more about ourselves by seeing ourselves through his eyes. It's like he only knows us as perfection, so we're all better people. I remember how many times he has made the sick feel better and stayed right with people, often in their bed through their transition time and then been a comfort to the family. Yes, he is part child, part spirit—all love."

"Mary, you always know just what to say."

"Thank you, and again, I can say, you're right, and I am so blessed to have the privilege of Howdy's love, and I am grateful. I know I can release him when it's time. I feel better. I didn't realize how much I needed to talk about the reality of releasing Howdy, and I know it will be so much better for him. I love you, Mary."

"I love you too, child."

"Now I had better wipe my tears, powder my face, and get to work."

"Yes, I know everyone is going to want their turn. They have learned list-making very well. They have a great teacher, so I'm sure you will find things in order, more or less."

"Thank you, Mary. Well, here goes."

*

"I do believe in miracles, and I've sure been a part of one today. We have accomplished so much. You guys are amazing. You work together like a symphony, every move in perfection. So now I know this project is going to be done in time, and even better than I had imagined."

"You did a good job today, Richard. You can be very proud of what you have contributed. We do this all of the time. Each time is a little different, but the basics are there. You absolutely kept up. Ask questions when you needed to. Kept quiet when you needed to. Joking. We will see you in the morning, and thank you so much for that great lunch. It was a good day."

"I will definitely sleep well tonight and look forward to another eventful day tomorrow. Oh yes, and I will have lunch prepared. We'll see how many more jokes you guys can tell. That was really fun. Good night, everyone. See you tomorrow."

"Howdy, we had best get up to the house, start the fire, and get dinner warmed up. I am so glad that Margaret prepared almost everything yesterday. I am definitely a little sore and stiff already. Small price to pay for what we accomplished. I'm sure Margaret will have a lot to tell us about her day, and that's great because I sure can't tell her about mine yet. The guys really enjoyed having you around. You are a good supervisor. It was kind of like you'd just give your look of approval, and we all felt better. Good job, fellow. If you're up to it, and I think you are, you'll be working at the library tomorrow. It's children's day, and I'm sure they will be very glad to see you."

✳

"I see you have your favorite place already. I'll feed you after I get dinner going. Welcome home, darling, and how was your day?"

"Hi, Richard, it's really good to be home. Although it was great to be back at work also.

"Hi, Howdy. You look comfy and content. Oh yes, I love you too. Yes, and you too Richard. My goodness it's nice to be greeted so warmly. I'm going to go upstairs and get my evening comfy clothes on. Be right back."

"Dinner was delicious. Thank you, Richard. Actually, you made most of it, darling. I just did the finishing touches, and if memory serves me correctly, you said something about a seductive dessert?"

"Oh yes, it will only take a few minutes, and I promise it will be worth waiting for."

"I'm intrigued."

"Well, what do we have here, and what is that wonderful smell?"

"We have spiced roasted nuts, red wine, dark-chocolate-covered coconut mango bites, and I mean rich dark chocolate, and chocolate-covered strawberries."

"Margaret, this soft chewy coconut with a tangy mango touch along with the dark chocolate is a powerful combination and could easily become addictive."

"This is a very seductive dessert, darling, and so are you."

"Margaret, do you want children?"

"Richard, you told me that you and Sylvia had decided not to have children. I have accepted that."

"That is not what I asked, darling, and remember, everyone can always choose again. I asked what you think about having children, or a child. I have watched you with children at the library and many other places, and I know you are genuinely a loving gentle person, but you have a special glow about you when you are with children. I'm sure that you must have considered the question. We have just never talked about it, so?"

"Yes, Richard, I had assumed earlier in my life that I would have children. I had even imagined how different this house would be with the sights and sounds of children. But on the other hand, my life with you is complete, and I am very happy."

"Margaret, I would really like for us to have children or maybe start with a child. When I started thinking about it, I had a few demons to slay. I honestly never think, or spend any energy considering the possibility of blindness. I'm too involved in living life to the fullest every moment, that there's just no time or space for negativity. However, that thought did occur, *What if?* And then just as quickly I thought, *Yes, what if?* And I truly am all right with that. I will never dwell on it. Yes, Margaret, I really do want us to have a family. Maybe just start with one and go from there."

"Oh, Richard, I am so happy. I truly was all right with not having children. Goodness know there are enough of them to love and care for in our community, and I do. But yes, or yes, I would love for us to start with just one, and I think that's generally the way it works, darling. That is unless you have a history of twins in your family."

"No twins to my knowledge."

"Mine too. What a lot to take in. Just think, we are actually planning to become parents. A whole different identity."

"Yes, it is awesome, and yes, it is a responsibility and one that I am looking forward to."

"Me too, and the sooner, the better."

"That's what I'm thinking. That seductive dessert was not nearly as seductive as you are right now, Margaret. There's no better time to start our project than right now."

"Richard, my darling, you are absolutely right. I love you, oh yes, I love you."

✳

"Good morning, Howdy. You look like you've already been outside. You have a few snowflakes on your head. They are so pretty, and so are you. OK, yes, I know it is time for me to get up and at 'em, and obviously Richard is already in the kitchen. I smell the coffee. Let's go."

"Good morning, darling. The coffee and Howdy brought me down here just like I am. My routine is crooked today."

"Well, you are beautiful today, my dear one. A little change in the schedule once in a while is a good thing. Priorities keep changing, you know."

"Yes, I do know, and many paths lead to the same destination."

"Well, you are bright and alert even though you are still in your pajamas."

"I'm even going to have my juice and coffee before my special morning wake-up drink. How about that for mixing things up? What is happening to us?"

"I don't know, but whatever it is, bring it on."

"You made biscuits? I find new talents all of the time, Richard. As a matter of fact, I found a few last night."

"So did I, Margaret. What was in that chocolate?"

"No, don't tell me. I like surprises. This is a wonderful breakfast, you are spoiling me, and I love it. I took Howdy for a short walk this morning. He looks pretty good, Margaret."

"Yes, he does, and yes, he is going to the library today. He has a favorite resting spot there also, and I am going to talk to the kids today about Howdy's special event. Everyone is excited about it. I'm also going to talk with them about Howdy's age, and let them know how much he loves them, but he won't be as active, and he takes more naps. I think they need a little preparation, and I also know they will understand."

"Margaret, that is a great idea, and I absolutely agree that it is timely. Do you want me to be there?"

"Thank you so much for offering, but no, you continue with your projects. My curiosity is mounting. Also Mary and I had a great talk yesterday, and it helped me a lot. Maybe we'll have time to talk about it tonight. Well, I'd better get in gear. I have a 10:00 a.m. staff meeting, so I think I'd better be on time."

*

"Come on, Howdy. Let's go. We have a full schedule today. Have fun, Richard, and do whatever it is you're doing. Oh, also Mary is baking chicken pot pies today, and I asked her to bake one for us. They are delicious. That is if you're ready for chicken."

"Yes, I think that sounds perfect. Have a great day, and I'll look forward to seeing you guys tonight. Love ya."

∗

"Good morning, gentlemen."

"Morning, Richard. We are having great luck with the weather. There was a little flurry last night, but he sun is up and the snow is gone. We should be able to get all of the outside stuff done today. Then if the weather turns, it really won't bother us. We could do it anyhow, but this is better."

"That's what I'm thinking. I'm so anxious to really get the inside design going. This is an exciting project, guys, and it's getting more exciting every day. Well let's get to work."

"By the way, where's our supervisor?"

"Sorry, guys, he had to go supervise the children at the library today. Well, I guess we'll just have to muddle through. But I'm not kidding now. We will miss him, I know."

∗

"Hi, Mary, I finally got a moment to come into my favorite spot, with my special people and breathe."

"Pretty full day, Margaret?"

"Oh yes, talking to the children was both rewarding and exhausting. They really had a lot of great questions, and they were very comfortable talking about death and dying. It's always so refreshing to see things from a fresh perspective. It was very good for them and me, but I'll tell you, I am really ready for a cup of whatever special tea you chose for me."

"Well, I do have a special blend that I think will be perfect for both of us. It's green tea with jasmine, floral chamomile, spearmint, and lemongrass."

"It's a delightful way for us to wind down the day."

"The chicken pot pie order turned out great. I'll tell you my granddaughter has a natural knack for cooking. She sings and hums while she works, and everything turns out to be perfect. I do believe this may turn out to be her passion. She's not really interested in going to college. We've talked about it a lot. Her grades are OK, but she's really not motivated to apply herself in any other direction. She is most alive and happy when she's cooking or baking, and I'm certainly OK with that. It's a blessing to my life, and I still get complete satisfaction everyday watching people's faces as they take that first bite of whatever it is that brings them pleasure."

∗

"I am sure she will make the right decision, Mary, and you know what we always say. We can always choose again."

"That's right, darling. That we can. And don't forget your chicken pie for tonight, and I stuck a few other tidbits in the package."

"Thank you, Mary. Someday, after Howdy's celebration and the staff Xmas party, you and I need to sneak away somewhere and talk about our wedding cake or cakes. I know you can do it, but I would like to work with you, just a little on the design. You do realize this will be for the community and on New Year's Eve. I know it's a big commitment, but I also know you can do it. You, your daughter, granddaughter, and whoever else you need in order to get it done."

"Margaret, you're right. It is a challenge, and I want it to be so perfect, and I'm sure it will be, and yes it would be very helpful for us to get together and create the design. It will also be fun. I am so excited about you and Richard. You are absolutely perfect for each other. And what a joy to have him become a part of our community, so easily he just absolutely fills what was a missing piece, and we just didn't know it. Do you know what I'm trying to say?"

"Yes, I do, Mary, and I totally agree. I also had better go get Howdy and get home, and when I say home now, it actually does have a deeper meaning. So good night, Mary. Thank you."

"And I'll see you for a few hours tomorrow. I am on my twenty-hour flex week now. So I will be in from 10:00 to 2:00 tomorrow. See you then."

∗

"Well, guys, we did it again. Another miraculous day. You are all so good at what you do. But you know that. I am so grateful that you were available at this time. It is perfect, and I think we're ahead of schedule. Do you agree?"

184

"Well, you know, Richard, we usually are. I tend to underestimate our projections, and then everyone is happy when the job is completed, not just on time, but earlier than projected. I like happy people."

"All of you obviously really like what you're doing. I am so pleased with everything. It truly is even better than I had visualized, and I know Margaret is going to love it."

"Well, that's what we like to hear. Now. When do you want us back to finish the job? I know Margaret's hours have changed. So we can be as flexible as necessary. We don't have another project until after the holidays, so it's your call."

"Unless something changes, her schedule is Tuesday to Wednesday, and a half day on Thursday next week."

"Then we will see you on Tuesday, and I think we'll be able to finish, if not, for sure by Wednesday. I think it's amazing that she hasn't been down here. I mean just plain curiosity is powerful, but knowing you have a big project going on, and then to be able to restrain from at least a peek."

"As you guys all know, Margaret is no ordinary person. Her word is as good as gold. I have no concern. I know she would never want to spoil the surprise, and she would not break a promise. That's just who she is."

"You are right, Richard. You know her very well. I guess you know this entire crew loves Margaret. There isn't one of us that she hasn't touched with some act of kindness. We really like you, but Margaret, she's our special angel, and we are very proud to be able to do this project for her, and you of course. And you do fix a really good lunch."

"Thanks, guys. I will see you on Tuesday, and I'll be sure to have a super special lunch prepared."

"Good, have a great weekend. I know it's going to be a very special one. So have fun, and I'm sure we'll see you somewhere during the festivities."

*

"Well, that's what I call perfect timing. Hello, you two."

"Margaret, you look absolutely vibrant. I'd say you had a very good day at work?"

"And you would be absolutely correct. There is so much good energy in town, Richard. The holiday spirit is alive and well."

"Howdy, I will have your fireplace glowing in just a few minutes. I missed you today, boy. OK, you too, Margaret."

"Sure you did. I know you get as immersed in your projects as I do mine, and yes, there are moments when I think about you and I'm always very happy to think about coming home because you're here, but we both know the time literally flies by, and then here we are. I love you, darling. And Mary does too. Remember she prepared our dinner for tonight, and we are in for a treat. Her chicken potpie is the best I have ever had. Of course my mother wouldn't ever make one because Mary's was so good. So while you're starting the fire, I'll put the finishing touches to dinner, and then we will have our evening teatime and we always have so much to share."

"I think that's because we have such full lives, darling."

"Yes, and fulfilling."

∗

"I know I had lunch, but I honestly don't remember it. That's probably why I was so hungry tonight. Everything tasted so good."

"Well, I know I had lunch, and a lot of it, and I was hungry. Also I think it was something Mary put in the food."

"Yes, she does that, Richard. It's called love."

"Well, that's a relief. We probably won't get fat if it's just love."

"You are silly."

"So I've heard, my dear. I think I had better get downtown tomorrow. I want to feel the holiday spirit that's filling the town, and I need some supplies. I'll stop by about noon, and see if you have a few minutes for lunch. What do you think?"

"I think that's a great idea, and maybe you could have Howdy with you tomorrow. He has a very big day coming up this weekend. I mean really big. That's part of the buzz in town. I hope we're not pushing him too hard, Richard. I am a little concerned about it."

"You want to know what I think, Margaret?"

"Yes, I really do."

"I think Howdy understands so much more than we can imagine. I've watched him with children. He reads them all individually and knows instinctively how to respond to them. He does that in so many ways. He knows people's moods and needs, and he demands nothing.

He just gives. I think this tribute is a very good thing especially now. We don't know how much longer he will be with us, but we do know the clock is ticking. This celebration will be wonderful way for everyone to show their gratitude, respect, and love. Howdy will feel that, so will it be demanding? Yes. Will he be over-tired? Probably. But I think his vote would be, 'Yes, let's do this thing, and revel in it. That's what I'm going to do.'"

"Richard, thank you. I was sensing a little guilt about the whole thing, and I don't usually experience that feeling. I sure don't like it. I think I was just being a little protective, and I surely don't need to be. Howdy has always belonged to this community. I just had the privilege of spending more time with him. This will be a very timely event, and it is the right thing to do. So between you and Mary, I have a lot of support and wisdom to draw from. Thank you, my darling. And yes, Howdy. You may thank us also. He is definitely a right-handed paw dog. He always has extended that strong right paw for many expressions. Such as now. I love you so much, Howdy."

*

"Good morning, Richard. I think this is the first morning we have awakened at the same time."

"I have been awake for a while, darling, just enjoying your beauty, the morning glow, and the fact that neither of us have to be on an early schedule this morning. We did forget to tell Howdy. He has been in to check on us several times. And yes, I have already been out with him."

"I certainly slept through that and thank you."

"That's OK. Howdy already thanked me."

"This is so nice, Richard, just being here with you. Listening to the morning sounds."

"Yes, it is, my dear, but I am getting very hungry, so I will go put the coffee on, and then we'll fix breakfast together."

"That sounds like fun, Richard. I'm so glad I don't go in until ten today. My perfect routine has kind of gone astray."

"Only temporarily, Margaret. We both love the rituals we do, especially the meditation and yoga combination. I actually do the short version of that several times a day."

"So do I, and fortunately, I have the privacy at work to accommodate those five-minute refreshers, and I am always so much more productive when I do."

"I will see you downstairs in five minutes because now I am really ready to eat."

*

"I love the smell of coffee and the anticipation of that first sip. I believe tea is still the most consumed beverage worldwide, but I'll bet coffee is a close second. Except for drinking water, of course. My grandfather used to talk about Turkish coffee, and honestly, it didn't sound very good to me then. I had tasted his coffee once and thought it was awful. As I recall from a previous conversation, coffee and tea both have ancient origins. Tea has been used for health purposes throughout the world for thousands of years, and finally coffee is beginning to be recognized similarly. How in the world did I get into that, Richard? I'm sorry."

"Margaret, I love our conversations, and when you talk about your family, you glow or maybe it was the coffee."

"Well, this has been a great breakfast, and now I see that I'm running late again. So I must eat and run. Richard, I think Howdy should stay with you today. People understand that he needs more rest, but especially the children want to be with him, and it's just too much stimulation. Bless his heart, I could tell yesterday that he was really struggling to respond. It's just too much."

"I'm sorry, Margaret. I know this is tough. I would be glad to have his company today. I have a very easy schedule, and if I do come in to town, it will be an easy trip."

"Thank you, darling. I love you. Got to go. Maybe see you around lunch, if not shortly after."

"Oh, I almost forgot. If you do get to stop by, we need to schedule a time to talk to Mary about our wedding cake. I have some ideas, but I'd really like for us to share ideas also."

"Great, I'll see you in a couple of hours. Love you."

"Howdy, I'm going down to the cottage to write for an hour or so. Do you want to go with me or stay here? You beat me to the door, so I will take that for a definite yes. Good boy. I love having your company. Let's go."

✳

"Good morning, Mary. I just finished a wonderful breakfast. I walk in here, and the smells make me think I'm hungry, when I know I couldn't eat another bite. My daughter is baking this morning, and you're right. She is creating some pretty amazing stuff."

"I just wanted to tell you that Richard will probably be by about 12:30 p.m., and if you have a minute, we'll schedule a time soon for us to talk about the design for *the cake*."

"That is so exciting, Margaret. I will make time, whenever it works for you, so check your schedule, and when he gets here, we'll confirm it, OK?"

"Sounds great. Now I'd better get busy. I'm mentoring Lizzie today. I've given her several projects, and we need to review progress. She's really doing well, Mary. I'm so proud of her."

"I'm glad darling. I know she will be fine."

✳

"Hello, busy lady, do you have a minute to spare for a couple of friends?"

"Hi, Richard and Howdy. How are you?"

"We are doing great. Easy day. How about you?"

"Lizzie is doing great, Richard. Of course, I knew she would. I saw Mary on the way in."

"Have you checked your schedule for a meeting?"

"Yes, actually I have, but I also wanted to check with you. Tuesday and Wednesday of next week are pretty full. Other than that, I'm very flexible."

"Yes, I know you are. I'm so glad you've noticed. I think we had better go see Mary and get that meeting set."

"All righty. Let's do that."

"Hi, Mary, get your calendar, and let's do this. I know you are really busy the rest of this week and weekend preparing for Howdy's special day and then the family Xmas event at the community center. It looks like next

Thursday when I'm through work, like about 2:30 p.m., that would be my first choice and Richard is available then. So how about you, Mary?"

"Sounds like a plan, darlings. I am so excited about Howdy's special day, and the weather is supposed to be great. I'm so glad, Margaret. I know Howdy's always at the center event right by Santa. Do you think he's up to it this time?"

"I have really given it a lot of thought, Mary. What do you two think about having a special Xmas sleigh for Howdy to rest in, and he could be behind Santa, close to the stove, and the sleigh could have some kind of sign or something. The children are so used to being right with him, and I know that would be too much, but I really think he would want to be there. Any ideas?"

"I can certainly build a protective Howdy Santa sleigh and then maybe a sign also. We'll think of the perfect thing. It will work, Margaret, and I agree, I think Howdy should be there. How about you, Mary?"

"Yes, bless his heart. I know there will be a lot going on, but yes, I'm sure it's the right decision, and it will work out fine."

"Ladies, Howdy and I have one more little errand to do, and then we're headed home. Anything I can do for you, Margaret?"

"No, darling, but I will be a little later than I thought. I've been a little slow today. Probably see you about four o'clock or so."

"Take your time, Margaret. Do what you need to do. This is transition time, you know. You can't possibly know exactly how it's going to go. You haven't done it yet."

"Thank you, Richard, and that's why I call it flextime. So I will try to remember that, and enjoy the process. See you later, love.

"Mary, he is a joy to be with."

"I know that, Margaret, and then again, so are you."

"Well, back to work. Lizzie is probably wondering if I left early. Thank you, Mary. See you later."

"Margaret, stop by on your way out, would you please?"

"You bet. See you then."

*

"Mary, are you still here?"

"I'm in the back, Margaret. Be right there. You did stay a little later than you planned, my friend."

"Yes, I did, but it will not become a pattern. I know this job-sharing thing is going to work out very well. It's just transition stuff."

"I know how that is, Margaret. I have a dinner box ready for you, and if Richard already has something ready, this can go right into the freezer."

"Mary, thank you again. I was going to stop by the market and get something, but this is so much better."

"You are so welcome. I know tomorrow evening may be a bit of a mixed blessing. A very special time for all of us. I do hope you and Howdy will have a restful day tomorrow, and I know that tomorrow evening will be a very memorable occasion."

"Thank you, Mary. I feel good about it. As a matter of fact, I feel wonderful. I will see you at the town square tomorrow evening. I'm so tempted to go over there right now. I know they are placing it tonight, and it will be very securely covered, so folks like me won't be tempted to see it before it is unveiled. So I'll be on my way with this wonderful box of delicious food."

"Good night, love."

∗

"Richard, Howdy, I'm home, and I see that you guys are too. You look so cozy lying there by the fire. No, stay, Howdy. I'll join you. Doing nothing for a while sounds good to me. Richard, you are almost as good a snuggler as Howdy."

"Well, thank you, madam. I will continue to get better as time goes by. Howdy is a good teacher."

"Yes, you are my friend. By the way, Mary sent us another care package. I have no idea what it is except to know that it will be soul food."

"That's so thoughtful of her. She is a very special lady."

"Yes, she is. Would you like a cup of tea or a glass of wine before dinner, Margaret?"

"Yes, I would. Red, red wine. Thank you, Richard."

"Good choice."

∗

"Richard, I know you will understand. Tomorrow I want to take Howdy to our favorite place, the lighthouse trail. We'll drive most of the way. And our favorite stopping spot is not far from where I will have to park. He and I need some time there together. Probably more correctly, I need some time with him, and I feel like it should be tomorrow."

"Absolutely, Margaret. Just let me know if there's any way I can help. By the way, I made his Xmas sleigh this afternoon, and he loves it. I found some red velvet out in the storage drawer, and his pillow fits the sleigh perfectly, by design of course."

"Oh, Richard, thank you. That is so sweet. We'll do the sign tomorrow. I have some ideas."

"I think tomorrow will definitely be one of those lifetime special memories."

"I am so happy to be a part of it, Margaret. I love you so much."

"I know you do, Richard. We are blessed. Shall we see what great surprise we have from Mary, who also is a constant blessing in my life?"

"Our lives, darling. I just opened the box, and the aroma escaped. I don't know what it is, and I don't care. Let's eat. I'm suddenly starving."

"Me too."

✳

"Good morning, Margaret. I can't believe you're up and obviously have been for a while, and I'm only partially awake now. You look absolutely beautiful, and it's so early."

"Not really so early, Richard, it's almost nine o'clock."

"I've been up for about an hour, but I just made the coffee, and I will go prepare breakfast now, that is, if you're ready to get up."

"With coffee brewing and Howdy nudging me, I think I am ready to get up now. I will be right down, OK? Howdy, let's go see what we can throw together.

"What a beautiful scene! This is a fairy tale setting for breakfast. May I help?"

"Thank you, darling but no, everything happened to come together perfectly and all at the same time, probably because it is so simple and quick."

"Perhaps quick, darling, but certainly not simple. You must have everything in that freezer. The strawberries look like they've just been picked, and they taste like it. You, my friend, are very easy to please. However, this is one of my favorite simple breakfasts—oats, yogurt, almonds, bananas, strawberries, real maple syrup, fresh orange juice, strong coffee, you, and Howdy. Who could ask for anything more?"

"Certainly not me, Margaret. I am a happy man."

✳

"When are you and Howdy going to go on your walk? Or do you know yet?"

"Yes, I think about noon will be a good time. We have another sunny day and no wind, and that will also give us some time to a rest before the big event."

"This morning, I would like to work on the sign for Howdy's sleigh. What time do we need to leave for town this evening, Margaret?"

"The dedication ceremony for Howdy is at 5:00 p.m. I am going to keep that very short. I will introduce the artist, and have him do the unveiling, and I will make a very short statement. As soon as I finish and Howdy has received his recognition, the Xmas lights and music will be turned on, which signifies the official beginning of the holiday season, which is always such a delightful time. Then the crowd follows Santa to the gathering center, where folks have been preparing food and decorating all day. This is really something special, Richard. I know it will be a lot of stimulation for Howdy, but I still feel like it is where he wants to be. So we will help him enjoy it, in his own way."

"Yes, we will, Margaret. What can I do to help?"

"I don't have a clear idea yet of design for the sign. It might help if we just talk about what we want to accomplish with it. I have thought about it Richard. I want especially the children to be able to see Howdy, and know that he is there, but to be reminded that he will probably at least pretty much remain in his sleigh and doze as he needs to."

"Margaret, since we have the sleigh, and red velvet pillow already, he will have been recognized as a VIP. How about 'King for a day,' and the kids could bow to the king, whether he was awake or sleeping. His throne will be right behind Santa's."

"Richard, I like it. I think that will work for the children and Howdy."

"I could work on the sign while you and Howdy are gone, if you'd like for me to."

"I really would appreciate it, Richard, and I know it will be perfect."

"Thank you! Thank you! That is a relief. I knew it would come together, but now I can see how. Would you like another cup of coffee, Mr. King?"

"Yes, I would, 'very soon to be Mrs. King'. How does that sound, Margaret? I mean actually, you haven't said if you want to keep your last name, and it's all right with me if you do. I know it has a lot of history attached. Maybe I should take your last name. It sounds like something we should think about."

"You're right, Richard. I had assumed I would become Mrs. Margaret King, and I love the sound of it, but I do think we should think about it. So we will, and the answer will come, and we will know when it does. Yes, we will, and now, I think it's time for Howdy and me to head out to the lighthouse trail. Are you ready, Howdy?"

"Yes, you creature of habit, leash in your mouth, waiting by the door. We'll be back soon, Richard. This is a journey more for me than anything else. We need this time together. I know I do."

"Yes, I think it's a good thing, darling. I'll keep the fire going and fix you some hot chocolate when you return. I love you very much."

*

"Howdy, my friend, I need your support once again, I know this journey is for me. We don't need to go far or stay very long. Here we are again, where we have been so many times before. I am so grateful to walk this sacred path with you once more and stand here on this rocky cliff above the ocean. The air is cold, and the wind a bit brisk as it blows off the water. We can feel the spray as the waves crash on the rocks, and once again, each breath brings renewed vigor. Just standing by the ocean with you, where we have stood so many times, seems incredibly calming to my emotional state.

"Howdy, my friend, I have always felt your support through any challenge in my life, as you listen with an open heart. Thank you. I truly believe you are a compassionate expression of God. You see me as I truly am. I feel your faith and complete trust in me when you give me your paw, as you are now, and look so deeply into my soul.

"I have felt your caring nature every time you have blessed me with love and reminded me that I am not alone. I am so grateful for this life we have been given to share. I know that you will always be with me. I truly believe love and devotion transcends separation and death spurred by your caring presence.

"I know I will not only survive, I will thrive, as you have taught me to do, as you have always done, to eagerly welcome the adventure that is my life. Once again, my dear one, I know you are cold and tired and ready to go. But never once have you put your needs ahead of mine. Thank you seems so small, but it is filled with love and gratitude. Let's go find that warm fire that Richard has waiting for you, and maybe we'll just snuggle and nap for a while. You have a very special evening waiting for you, my friend, and this has been a very special time for me. You have truly taught me what it means to be and have a friend.

*

"Hi, Richard, we have returned. Your timing is great. I have the fire going, and the rug is warm and ready for you, buddy."

"I'll bet it was a little cold and windy on the hill."

"Really not bad, of course. I had Howdy to keep me warm. We had a very good time, Richard. I needed to do that."

"I'm glad, Margaret. I will fix you that hot chocolate I promised. But first come and see the sign and stuff I fixed for Howdy."

"Oh, Richard, you made a special place for his crown. That is so cute. I love the sign, and I'm sure the kids will too. You did a great job decorating the sleigh, sign, and crown holder, all matching. I love it all, and I feel so good about the evening. I know it's going to be another great memory maker. Now do I get my hot chocolate?"

"Indeed we do, and a special strawberry delightful thing that was in the package from Mary. Yes, I did have a bite, and that's how I know for sure it is a delight."

"This hot chocolate is fantastic. What did you do to it? A dash of cinnamon and cayenne pepper."

"You are the brave soul. I've never used the pepper. This is really good."

"I'm glad. I thought maybe it would keep your circulation flowing, or maybe I was thinking about me."

"I promised Howdy that we would just cuddle, relax, and maybe even doze a bit. How does that sound to you?"

"Absolutely wonderful. I guess there wasn't too much pepper in the hot chocolate. I think you and Howdy are already napping."

"Uh huh."

∗

"Margaret, I think we had better rise and shine. It's four o'clock already."

"Oh really! That just doesn't seem possible, but you're right. It's time to get it together. I'm going to go shower and dress, and it will be cold tonight. I'm so glad Howdy has his warm cape that you made for him. However, I think the crown will be for show only."

"Yes, I think so too. I really can't see Howdy going for the crown thing, but the cape is really classy. I think he'll like that. He hasn't seen his bronze likeness, but I really think he will understand the general concept, and I know he will feel and understand the love. I would like to have you up there with us, Richard. We are a family, you know."

"Well, that was a nice kiss, Margaret. Yes, we are a family, and this is home, and I am just so very happy and I would love to be beside you anytime, anywhere."

∗

"My goodness! What a crowd, I think the entire community is here, and I'm not really surprised. Well, Mr. Howdy, you look very perky this evening and quite regal. So do you, Margaret."

"Thank you, Richard. We are quite the team, aren't we?"

"Yes, ma'am, and it looks like everything's ready, and every one is in place. Showtime, Margaret?"

"Good evening, everyone. What a perfect evening for a community gathering. Let us celebrate together the fullness of life which is a gift that Howdy has shared with all of us. Let us celebrate the moments that lift us up, as well as the challenges that allow us to grow, appreciating the full spectrum of life's experiences. Howdy celebrates all points along the way filled with joy and enthusiasm for loving all that life has to offer. Let us thank Howdy today in recognition that the fullness of life is a gift from God. Thank you, Howdy, for sharing that love with everyone and all of the time, not just when it was convenient, or as a reward, but rather as a way of life.

196

"I thank you, with Howdy, for your applause, for being here, for creating such a wonderful community to live in. Let us now also thank Mr. Anthony who has honored Howdy and our community with this magnificent bronze replica of our own special Howdy. Thank you. Now for the unveiling of this wonderful piece of art that will enhance our town through the ages. Howdy, if you would please sit right there, Mr. Anthony will unveil the statue. Oh yes, this is an amazing likeness, of an amazing being, Mr. Howdy. And now our community council leader will wave his Xmas wand and officially declare the holiday season. First the lights, followed by our traditional Xmas carols.

"After that of course we will follow Santa and Howdy's sleigh to our spiritual life center for food, music, games, and Santa's stories around the fireplace. Again, I thank you, and Howdy thanks you for your warm presence and support. We'll see you at the center."

*

"Margaret, that was beautiful, and the statue is perfect. He really captured the Howdy spirit. It certainly will always be a favorite gathering spot for the community, visitors, and, of course, for us."

"Well, we're here and what a sight! Richard, there must be at least a thousand Xmas lights."

"Yes, it is spectacular. Do they do this every year?"

"And I say 'we,' because usually I am a part of the team. Yes, we always have a great time decorating. However, this year is exceptional, and I just noticed that the gate has lights in the shape of a dog, of course a special one. How thoughtful! Let's go inside and see what else we find. This is your first Xmas with us, Richard, and it's really challenging for me to truly grasp that. It just seems like you have been a part of my life forever."

"That bad, huh?"

"You know what I mean."

"Yes, I really do, Margaret, because while I know I still have so much to learn about everything. I feel so comfortable with you, Howdy, the community, and I think, most importantly, with myself. I love the way I am now. I have nothing to prove, no pressure, so many real friends, and very soon to be wife that I love with all that I am, complete honesty, with deep admiration and respect."

"Oh yes, my darling, you do understand, and thank you for being you. I hear the music and merriment. Let's go see what's happening. By the way, do you square dance?"

"Well, maybe. It's been a long, long time. I'm talking about when I was a child, living with my grandmother. My sister and I would join the group at the barn gatherings. I think it was square dancing or round dancing. So let's keep our expectations of me square dancing rather low."

"Richard, you know when you said you have friends here, you are right. Everyone supports one another. If you want to dance, we will dance, and you will have only love and gentle guidance, that and a whole lot of fun."

"I know you're right, Margaret. Bring it on. Right now, I believe I can do anything."

"So we shall. In every room, there will be something different happening—table games, dancing, conversation, children's room for stories, and games. The dining room is open. People eat when they're hungry, drink when they're thirsty, and, believe me, the food group will keep that table full all night."

"It's like magic, only I have worked with that group also, and I know it's not magic, but I also know that everyone cooks, cleans, decorates, entertains, and whatever needs to be done, because they really want to, so there is no frustration, anger, or resentment which leaves joy and reward, and we will definitely be part of the program next year. This time, we just enjoy. We rotate—one year give, the next year receive. You came in at the right time, because you are a part of my team."

"I certainly am, my dear. Shall we check on Howdy and see how well our plan is going?"

"Yes, Richard, I was thinking about that, and I am so hopeful that he is really OK with this. I know he loves it, so let's check it out."

"Margaret, do you have your camera."

"No, but we have a couple of photographers here. Why?"

"Look at Santa and Howdy. They have a sign that says Santa and Howdy are taking a short nap and to check back in ten minutes, and there they are. That is so cute, and that's why it's so quiet in here. I'll go get the photographer and be right back."

"They haven't moved. I think maybe their ten minutes are magic minutes. However, the children are getting restless. I think you'd better get the shot while you can. This is classic. Santa and Howdy both look so peaceful, and in the midst of all of this activity, nothing else exists for them right now."

"I got some great shots. Thank you for finding me."

"Margaret, I will give you a set of pictures that I have taken, at the unveiling, and here and there are some great ones. Of course, on Xmas Eve, I will show the video here, and you can have a copy of that also. Well, Howdy and Santa have come back to the party."

"Ho! Ho! Ho! Is everyone having a good time?"

"Yes!" The chorus of children, everyone said in unison.

"Look, Richard, Howdy is taking his place right behind Santa. The children can see him and love him, but they are not roughhousing with him. They do understand, and they are respecting the unseen protective barrier."

"Yes, Margaret, it has worked out very well. I don't think we need to be concerned about Howdy. He and Santa are quite a team."

"Yes, they are, Richard. They have both been doing this for at least the last thirteen years. Well, they have their parts practiced well."

"Santa has the children spellbound with one of his wonderful and unique stories. I want to find out, later of course, if he has these stories written. I certainly have never seen them, and they are very good. Richard, perhaps you could work with him to create a Christmas book in time for him to give all of the children, one next year."

"Yes, and maybe even more than that. We'll see. He really is a very talented storyteller, and I could sit here and listen for a long time I'm sure, but do you know what I'm going to say, Margaret?"

"I sincerely hope I'm right, and it's about food because I am so hungry."

"You are right, and it's about food, because I am so hungry as well."

"Let's go forage."

*

"What are you thinking about, Richard? Care to share?"

"I was thinking about my sister and family and kind of wishing they were here to enjoy this evening, and they really would."

"I wish they were here too, Richard. I am so looking forward to their visit. Have they confirmed travel arrangements?"

"Yes, I'm sorry, darling. I talked to Sis this afternoon. The day has been so full. I haven't had a moment until now. They will be here on Xmas Eve."

"Really? That's great! I thought they wanted to come after Xmas. I'm so glad they are going to be with us for Xmas."

"So am I. They decided as a family that this is exactly where they would like to be for all the holiday time, so they will be here early afternoon of Xmas Eve, and they will go back on the evening of the first. They were concerned about interfering with our honeymoon arrangements, which I admitted we really don't have any real plan yet, and of course, my sister gave me a really bad time about that. I am excited about going away with you. Why do you think we haven't talked about it, Margaret?"

"That is a very interesting question, Richard. I'm of the same mind. I'm really not in a hurry to run away just after our wedding. I believe there are several considerations. We are quite frankly going to be quite tired, after all of the activities, events, guests, which is all good, but I am glad, actually relieved that you are not feeling an urgent need to run away on a honeymoon just because that's usually what happens. Also I am somewhat preoccupied with Howdy and a bit reluctant to leave him right now. So that's kind of where I am."

"I am so glad, Margaret. I absolutely want us to plan a trip together to take our time, and of course, Howdy is our priority. We'll see how that goes. In the meantime, we can share our dreams of travel and perhaps even create some new ones together. So I think we're both greatly relieved to have had this conversation? So thanks, Sis."

"Yes, we will both let her know how grateful we are to not be running away to somewhere for something when we really have everything we could ever want right here."

"Right."

"I do love you, my darling Margaret.

"And I you, my handsome Richard. That was almost a wedding vow. I am totally committed to us, Richard. I am looking forward to our wedding."

"So am I."

*

"The food was delightful, the conversation stimulating, and now, I'm ready to try the square dancing thing. How about you, my dear?"

"Let's go, Richard. The music has started."

"What a physical workout this evening has been. I am really out of shape, Margaret, and you were still going strong. I think I had better increase my exercise time."

"You will, darling. I will see to that."

"Well, we're almost home, and Howdy is actually snoring. Shall I carry him in?"

"We'll see, Richard. When you open the car door, he usually will respond. Yep, there he is. Yes, Howdy, we are home, and you have had a very special but long evening. Tomorrow, all of us will relax. No schedule, just eat, sleep, play, and then do it again."

"Margaret really!"

"Silly, I didn't mean that necessarily. Let's go to bed and warm up. I think I already have warmed up, that is. Richard, you are such a good bed buddy."

"You too. Umm, Margaret, when you said I would increase my physical exercise, you weren't kidding, were you? And I love it."

"Good night, love."

∗

"Good morning, Howdy, or should I say, Mr. Howdy? Or His Highness Howdy? What a wonderful day we had and evening. It was perfect, but today we will be relaxed, enjoy the fire, each other, and good food and drink. Umm, sounds delicious. Did Richard send you up here to get me out of bed? Well, it's going to work. I smell coffee, cinnamon, and other great aromas. So let's go see what's happening. If we have time, we'll do some stretches before breakfast. We both love doing that.

"You know, Howdy, a couple of my favorite yoga movements are actually ones that you have taught me. You do them so naturally, and they feel so good. So thank you, my friend. Richard will probably want to join us, and he really does need to. He could use a little loosening up."

"Good morning, my friends, and what brings you down so early, Margaret?"

"Well, first of all, it's really not that early. Richard, you remembered to put the touch of cinnamon in this wonderful coffee. Thank you so much, and it smells like you have breakfast under control. Anything I can do to help? I know that I am still in my pajamas, but I have washed my face and hands thoroughly, so is there anything I can do?"

"Not a thing. Why don't you and Howdy just relax, enjoy your coffee, and breakfast will be ready very soon."

"Oh yes, I fixed your special morning drink. It's on the counter by the coffee."

"Thank you so much, Richard."

"This has been such a cozy day, and very productive in such a quiet relaxing way. I think we have the house ready for guests, although I really don't think of your family as guests and certainly not Aunt Betts. I think this holiday is going to be such fun."

"Margaret, my beloved, I am so grateful to walk the pathway of life with someone as caring as you. You are truly a compassionate expression of God, as God. I feel your caring nature every time you bless me with love, which is truly a natural part of your presence. I am filled with hope as I breathe in the fresh air of each new day and feel fully alive."

"My dear Richard, you have such courage. You have faced fear, loss, and major challenges, ones known and still to be known, and have refused to be conquered by them for more than a moment. I believe you have the courage to climb any mountain, however insurmountable it may appear. You make wise choices and use good judgment. We are open to new adventures and respond to life with awe and joy. We will continue to embrace life with gratitude. We are so blessed."

*

"Thank you for taking Howdy out, Richard. I finally managed to shower and dress. I have really pampered myself today, as you may have noticed."

"Didn't you know, Margaret? King Howdy declared this a no-work zone or more accurately and indulge yourself in food, drink, and pleasure day."

"I think I must have known that. I just put on water for teatime. I took a package of Mary's frozen surprises out of the freezer, and they are ready to go into the oven."

"What do you mean exactly? Surprises. Just that she and her daughter had a bake day at home and several items were not labeled, so I became the lucky recipient."

"Whatever it is, it will be great, and yes, I love surprises. Howdy is really taking the day off seriously. He has hardly moved anything but his tail."

"Yeah, he's a little tired today. His outing this morning was very short, but then look at us. We're not bounding up the mountain either."

"No, we're not. I am very happy to sit inside today and watch the snowflakes fall, and from the amazing aroma coming from our cozy kitchen, we will further indulge in a heavenly concoction from Mary and a special tea that has the spicy aroma of freshly baked gingerbread."

"What a wonderful way to spend a frosty winter day, and your choice of music is perfect, Richard. I love it, and you know what? I think it sounds like a game of chess. What do you think?"

"Beethoven, chess, of course. I'd be happy to take the challenge."

"Richard, we have a never-ending game. It's fun though, huh?"

"Yes, however, I was sure I'd have you by now. Well, you know we don't have to finish right now. It's kind of like a puzzle. We can always pick up where we left off."

"OK, a time-out, we'll have dinner and then either resume or delay for another time. However, after I have eaten, I believe I'll be ready to go another round."

"Game on, Margaret. I love it. And I love you."

"We are very well-matched."

✳

"Now that we have had a delicious dinner and conversation, I am ready for a glass of wine. How about you?"

"Sounds great, and since Howdy is not going anywhere, let's join him. Howdy, my dear, you are a very tired king, aren't you? However, you are still very regal. Yes, you are. We're going to do some yoga stretches in a few minutes. I know you really like those. So think about it."

"Oh, we're going to do yoga, not chess, huh?"

"Yes, I had a mood swing, Richard. I've stretched my mind but not my body."

"Yoga sounds like a very good idea to me too."

"You're right. We have been very sedentary today, which is fine, but my body needs a little stretching. No, actually a lot. I kind of feel like a pretzel. That would be a great yoga position."

"Sure, shall we have music or quiet?"

"I would like music, and after yoga, some quiet meditation time."

"Perfect. This is a better choice than chess right now. Thank you for knowing that, Margaret."

∗

"Good morning, Howdy. I'm so glad to see that you are moving around today. Thank you for coming in to get me up. I needed the nudge. I am so lucky. Richard likes fixing breakfast, and you like to gently awaken me. What a team."

"Good morning, Richard. That was a nice before breakfast—the morning kiss. Thank you for those wonderful smells coming from the kitchen."

"You are oh so welcome. I love it when you fix breakfast also, Margaret, but I figure whoever gets up first gets the pleasure."

"I like that plan. It works for me. Did you send Howdy upstairs to check on me?"

"No, my dear, he did that all on his own."

"I'm so glad. He looks so much better this morning."

"He had a pretty demanding schedule, which he appeared to love every minute of, and he and Santa did get to take their breaks."

"Yes, that was so special. We really had a good time, didn't we, especially the dancing?"

"You know, Margaret, I really did. I actually felt like a kid again. I love knowing that there is no judgment or expectations. I have truly been able to finally trust that as real. At first, I was skeptical. I kept looking for the egg to crack, so to speak. I immediately felt your authenticity, but I couldn't imagine an entire town based on trust, acceptance, and love. No wonder it is so solid. By the way, is this a good time to get another lesson about community life?"

"Absolutely. I only have a small work project to complete today, and I'm doing it from here, so I have a very flexible schedule. What do you want to know?"

"It's regarding finances. I haven't been in a hurry to transfer funds, but it's definitely time to decide how I'm going to handle my finances. I haven't seen a bank, people accept my checks, but how does that work?"

"Richard, I'm so sorry. I didn't even think about our system being different. You do have options. There are banks in several towns within thirty to forty-five miles from here. So, of course, there is that option. The other one may be a little complicated for me to be clear enough with my information. It seems so simple to me, but that's because of my familiarity. So if I'm unclear, we'll go to the council, and they can thoroughly discuss the system with you. As a matter of fact, that's exactly what we should do. However, I will give you a thumbnail sketch.

"So let's get a cup of tea, get comfortable, and I'll give it a go. The founding council created a system for financial independence as well as everything else that it takes to sustain a community. Fortunately, the folks that were our founders were pretty much like-minded, although very independent individuals. They were spiritually based, and I find it very interesting that my great grandmother was chairman of the financial committee. As a matter of fact, she was very active in the entire project, but back to task."

"Margaret, I love hearing about those folks, and how this amazing town was founded and has thrived. So please share as much as you wish."

∗

"There is this financial resource vault, a system that was created by the committee. I believe there were, and still are, seven members. I'm sure the system has been adjusted, as is everything. Things are either changing or stagnating. However, my understanding is that the basic foundation has worked so well for this community that it has essentially survived.

"Members donate ten percent of their income, which goes into an investment account which is decided by the council and may be changed at any time. These are designated funds under a 501c-3 non-profit status, a college fund that continues in perpetuity.

"All youth that choose and are accepted by a university have access to scholarships. If they choose other training, the same access is provided.

"Another 10 percent of income is also provided and invested. That money is available to anyone who has either a personal or business need. There is no interest charged, and the individual creates a proposal of how, maybe labor, and when to return the funds. That can be adjusted as necessary, and the council can choose to forgive the transaction if they find it to be in the best interest of the party or parties involved.

"This system has been very effective. It is built on trust and respect. And to my knowledge, it has never been abused. Another element that has been added is the ability to hold in trust an agreed upon amount to accommodate our summer visitors primarily, although anyone may use it.

One ATM machine has been installed in the post office of our town, and one window space in the post office is designated for banking services. Community members seldom use it. We actually have very little need for money. We just sign the receipt, and the business sends it to the financial council monthly, and we receive our statement.

*

"I always keep some money available. I often have meetings in another county, so it's convenient. As I imagine you already know we donate at least 10 percent of our time in a community activity. Oh yes, there is also a savings option. We have maintained a sound financial structure. No business goes bankrupt and no homes are foreclosed. No one has ever needed to be hungry or uncared for. There is an annual audit and a report is posted at the spiritual center, and anyone may have a copy and can attend the annual meeting.

"I hope I have been helpful Richard, and have given you enough information that you will be prepared with your questions to the council. I know there are more technical things like being insured and structural related information. To my knowledge, everyone in town is a member of the cooperative system, and I have never heard a complaint.

"Oh yes, we do train the children in economics and have them become very familiar with the system as it functions outside of our community. We want everyone to understand that our way is not the only way."

"Margaret, I continue to be amazed at how this all works. It seems both very simple and yet my mind keeps thinking it must be more complex, but I love it. I definitely want to become a member. So give me a name, and I'll take it from here, and yes, as always, you were very helpful. I am actually falling in love with this town."

"That's a good thing, Richard, since you have pretty much committed yourself to living here. I'm glad you're becoming immersed. It takes time, and those of us that have a history here, take things for granted, so it is so refreshing to see things from a new perspective.

"We have time if you'd like to hear about our auto and bicycle system. I'm cramming a little because your sister and family will be here soon, and the more you know, the better."

"So shall we have another cup of tea with scones and continue?"

"Absolutely."

"I'll get them, Margaret."

"You're doing all the work here, and I am definitely being entertained. Again, Richard, my familiarity may make me a bit myopic, but generally speaking, we have a carpool. The council has purchased five cars, again under a non-profit business. They belong to the community. Members may use them by the day or up to thirty days if they are going out of town. Tourists may use them also and pay a maintenance, insurance and replacement fee, which are $20 a day or $100 for a week.

"There is also a bicycle option. That is a very popular item for our summer visitors. Those are $10 a day. That fee is utilized the same as the cars. Those are designated funds."

"Margaret, that is a fantastic plan. Is this a newer concept?"

"Actually not. There were horse and buggies or just horses. When the community was smaller, everything was collective—all the equipment and building materials. Most folks need their own equipment now. Although there are still a lot of items available to check out."

"I love it, Margaret."

"Enough information for now, Richard. I need to get some work done, and Howdy is standing by the door patiently waiting. Would you be willing to take him out?"

"I'd love to, Margaret. I love you, you know?"

"I do know, Richard. I am very happy."

✳

"Howdy, I am a very grateful man. I love living here and everything about it, and the more I learn about this community, the more I want to know about the founders and how this has been preserved so well. It's like the town has a protective bubble around it and yet, I have never felt like a stranger here. There was an immediate feeling of peace, which has never left.

"Shall we rest for a few minutes, fellow? I was so involved in my thoughts, I picked up the pace a bit. Sorry, Howdy, come here and warm up a bit. We'll take our time going back. I'll let you lead. You really love this spot, don't you? You are totally here."

Such a gift. I love sharing information about our town with Richard. He is so open and anxious to know everything. I tend to forget that he doesn't. Actually, there is so much more. I do need to prepare him for the

Christmas traditions. This month always has wings, especially this year when the house and the cottage will be full of life and laughter.

I am so looking forward to having family to share with. It is really hard not to go down to the cottage. Whatever Richard is doing with it is definitely top secret. I am sure it will be a delightful surprise. Just a few more days. Patience—I am learning to understand the word a little better, but I do have a ways to go before I can honestly say it's a treasure. Time to get to work. I do have a deadline, and it is here. I will talk with Richard about the Xmas traditions later but certainly not much later. Also I think it is time for me to get back to my list-making habit. I need a little more structure, and that's one way that I know works for me.

*

"Something smells so good, and I am very hungry. You two were gone a long time I finished my project. Made a task list and this heavenly dinner. Howdy, are you all right?"

"Yes, Margaret, he's fine. We stopped by the Millers' place, and he got a lot of gentle loving care and a few treats. Sorry, we were gone so long, but unlike me, I totally lost track of time."

"Richard, that's my line."

"Yes, I know, but it is true. What a great family! When I smelled the bread baking, I realized that we had probably been gone for longer than I thought, and by the way, I still smell break baking and some other wonderful aromas. What is on the menu for this evening, and can I help?"

"We are having Balsamic-garlic pork tenderloins, roasted vegetables, and sweet potatoes with coconut oil, cinnamon, and other spices and, of course, dinner rolls. Yes, if you would be willing to set the table, and check on the fire, that would be great."

"Margaret, I'll clean up in the kitchen later. Dinner was delightful. Thank you. Howdy is sleeping soundly, and he looks so peaceful."

"I'm so glad you had a nice visit with the Millers', darling, and yes, let's join him, and if you'd like, I could tell you about some of our Xmas traditions. That would give you a little time to consider some options."

"Sounds intriguing, Margaret. Yes, my dear, spin your web. I will gladly enter the circle. Really, I am eager to learn."

*

"I love this season and all of the activities so I get really involved. Just remember there are no expectations, and you need to go at your own pace. We have a three-day workshop event at the center, and yes, it is kind of like I would imagine Santa's workshop to be. We start on the twentieth. The center is open from 9:00 a.m. to 10:00 p.m. for three days. And there is a resource team available for all of that time. However the real events are from 9:00 a.m. to 12:00 noon, lunchtime, and again from 1:00 p.m. to 4:00 p.m. Dinner is served also. There are a variety of options, such as making jewelry, woodcraft, sewing, writing, and baking, making cards. For every interest, there is a craft coach and several assistants. All of the materials are there. This is where Xmas gifts are created. Gifts can be made for family and friends. One of the traditions that continue to work well for us is that children may ask Santa for one gift—a bicycle or a special game, or a doll and a gift of clothing. Everything else is handcrafted at the center, and I am always impressed with the creativity, quality, and teamwork that happen at these workshops.

"I will be one of the coaches for making cards and creating poetry. We never buy or mail cards to anyone in the community, and we make Xmas tree ornaments out of the old ones. It is so much fun. Primarily, the children are there for the morning and afternoon workshops, and after dinner, they go home and the adults get to play. That's when the sleighs, doll buggies, high chairs, and beautiful things are created. So what do you think, Richard?"

"As usual, darling, the beauty of this place and the simplicity, which is so honest and has such clarity of values, blows me away. So does that mean you are willing to be a coach?"

"I am willing, but am I capable? What would I do?"

"I think you have several choices, Richard. I know you are very good with building things, and you love it, and writing would be a natural. The children actually create storybooks as gifts or write special letters to their parents or loved ones. It is really a rewarding experience. I always feel like I get much more than I give. The energy is great and seeing how proud they are when they complete a project, and there is also the wrapping station where they choose the paper, and they can choose a card or create one.

"I just have one dilemma myself this year. What in the world will I create for you?"

"My darling, Margaret, you have already created it, and it is you."

"Thank you, Richard, but I really want to do something, and I'm sure it will come to me at the right time."

"Yes, I am sure it will. I am really excited about this, Margaret. I've never been much of a Christmas person, but I am now."

"Richard, I have to ask again, when do I get to see the cottage?"

"Very soon, darling. There have been a few delays, but everything is back on track and probably will be ready for the unveiling by mid-week or so soon. You have been so patient. I know it's a challenge for you and also I appreciate your complete trust in my judgment with making changes. I know that had to be somewhat challenging, and I certainly understand and marvel at how you could be so trusting."

"Yes, to be perfectly honest, it was a bit of a struggle at first, but after mediation there was complete release, except for curiosity."

"Oh, Richard, I am so sorry, I forgot to tell you your sister called. She said for you not to call back this evening, they will be out. We had a wonderful conversation. I am so comfortable talking to her. It's like we have known each other forever. I am so excited about their visit, and she asked if we could Skype which I think would be wonderful, and we do have the computer system at the library. So you guys can figure that out when you call her tomorrow."

"I am so glad you two are having conversations, and Skypeing is a natural option. That's exciting. I haven't actually seen them for quite a while. The children are probably not really children anymore or probably don't think they are. What evening would be best for library access, Margaret?"

"We have family game night on Tuesday, poetry and reading group on Wednesday. Thursday is a quiet night if it works for them. If not, we'll find a way to make it work at their convenience."

"What is your work schedule this week?"

"I plan to work tomorrow probably from nine to three and Tuesday about the same, and Wednesday from eleven to five. I have meetings scheduled that day. I have already worked at home for five hours. It's kind of a challenge to keep myself scheduled with my new part-time position. I love it but, during this training period, I may need to expand my commitment for a short time. I am planning to be free for the week before Xmas, and most of the week after Xmas."

"Margaret, very soon we will be husband and wife. I am so looking forward to that time."

"So am I, Richard. So many emotions and activities. Fortunately, my energy is very solid throughout this entire season. It has always been a magical time for me. There is so much love shared throughout this month, and as a spiritual community, everyone seems to absolutely glow. The energy is contagious, Richard, so be prepared."

"I am ready to receive and give, Margaret. I have already felt the surge."

"I'm not surprised, darling. You are a solid source of warmth for me."

"Now you're just trying to seduce me, woman, and if even you're not trying, you're still doing it. Let's leave the dishes. I have a much better idea for now."

"What dishes? Richard, I love you so much, and I love your better idea."

＊

"Well, that was fun. You do have a lot of energy."

"So do you, darling. It's a good thing because now we get to go downstairs and clean the kitchen, remember?"

"Honestly, no. I didn't remember anything but how much I love you."

"That's sweet, and I love it. Now move your body and let's go do it."

"You are a slave driver, woman."

"I'm glad you know that about me, Mr. King."

"You must be really serious. When I get the Mr. King honor, I'm up, and I'm moving."

"Let's go."

＊

"Good morning, Richard. Coffee's ready. Blueberry hotcakes on the griddle."

"Hi, darling, you smell like laundry freshly picked."

"Thank you, but I'll just bet
I run a close second to the bacon, and hotcakes."

"Close call. I'll do the orange juice."

211

"By the looks of Howdy at rest, I would say you two have been out already, right?"

"Oh yes, we did our yoga routine, our quite short walk, and he was ready to snuggle by the fireplace."

"Well, I know I love snuggling by the fireplace, with you."

"Oh yes, there is magic to that spot."

"Which spot are you referring to, Margaret?"

"OK, don't get me started. Let's have breakfast, and then I am ready for the day. I have a meeting in about four minutes. I'm a very busy woman, you know."

"Yes, I do know that. I will prepare a feast for you tonight, and yes, Howdy and I will be fine. We have a full schedule today also, and I will definitely be conscious of his needs."

"I know you will, Richard, and I am so glad he has both of us now. Have a great day, darlings, and I will see you around four, maybe five. I have some errands to do for the center."

"We'll be here, Margaret."

✻

"Howdy, my friend, we are back to the cottage project. The supplies have all arrived, and the crew is ready to go. This is really a big day. I am a bit overwhelmed from time to time, but that amazing group of skilled guys is so reassuring, and so far, it is like they are reading my mind and are ever at least one step ahead, which is a good thing because time is of the essence. Yay! The sun is out, no clouds, or rain in sight, perfect. Let's go, buddy. I see the trucks pulling in with lots of good stuff. We will have fun today."

"Hi, guys. Everyone ready for a miracle?"

"Mr. King, we are a miracle. We have the reclaimed timber, and it is perfect. We also have bamboo for the floors and the complete array of solar equipment. Man, we are cooking!"

"Wow! I am impressed and the entire crew is here. This is exciting, and Margaret is getting very curious. I wouldn't be able to stall her much longer."

"Well, my friend, you won't have to because we are good to go."

"Guys, you all know what to do, so do it. Richard and I are going to review the plans one more time. I've added just a few things I think you're going to like."

"I am pretty sure I will. Margaret trusts me, and I really trust you, guys, so let's take a look."

"Basically, we have an thousand-and-two-hundred-square-foot area to work with, so obviously every foot counts. Fortunately, most of the newer homes around here, as you may have noticed, are rather small, and they are all what is now known as green. We've just always tried to be creative and efficient. Fortunately, more choices are available now as for as supply options go. So we can work faster, and we have great options. So just to review, we have the high ceilings in the living room, which reflect light flooding down the hallways through the front entry doors. The timbered knee braces create the illusion of arches, separating the living room and kitchen lofty yet cozy. Your idea, Richard. A darn good one, and this is a new suggestion—single light glass doors for both bedrooms and the bathroom. Margaret can choose fabric to cover them for privacy. What do you think?"

"Yes is what I think. What else do you have?"

"We do have the solar water heater system you wanted. It will heat both your domestic water needs and water for the floor, which will run through a self-contained loop. A gas furnace provides supplemental heating, which you probably won't use very often, but it's nice to have options. Another plus for using the reclaimed lumber, which is all local, by the way. There will be a really pleasant smell to the cottage, and our cabinet makers are magicians. The grain will look continuous and panels mirror each other. They plan to make the all-purpose dining-cum-game table from a peach tree that fell over in a storm.

"Did you remember that I want extensions for the table and benches, which will add storage?"

"Oh yes and more. We have been able to fit in a mini pantry in the kitchen as well as the window seat at the end of the living room which has a spectacular view of the ocean and has pullout shelves underneath for game storage, and we added bookshelves on either side of the seat."

"All of this is absolutely perfect and of course Margaret and I have our writing desks in a nook, between the two bedrooms. This is a happy house."

"It always has been, Richard, because it's always been filled with love. We're just providing some conveniences."

"You are absolutely right. We also received the garden window for the kitchen and the seen room material, you know for expanding the front porch and having the option of opening it in the summer or closing it when you wish and still having your view completely unobstructed. I think this part of the project I want to do because it is so special. You know we are probably going to be having a lot of guests when they find out about this."

"My sister and family will really enjoy it. They all love the ocean, and I know Margaret and I will spend more time here, writing, and on other projects. This will be a work of art itself and would bring much joy to many. I love everything you have presented. Now I hear the music and the sound of happy people doing what they love to do. Shall we join them? I am a very good gofer as well as a great lunch provider."

"OK, Richard, full steam ahead. We will get this done. Has Margaret's schedule changed?"

"Oh yes, actually it has, and it gives us more time. You, guys, can swing it. She's working until about five this evening and much the same for the next few days."

"Well, I'm estimating we'll only need about that much time to finish. So we may have the unveiling by the end of this week."

"Sounds good to me. We'll have a really big party, only we'll have it in the big house, not here. We'll save this one for now."

"Good idea, Richard. You, Margaret, and Howdy need to spend some time here together before anyone else does. It is a very special spot, and I feel privileged to have an opportunity to be a part of its rebirth. Now I had better get to work and let you do the same."

"Yes indeed, a labor of love."

"Guys, I didn't even ring the bell for lunch, and here you are. We just had to follow our noses. Whatever it is, it smells delicious, and we are hungry."

"Good, I made enough stew for an army, which you sort of are. So grab a bowl and help yourself—fresh bread from the oven on the stove by the stewpot, and that's it."

"What! No dessert?"

"Oh yes, I didn't forget that I brought cookies from our freezer. They're in the oven. How late are you guys going to be able to work?"

"Most of us will be here until four, and tomorrow, you and Howdy are evicted. We will be in here, and it won't be a pretty sight. We need to have you box and move everything to the back bedroom, Richard. Sorry, I didn't mention that this morning. Will you need some help?"

"No, I have the boxes labeled and have actually already started, except for the kitchen, and that won't take long."

"I'm not surprised. You're always a step ahead. That's great."

"We may need to have you pick up some things from town tomorrow, if you don't mind."

"I would love to do any and everything I can to help. This is really exciting and scary."

"I know what you mean, Richard, but it is going so well, and Margaret is going to love it."

"Thank you, I needed that. OK, guys, grab your cookie. Break time's over. Let's do it!"

"Howdy, we are totally committed to this project. Somehow it hasn't seemed so real until today. I'm glad I won't be here tomorrow. I have a feeling it will look and be total chaos. I know from that chaos will be order. You and I may just curl up on the rug in front of the fire and sleep the day away. What do you think? Good plan, right? What a day. I believe I told Margaret I was preparing dinner tonight. Boy, am I glad I have leftover stew. I'll just make a salad. Pour a glass of wine, and we're good. Move over, Howdy. I need a little room here too. That's better. This is a special spot, and it's really great for napping. I probably snore as loud as you do. You are getting louder fellow. Maybe because you're just getting really tired. You are a good friend, Howdy."

"Well, look at you two sleeping in the middle of the day, while I've been working like a dog. Did you get that, Howdy? Really, you look very comfortable, and I just had to come in and rouse you out of your reveries."

"Sorry, Margaret, honestly we just lay down, at least not long ago. What time is it anyhow?"

"About 5:30 p.m. I had several errands after work. I'm thinking that was a good thing."

"Come here, my dear sweet hardworking lady. Come, rest with us. I love you, umm you too. Yes, you too, Howdy."

"It's good to be home."

"You and Howdy hang out together. I made stew for dinner tonight. So I'll go toss a salad, heat the stew, and rolls, and dinner will be ready."

"Sounds great. Howdy, my friend, I'm going to go change clothes, and I'll be right back."

"Dinner was perfect, Richard. I love the way we just do what needs to be done without missing a beat. Do you know what I mean?"

"Yes, I think I do, Margaret. We have both been independent for so long that we just know what it takes to keep life flowing. You know, food, shelter, love. We both know how to cook, clean house, do laundry, shop, and I'll bet that you even know how to change lightbulbs and probably a lot more. I'll admit I do have limitations, when I need an electrician, or a plumber. I know whom to call."

"That's great because I don't know how to do either of those things, so we'll keep the numbers handy. How was everything at work today?"

"Flowed like a river, a calm river. I had a great day, and Mary made her very special bread pudding today, and I just remembered she sent some home with me, but I left it in the car."

"It's certainly not going to stay there. I'll be right back. I'll turn the oven on. It's so good warm, and she also sent some raisin sauce with it."

✳

"This is so good. Honestly, I only had a tiny taste earlier today. I wanted to enjoy it here with you tonight."

"Thank you. I missed you today, but I was very busy with my project. That's why I was taking a break when you came home."

"Your project? The cottage?"

"Yes and no. You can't see it yet, but very soon, I promise."

"OK, I'll be patient, sort of. By the way, when do you like to decorate and put your Xmas tree up? We haven't really talked much about that."

"Honestly, Margaret, I haven't done very much in the way of holiday festivities since Sylvia and I were together, but I definitely am in the holiday spirit now, and I am really very interested in what you usually do, and I'm betting it's a lot."

"I think you're right, Richard. I start with the lights outside. Now don't be nervous. We always have a lot of help. I have about probably two or three thousand lights."

"Really!"

"Yes, darling, really. They are spectacular, and I love them. I'm sure I will too at some point. My parents started the outside light tradition and after they died, I started the house decoration potluck party tradition. Xmas has always been so special to me, and it was to them. The first year was a bit challenging, but it was wonderful to have friends close. Actually, they are family also. At the next event, we get lots of fresh garland and pinecones and start decorating the house, and we have a decorating party for that, and everyone brings food. We have hot cider, hot chocolate, and it's a great party. Usually about twenty to thirty folks come for that, and they all know what they're doing, so it goes well. We sing carols, and someone plays the piano."

"Margaret, is this for real, or are you teasing me?"

"Oh, this is for real, Richard, very real. The last thing we do is decorate the tree, and then it's like a magical change. Everything is bright, and shiny. This year what we'll do that's different is only you, I, and your family will decorate the Xmas tree at the cottage, if you'd like?"

"Margaret, I would love it, and I am a little awed by the activities. However I am also absolutely positive that I will love every minute of it. I knew it would be special, but I can't begin to imagine how special it will all turn out to be. But I'm ready."

"You certainly are, Richard. I love you so much."

"Margaret, you feel so good and fit so well right here in my arms."

∗

"Good morning, Howdy. I've missed you the past few mornings. I probably have you confused with my new schedule. I know I am. I'm not really sure what schedule is anymore, but I am sure that I love it when you're waiting patiently for me to awaken. You know the month of December is always a little crazy. Well, it promises to be a bit crazy this year. But in a good way. When there's too much going on, you can always come in here and rest. It's quiet, and your bed is nice and warm. You'll be fine, and I had better get a move on. Lots to do today. Just a few more days, and the guys will be by to check out the Xmas lights. We replaced a lot last year, probably not so much this time. We'll see. One thing at a time. Deep breathing time, Howdy."

∗

"Howdy, I'm going to do you a favor, fellow. I'm going to let you stay here by the fire. It's pretty cold today, and I could see you shivering on our outing. I'll check back with you after lunch. It's going to be really kind of crazy at the cottage today. As a matter of fact, if I feel like I'm in the way, I'll be back sooner. Everyone will miss you, but they are really going to be loud, and moving fast, so you just take it easy. Stay warm and I'll see you shortly."

"Good morning, everyone. I could hear you before I could see you. Good thing Margaret left early this morning."

"Actually, Richard, I checked to make sure her car was gone before we really got into it. We all really want to be in on the surprise."

"I think I know what you mean, but I am sure it's going to be a great surprise. If not, I'll just blame you, guys."

"Oh no, you don't I have your plans in my possession."

"You got me, so we had better just get this right."

"So we shall. Do you guys want me to be a gofer or help with whatever or get out of the way?"

"Probably all of the above. Everyone's started on their part of the project, so we'll soon know if anything is needed. Also we could use you to help out with the front porch redo."

"Great! I'd love to. I just really don't want to slow you down."

"Richard, I have seen your woodworking skills. You are very precise, and you are not afraid to ask questions. You will be a great help."

"OK, I'm ready to go, and by the way, I made sandwiches for today, and a great soup is cooking. So lunch is easy."

"Good thing, you do not want to see these guys when their lunch is late. Not a pretty sight."

"I can only imagine, never really want to know."

"There's Bob now. He's the lead guy for the project you're going to work on. Bob, I found a volunteer for you. I know Bill had to be away today, so Richard is available."

"Great, Richard, come on, let's go, we have a lot to do, and we are really glad to have you on our team. We are just ready to have our meeting, so we're sure everyone knows the plan, and if there are questions or suggestions about what we are doing, you can ask us. Charles, you will be Richard's coach, and you can work together. Is that all right with you?"

"Absolutely. Glad to have you, Richard. Maybe you can help out tomorrow also."

"I would love to. We plan to finish tomorrow, and that's always a time for celebration. Hallelujah. Let's go circle up. Bill left a few suggestions for me to pass on to the team. This five minutes or so that we spend in preparation for the day's work is so worth it. I doubt that we would really be a team without it."

"Sounds like a great idea to me. Of course anything probably would. Well, almost anything."

"I am really excited to be an active part of this project. Especially this particular part. There is such a spectacular view here, and now it can be enjoyed year round. I don't mind telling you, Richard, it was a real challenge to design and a bigger challenge to find everything we needed for it. Our building goal is always to think sustainability and to get everything we need as close to home as possible. So we often have to spend a little time on researching options.

"This was one time I was grateful for computers, and I am glad that I finally can honestly say that. I have had a block about using the computer. Now I know and accept the value of the tool. Doesn't mean I'm going to jump right to it as a first choice, but it's good to know it's here, and I feel good about it."

"Lots of good ideas, guys. Thank you very much. Now to put those plans into action."

"Let's do it. Richard, I'll check back in with you shortly. Now I need to move around. We have cabinet team, skylight teams, flooring teams, and I'm not sure what to call this team, I guess I'll call you guys the visionary team. Anyhow, I'd better keep moving. See you later."

"You bet."

"Howdy, lunchtime came too soon. I was really getting into the rhythm, when I was reminded about the time. I am having a great time. It's noisy and looks like mayhem with people moving in all directions. I swear I don't know how they do it, but they do. I think it has to do with concentration. I know that is true for me. I have a certain thing to do, and as I really get into doing it, everything else fades into the background. It's all kind of like a puzzle. I am beginning to see the outline, and gradually the pieces are beginning to fill in.

"Howdy, you are the best listener I have ever had. You always look interested, and never go to sleep while I'm talking, and sometimes I'm sure you're nodding your head in agreement. Thanks, fella. Well, I'd better get this food down to the zoo and feed the animals. I'm really glad that they have that portable greenhouse for shelter. It's actually pretty warm in there, and we couldn't eat in the cottage right now. It is a mess. I sure wouldn't want Margaret to see it right now. See you later, Howdy."

"Dinner bell gong time, you guys in the greenhouse, come and get it. It's getting colder out there. We really need one more clear day. For now, we are fine. Embrace the moment. I can hear Margaret saying, be grateful for this moment right now, and so I am. It is a perfect day."

*

"Mary, I love having this Book Nook Bakery here, although I'll admit the alluring aromas that escape into my office often entice me to take a break."

"Yes, and a much deserved break it is, Margaret. This is the time of year that we always celebrate. Time for laughter, remembering good times past and creating memories in the moment. I believe it's time for us to have a tea and talk break."

"Mary, I can always depend on you for honesty, and holding up the mirror so I can take a look. So yes, let's go into the inner room, so you can have a go at me."

"It's nice to have your permission to fire at will, my dear girl. You appear to be missing the point of Xmas, quite frankly you are actually putting a damper on the whole place. You always set the tone around here, and that's a good thing. So I believe you need to take a few deep breaths and then share with me what you think about what I've said and how you feel about it, and get to the core of what's bothering you."

"As always, Mary, you know me, perhaps better than I know myself. Here goes. I'm just going to open my mouth, and we'll both see what comes out without a filter. Basically, I am healthy and very happy. I love the changes in my life and work. Sharing is a great thing, and that's going well, it's just a little demanding right now. Perhaps I'm trying to rush it, and I really don't need to. I know it's going well, and there is not a deadline for anything. So there's that. Next thing that comes to mind is Howdy. He is very frail, Mary. His spirit is still there, but I feel him slipping away. Again, we know that's happening, and I am really prepared, as much as one can be.

"He and Richard have become so close that I really don't feel guilty about leaving him while I am here because I know they have a special bond also. Mary, I already feel so much lighter. I think just taking time to clear my head and heart is something I really needed."

"Yes, my darling girl, and I'm going to get us another cup of tea and a fresh-out-of-the-oven muffin, and you take a few more deep breaths, and I believe you will find a few more things to clear out the cobwebs."

"Mary, you are a saint."

"Oh no, let's not go that far. I'm a talker, as everyone knows, but, Margaret, I'm also a very good listener, and I know you and love you like you were my daughter, so I can tell when you start getting all bottled up, and Richard will learn that about you. However, I think you are learning that you need to open up, before you get a full head of steam going on inside, don't you think?"

"Yes, I do, Mary, and you're right, Richard is learning to push my open-up buttons. I think to sort of sum it all up. I have not been keeping my routine, I mean, my spiritual ones, especially meditation which really helps me live in the moment. Mary, that's it! That's what all of this is about. I am off track, and my energy is scattered. Oh bless you, my dear mentor. I feel so grounded now, Mary, and definitely back on track. So indeed it is a time for celebration, gratitude, and appreciation, and we shall get about brightening this place up. Thank you, my dear friend. I love you, Mary."

"And I you, my sweet girl. Here's a care package for you to take home tonight, and tell that handsome guy of yours that we miss him around here, and give my love to our Howdy. I put something in there for him as well."

"Again thank you, Mary. I do have just a few more things to do then I'll be out of here. I'll see you tomorrow then I'm off for five days, and I won't think about work at all, and there's no need for me to."

"See you in the morning, love."

✶

"What a productive day. Honestly, when we started this morning, I was a little concerned that so many people in such a small space, doing so many different things at once, well it just looked very confusing to me. Until I started focusing on my team, and my part of the job, then nothing else existed. Now I look around this place, and I am astonished. It is perfect, and we are just about finished, aren't we? We have a pretty full day tomorrow Richard. We still do have a lot of finish work to do. As well as the cleaning up, although we have learned pretty well to clean up as we go, but yes, we are on or very close to the finish line. So celebration time tomorrow for sure. So we'll be off now and see you in the morning. Thank you, guys. You are the best."

"Hi, Howdy, do you want to go out for a stretch? Let's go. Margaret will be home very soon, and I don't have any idea what we're doing for dinner, but I do know I had a terrific day. You're going to love the cottage, pal. I know I do. It was already a great place, but now, it is truly a refuge for us. It's a great party place and guest quarters. I think it's going to bring joy to a lot of people. That didn't take long, I'm glad, it is getting really cold out here. I feel a little ice rain. Back to the fireplace for you, and I'll go clean up a bit, and hopefully think of something creative and easy for dinner."

*

"Hi, Margaret, are you home a little early or am I just running late?"

"I am a little early, and how in the world could you be later, Richard? I'm considering tossing our clocks and watches."

"Well, what brought this on?"

"Mary and I had a little mother-daughter chat sort of. It was very good for me. I was forgetting the most important things and focusing on details. I realize there needs to be details, but not to the point of blocking the love and light of life."

"Sounds like you two had a real discussion."

"Mostly me, darling. Mary holds up the mirror, and I just see what's reflected back. Anyhow, enough of that for now. It's really good to be home."

"I love you and Howdy."

"Yes, I missed you too, and I am so glad to see you."

"Margaret, darling, I haven't even started dinner. I hope you're not starving."

"Mary the magician sent another care package home, Richard. I am so glad you haven't started anything. That's perfect. I have no idea what she sent, but I do know it will be a wonderful treat. You can find out what we're having for dinner if you want. I'm going upstairs to get into something more comfortable. Tonight I am getting back into the yoga and meditation routine. You two can certainly join me if you'd like. Be right back."

"Dinner was so good, comfort food, chicken and dumplings, green beans, and that great salad you made, and then of course Mary's famous apple cobbler with caramel sauce. Thank you, Richard, for putting it all together."

"I know you're very busy this week also. It was a pleasure, and I also really mean it was a pleasure. Thank Mary for me, will you, darling?"

"Next week, I'll bring Howdy to the children's story time, if he's up to it, and I'll see Mary then."

"Richard, you'll see her tomorrow, remember? We are Skyping your sister and family. I believe you said five o'clock, unless it's changed."

"Oh no, Margaret. It hasn't changed. I had simply forgotten. That doesn't sound very good. I really am excited about talking to them and especially seeing them. I know the children are probably not really children anymore. Thank you so much for reminding me and for being a list maker. I'm almost convinced that I should become one. I have boasted more than once about my wonderful memory, and time management, however not so much anymore."

"Richard, you are so organized and naturally thoughtful. I'm pretty sure you would have remembered. But if not, we make a pretty good team on all levels."

"Yes, that we do. Tomorrow is Thursday, right?"

"Yes, my dear."

"Well, you will get a tour of the cottage on Friday."

"Richard, I have been trying to be patient, but honestly I was ready to sneak down there and have just a little look. So now you have saved me from myself. I can wait one more day."

"You have been an angel about this entire project, Margaret. I am sure you will love it as much as I do."

"Maybe even more, Richard. I haven't shared this yet, but I have longed for the time, energy, and the real motivation to renovate the cottage. It is such a jewel. I know you and that fantastic team have enhanced it the way it should be. However I am really, really glad that Friday is the day for the unveiling, and thank you. Yes, Howdy, thank you too. I'm sure you were a good watchdog, and I'm sure there were times when that creative bunch of guys needed watching."

"They really are special, Margaret. I swear they are magicians."

$$*$$

"Good morning, Margaret. Everything is ready. Howdy and I have been out in the brisk morning air. Really, you should dress in layers today. It's supposed to warm up, but it is very cold right now."

"I am such a pampered person, Richard—a great breakfast, a grateful Howdy, and a weather report. What more could a person want?"

"I'll just bet if we put you to the challenge, you could come up with quite a list."

"You know me very well, my friend."

"Shall I meet you at the library about five or so, Margaret?"

"Yes, darling, that would be great. I think your sister said any time after five, and I have plenty to do to keep me busy, so if you're there between five and six that would be fine. Speaking of plenty to do. I'd better be on my way. I have a nice fully packed day."

"As a matter of fact, so do I. So be on your way, woman."

"Howdy, you can come to the library this evening and meet the family, and Mary really misses you. So I'm sure you will get special treats, as always. Love you, guys. Later."

"Howdy, we're working inside today at the cottage, so when I come back for lunch, you can come back down with me, so I'll see you soon."

"What a great surprise! This is a piece of art, guys. Where did you get it?"

"We created it, Richard. It was Bill's idea at first, and then we just got on a roll. We used concrete pavers and landscape wall materials, and we always have pre-built brick ones and grills. Our ulterior motive was to build an outdoor cooking option that could accommodate a large number of people.

"I know Margaret already has what we call the Egg, and it is great for indoor or outdoor use. It works well for small family gathering, but this will work for your very large extended family gatherings. You know, like us."

"I am overwhelmed. This is absolutely beautiful, and you have found the perfect spot for it, and you've made tables and benches from pallets?"

"That's right, and they all fold up for easy storage. We are all blessed. All of you have such skill, imagination, love, and it shows in everything you do. Thank you. Margaret and I will treasure this. It is a masterpiece, and yes, indeed our extended family will definitely be invited to many gatherings, and I hope at least some of you know how to cook on it, and I'll be glad to help."

"Speaking of help, we had better get inside and finish the job. I promised Margaret she could see it tomorrow. I am going down to the library about 5:30 p.m. Then I'll take her out to dinner, so if you need it, you'll have until about eight o'clock tonight. I don't think we'll be running that close, but there's always the little things that sometimes give us a challenge. So it's good to have a little cushion."

"OK, everyone, team up, and let's get this done."

*

"Good morning, Mary. I don't have time right now, and I know you don't, but let's try to get together for lunch. Would you be willing to call me after your lunch crowd is under control? I really want to talk to you."

"You bet, darling. I'll give you a ring probably just a little after one o'clock. Can you give me a hint?"

"Yes, my wedding gown, and we're Skypeing Richard's sister and family tonight. I am so excited I can't think straight. Maybe I can help, I know I can listen."

"Thank you, Mary. You do know that you are my surrogate mom, don't you? I really am missing her. She was so excited about Chad and I planning our wedding. I really am feeling her presence. I have to go. You have a full house gathering, so see you later, Mary."

"Margaret, is this a good time for you? People kept coming. We finally actually ran out of food, except for what I stowed away for us. Sorry it's so late."

"Perfect timing, Mary. I just finished the calendar through June. That was my major item for today. I'll be right over, and I am so glad you saved some food for us. I am ready to eat. Come and get it."

"Oh, Mary, this is delicious. You make the best bread I have ever tasted. I don't care which kind you make, it is the best."

"I've been at it for a long time, darling. I started making bread when I was seven years old. I'm sure my mother knew something was wrong with her, although I never remember a complaint or a grimace. She was always up early, worked hard, sang songs as she worked, and had a smile on her face and in her voice. She was very serious about my sister and I was learning how to do things. Everything—canning, cooking, and laundry—but she made sure we also had some time for playing.

"My specialty always was bread-making. Probably because everyone bragged on it so much and really loved the feel of dough."

"I still do. People are not only bragging about it, they are always lined up to buy it."

"Thank you, Margaret, but we're here to talk about you and the exciting things that are happening to you, like a wedding and a new family."

"Mary, I am so blessed, and I am not having any challenge with writing in my gratitude journal. There is so much. Okay, first thing, my wedding gown. I know everything is going fine, but I haven't heard a word, since we designed it. Betty got my measurements."

"Now what do you need to know?"

"I'm not sure, just that everything's going well, and when will I try it on? I guess primarily, when do I get to see it?"

"Almost any time now, Margaret. We have some fine finish work to do, and it will be complete. So I can see it next week?"

"Yes, darling. You can see it, try it on, feel it, touch it, and smell it if you want. We've put it in a box with lavender."

"Oh, Mary, I love you so much."

"Thank you. I know it's perfect, and I am so happy."

"Now what is this other thing you're doing tonight, about Richard's family?"

"Are you familiar with Skypeing, Mary?"

"No, I can't say that I am. Unless it has something to do with food, I probably don't know much about it, and no, I don't have any idea about whatever it is you said."

"Well, I wouldn't either, except I've been able to use it several times for conferences instead of going out of town. That's why, and how I am familiar with it. You can see and talk to people wherever they are, and usually the reception is very good, and it is conversational, and that's how I'm meeting Richard's sister, brother in-law, and their two children tonight. By the way, Richard said to tell you hi, and he misses seeing you. He and Howdy will be here between 5:30 p.m. and 6:00 p.m. tonight. He was hoping you might be around."

"I definitely will be, at least long enough to give them both a big hug and a special treat. Are you nervous about meeting the family, Margaret?"

"You know I thought I was, but no, I'm not. I've talked to his sister several times on the phone, and the conversations have been so easy. I really like her. I'm sure the rest of the family will be the same. Maybe I'm a little nervous about the children."

"Margaret, you are a natural with children, always have been, and they are just naturally drawn to you. So all you have to do is be yourself."

"Mary, you are my rock. Thank you, the lunch was great, the conversation almost as great. I'm ready for tonight. Thank you, Mary. When Richard and Howdy get here we'll find you."

"Thank you, darling. See you then."

✳

"Well, hello, you two. Yes, Howdy. I can tell you have missed your spot here, and everyone is looking forward to your visit. You too, Richard, of course."

"Oh sure, I can tell. Mary said you and Howdy should go right over to the Nook. She will be leaving soon, and she has a hug and a treat for both of you."

"We will see you later, right, Howdy? Let's go."

"Richard, I will be in the small media room. That's where we will call your sister. I even have a pot of tea brewing. Great! We'll be there in a few minutes."

"You have the tea, and Mary sent pumpkins, raisins, and sour cream bread to go with it. So, Margaret, are we ready to make the call?"

"Absolutely. I am looking forward to seeing my new family. Most of the time this works, Richard. I'm not really skilled with the new system, but generally am able to navigate it enough to get by."

"You know I don't use the computer for most of my work. Only when I have to. So the pressure is on you, Margaret."

"No, not really. If I run into a challenge, I made sure the tech man is here tonight, and he knows. I may need him. We'll see."

"So what do I do?"

"Just call them like always. Yes, and your sister sounds like she's very familiar with the process, so let's have a nice visit. Here goes."

"Hi, Sis, you're already online? Good, Margaret, are we online?"

"Yes, Richard, the microphone is right here, and the camera is right beside it. There, our picture is very good."

"How about you, guys? Can you see and hear us?"

"Oh yes, Margaret, this is wonderful. You are as beautiful as you are gracious. I have enjoyed our phone conversation so much. Richard, you look great. Living the good life agrees with you. And where is the other member of your family?"

"Howdy, move right in here beside Richard and me."

"Oh yes, hi, Howdy. I am so excited about spending Xmas with all of you. Here comes the rest of the family, so Margaret get ready. There will be questions, probably at the same time, so take your time, and I will try to keep them in order, somewhat."

"Richard, what a wonderful family! But you're right, the kids are not exactly children anymore."

"Margaret, they have grown so much. I can't believe I haven't seen them for so long. I have certainly missed a lot."

"Yes, but we will not be out of touch anymore. After this visit, we will schedule regular times to visit. Computers are not all bad."

"No, they definitely are not. This was a great idea, and I am so glad that you are tech-savvy, my lady."

"I think we should have this system at our house. What do you think, Richard?"

"Absolutely, whatever or whoever makes that happen. Let's get it done."

*

"Today is the day for the great tour of the cottage. Mom used to call it the Sea Escape."

"That's a great name, Margaret. I am beginning to think I know your parents."

"You definitely would have enjoyed knowing them, Richard. They loved life, family, community, travel, history, writing, painting, music, and, most of all, one another. They stayed passionately in love with each other."

"I believe that's the way we will be, Margaret. As a matter of fact, I know we will. Yes, I know you've been patient long enough. I am so ready to see your response to what we have created. So let's go do the tour, and we will take our time and absorb the project step by step. Howdy has already approved, not that you have to. Really, Margaret, if there are any changes you want to make, everything is possible."

"I'm ready, Richard. Let's go on this adventure."

"Margaret, I want to take you in through the back door and work our way through to the front."

"This is really exciting, Richard. It feels like Christmas morning already, and I'm going to unwrap this giant package."

"Well, it is almost Xmas, and this is a rather large package. There is a lot to see, Margaret. The team and I kind of kept getting one more idea, and they all seemed like great ideas, so I'm absorbing the project along with you. I may not have all of the answers either, but you will have time to talk to all of the guys. They are coming over for a barbeque tomorrow, but now let's do it."

"The first feeling I have as I come inside is what a cozy comfortable place to be. The dining area is a symphony of natural materials, and the smell is so rich. I love the floors, and I can feel the warmth. I mean literally."

"Yes, you can. It's an advanced climate control system. It's a geothermal heat pump in the ground. It extracts heat, repurposing it, and the energy it creates warms or cools the house, no HVAC unit necessary. Just one more technical thing, and then I'll wait for questions, but this is something you don't see and adds to the energy efficiency: the cottage's double thick windows are insulated with argon gas and almost invisible (now-E) coating does double duty, admitting warm sunlight while also reducing radiant heat transfer to the outdoors.

"In addition, in the loft above, on the top floor along the west-facing side, and forgoing window treatments, bathes the room in natural light all day long so there's no need to flip a switch until evening."

"Richard, I am a bit overwhelmed."

"I'm sorry, Margaret, I get so excited about the sustainability part. Let's just let the beauty soak in. OK?"

"Good idea, darling, and there is so much of that, like the dining area. I love the table, it is unique, and the benches have hidden storage areas and that magnificent mantel over the fireplace. I know there's a story with that, but let's wait. I love the glass doors. They let light flow between rooms. I really like the color of paint you chose, and I'll just bet you did choose it. It happens to be the color my mother and I had chosen. We just didn't get that far. It is robin egg blue, isn't it?"

"Yes, it is, Margaret. I'm glad you like it."

"No, Richard, I love it. We see it in the sky and water all around us, so it's very pleasing to the eye. The layout, flow, and livability of this cottage are perfect. I found another gem. This is a mini pantry, right?"

"Yes, and that wasn't my idea. Bill redid the stairway to the left, and was able to create the pantry from the back of the stairs."

"Are you sure this isn't larger than it was, Richard?"

"Well, the square footage in the cottage is the same but with so many built-ins and space-saving techniques. I agree it is spacious and yet compact. I know it doesn't make sense, but it works."

"I can really visualize family and guest time, playing games, talking, and watching the ocean. Enjoying the moment and you and I being creative. This place will always be a castle to me. I love everything I've seen, Richard."

"Next is the bathroom. A very important place."

"Oh my God, a soaking tub. You know how much I've wanted one in our bathroom, and of course, still do. But this is great. I love the ledge to sit on, and the shower handle is on the side, so you don't get wet turning the water on. There are even double sinks, and beautiful tile work. Everything fits, and the skylights and garden window. So much natural light."

"Remind me to tell you all about the skylights when we do our more technical discussion. They are amazing, and super energy savers. But later. Shall we continue?"

"I feel like I'm touring a mansion, not a cottage. It's all so perfect and so natural."

"Yes, let's continue. Just let me take a few deep breaths. Now working our way to the grand finale. You did see the window seat and shelves, I believe."

"Oh yes, and I can see that it can also become a very comfortable bed and again more shelves and drawers. You are right, Richard. That wonderful construction team, they really are magicians. Richard, there is no wall here. It's all open. I can stand right here by the fireplace and see the ocean and everything. We really do have more room. This is not an illusion."

"This part is my design, Margaret, and I actually got to work on it, and I loved every minute. I will have to give you a little technical information, but I'll try to keep it brief."

"I certainly won't interrupt because I am speechless. This awe-inspiring view and natural light is like the outdoors is indoors."

"Margaret, let's go through these beautiful French doors, which open out and go back to the wall, allowing total space in our all weather sanctuary. When I first saw this cottage, I visualized this as a part of it. Other than being absolutely awe-inspiring, it is extremely practical. We have a 180-degree open system. A specially designed hanging system which allows the fiberglass doors to open as we wish—we can, and will, utilize this year round. This spot is just too special to not take full advantage of it. What do you think?"

"Richard, I think we are going to spend a lot more time here ourselves, and we are going to have lots of gatherings and guests, and the cottage has come back to life. Thank you, darling. I could never have imagined what you guys were doing, but I am so very grateful that you did. This is like a giant garden window, only better. What in the world is that magnificent creation over there?"

"That, my darling, is indeed a creation the team built that for us. They knew we would have many occasions to use it. It is a barbecue, and it has a brick oven and many other amenities. They are going to show us how to use it when they come over for the first gathering. And they also gifted us with I don't really know how many truly unique tables and benches and they store very easily."

"Richard, I love you so much. I am so grateful for your love, your spirit, skills, and everything. I do have to reassure myself occasionally that everything is real, and this life we have is the normal way to live. This moment is so very full of life. I feel like I'm bubbling inside."

"And how does that feel to you, darling?"

"Alive and rich. Howdy has settled in, sleeping in front of the fireplace even though there is no fire in it. I'm sure he loves this warm floor. I know I do. I do want to know how everything works, Richard, but right now I really don't care."

"We can put the finishing touches on tomorrow. There's really not much to do, and it will be ready for the first guests. I was concerned about it being able to accommodate the four of them. Now I can see that they will be very comfortable and certainly have an ocean view. So what do you think, Richard? Do you think they would prefer here or the house?"

"Definitely here, Margaret. They will absolutely love it. Who wouldn't? I feel like I have known Aunt Betts forever and you have mentioned how much she loves the house. I know we are all going to have a memorable time together. I am so glad this came together so well, and so fast. I was a little concerned. We had a few challenges, but here we have it, and you will hear the laughter, music, the games, the life that you remember so well, being here again, and this time, I will be here with you."

✳

"Richard, I think it's time to go home and have a cup of hot chocolate, and cookies, and then relax, let go, release, and surrender. All is well. I love that meditation, and I love you. Come on, Howdy, wake up, fellow. One more trip up the hill. You can make it. Let's go. Oh good! The fire is still glowing."

"So are you, Margaret, you are a very sexy lady."

"If you're trying to seduce me, Richard, you are definitely going to be successful."

"Margaret, do you really want hot chocolate?"

"Not as long as you have your arms around me like this. No, I really don't."

✳

"Good morning, darling girl."

"Oh my! It is morning, isn't it? I slept so soundly, and I feel so refreshed."

"Me too, Margaret. We work hard, we play hard, and it's all so easy. I remember we didn't get to do our meditation routine."

"Are you really sure we didn't, Margaret?"

"Pretty sure. Meditation has many forms. I think we just did it differently last night."

232

"You mean the meditation routine?"

"Yes, Margaret."

"Well, I'll think about that. Anyhow whatever we want to call it is OK with me. Now we do have a lot to do, and I am looking forward to doing it. So let's jump up and get this day moving, shall we?"

"Yes, ma'am. On my way. I'm surprised Howdy hasn't come up by now."

"Darling, it's getting really hard for him to do the stairs. I've watched him the past few days, and he is still willing, but it's challenging."

"Richard, I know, it's really hard for me to admit it, but I do know. Will you check on him, darling? I will be down in just a few minutes."

"Of course I will. I always do, and if he wants to go out. I will do that also. See you in a few."

"Thank you, darling."

"Good morning, Howdy. Bless your heart. You're shivering. I know it's really cold out here. Our routine has changed, Howdy. We don't need to climb the hill today. You can spend as much time as you want right there on your warm rug, and we'll keep the fire going for you. How about that? Howdy, when you look at me like that, I really do physically feel such a strong vibration. You may be kind of old in years, but your spirit is still so strong. I love you, my friend. Yes, and I know you love me. Now go get, warm friend, you're still shaking."

"What are you two up to?"

"We were kind of talking about life and changes. Philosophies before breakfast."

"Sure, why not? Let's do some yoga stretches before breakfast. What do you think?"

"I think yes. Good idea."

"Breakfast was especially good today, Richard. Of course, it always is, especially when we work together. You are a very good intuitive cook, Richard. You almost always anticipate what I need, or am going to do next, and we just really create good stuff. Don't you think?"

"Yes, ma'am, I do. So do we have a game plan for today, my dear?"

"Oh yes, I have a check-off list started for the cottage. I'd really like for you to look it over and add anything you can think of, and especially the grocery list. I know we will be eating together most of the time, but we will all also be spending time at the cottage, probably quite a lot, especially in the evenings. Oh yes, the cottage will definitely be a family gathering spot. So yes, I will start a list and then we will review it."

"I may have told you the guys were coming over tonight for a celebration party, did I?"

"Yes, I believe you mentioned it, but we haven't really talked about it. What's happening?"

"Well, as it turns out, nothing. I had a call from Bob this morning and since all of them are coming over tomorrow night to put up the thousands of lights, and we will have a buffet then. They wisely suggested we skip tonight. I hope I didn't sound as relieved as I felt. We are both a little overextended, so I am glad also. It would have been fine, but I am very glad we have a quiet night. We can have lasagna, salad, and wine, and hang out with Howdy."

"This will be our last night of quiet. The next two weeks will absolutely fly by, Richard. Xmas, family, lots of friends gathering, I really love it, and I am looking forward to sharing everything with you and your family, actually our family. Yes, every tradition I've shared with you so far has been inspirational. I can't even imagine what this season will bring. However, I can tell you, I am really looking forward to whatever we have waiting for us to discover, especially me."

∗

"Let's get to town, Richard, and we'll stop by the library. I'll just bet Mary will have something really Christmasy for us. We really don't have much to get from town. So we'll have a little time to visit."

"Great, let's go. Shall we take Howdy?"

"No, Richard, if he wanted to go, he would already be by the door. He always knows when I'm getting ready to leave."

"Yes, you're right, he does. We'll see you in a little while, Howdy. Enjoy the quiet. Margaret, are you concerned about having so much company and Howdy having so little energy?"

"No, I'm really not, Richard. I think Howdy will enjoy the holidays. He always has. He may not be running around, greeting everyone like he always has. Honestly, it was usually like Howdy was the official host."

"I know. When I first came to the library, he was the host. I don't mean you weren't. However, he was obviously the one that knew how to keep things flowing. I think he will actually get energy from the events and company. He knows he can completely relax with us, and that's good, but I think he will rally at least for the week or so of Xmas-ing."

"Where shall we go first, Margaret?"

"If you don't mind, Richard. I would like to stay at the library, while you do your errands. When you get back, it will probably be lunchtime, and we can have lunch with Mary. Richard, I know Mary will ask me because she already has once, and then I forgot to ask you. What's happening with whatever it is you're wearing to our wedding?"

"We really have been busy, haven't we? We actually haven't talked about our wedding very much at all, and it is a very high priority. I have been measured and mauled several times. I don't know what the tailor is doing. The guys all said that I just stand still and that he knows what he's doing. He did it for us, so I really just totally trust that is true. Can't tell you any more than that."

"Good enough, Richard. They are right, and it will be perfect. See you in a little while. Love you."

"Me too."

"Hi, darling, I thought you might be by today. I just had a feeling."

"Mary, you are always having a feeling, and yes, that feeling is almost always right. Are you going to be able to have lunch with Richard and me?"

"Absolutely. What time are you thinking, darling?"

"Richard should be back in about an hour or so. How does that work for you?"

"Perfect. I'll have my stuff out of the oven by then, and we can relax and catch up a bit."

"See you then, Mary. I have a few calls to make and check on a few things. So later."

∗

"Richard, your lady will be right back. I'm getting our lunch ready now. I hope you haven't eaten."

"Mary, I think you know that I would never miss a chance to have lunch with you."

"Flattery will get you the best food I have already prepared for you."

"Thank you, Mary. It is so good to see you. So much is happening so fast. All good! But fast. I feel a bit dizzy sometimes, and you are so solid. Your food is superb."

"Richard, have you been drinking?"

"Only the elixir of love, Mary. My life is so full. I am a very happy man."

"You look it too, I'm happy to say. Both of you are glowing like you've been dipped in glitter."

"Tea or coffee, Richard?"

"Hot tea. I'll ask you to choose for me, Mary. I love a mystery, and you always serve great tea."

"Margaret, I am so glad to see you, darling."

"Me too, Richard, but really it's only been a little over an hour."

"All right, you two, lunch is served, and I will be right back."

*

"What a nice visit we had with Mary. I don't know how she does it, but she always anticipates what's on my mind, sometimes even before I know."

"She is a very intuitive person, Margaret. I haven't known her for very long, but like most people in this town, she is a definite part of my life now."

"Yes, Richard, you have been so open and totally receptive to every challenge presented and truly there have been a lot of opportunities to be overwhelmed, but you have welcomed everything and everyone."

"There is a special one that opened the first door for me. You really did, Margaret, you and Howdy, and then everything else just fell into place."

"I am so grateful, Richard, and by the way, before we get started, were you successful in getting the replacement bulbs for the grand event tonight."

"Oh yes, it was like Steve expected me. Of course, he's going to be there this evening, as he says he has been for the past ten years. He even knew almost exactly how many bulbs I wanted."

"Yes, he usually does. Thank goodness, because I never did. He has always anticipated the amount and ordered them for me."

"Well, I'm glad I just plugged them in and did a quick estimate instead of counting each one."

"Yes, darling, I'm glad you did too. I just can't remember that you haven't always been here, really."

"I know, Margaret, It's kind of weird and a lot wonderful. By the way, what in the world are we feeding this hoard of people?"

"Mary again was way ahead of me. She already had the bread and cookies made. They are in the trunk, and I have gallons of frozen Gumbo base. Well, it's not frozen now. I took it out of the freezer last night, and I have pounds of pork already cut up and thawed, so all together it will only take an hour or so to prepare the Gumbo and rice."

"You are absolutely an amazing woman, Margaret. I had no clue."

"Remember, I have been doing this for a long time. I think that's part of the beauty of tradition. It creates a foundation, and then it's very easy to adjust from there. So how many people are we expecting?"

"Never totally sure, Richard. Always enough to have fun and get the job completed, usually within two hours. Also, there are always young ones, usually teens. Of course, they have to learn the tricks of the trade, and boy, can they eat! So far I've always had enough and usually some to send home with at least a few of the guys. I just pack it in containers and let them decide who's taking what. It always works."

"I'm sure it does, darling. This community is like a fine Swiss watch. It runs well."

"It's good to be home, and I can tell the fire is still going. I'm sure Howdy is glad about that. Speaking of Howdy, yes, I am so glad to see you too. Richard, before I start preparing stuff, I want to take a few minutes here at our favorite gathering spot. Do you want to join us?"

"Absolutely. Would you like anything before I do that?"

"You are a mind reader. Yes, I want a glass of red wine, and I have a small tray of cheese cubes and the crackers are, well, you know where they are. Thank you, darling. Howdy and I are going to do some stretches. Join us if you like."

"I like. That always feels so good, and this cheese and wine tastes so good. Thank you, darling. I love doing things for us, Margaret. This is really our last day before the official holiday rituals start, right?"

"Actually, darling, tonight is the beginning. The team that puts the lights up for me. They do the same thing for everyone. Actually, they are the same ones that decorated downtown on Howdy's special day. They leave me until last because I'm usually working, and my house has about as many lights as the community spiritual center. A lot. So they started early this morning. Split up into teams, always at least two and one trainee, and we all turn our lights on officially at approximately at six o'clock tomorrow night. I love it that they come here last, and amazingly enough, they never seem tired. They are always in a jolly mood when they get here, and they never have wine until we have a toast when they complete the job here, and all of the lights are working."

"Margaret, I could have helped them today. I didn't know."

"Of course you didn't, darling. Enjoy it. They are giving you some room because they know that you have a lot going on this year. The cottage, company, Xmas events, and most importantly, our wedding. Richard, I honestly think most folks thought I was going to remain a single lady. Actually I kind of thought so too. Anyhow, they are jubilant that not only are we getting married, but everyone approves of you. So please just enjoy the respect they are showing, and believe me, the next holiday season, you will be on the list."

"Thank you, Margaret. I still do have a learning curve, and you continue to be a wonderful teacher. Shall we take the supplies and things down to the cottage and put on the finishing touches?"

"I still kind of think, I dreamed that cottage vision, and when I go down there, it will not be changed. It's just so challenging to comprehend all of the amazing and wonderful changes in such a short period of time. So I'm ready to go but a little bit nervous."

"It is all real, Margaret, but I know what you mean. I was involved completely, and I'm still awed by the outcome. So let's both be brave and go make it company ready, shall we?"

"Absolutely. I'm ready. I did leave a couple of bags in the car, Richard. If you don't mind getting those. There are some things upstairs that I have ready to go. I can carry them, of course, if we need to come back for more. I think we know the way. Let's do it. Well the magic is definitely still here. Even more so, now that we have the beds made, the bathrooms readied and food in the cupboard. I had to bring a few of the traditional Xmas decorations, but I am glad we decided to wait for them to decorate the tree, and of course we'll help. Oh, Richard, wait until you hear about Aunt Betts sing. She has this natural commanding presence and voice and has used it professionally."

"She is a treasure. Margaret. I am completely captivated by her already, and I haven't even seen a picture."

"Yes, actually you have. We just haven't gone into detail about a lot of the pictures, especially the one upstairs. My mother and Aunt Betts were quite the pair. Their pictures were usually taken when they were off on an adventure. I especially like the ones of the trip to India. I love elephants as you probably have noticed. I have been collecting them since I was about five years old. I am sure that you will learn a lot about my family from Aunt Betts. She has a way of mesmerizing people. She has a very big life. I never know where she will call from next."

"I think we're through here for now, and a good thing we are because we need to get back and start the food. The troops will be here soon. Do we have lights for the cottage also?"

"Darling, we have lights for everywhere—the storage buildings and the garage too. Yes, we do have lights. Sometimes we end up with enough lights for a couple of outside trees. I have lights for the cottage tree put away. They're safe. Everything else is going to be used. It is so beautiful I get goose bumps thinking about it."

*

"Margaret, what can I do to help?"

"If you would be willing to go out to the storage building by the garage, there is a cupboard just inside the door. I have Christmas plates, bowls, cups, napkins, and serving trays. This holiday season I break my rule about paper products. Tonight and tomorrow night I use them. I know they are recyclable, but I just don't like to use them. Except—"

"There are always exceptions in life, Margaret. I'll go seek, search, and return. By the way, how many do you want me to get?"

"Let's start with forty. You can watch, and if necessary, you'll know where they are, and by the way, tomorrow night for the open house decorating, potluck party, it's more like two to three hundred, maybe more."

"You are so calm about it."

"Darling, remember, this has been my life forever, and I know I can trust the process. It's so rewarding."

"It is already smelling so good in here, Margaret. Did I tell you I love Gumbo?"

"I believe you did, and I am glad."

"Margaret, did I tell you I love you?"

"In so many ways, but I still love hearing it, and I love you. Let's never take it for granted, Richard. Life is so precious and moves so quickly it's very easy to let priorities blur."

"We'll help each other with that, as everything else. We'll never get far off track, Margaret."

"I know you're right, Richard. We also have Mary and probably a number of others very willing and able to see that we are being our very best selves. Richard, do you want to be my Gumbo taster."

"Honey, I have tasted Gumbo from many places. The best so far was in Louisiana, Cajun country. So with you understanding that, I am ready to taste and tell."

"Here you go, Mr. professional taster."

"Oh my God!"

"What, Richard?"

"I think I'm having a food orgasm."

"Maybe that's why the guys get so noisy and robust at dinner. And I thought it was the wine."

"Sure you did."

"So to answer your question, being a professional taster, I must say it is the best Gumbo I have ever tasted. Now I can also tell you that was a magazine assignment for me to seek and find the best Gumbo and write an article on it. Believe me, if I had tasted your Gumbo, the article would have been much more sensuous. Let's just keep that part our little secret, shall we? Oh yes, I want to preserve the essence of the Holy Grail."

"Richard, now you are going too far."

"I think I tend to do that when I put my writer's hat on."

"You and Auntie Betts are going to have quite a good time. Speaking of a good time, I hear the approaching herd. Get ready. Here we go."

"What an experience! I love this community, Margaret. I mean it. This cooperative community living is so simple and so very powerful. It would have taken us days to do what they did in hours."

"You're right. A good time was had by all. I know I take so much for granted, Richard. I think that's why I've never been concerned about anything, really. If something needs to be fixed, it gets taken care of. And that's true for everyone. If you need help, you have it. If you don't need it, no one is assuming you do."

"I still marvel at the beauty of it, Margaret. How beautiful, how grand, and liberating this experience is, when people learn to help each other."

"We have several generations invested in creating, what I tend to take for granted. Speaking of generations, tomorrow Aunt Betts arrives, and when I say arrives, I mean it. She is at home immediately wherever she is. She loves this house. She is very sensitive spiritually. She has a bit of a reputation for being a seer, and she really can tell a lot about folks, so don't be too surprised if she goes on about you a bit."

"I sense that she is a rather large person. Is that correct, Margaret?"

"You know, that's an interesting question. She and my mother appeared to be pretty much opposites. My mother appeared to be very much the refined petite beauty that one would admire immediately. In fact, she was all of that, but so much more. She had an infectious giggle and loved to play, almost anything, games with me, mental sparring at parties, chess, and making up stories was a favorite. By the way, I'm sure Aunt Betts will get that one started. I've always loved it. Someone will start the first sentence, and there's a recorder who writes everything down so we can see it, and we keep going as long as we wish. It's pretty amazing how it works out. Often hilarious, sometimes a bit spooky, but always entertaining. Anyhow, Aunt Betts is a large-framed person, very solid, not obese, just like her personality—robust. I think she is absolutely beautiful.

"She and my mother were extremely intuitive with each other. Apparently, they had been, even as children. My godmother told stories about them finishing one another's sentences and being very protective of one another. They never lost that closeness. After they both had married, they often went on excursions together. I'm sure Aunt Betts had a major void in her life after Mom and Dad's death. She avoided coming here for a while. She has always called and gradually started stopping over between trips. She has always had a special place in my heart. I love her very much."

"She sounds so interesting, Margaret. I am so looking forward to tomorrow. By the way, is she flying?"

"No, she is driving this time. She loves the adventure of winter travel. She has a beast of a car. I swear it's just like her. It will go anywhere and does. She expects to be free about noon or so. I know she won't miss the potluck party. She loves to decorate. She also loves to eat. So are you up to all of this, Richard?"

"I am way up to it, my darling. I am in wonderland, loving every minute."

"I always love it when the lights are up, and then, by this time tomorrow night, the Christmas decorations will transform this entire place into a magical fantasy land with a fresh pine scent. There will be fresh garlands everywhere. It does seem like a magic wand passes over, and then everything sparkles."

"Nothing could sparkle more than your beautiful eyes are right now, Margaret my precious love. You are so vibrant."

"Richard, I do love you so very much, and I feel so content and excited at the same time. You hold me so gently, and the room seems to vibrate with our combined energy. Let's lie here with Howdy for a while. He looks like he could use some of that energy. Bless his heart. He looks so content."

"I think he is, Margaret. He knows he is loved."

"Richard, I am so aware of the loving presence of the spirit. In this moment, I understand Howdy's condition, but I am also comforted as peace washes over me. I am enfolded in unconditional love, safe and protected. And I believe that is exactly what Howdy is feeling."

"Shall I carry him upstairs to his bed, Margaret?"

"Yes, Richard, I'm sure he would manage. I also think he would appreciate the lift."

"Yes, Howdy, we're going upstairs now. We can all use some rest, and restoration. Tomorrow is another adventure."

✳

"Good morning, Howdy. You look hale and hearty. That's what a good night's rest does for us, right? We have a great day to experience. Auntie Betts will be here. Yes, I know she's one of your favorites. She's always so different with you Howdy. It's like you two share a secret, which you probably do. Then we have the holiday decorating potluck. I think you may prefer to spend part of the evening at the cottage. We'll see how it goes. But for now, it's breakfast time. I hear the call and smell the coffee, so let's finish this stretch and go for it."

"Good morning, you two. You both look like you're ready for anything. In other words, you look wonderful."

"Thank you, kind sir, and so we are, and so are you. Look at this. Everything is ready and so beautiful. You are an artist, Richard."

"We're having Dutch babies."

"I recognized the smell, but it's been a while. You remembered it's one of my many favorites—blueberries, juice, and heavenly coffee."

"Richard, I am so grateful. What a glorious day! By the way, Dutch babies are Auntie Betts favorite also. She loves to watch them in the oven as they rise and brown. She loves to eat, but then again she loves to do whatever it is she's doing at that moment. I swear I think she and Howdy are kindred souls."

"Well, that's quite a compliment huh, Howdy?"

"You sure look alert and energetic today, my boy. Richard, I really think Howdy knows that Aunt Betts is on her way, and he certainly is recharged, as we probably should be about right now."

"Do you have a list for this morning, Margaret?"

"Actually, I think we are fine, Richard. Aunt Betts's room is ready. The house is ready for decorations. And all of the folks that are coming know where their boxes of decorations are. They are the same ones that they have taken down, labeled, and stored.

"I am making Manhattan Clam Chowder for tonight. Yes, it's tradition. Mary brings the sourdough bread and fresh butter. I usually make about three batches. Folks start to arrive at about five o'clock. All will have arrived by seven, and folks eat as they wish. So I have one pot ready by five, another by six, and usually the last one by seven. It is a potluck, so you can imagine the amazing choices. It is truly decadent."

"Great! Shall we start now?"

"Yes, my dear, but not what you're thinking. While I'm creating chowder, if you'd be willing to put all of the extenders on the dining room table and the made-to-order Xmas tablecloths are on the buffet. Food will fill the dining room table, the buffet, the special table that's in the storage room, and probably some other places. It will just work out. It always does. It is so exciting, Richard. I get goose bumps all over just thinking about it.

"When Auntie Betts starts the Xmas carols, I feel the spirit of Xmas throughout my entire body."

"Margaret, I am sure this is going to be like a first Xmas for me. I have had some great ones, but they were never anything like this."

"We haven't even started the events at the spiritual center yet, which I'm thinking must be like Santa's workshop."

"Sometimes, I think this must be one of my stories or a dream, and I'll wake up. Fortunately I never wake up, so if it is a dream, or a novel, I just want it to be never-ending."

"Me too, Richard. However we had better get to cracking, so to speak. We are having a party, and she will be here very soon. Also, Richard, would you be willing to keep an eye on Howdy? He loves the event, but it may get to be a bit much for him. If so, he could go down to the cottage for a while."

"Sure, I can do that, Margaret, and I think it's a very good idea."

"If you need help with the table, let me know. I'm going to be in the kitchen."

"Well, Howdy, I see you're going to watch me try to work this puzzle. It sounded so easy, but this is a really big table. I'm going to give it a go, but I can see where I may need some help. Margaret, I need a consultant please."

"How can I help, Richard?"

"Have you actually put this table together yourself?"

"Actually, no, I haven't. I've always had enough people around that I just never even thought about it. I can see right away however that it definitely is a two-person job. Sorry about that, darling. Let's see if we can manage this. If not, when Aunt Betts gets here, I know she will be very helpful. "Well, Richard, we are pretty strong people. That was a test of endurance. I can certainly appreciate the folks that have always just taken care of it."

"Thank you, darling. I'll put the tablecloth on and get the tableware out of the storage room, and then I can help you in the kitchen, if you'd like?"

"I would definitely appreciate it, darling. I want to have everything going, when she gets here, because I know she'll be wanting a teatime chat with us, and I do mean a chat, no holds barred. She does very little of any filtering conversationally. She pretty much says what she's thinking as she's thinking it. I love it, but some folks are not quite prepared for such absolute curiosity, honesty, and genuine love. It seems to me she would fit in to this community very well. I think almost everyone has that approach."

"I love the congruency that I find everywhere."

"You are right, Richard. This is her hometown, and she is so loved. I think she probably reflects a lot of traits of our founders. She is strong, intelligent, spiritual, independent, full of awe and wonder, collaborative, and a natural leader. As you can tell, I am her greatest fan. For a change, I'm actually watching the clock. It seems to have slowed down. However, it will speed up once she arrives. Time is so strange. I accept that, I just don't understand it."

"Margaret, I have the tea ready. Shall we join Howdy by the fire and just relax for a few minutes?"

"Oh yes, Richard, I would love that. Thank you."

*

"This is so nice, being so close to you and Howdy—the warmth and beauty of the fire burning, the smells of herbs and spices, the delicate taste and aroma of jasmine in the tea. The only sound is of our breathing, which somehow creates such a wonderful state of relaxation. Richard, you always seem to know what I need, even before I do. This is so restorative. I am centered now. I was getting a little scattered."

"Yes, I think you were just a little bit, and that's all right, but this is so nice."

"Oh yes, it is."

"Richard, I have been sleeping."

"Yes, all three of us took a power nap. What time is it?"

"It's time for us to check on the chowder, I think. Margaret, I hear a pretty powerful motor coming this way. I think we are ready to awaken."

"Oh yes, my dear, so we are. Auntie Betts, welcome! You have always been the best hugger in the world. When you hug me, I know I've been hugged, but let's get inside out of the cold. Richard will get your bags in a bit."

"Maggie, you are even more beautiful, and I didn't think that was possible. I missed you, darling. And I miss this community, and Richard oh good, you are a hugger also. I am so glad, there's just something so right about getting and giving a hug. Well, Margaret, you certainly didn't exaggerate about this one—handsome, engaging, gentle, strong, and honest. Yes, I can see all of that in your eyes, Richard, and feel it in your energy. You are a good person. Welcome to the family. I am so happy for both of you. And there you are, my furry friend. Oh, Howdy, it is so good to see you. Come here, fellow. Let's touch noses. You haven't forgotten, have you? You do feel so good, Howdy. It is wonderful to be home, Maggie. I felt home the minute I walked in the door."

"Aunt Betts, I will go get your bags and take them up to your room, and I'm sure you know where that is."

"Yes, I do, Richard. Thank you so much. They are a little heavy, but I think you will be able to handle them fine. Maggie, he is a sweetheart. Really I feel like I've known him forever, and who knows? Maybe I have. You are glowing, my girl, and I love it. I have been a little concerned about you. You have so much love to give, and you give it. I know that, but I'm so happy that you have found a partner, and I know your mom and dad are happy also."

"Yes, I know they are, Auntie. It's so good to have you here. Now it really feels like Christmas."

"Oh yes, tonight is the big party—potluck, decorating, singing, playing games, all mixed with a whole lot of laughter. Oh yes, all of that and more, but for now, I have one of your favorite soups ready—Shaker Potato Leek Soup."

"Oh yes, Maggie, I can smell it. Bless you, darling. I am hungry. I knew you would have something wonderful waiting. Do you put the caraway seeds in the soup, like your mama did?"

"I surely did. Wouldn't make it any other way. Some things you just don't mess with, and this is one of those things."

"Maggie, darling, if you don't mind, I'll run upstairs, and freshen up just a bit. I'll be right back, ready for soup for the soul."

"She calls you Maggie? I've never heard anyone do that. I think I remember you saying you preferred to be called Margaret even as a child. I was just surprised."

"Interesting observation, Richard. I've never consciously thought about it. I think what's important much more than the actual name itself is the emotion from one person to another. All I have ever felt from Aunt Betts is complete acceptance, love, and respect. To some folks she is seen as Lady Elizabeth, or professor, depending on where she is and what she's doing. However, here she is Auntie Betts, or just plain Betts, and to a few, Betsy. So, Richard, to answer your question, I suppose I don't have a strong preference of Margaret. It's just familiar."

"Well, I am instantly enthralled with her, Margaret. I can see why you couldn't really define her. She is indefinable. She has so much energy she fills the room, and I don't mean her physical size, although she definitely is a robust lady. It's hard to describe. Let's see, if I was writing about her, she has a commanding presence, although not in a domineering way, more from a sense of awe and wonder. She is a very attractive lady, I think primarily from her eyes and posture. Her eyes are such deep violet velvet with a look of the ages reflecting the best of humanity. Her posture says to me, 'I am sure of where I am and prepared for sun or storm and will equally value and be grateful for both.'"

"My goodness Richard, remind me to ask you to define me someday, as if you were writing. That was a beautiful description and said pretty much what I believe to be true about this lovely and loved lady. I think the next few weeks are going to be quite a ride, and I am very glad we bought tickets."

"Me too, Margaret."

✱

"I am famished. How can I help?"

"You can help this time by sitting down and being served. I know I won't have this opportunity again, so let me enjoy it for now. You are always waiting on everyone, Richard. This lady anticipates what folks want before the thought has formed. That's why they call her the seer. She reads minds. So watch your mind. Richard, my friend you're a writer, so we all know that your mind is of its own. So I will tread lightly around it, rest easy. By the way, I have read your books. You have a great style, which I feel has only continued to get bolder and brighter as you have obviously experienced life. You understand and love children. With your children's books, you have a very different writing style, humorous, witty, encouraging curiosity, beauty, and love, which leads me to my next question. Are you two planning to have children straight away or travel for a bit or both?"

"I told you, Richard. She's an open book. I know you were asking both of us about that decision, Auntie. First, yes, we have decided to have children. Secondly, we haven't really thought or at least talked about when."

"By the way, my darling girl, this soup goes back through the ages, back to my childhood, when my grandmother made it. I can imagine you making it for your grandchildren, and if there's ever one of them that doesn't like it, you had better just go ahead and drown it or something like that. Well, either drown it or just love it until it gets its taste buds."

"Oh, Aunt Betts, it's so good to have you here. I love and miss you so much."

"Darling, you know I'm with you even if I'm not always physically here. You are in my heart always."

"I know, however I can share your energy better when your body is here also."

"I know what you mean, Margaret. Yes, I am glad to be here."

"Aunt Betts, I really appreciate what you said about my writing. I am so grateful that you have read my books and especially your perspective regarding the children's books. I haven't felt as clear about those as I would like. I had to really let my writing guides take over for those. I think I'm getting better at doing that. It's a lot more fun."

"That's the difference, I felt Richard, more joy and freedom in your style. However all of your work is excellent."

"Thank you again. Coming from you, that is a real compliment. I'll make sure you get one of the first copies of my next one. Actually what I would really like, that is, if you have time, and would like to, I would love to send you a copy before printing. I think your feedback would be invaluable."

"That's exciting, Richard. I would love to do that."

"Thank you. I will look forward to it. Now, Maggie, let me tidy up and get the kitchen ready for the grand finale potluck event."

"I'm going to be firm about this, Auntie Betts. After tonight, you can reign, but for now, I am going to insist that you go cozy up with Howdy in front of our wonderful massive fireplace, and you two just relax, enjoy, and perhaps even nap a bit. Richard and I may join you after we get things going, which is very quick and easy."

"Thank you, Maggie, Howdy, and I do need some alone time. I sense he has a lot to tell me, and I am here to listen."

"Magpie, I will get the supplies form the storage room, OK?"

"Richard, my love, you may call me a lot of things, but trust me, Magpie is *not* one of them. Do you really think I chatter nosily?"

"Just testing your sense of humor, darling."

"It's intact, right?"

"I kind of thought that one may not fly. I'll just bet you did."

"Yes, please. Fortunately, my sense of humor is intact. Start the setup process and humor me, my dear."

"Touché. I can hardly wait for my next term of endearment."

∗

"Margaret, when you have time, would you be willing to check out the supply stuff? I did make myself a list. However, I am still a fledgling."

"You really can't use that for much longer, my dear. You are just about ready to fly. As long as you will still catch me if I fall."

"Always, my darling. Everything looks great."

"Thank you. Auntie Betts and Howdy are in harmony even with their nap noises."

"Yes, they really are. I'll bet that is the way we are when we're in slumber. How will we ever know, darling?"

"We could be creating another symphony. We'll call it the Slumber Symphony. Shall we practice now?"

"I'll check on the chowder and then we can. We are ready, and we have about two hours until we open the doors. I love you, Richard."

"I love you too, Margaret."

"Well, you two lovebirds, are you going to sleep through your big event? Never mind ignoring your VIP guest. By the way, Margaret, I stirred the clam chowder. I really just wanted to smell it, and of course I had to taste it. As always, it is superb."

"Thank you, Auntie Betts. You and Howdy had quite a duet going, you know? It was just like you had practiced it before."

"That we have."

"Maggie, I am so excited. I want to see everyone all at the same time. I miss all of this, you know."

"Someday, you may want to settle in here, Auntie Betts. I know a great portion of your heart is here."

"Yes, my dear, but there is still so much to do, and oh, how I love my island. Richard, I haven't bored you to tears about Galapagos yet, you have fresh ears. So we will have a chat about it, which I am really looking forward to."

"That is one place I have actually dreamed about, Betts, literally."

"I knew he was a good one, Maggie. When is your family joining us, Richard? I understand we'll have some youthful energy around here."

"Oh, Margaret, I am so sorry. I forgot to tell you my sister called, and they have changed their plans. Oh no, don't look like that. It's not bad. As a matter of fact, I think it's wonderful. Thank you so much for asking, Auntie Betts."

"Well, Richard, hurry, get on with it. They have arranged to arrive on the twenty-second, late afternoon."

"That's wonderful, Richard, I'm so glad. I had written a letter so they could have at least a glimpse of this amazing place, and of course,

I mentioned the spiritual center and activities. So they rearranged their schedules, and they will be able to be involved in some of the festivities there, and of course they are looking forward to all of our family time, and traditions. Richard, I thrive on storytelling and adventures, so, of course, I'm hopeful that they are the adventurous type. Unless they have changed a lot, they are indeed."

"Maggie was one of my best adventure seekers. Do you remember, Maggie?"

"Auntie Betts, how could I forget? I have always looked forward to your visits so much. My folks wouldn't tell me until you were practically here. Because, I guess, I pestered them incessantly with, 'Is she going to be here in a few minutes?' So, yes, you and I found fairies and toadstools, and everything in between.

"Well, this has turned out to be quite the day, and it's just beginning. It's time for the lights to be turned on, and I'll just bet in five to ten minutes, we will meet and greet and turn this place into a holiday paradise. Let the party begin. Before we do that, Auntie Betts, Howdy has been needing a little more quiet time for a while. He loves company, but it really wears him down. So Richard will be watchful, and take him down to the cottage when he thinks it's time."

"Yes, darling, I know his energy level is low. I figured you were aware of it. I'd be glad to take him down to the cottage."

"Oh no. You, my dear, are restricted. You will see the cottage tomorrow with Richard and me. Do we have a surprise for you?"

"It's just like you to tease me like that, Maggie. You know I love surprises, and it sounds like I'm going to have one."

"Yes, and it is a good one. I hear merriment arriving, and I smell the food already."

"Yes, it has begun. I am so happy that I got here in time for this glorious occasion. I love you, Maggie."

"I know, and it's right back to you, Auntie Betts. The doorbell ringeth! Come in, come in. You are welcome."

"You all know your way around and where to put coats and such. Nothing's changed at least not in that way. Richard, what do you think about this wild bunch?"

"Quite frankly, Margaret, I can't believe it's real. This is unbelievable. Everyone know exactly what to do and how to do it, and it's working, the entire house is being transformed flawlessly and it's a real party. People eating, laughing, working in teams, and loving every minute of it. It's magical."

"I know. I feel that way every year. Actually, every year of my life, so don't expect to get over it. Even the food it seems like the more it's eaten, the more there is. Yes, it's not something I would ever try to explain to anyone. Although I did attempt to prepare you somewhat."

"Yes, you did darling, but you're right. It's something you just need to be a part of to truly appreciate it. And Aunt Betts is the belle of the ball. She's flitting around like a fairy with a wand. Everywhere I look, she's upstairs, downstairs, out in the storage room. She is a large woman but she can move."

"Yes, she is a very special lady, and you're right. She has always been right in the middle of everything, and that's always exactly where she needs to be. Richard, I am still thinking about your family and their change of plans. I think it's absolutely perfect that they can be here for the center's activities and have a little more time with us. We just got the cottage ready in time. Of course, you notice how easily I can now say *we*."

"It is we, darling. I just helped implement some of your ideas and a few of my own and a few of the guys'. Like everything that happens in this community it was a collaborative effort. Yes our timing was actually perfect.

"Margaret, I'm going to take Howdy down to the cottage. I think he's said his hellos, and he's beginning to wane."

"Thank you, Richard. Yes, I think he's ready for a little quiet time, and he's sure not going to get that here. Isn't it miraculous how this magic happens, Richard? The house is almost finished. Outside is complete, and there is still food. You and Howdy had best be going. I believe I hear Auntie Betts rounding up the troops for our song fest, and trust me, you don't want to miss that. She starts us off with her singing of a couple of songs, and then we all join in and honestly the house vibrates, and that's a good thing because the energy is harmonious. I swear the room lights up, literally."

"I don't doubt it for a moment. I will be right back. Don't let them start before I get back, OK?"

"I'll try, Richard, but it's a bit like a stampede. Once they start, it's hard to control, but oh so lovely. Hurry back, also I made fresh hot chocolate and of course spiced apple cider."

"Oh yes, I could smell the cider, even with all of the many aromatic aromas mingled in with it. So that's for me."

"Be right back, and thank you, darling."

✳

"My goodness the house is beautiful. I am awed every year by the sheer magic of the Christmas spirit. Everyone and everything sparkles. I am so happy to be here with you, Margaret, and Richard, not only are you an excellent writer but you can sing. You and Margaret create perfect harmony together, and I mean that in every way, and my sweet Howdy. What a package you have here. I'm so happy for you."

"Thank you, Auntie Betts. I love you so much."

"I know, darling girl. We do have fun, don't we? I know I can truthfully say I have never experienced a day like this before, and I have led a pretty full life, or at least I used to think so."

"Aunt Betts, you are a master storyteller. I know my family is going to be completely mesmerized with you just as I am. They are great people."

"I'm sure they are, Richard, and we love filling this house with life and laughter. That's the way it's always been, and thanks to you, Margaret, the legacy continues."

"Thank you, Auntie Betts."

"Richard, I don't think Howdy has moved since you brought him back from the cottage."

"Oh, he has moved all right. You can't make that much noise without moving something."

"Shall we bring his bed down by the fireplace, and let him sleep down here, Richard?"

"I don't think so, darling. I'll carry him up, but I think he should be with us, and we're used to his night noises. He'll let us know if he needs anything."

"You are a very sensitive person, Richard."

"And I think you are absolutely right, Margaret. I am sure Howdy knows you two are close, even if he appears to be asleep, and yes, Richard, I really think he wants to be upstairs. You two are so right. I realized that almost as soon as the words were out."

"I knew that it was not the right thing, and if he stayed down here, that's where I would be in the morning also. So yes, we are in complete agreement, and thank you, both of you. Now let's call it a night, and

Auntie Betts, sleep as late as you'd like in the morning. Breakfast will actually be brunch and a very flexible schedule."

"Right now, child, that sounds delightful. However, I generally rejuvenate pretty quickly, but it's great to have the option. So a very good night to the three of you. Rest well."

"Good night, Auntie Betts."

"Good morning, Howdy. You certainly are perky this morning, and apparently so is Richard. I never heard him get up. Oh my goodness it's nine o'clock. I really slept in, and I feel wonderful. Yes, Howdy, I hear Auntie Betts and Richard talking, and you are really getting anxious to see them. Go on downstairs, I'll be right there."

"Richard, look who's up and about."

"Good morning, Howdy. You look like you're ready to go for a little walk. Shall we do that? Oh yes, the leash by the door trick, never fails eh, Howdy?"

"Richard, we'll be back shortly, and I'll help you with the food."

"Oh no, you don't, Betts. I have that covered for this morning. Your turn will come. I've heard about some of the wild and wonderful recipes you create, and I am truly looking forward to the experience, but for now you and Howdy go appreciate the beauty of the morning, and I'm sure I will see my beauty of the morning appear any moment now."

"Thanks, Richard, we're off. You lead, Howdy. I'll try to keep up."

"Good morning, sleeping beauty. Howdy wasn't the only one sleeping soundly last night. I think every one of us did, and how are you this morning?"

"Richard, I feel wonderful—rested, refreshed, and ready for another day of magic. Speaking of magic, right now that coffee smells like it may be some kind of magic potion."

"Have a seat, my lady, and let me attend to your every desire."

"Oh, Richard, do we really have time now?"

"Well, maybe not your every desire, but I will bring you coffee with a hint of cinnamon, honey, and cream, just to get you started."

"Darling, I love you."

"Thank you, Margaret. That kiss was sweeter than the honey."

"By the way, where's Auntie Betts and Howdy?"

"They have gone on an adventure. Howdy is really perky this morning. He was eager to go outside, and it is really cold. Aunt Betts has quite an effect on Howdy. Well, everyone really. She truly is a magician.

I believe you, Margaret. This is the first day of the activities at the center, so what is our plan?"

"We definitely want to be there for dinner. That's the major gathering time, and Auntie Betts will be the belle of the ball, and I think we should be there in time for you to get the lay of the land. I have some ideas about gifts, but I always get so inspired when there is so much creative energy flowing and Auntie Betts flits about everywhere. I don't know how she does it, but she has always managed to visit with everyone and get everything accomplished. I'm ready anytime you are."

"I'm looking forward to uncovering my hidden assets."

"Richard, everyone can see your assets. They're not really covered."

"Margaret!"

"No, really, your talents and skills are quite obvious. Perhaps you need to focus a bit, but you will."

"You make me believe that, Margaret. You have such honesty."

"Well, you two, good morning, and let us get to the fireplace. Right, Howdy? It's really cold out there, but we had a great time. Howdy has been catching me up on everything, and now we are hungry."

"Good because breakfast is ready."

"Richard, did you cook this morning?"

"Yes, ma'am, I am proud to say I had the honor, and I am going to get the Dutch babies out of the oven right now. It is a piece of art."

"You knew this was one of my favorites, didn't you?"

"Perhaps, I remember it being mentioned. Fresh sliced lemon, powdered sugar, cooked apples, and hot coffee."

"May I help?"

"Both you ladies be seated, and I will be honored to serve you."

"Richard, you are going to spoil me. I may expect this every day."

"Madam, I must tell you that we all take turns, and I am really looking forward to your turn."

"Margaret has told me about your culinary skills, so my expectations are quite high."

"Then I shall not disappoint you, Richard. I shall rise to the occasion. Now, you two, what is our plan for the day? After eating this wonderful breakfast, I feel like I could do anything."

*

"Today, my dear Aunt Betts, you get to see the cottage. We want to make sure everything is prepared for our guests, although that doesn't sound right at all. For our family, there that feels right."

"Indeed, it does, my girl. That is what we are all about. Always being there for one another. You both know that I love surprises and adventures, and you have really got my curiosity roused about the cottage. I can't imagine what you've done, Richard. However, I can tell by the glow of Maggie's face that it's something pretty special. So let's see what's going on."

"You, ladies, give me a ten-minute head start please. Come on, Howdy let's go down the hill. See you in a few."

"He and Howdy have quite a bond, Maggie."

"Yes, they do have. Richard is very sensitive about Howdy, and his energy, or often his lack of energy."

"Yes, I've noticed that he is very intuitive, and he certainly can read you, my dear, and that's a good thing."

"Yes, he really can. We have such an easy flow of life and energy between us. We both know we are blessed."

"And so you are, and I am so happy for both of you. Now let's get down the hill. I can't wait another minute."

"Oh my goodness! Maggie, your mom and dad planned to do this. Do you remember?"

"I do remember watching them sketching on paper, and yes, one time when you were here. We had a great bonfire on the beach and all of you were laughing and talking at the same time, which you actually did a lot, but yes, I do remember the excitement and energy about the cottage plan. You called it a redo."

"That I did. I thought it was rather elaborate, and the cottage was cozy. Richard, may I tell you, my dear. You captured the dream and then added even more to it. It is still cozy and full of love. Everything is here. I can hear the chattering and excitement of your family, our family, as we gather here for memory building. I absolutely love it."

"Thank you, Aunt Betts, I am so glad. Now if you ladies will excuse me, I am going to take some pictures."

"Take your time, darling. I have so much to show you, Auntie Betts. You just can't see it all at once. I love the table, Maggie, and you know we are going to spend a lot of time there. Everything is so open, and Howdy, of course, has his favorite spot right in front of that magnificent fireplace."

"Maggie, the view always takes my breath away."

"Oh my God, this used to be the porch, and now it's an all-purpose room enclosed, but it feels like we are right out on the beach. It is perfect for napping or games, reading or maybe everything at one time."

"Yes, I know this will be a major gathering place, as it should be. Now come with me, I have much more to show you."

"Margaret, Aunt Betts, are you still here?"

"Yes, darling, I have discovered even more this time, and Auntie Betts is lost in the magic."

"Well, it's after one o'clock. How are we doing with time?"

"Well, as usual, I have lost track of time completely. Fortunately, everything is ready for the family, except for the tree, and we're only going to put it in the stand, and the decorations are here. So if you would be willing to do that, we'll go get lunch ready and prepare something to take to the center for dinner. I think we should be ready to go by four o'clock. Sound OK?"

"Perfect, darling. I'll see you in about twenty minutes. I love you, Maggie, and I am so glad that Aunt Betts approves of the changes."

"Oh yes, darling, and she certainly approves of you."

"There you two are. What a lovely couple you are! You make me tingle, just looking at you."

"Well, let's tingle our way up to the house and have some lunch, shall we?"

"You know, I'm ready to eat anytime, anywhere. Let's go."

"Maggie, I love this kitchen and how it flows into the eating area and how full of love it always has been and still is. This is where I feel their presence so strongly."

"So do I, Aunt Betts. I feel the laughter and sheer joy of life."

"You have it too, you know that, don't you, Maggie?"

"Yes, and I certainly understand it more clearly since Richard arrived. He definitely creates a spark wherever he is."

"I am so happy for both for you, actually all three of you. Howdy obviously has completely welcomed Richard into the nest."

"Yes, that he has. Speaking of Richard, I hear him singing his I'm almost there song."

"Great timing, darling. Lunch is on the counter. We're all on our own. Aunt Betts and I am getting very excited about getting to the center. So do you mind if we leave a little earlier than four o'clock?"

"I am ready this very minute. Well, maybe I will finish my dessert and coffee, but yes, I am really looking forward to seeing this Christmas workshop in action, and of course the food and singing, and everything. I need about an hour to finish up and get ready."

"How about you, Auntie Betts?"

"An hour sounds just right for me, and I am, like Richard, ready to see my people and get to work on whatever it is I'm going to do. Inspiration will strike. It always does. Maggie, we are really going to do some memory-making this Christmas."

"We already are, Auntie Betts. Just look at the magic in this house. It is totally transformed into a holiday miracle. And we have just begun."

"Time flies so quickly. I think I'm glad I've never understood it. It just doesn't make any sense."

"You are so right, Maggie darling. You and I have always shared that awareness, and personally, it's always worked for me, and some of the cultures that I have been privileged to live in and study live as a part of nature—no clocks, watches, and very little stress. I always found such peace and gratitude during those studies. Aunt Betts, I'm sure you did. But honestly, don't you have that wherever you are?"

"Well, Maggie, as usual you got me. You have always been able to see right into my soul, girl. What I see is always the same, a vibrant, exciting, energetic wild thing, and thank you for being a magnificent model."

"Are you two ladies going to stand around hugging one another all day or are we going to literally get this show on the road?"

"We are ready to go, darling. Auntie Betts, if you will get the materials, I'll get the food and I will be glad to drive. I'll even open the doors for my ladies."

"Thank you, sir. Here we go. Auntie Betts, lead us in some Xmas carols please, then we'll be all warmed up by tonight."

∗

"I absolutely love the decorations. They seem to be more meaningful every time I'm here. The town shows its loving personality so well, and of course, that amazing tribute to our Howdy adds so much to the town park and gathering place. It was so rewarding to see folks playing checkers and laughing, and children playing, seemingly unaware of the winter chill. Here we are."

"Oh, Maggie, this place always gives me God bumps. I am shivering with excitement and love. The lights are so beautiful inside and out. Let's just sit here for a moment, and let me just listen and watch."

"I know what you mean, Auntie Betts. We can see the happiness, and spirit of Christmas and hear it."

"Ladies, I am respectful of your wishes, but I just need to remind you that this is my first time here, and honestly, I would love to join the party."

"Of course you would, Richard, and so would we. We were just soaking in the memories. So let's go crash the party, folks. Yes, let's. Come on, Richard. We are on our way. You are in for quite a ride."

*

"Maggie, you were right again. I swear that lady can be in two or three places at the same time. Yes, and I know we will both be surprised at how much she gets done."

"I forgot to tell you, Richard. Please don't mention Galapagos. We kind of keep that discussion for more quiet times. Everyone just seems to know and respect that she will share that when and where she feels the time and place are right. It is certainly not during this time. This is Santa's time and place. And by the way, how are you doing?"

"I am trying to follow your advice and visit the different workshops, watch, and listen. I am learning so much, and I can feel the creative juices start to flow. How about you?"

"I am working relief for the children's card making projects, and then I'm helping Mary with dinner. We'll probably start dinner by six. The children usually leave by around seven, at least the younger ones do. So have fun, and I'll see you soon. By the way, Auntie Betts is the guest of honor tonight. So she will be sitting at the head of the table, which is exactly where she should be."

"Do you need help, Margaret?"

"No, darling. We're fine. You just have fun. Love you. It's so exciting to think about your sister and family being a part of this tomorrow night. I trust they will not be overwhelmed."

"I can assure you, Maggie, they may be momentarily speechless, however they will catch up quickly."

"Just like you, my darling."

"Truly, Maggie, I think this event, this community, this way of life is what everyone is looking for. It is like the pot of gold at the end of the rainbow. How lucky am I!"

"Richard, I think you are on a creative roll, so go with it."

"I just believe I will, my dear. See you soon."

"Have you been creating, darling?"

"Oh yes, the energy here is so high, and everyone is focused on a project, but still somehow working with others as well. I know it's pretty awesome. While we were creating Christmas cards, at first, each child wanted to do their very own, and they were very clear about how that was going to happen, and then the process just evolved into becoming a group project and became so much more, and the cards are still so individual. I am looking forward to meeting with them tomorrow."

"Margaret, have I gained weight, and just don't know it?"

"Why would you ask a question like that, Richard?"

"I know I am eating more. Everything is always like a grand buffet, like tonight."

"No, darling, you haven't gained weight. You actually don't overeat, Richard. Your portions are really quite small."

"I am consciously doing that because I want to taste everything, and I just can't."

"I know, neither can I. But the good news is that we don't need to because there's always another opportunity."

"That's right. Thank you.

"Richard, have you noticed how Auntie Betts is absolutely glowing? She is obviously so happy to be here tonight. After mom and dad's death, it was really hard for her for a while. She and Mom really were close. They actually did answer questions for one another, and the questions hadn't actually been asked. They truly were of one mind. I always found it quite funny and not unusual at all. Now I realize how very special their relationship was."

"I'm so glad she's with us, Maggie. I know my family will totally fall in love with her just like I have."

"That reminds me, Richard. I need to share another tradition with you. I'm sure you will be fine with it."

"I am a bit concerned about overwhelming everyone else. On the twenty-third, after dinner, the children have an overnight sleepover in the barn which is very comfortable and heat regulated. The elders take turns sharing the honor of staying with them. They all have sleeping bags, and it is indeed a highlight of the season for them. The elders tell stories and sing rounds with them. I'm telling you this because while the children are gathered in the barn, there is a very special meeting happening in the large round meeting center. We have several speakers. Auntie Betts is one of them this year. The purpose is spiritual in keeping with the season. As members of this community, we understand that we are representations of past generations. The seeds were planted by our forefathers and mothers, both physically and morally. This is a great time of celebration for us, our community, recognizing the love we have for one another. It is truly an inspiration to renew the values of our sacred commitment to continue the patterns that have provided us with such joy, abundance, health, and happiness. It is a gathering that we all look forward to. My concern is that it may be a bit overwhelming for my new family, and I do so want them to be comfortable, Richard. That's why I may have seemed a bit shaky when I learned they were coming on the twenty-third. I just don't know exactly how to handle it, and I know it's a lot for you to manage as well."

"Darling, Maggie, you are thinking too much."

"I know I need a little time and quiet meditation to sort this out, and it will sort out."

"I know my family will be fine either way. Thank you, Maggie, for sharing with me your concerns. Let's always do that. The family arrives at around noon tomorrow. We will have time to share lunch, and they can settle in and explore the cottage a big before we go to the center which they have already expressed excitement about doing. We can leave a little early if we choose to. I suggest we practice what we preach."

"Live in the moment is what you were going to say, weren't you, Richard?"

"Yes, my darling."

"I have a great teacher. Thank you. However I think we are taking turns being teacher and student, and I think that is a perfect blend. Also, in case, I haven't actually said it, you are absolutely right, and I know it. I feel so much better. I certainly don't know how everything will happen, however, I do know it will flow like a river."

"My goodness, time has flown again. Aunt Betts is playing the piano. Soon everyone will gather, and we are in for a treat. Honestly, Richard, she has the voice of an angel, and when we all start singing, it is so beautiful. The sound does fill the air, and it is indeed the sound of love and joy. I am enjoying the piano piece. She is a fine pianist. She is an excellent speaker as well. She combines humor with wisdom, and she is absolutely spell-binding. But for tonight, it's all fun and games time. Let's join her before the crowd gets here. I love to watch every expression."

"Ladies, your chariot awaits."

"Thank you, darling."

"Are you ready too, Auntie Betts?"

"I am ready, child. What a wonderful evening! Richard, you are a natural baritone. What a voice! Your talents just keep revealing themselves."

"Thank you, Betts, coming from you especially. I truly appreciate the compliment. Before I came to this community, I hadn't sung since high school, not really. I would sing in church, and yes, in the shower."

"In high school, I was in several musicals, and I loved singing. Tonight, singing with you and Margaret was such a gift. Thank you. The energy that everyone brings to this gathering makes singing such a joy."

"This has been another perfect day, Maggie. I am pleasantly tired, and, at the same time, eagerly looking forward to tomorrow. With our new family arriving and the creativity really started flowing today, I have all of my projects clearly finished in my mind. I have a vision of every gift I am making, so no time or energy will be wasted thinking about how it will happen. I am ready to proceed with clear intentions, and I know the steps necessary will flow in divine order to create the finished results. You are such an inspiration, Auntie Betts. You always have been and I have always been surprised and pleased with all of the many gifts I have seen you create, and again it seems like magic because you're always everywhere, talking and encouraging everyone, and then somehow you bring those unique beautiful gifts out of your bag, and I am once again surprised that you have created such masterpieces, while laughing, telling stories, helping others, and still manage to get everything completed. Richard, you help me keep an eye on her this year. I know she must have some elves stashed somewhere."

"You bet. I would love to have a few of those myself."

"You two are a pair, and I really do mean that. You are so right together. I just love watching you, however we are home now, and if you don't mind, I think I will go up to my room straight away."

"I think we are going to do the same thing, Auntie Betts. That is, after Howdy and I have a little time to catch up on the day's activities.

If he's up to it tomorrow, I think we'll take him with us. I know he loves this time so much. Good night, children and Howdy, love. I'll see you in the morning. Howdy, I missed you so much, I kept looking for you. Yes, I know you missed us too. I found a special place for you to have quiet time when you need it, and I'll probably join you."

"Richard my love, remember you are the number one host tomorrow."

"Yes, oh yes, I know, family. Maggie, I am so excited and a tiny bit anxious. It's been a while, and I feel like a different person. Maybe they won't recognize me."

"You are a silly goose, Richard. Everything and everyone is going to be absolutely perfect. Now just take a deep breath and talk to Howdy about it. He always knows everything, don't you, boy? Richard, Howdy and I feel like we already know everyone, and we are ready for this next adventure. So we will sleep well tonight and be ready for a full and wonderful day tomorrow. How about you? Are you ready to relax and enjoy?"

"With you, Howdy, and Aunt Betts on my team, absolutely."

"I love mornings—getting up early to enjoy the quiet time before everything starts. The aroma of coffee and the anticipation of savoring the smell before the first taste of exquisite rich hot black coffee with just a hint of cinnamon and honey blended with the newness of the morning, and you, Howdy. Every day, actually, every moment is new to you. You are so alert and aware of everything. I'm still struggling to live in the moment, but you my friend are a great motivator. Speaking of motivation, it's yoga time. I am so glad I really paid attention to your version of what I was doing. Your form is much better than mine, just one more thing you have taught me. I love Saturday morning especially. It's my day of self-indulgence, no structure, and today no errands. I didn't bring any work home with me. Even the weather has cooperated. There is a bit of a nip in the air, but the sun is bright and warm, so our special Saturday walk will be perfect. Now that we have finished our routine, I love watching you meditate. Howdy, I often get to hear you as well. That's really deep meditation. I've worked it into my routine. It's something like 'Om'. So now for my really special breakfast this morning, and that's going to be sourdough hot cakes, delicious Maine blueberries, with maple syrup, and I am also going to have an egg and some of that wonderful fresh honey-cured ham. I really hope you're up to a nice long hike today. I'm going to need it. However, after breakfast, you can curl up in your favorite spot by the fireplace, and I will spend about thirty minutes writing. Poetry night is coming so I will use that for stimulation. I have really had a block for a while. Oh well it happens. This too shall pass. I know myself well enough to understand that I am not naturally a disciplined person, so I continue creating ways to compensate. As a child, many times my parents, teachers, and friends often told me I was a dreamer. Not in an unkind way but rather to wake me up so I could pay attention to what was happening in the moment. I am aware that I still have a tendency to shift into my other worldliness. As a matter of fact, that's when I find most of my inspiration. However I do function much better with routine. I certainly found that out after my parents died and then Chad. That's the only way I could function. Routine, you, Howdy, and this wonderful spiritual community kept me moving. So my life is pretty predictable. Monday through Friday, up at 6:00 a.m. Drink a glass of cold water, then have a cup of hot water with vinegar and honey, then you and I do our stretches, yoga, meditation, and then we are ready for our walk. Especially you, Howdy, I think you endure the rest of the activities, knowing that your reward is close. What a joy you are, so full of curiosity and unconditional love for everyone and everything."

"Good morning, Richard, my you look chipper this morning, and the coffee aroma traveled all the way upstairs into my bedroom, and I had no choice but to come down here, ready or not."

"Good morning, Betts, and yes, I feel fantastic. I am so excited to see my family, I just want to tell them everything about this wonderful community, and Margaret, and you, and of course, Howdy, and the holiday traditions and find out what they have been doing since I last saw them."

"And wait just a minute, Richard. Sit for a spell and let's savor the coffee and the moment. A couple of deep breaths do wonders for perspective. Richard, you may want to consider taking a moment at a time. There's no need to rush. Everything will evolve in a timely manner, no pushing or pulling. Just be, Richard. Trust me they will have questions, and probably as the question is formed, the answers will be understood. Do you know what I mean, Richard?"

"Yes, I do Betts, and I know you are right. Howdy and Margaret tried to tell me last night, and I knew then, and I know now. Live in the moment, and each moment will be complete. Speaking of complete, I have a breakfast casserole in the oven, and it very well may be completely cooked."

"Whatever it is, Richard, it smells very good, and I'll just be. Margaret will be down here any minute now. Your casserole has a wonderful breakfast smell to it, and here she is right on cue."

"Good morning, Maggie girl, your betrothed, and I have been chatting a bit, and I think I delayed breakfast. I'll pour the juice, after I have my coffee, at least a sip."

"What can we do to help, darling?"

"You just did, Maggie. A good morning kiss may be all that I need in exchange for breakfast."

"Yes, right, good thing you said 'may need'. Breakfast is served, ladies. Auntie Betts, would you be willing to say the blessing? Thank you, Richard. I would be honored."

"I draw in deep calming breaths that spread through my body. I breathe in gratitude for all I see, hear taste, smell and touch. I am grateful for my loved ones, and the many blessings in my life. As Psalm 86:12 says, 'I give thanks to you, O Lord my God, with my whole heart.' And so it is. This is certainly a day for celebration. Our family is increasing today. We all have so much to be grateful for."

"Yes, Maggie my love, we surely do."

"Thank you for this wonderful breakfast, Richard. You seem to be the first one up recently, and it's certainly working well for me and Aunt Betts. Works well for me also. I really do enjoy cooking breakfast, especially when I have so many choices that Mary has prepared for me."

"So that's your secret. However it happens, it's all good. What time do you need to be at the airport, Richard?"

"What do you mean me? Don't you mean us?"

"I have really thought about it, and I think it feels right for you to meet them and have a little time together and perhaps stop for lunch. Aunt Betts and I will prepare something for the dinner gathering at the center. We'll have tea and muffins together after they have settled in to the cottage. We have time. No need to rush. What do you think, Richard?"

"I think I assumed you would be going with me, however, I certainly respect your perspective, as usual, and no, I don't get tired of saying it. I think you're right again, Maggie. They arrive around noon, so lunch is also a great idea. I think it would be good, if it works out for us to go to the center at least by four o'clock. Then they will have a little time before dinner to get the lay of the land."

"Richard, you could show Kevin around, and maybe get an idea of his interest. Aunt Betts, young people adore you, so Kara and Jamie could be our charge. Mary Beth and I will check things out. How does that sound? Or another suggestion?"

"Sounds great to me, Maggie. Count me in. Thank you, Aunt Betts."

"Me too, Maggie. I'm not sure what my plan is, but I know there will be one."

"Yes, Richard, I am sure there will be. OK, Howdy, I see the leash. It looks like Howdy has a plan for me, and I will tell him all about the family while we're on our little walk. Thank you, Richard. I love you."

"Richard has a little anxiety today, I think. He has a natural exuberance, but I sense a bit of tension with it, which of course is understandable. Yes, he and I had a little talk before you came down. He was a little over the top, but he is fine, Maggie. I am glad that he is getting his feelings out now. Once he sees everyone, everything will just pop into place much like a dislocated shoulder."

"You do have a unique and colorful way of explaining things, Aunt Betts, and you always have, at least all of my life. You and Howdy are like beacons in the night. Every time I needed to find my way, one or both of you were there."

"Thank you, my sweet girl. Now I think we have some stuff to do. Would you be willing to create one of those guiding lists that you do so well? I'll get ready, and we can get about it. This is a special day, Maggie. Of course, every day is. But this one will be one of those memorable times to take out of our treasure chest in the future and fill us up with joy. That's one of the ways we continue creating great energy, darling. Live in the moment, create treasured memories, and within those memories are the very energy that was there at the time it was happening."

"That's why I still have my trusty old camera. It's been with me for a long time and seems to know when it's time to capture the moment."

"I have a great camera at Galapagos, and boy, has it ever collected the memory moments, many of which I am proud to say have been published and enjoyed by many. It is part of my 'pass it on' mission. Oh my and I am the one that said let's get to it."

"Thank you, Auntie Betts, there is nothing I enjoy more than sharing time with you."

"Bless you, Maggie. See you in a few."

"You two look like the cat that swallowed the canary. Looks like you had a nice walk and talk."

"That we did, Maggie. Howdy is a wizard, you know?"

"Yes, I do know that, Richard. He always allows us to be our best selves."

"Yes, that's it. I look forward to our little walks much more than he does."

"I don't know about that, Richard, he looks pretty proud of himself to me, and you look very calm, cool, and collected."

"I am, Maggie. I do know everything will flow today. I know my family. I just forgot for a few minutes. A twinge of guilt showed up in the form of anxiety. I was out of touch for quite a while, and Sylvia and I had the kids over most weekends. We were kind of like alternate parents, and then I was just gone and have had very little contact since. I was truly a lost soul."

"So are you really ready to pick them up by yourself, or do you want support?"

"I am ready, Maggie, and I know it's going to be great, but thank you for understanding. Now I had better get myself ready, and be on my way."

"You are well on your way, darling, have a good time, and we will look forward to seeing our new play pals."

"Maggie, Howdy and I were meditating, and the next thing I knew I was waking up. What time is it?"

"Like you would know."

"Actually, Auntie Betts, this time I do know, I just put the muffins in the oven, and I set the timer. It's a little after one."

"Oh my goodness, I had no idea. Richard will be back any minute now, and I must be a mess."

"Relax, darling, they won't be here until around two or a little after. Richard is taking them to lunch, at the Pharmacy."

"I know they will love that."

"And then he will give them a thumbnail sketch of town, saving most of that for you and me to fill in. So actually we can have a cup of tea and relax for a few minutes. Everything is prepared for the evening. Maggie, my dear, you are so organized, and it's so natural. Your mother and I used to marvel at what an old soul you are, so wise and witty, and thank goodness you loved to play games and have fun with storytelling."

"I still do, Auntie Betts. Sometimes at the library, I get a little too focused. Fortunately, I have Mary there to let me know when I need to loosen up a bit, take a deep breath, and know that everything is as it should be."

"Well, I know those muffins are as they should be. They smell heavenly. They are ready to come out of the oven, that's for sure."

"Auntie Betts, I really feel like another chapter of my life is beginning, and it feels so right. You know Richard and I have discussed having children and much to my surprise, I think actually for both of us, we really do want to have a family."

"Oh, Maggie, my love, I am so happy for you. I know you and Richard will have a rich and happy life either way, but perhaps somewhat selfishly, I am very pleased that our family will continue. I have felt a twinge of guilt occasionally for choosing not to have children. However, only occasionally, and I do know that I made the right decision. My work has been, and will be, my legacy. It is so nice to have these chats, Maggie. I love you very much, my girl"

"I know you do, Aunt Betts. I look forward to our visits, always have and always will. And I am especially glad you are with us this Xmas. I know it will be one of great joy. You have a lot to share, especially with Jamie and Kara."

"So do you, my darling."

"Yes, but you have such a gift with young ones. Speaking of young ones, Maggie, I think they are here. So they are, and Howdy is right there to greet them. Bless his heart. He is still doing his 'welcome to our home' job that he does so well."

*

"Richard, everything is just as I imagined. Everyone was immediately at home and comfortable. It seems as though we have known each other forever."

"Yes, it does, and Maggie, when I met them at the airport it was like we had never been apart, even the kids. There wasn't a second of hesitation or a moment of awkwardness. My sister had explained my need to have some time to heal, and they understood that. We had a great time at the Pharmacy, and yes, they loved the chocolate phosphates."

"Were you able to show them at least a little of our town?"

"Yes, and I was very pleased with my familiarity. Of course, I chose carefully, and it was a very quick overview. I chose one of my favorite streets where the older homes are, many of which were built for Port Haven sea captains and lead to the waterfront. And of course we went by our downtown favorite gathering place, the Seascape. They are really looking forward to having you give them a tour, and of course to meet Mary."

"They will indeed meet Mary shortly. She has already called to make sure they had arrived, and when we would be coming to the festivities, which by the way, is about now. Oh yes, everyone is ready for that. Richard, they obviously fell absolutely in love with the cottage, and of course, with Howdy. I don't believe I have ever seen anyone settle in to a new place as quickly as they did. They didn't really need any help at all. They found their sleeping areas immediately and are obviously very pleased with the Xmas decorations and loved the tree. We are going to have such a delightful holiday. I love the sound of laughter, and excitement. The cottage has come to life again. Thank you, my darling Richard. I love my new family."

"I am so glad, darling, but not surprised. Now let's get this caravan headed in the direction of the North Pole and Santa's Workshop. We have things to do, food to eat, and songs to sing. Let the party begin. I'll go down to the cottage and get the family. Is there anything that you would like for me to put in the van, on my way?"

"Thanks, darling, no. Auntie Betts and I have that part under control. I do want to take Howdy. What do you think?"

"Maggie, he loves being there. Everyone loves him and he knows he can get behind the stove in his safe spot if he needs to rest. I think he should go if he wants."

"Thank you, Richard, I know you are right. I just needed to hear you say it, so let's do it."

"Wow, look at the lights, Auntie Maggie! Your place is beautiful and bright, but this place is gigantic. Is it a palace?"

"No, Kara, well now, maybe it is, perhaps more like a magical castle. This is our community spiritual living center, and we do a lot of living in it. You will all find many new friends here tonight. This is our, well, one of our favorite times of the year. As a community, we are family, and for this week or so of celebration, we get to be together often, so it's very special, much like it is having all of you here to share it with us. So let's go explore the castle with its many rooms full of adventures. Tonight we are all Santa Claus's helpers. Yes indeed, Jamie and Kara, we will be a team tonight, and I'm sure we'll have many other elves joining us. I'll give you a tour first, and we'll all gather when the dinner bell rings."

"Auntie Betts, I'll just bet you could make anything."

"Thank you, Jamie, but fortunately I won't be put that test. We have master craftsman and women at our disposal. See you folks at dinnertime. Now let's be off."

"Mary Beth you look a little overwhelmed. Are you all right?"

"Oh yes, Maggie I'm much better than all right, I just feel like I need to pinch myself occasionally to see if this is all true. Richard is so happy, and when we would talk on the phone, I could tell that he had found a very special place and of course a very special person. He also told me there was no way he could explain this community to me. It was something I just had to experience. We have missed him so much, but seeing him happy, so complete. I am so glad that his journey brought him here. You and Richard are a perfect fit."

"Thank you, Mary Beth, and I have always wanted a sister so now I have one, and big bonus of a wonderful brother-in-law. Actually, I don't like in-law. So I'm just going to drop that right now. And Jamie and Kara are absolutely delightful, and what a wonderful holiday gift to share this time together. Now let's get on with the tour. We have some gift-making to do. Kevin and Richard have absolutely disappeared, and so has Howdy."

"Maggie, this is a magical place, full of cinnamon and spice, laughter, and oh so beautiful. Everything and everyone sparkles."

"Speaking of spice, I promised my friend Mary that I would bring you by to meet her first. And wherever Mary is, there will be food and drink. Her hot cider is very special. However, the hot chocolate is also. It's a win-win situation with Mary, in every way. I probably should warn you, you will get a lot of hugs tonight, starting with Mary. I hope you're ready for that."

"Oh yes, Maggie, I am more than ready. Let's go. There she is right by the ovens as usual."

"Maggie, child, it's so good to see you. Happy holidays, and this must be Mary Beth. I can see a resemblance to Richard. Mary Beth, welcome to our home and heart. I love Richard, and I am so happy to meet you, child."

"I told her you were a hugger, Mary, but you had better make sure she's still breathing."

"Oh, you're just jealous. Come here, Maggie girl. I have missed you so much. I am glad we have some time off for the holidays, but I already miss our morning coffee time."

"Yes, I do too, Mary. And speaking of coffee, I want some cider. And what would you like, Mary Beth?"

"I'll have the same, Maggie. Thank you."

"Do you want some help with dinner, Mary?"

"Absolutely not, Maggie, thank you. Our dinner team is top notch, and as usual there is enough food to feed an army. You just see to Mary Beth and the rest of the family, which I am anxious to meet, especially the young ones. Anyhow, you two have plenty to do, and Mary Beth you have a lot to see and people to meet. The dinner bell will ring at 6:30 p.m. Until then, have fun, you two."

"Mary is a delight, just like seeing our old friend, and that's really what she is, Mary Beth. She is an old friend. And she will always be your friend, that's Mary. Now, for the tour."

*

"It seems impossible, Kevin, but that is the dinner bell. So it must be 6:30 p.m."

"Rich, I want to thank you for inviting us to share the holidays and this amazing community with us. At first we were pretty sure we wanted to be at home for Xmas, and then all of us kind of at the same time decided that you are home and being together was like a special Xmas gift. Boy, were we right. This experience is like an Xmas miracle."

"Thank you, Kevin. It is so good to be with all of you. I have missed you so much. We are so glad you changed your minds. Now let's go join the others for dinner, and just a word of warning, be prepared to see more food than you've probably ever seen at one time in your life. And there they are."

"Hi, Sis, you look radiant, and you, my darling Maggie, have even a brighter than usual glow tonight."

"Oh, Richard, we have been having so much fun. We have already started our gift projects. Kevin, this is like Santa's workshop. The kids and Auntie Betts must be having a wonderful time."

"Yes, Auntie Betts is usually one of the first ones here. She's kind of like the informal greeter, although like me, we do have a challenge of time. There they are now. Kara and Jamie are obviously having a great time, as is Auntie Betts, which of course for her is not unusual."

"Aunt Maggie, I have never seen such a lot of food. It's everywhere, and the smells in here are awesome."

"Yes, they are Kara, and what have you all been up to? Now that, my dear, I will answer for them. It's all top secret stuff, you know. That's the way Santa's workshop is."

"You are so right as usual, Auntie Betts. I don't even know who is going to say the gratitude blessing for dinner. Are you going to start it, Auntie Betts?"

"No, my dear, not this time. We have a special guest with us tonight. He's not really a guest. It's our Amish friend from Ohio, Galen Irven. We're going to ask him to say the blessing tonight."

"Auntie Betts, I haven't seen him since my high school graduation. He spent the summer with us. It will be wonderful to visit with him. He helped a lot of folks, something to do with farming. Of course, Chad and I were busy with other things that summer, but Mr. Irven stayed at the cottage often, and I remember he looked so serious, but he had a great sense of humor and a very deep 'belly' laugh."

"He still does have, my dear. He and his family before him have been very good friends to this community. By the way, Mary Beth, Kara, and Jamie made excellent progress this evening. They have both made decisions about the gifts they are making. As a matter of fact, they have already started on them."

"Aunt Maggie, Uncle Richard, this is so great. The people that are showing us what to do are amazing. I'm not even afraid to try anything, and Jamie has already started a really neat project."

"Well, you two are ahead of me. Mary Beth, I think you and I had better shape up. After dinner, we'll get serious."

"Sounds like a plan, Maggie."

"How are you, Richard? Have you and Kevin started projects?"

"As a matter of fact, yes we have. Saved by the bell. I think Mr. Irven is getting ready to speak. Auntie Betts, he doesn't look any older than did when I saw him so long ago."

"I doubt that he is, Maggie."

It is a pleasure to be here surrounded by all of you at this most precious time of celebration. I am honored to have the privilege of sharing this evening with you. We all have a place at God's table. The bread has been broken, the wine will be poured. You are welcome to share all of the love that is here. The candles are glowing, but the light from within each of you is the brightest of all. This is the season of love. This community was built on love and has been sustained through love. As we continue to progress on our spiritual path, we will continue to understand that nothing is more powerful than the love of God in the human heart. As we continue through this time of celebration, let us remember that divine love and wisdom is within each one of us, in every person, and circumstance. The more we focus on the fullness of life, the more gratitude we will feel. Let us gratefully acknowledge our abundant blessings and give thanks. According to Colossians 3:16, 'Let the word of Christ dwell in you richly. With gratitude in your hearts sing psalms, hymns, and spiritual songs to God.' Now let's enjoy this bountiful feast set before us, which was prepared with love and labor by our brothers and sisters. A toast to one another and this wonderful season which celebrates the gift of life through the ultimate gift of love. Enjoy."

"Mary Beth, I don't know where to start. Everything looks and smells so good. Kevin, I have never seen anything stop you from eating. Here, start with this. And I know I am going to start with a tablespoon because I want to taste everything."

"And I know I really can't. So maybe we should start with a teaspoon? What's up, Kev? You don't like the food?"

"Sure, Rich, that's the problem. Wow, this is quite a feast for the eyes, the nose, and ultimately for everything. We may not eat again."

"Sure, Kev, at least not until brunch tomorrow."

"Brunch! Get in the moment, you guys. Be here now. Breathe."

"Thank you, Margaret. I think we really needed to hear that."

"So did I, Mary Beth. Richard and I take turns with the centering thing. It's kind of like sailing a ship. Keep an eye on the way the wind blows, and be ready to correct. Auntie Betts, you have been very quiet. Are you all right?"

"Maggie, my girl, I am doing what I just heard you talking about. I am in the moment, totally enthralled with the food, laughter, and the gift of life. Kara and Jamie are also. They have blended right in with the group. They look like they have been friends forever. They probably have. It was a joy taking them around to the different project groups. Everywhere we went, they were complete."

"Thank you, Auntie Betts. They really admire you. And usually Jamie is kind of reserved at first. He generally doesn't seem to like crowds. But you certainly wouldn't know that by seeing him here. I don't think he is a follower. He will definitely find his place and make his contribution."

"Well, I am full as a tic, and I want to find Galen. We have some catching up to do. And those young ones don't need a shadow. They are focused. Have fun. I'm sure we will all drift back for dessert about the same time. Kevin, don't say, not now, just wait. After you have worked a while and you start smelling the cinnamon, ginger, nutmeg, and so forth, you'll be here. It is like a magnet. We all manage to be drawn back, and it's oh so wonderful. See you all later. Have fun with your gift-making. You are allowed to whistle or sing while you work, you know."

"She is an absolute angel, Maggie."

"Yes, I agree. I have always had fun with Auntie Betts. She is a free spirit. I am never surprised when I receive cards from her. She lives fully, and yes, she has a lovely bed-and-breakfast cottage on one of the Galapagos islands. She was one of the few that were allowed to be there initially. She was doing a research project and fell in love with the island, so it's her refuge. I really want to go there to visit sometime. I've seen and felt it through her stories so many times."

"When Richard and I were children, Richard was always traveling to faraway places in his imagination. I, on the other hand, loved familiar places. I went to college to become a home economics teacher, and Richard became a journalist, first writing about places, and then after Sylvia died, he wrote about food and travel pieces and stayed on the road, actually mostly in the air for several years. We kind have lost Richard for a while."

"Mary Beth, from what I've learned from Richard, he pretty much lost him for a while. Both he and I share experiences in grief and grieving. Everyone does it in his or her own time and way. I do know that Richard's love for you, and the family, has never wavered. I am so happy that we have this special time to celebrate together. Thank you so much for changing your plans and traditions to be with us."

"Maggie, I can't begin to tell you how happy I am that we did. Now, girlfriend, we had better gets ourselves over to the workshop."

"Yes, let's do it. I am ready to roll although I am not exactly sure whether I'm rocking or rolling."

"We will probably do a little bit of both before we're through, Mary Beth."

"Is it really time to go, Uncle Richard? I need just a little while longer to finish my last piece."

"Me too, Uncle Richard. We just can't go right now."

"OK, guys, I hear you. I'm sure everyone will be willing to stay a little longer. Do you need a little help with your projects?"

"Oh no! Just a little more time."

"Kara, would you like some help?"

"No, Uncle Richard, thank you, but I am really just about through, and I am so excited about the gifts I made. I know now what it means when people say giving a gift is better than receiving one, or something like that. Anyhow I had better get busy."

"Well, I'll check in with you guys in about thirty minutes. Kev and I will go check on the ladies. Obviously, he and I were through first. I'm not sure if that's a good sign."

"Richard, honestly now, how could it be anything else? Mary Beth is as excited as the kids. Earlier when I went by, she, Maggie, and Aunt Betts were totally oblivious to anything else. When I saw them earlier, they were laughing at something Mary Beth had done. Richard, I think I may have asked you already, but if I haven't, I would really like to know more about this town."

"I know what you mean, Kev. Sure, we'll take a tour, and I'll show you some of the sights. Maggie, and, of course, Aunt Betts can really give you an overview and of course answer questions. I think the ladies are finished with their projects, not the laughter. What a great sound you, ladies, make. Auntie Betts, I think you have created a trio. You all sound great together, and so we are, my friends."

"Where are the young ones? Have they found a napping spot?"

"Oh no, they are focused on their gift-making. They need just a little more time. Howdy certainly found his napping spot. Yes, but he had a great time for a while. He made his rounds as usual and then found his safe spot. He's been dosing ever since."

"Dozing? He couldn't snore like that while dozing. He is really pretty loud for it to be called dozing."

"That's true. He is so comfortable. I really hate to awaken him. After Kara and Jamie get here, I'll carry him out."

"Maggie, thank you, darling."

"Did you and Kevin have a good time?"

"Absolutely. And we got a lot done. It's so good to see the kids so involved. They are really into their projects."

"Now you know why this center means so much to me, Richard. And having all of you here to share it with, well, it's just that much more special. Auntie Betts, would you like some hot chocolate or something?"

"No, child, I am complete. I just like sitting here and soaking it all up."

"I know. So do I."

"How late is the center open, Maggie?"

"Kevin, there are folks who stay here all night. The center never really has a specific time for opening or closing. When we have a game night or special performance, of course, we know what time those are scheduled. Otherwise, it's pretty much just home."

"Kev, you and Mary Beth should have been here for the harvest festival. It was great."

"Oh yes, Richard, and for the food preparation after the festival."

"Mary Beth, I think you would really love that. You could certainly practice all of your home economics skills. It's pretty intense, but oh so meaningful and fun."

"Also, Maggie, we get the benefit year round."

"Richard, when the time is right, I think the family would enjoy a tour of our storehouse and perhaps a tour of the community storehouse, which is immense."

"Maggie, we love your community. It is a haven. The name fits perfectly—Port Haven. I know I can speak for all of us when I say we would love to come back this summer."

"You and Richard talk about it, and if it isn't convenient, we will understand."

"Richard, I don't think we need to talk about it, do we?"

"I know I don't. We would be delighted to have you anytime. That's what the cottage is for, and there is so much more we can explore in the summertime. This is the best Xmas present ever, Mary Beth. I think I hear Kara's laugh."

"We finished. All of our Xmas presents are made, and boy, are you guys going to be surprised? We can make anything. I am so excited. I don't think I can wait until Xmas for you to get your presents, but, Aunt Betts, we did wrap them just like you showed us. At home, we always opened one present on Xmas Eve. Are we going to do that here?"

"Actually, Kara, we have that tradition also, don't we, Rich?"

"Yes, we do, and I think it's a great tradition to honor. So tomorrow night starts at about seven o'clock. Don't you think, Mom?"

"I think we will not place a definite time on when evening starts. We will know when the time is right for the gift opening. Until then, you can just look at them and decide which one you will choose. You know, we will be trimming our tree at the cottage tomorrow evening also. Will we all be doing it together?"

"I certainly hope so, Richard. Auntie Betts and I especially love to do the popcorn and cranberry strings."

"Really! We're going to make our own decorations?"

"Yes, we are."

"Jamie, do you think you can manage to make at least one more thing?"

"Oh yes, and I'm tall enough to put the treetop on also."

"Yes, you are, and that will be yours to do. That means, of course, that you have to create it first."

"Great! I can do that. I think it's time to load the van. We can get all of these in the back. If not, I'll come back in the morning and pick them up."

"Oh no, Uncle Richard. They will fit. I'll help you."

"Thank you, Jamie. Let's do it."

"I want to help too."

"Come on, Kara, start bringing them out, and we'll arrange them."

"What a beautiful day and evening this has been. Have I told you how grateful I am that you kept pestering me to come for Xmas and especially to meet Richard?"

"I am so glad I did, Auntie Betts. I just knew you had to be here to make this the most perfect holiday, and it is. I love you so very much. Thank you for coming home."

"Thank you, child. I needed this more than you, and I'll tell you, Jamie and Kara are the icing on the cake. They have great energy and are truly the spirit of Xmas."

"Yes, Aunt Betts, we have much to be grateful for. It's almost Xmas Eve—one of my very favorite days."

"Ladies, we have accomplished our mission. Everything is in the van but you."

"Yes, Richard, and who else?"

"That's it, darling. Kev and the kids are in and buckled up, as we shall be shortly. However there is one more pretty important parcel. Maggie, you didn't think I would forget Howdy, did you?"

"Of course not, darling. Just checking. Let's go folks."

"I think we're going to have a very cozy drive home. At least we will definitely be warm enough."

"That was the quietest time we've had. All of you guys slept the entire way home. I think you were all sleeping before I pulled out of the driveway. We're home now, and we'll leave all of the gifts in the car until tomorrow, or, more correctly, until later today. It is past midnight."

"Mary Beth, I think I told you but maybe not. We'll have Xmas Eve brunch at around 10:00 a.m., and then we'll talk about the rest of the day. I can tell you we stay very casual all day and evening. So dress comfortably."

"That sounds wonderful, Maggie. I am sure we are all going to sleep very well tonight. So good night all, and thank you again for such a memorable day. See you in the morning, or this morning whatever, good night all."

"Auntie Betts, do you need anything?"

"Oh, Maggie, my love, I just need to get upstairs and let that wonderful feather bed just let me melt into it. I will see you two in the morning. Good night, loves."

"Good night, Aunt Betts."

"Richard, did Howdy wake up at all?"

"Oh yes, Maggie, and he took advantage of being outside fortunately because I think once I hit that bed I'm not going to want to get up and take him outside."

"Nor would I. What an absolutely perfect day and evening this has been."

"Yes, it was love. Good night, darling."

"Good night, Richard. I love you."

✳

"Good morning, Maggie. I don't think either one of us moved all night. I know I literally passed out, I think, and certainly not from drinking. How are you this morning?"

"Richard, I feel completely regenerated."

"So do I. Isn't this a wonderful way to start the day?"

"Yes, and what a day it will be. Our first Xmas Eve together. Yes, the first of many to come. Shall we begin the day?"

"Let's do it. I'll go start the coffee, Maggie."

"Take your time, love."

"Good morning, Richard."

"Good morning, Aunt Betts. You are looking chipper this morning."

"Yes, I had a good night's sleep. I hardly remember getting in the bed, but I'll tell you when I opened my bedroom door this morning, I thought I caught the whiff of the sweet aroma of delicious Galapagos coffee, and the thought of it was enough to get me down the stairs."

"Well, I'm afraid it's not Galapagos coffee, but it's very good and here you are."

"Thank you, Richard."

"Do you miss Galapagos, Betts?"

"Oh sure, I do, at times, but most of the time, I just enjoy wherever I am at the moment. Galapagos does have a special place in my heart though. I love my cottage. It's the last place in that area, so I'm surrounded by the special creatures of Galapagos and of course the bed and breakfast is close. That was my home when I first went to the island. The village built it for us. When we were there, the area wasn't open to tourists. It has six bedrooms and was large enough for the whole research party. After the project finished, they all moved on. I had my friends Aleya and Lenoli move in. They and the other islanders helped me build my cottage, and they have been managing the bed and breakfast ever since. Aleya is a wonderful cook and loves to clean everything, singing all the while. Lenoli is the epitome of a handyman. They are pure love. My you really must have pushed a button, Richard. I should be up helping you with brunch, instead of bending your ear."

"Oh no, Betts. I love to listen, and I am especially intrigued with Galapagos, so thank you for sharing. Have you ever considered visiting there, Richard?"

"As a matter of fact, when I was doing articles for a variety of travel magazines, I really wanted to do a piece on the Galapagos, but it just never worked out."

"So yes, Maggie, I do want to do some traveling, and that's high on our list."

"Great! I was hoping you would say that. Now seriously, I do know my way around this kitchen so let's get this show on the road."

"Very soon, we will have more help than we could possibly know what to do with. What is on our menu?"

"I know we have traditional Xmas Eve brunch, but I'm not sure I remember it correctly or which tradition it is this year. It's been a few years since I've had the pleasure."

"Oh good! I hear Maggie. I guess I'll have to confess. She and I have talked about the brunch and I did listen but I'm not sure I remember, or understand. I do know we have everything available. I'm just not sure how it all goes together."

"Good morning. Maggie darling, and yes, I can tell you slept well. You are radiant."

"Morning again, Maggie love."

"Good morning, and Merry Xmas Eve. What special thing did you do to the coffee, Richard? It smells magical."

"Really, I just opened a new package that was in the freezer and made it as usual. That's the coffee you brought, Auntie Betts. I was right, Richard. I told you it smelled like delicious Galapagos coffee, and it is. What a special treat and perfect timing. It will probably last us through to the New Year."

"Thank you again, Auntie Betts. It is truly my treat, and I mean that literally. Now that we have our mastermind, we need to review the menu. So Richard and I can be useful instead of just beautiful. I did some prep already."

"Good idea. With the three of us we can have everything ready by the time the troops arrive. Aunt Betts, would you be willing to start singing Xmas carols? Rich and I will join in. I love this season and it's over so soon."

"Just like life, my darling. Let's seize the moment. I will get the menu, and we'll divide or unite and conquer, and we'll get it done as we sing or hum our way through. Let's let Kara and Jamie set the table."

"Richard, would you set everything out for them?"

"Thank you, love. Mary Beth and Kevin can be in charge of making fresh orange juice, and all of them can arrange the table decorations together. Now, the menu. Richard, during this season we honor many customs. I'll explain more about that when everyone's here. I did decide to combine a mix of familiarity, and new things so we will have fresh orange juice and some choices of those nice bubbly drinks from the storehouse. Buckwheat cakes, sausage, sliced cooked spiced apples, fruit cups, cracker pudding, those are all recipes from our Amish friends; Fungi Ripieni, cheese stuffed mushroom caps, Italian origin, I have those ready for the oven. And for platter, chicken potpie, Pennsylvanian Dutch style. One of the secrets is the saffron. Auntie Betts, you taught me how to make this. Would you be willing to prepare it?"

"We'll have it later, but we'll be able to enjoy the smell even as we're eating."

"Oh yes, Maggie. I love to cook it and eat it, so I'll get started on that right now."

"And lastly, the Moravian Sugar Cake, which we'll also have later, and later. So, Richard, if you'd be willing to start the cake, I'll prepare the first course to get us started on the feeding frenzy."

"Good morning, Howdy. You got here just in time to greet the family. They will be here very soon. You can join in with the Christmas carols if you like. Yes, I know after you go outside. Come on, buddy. I could use a little cold air to clear my head. Let's go."

"Thank you, Richard. The cake recipe is on the counter, and I'll put the potatoes on to boil."

"Yes, potatoes for the cake. It works every time."

"Yes, Richard, most of these recipes have been with us for at least hundred years, family to family treasures. Thanks, Betts, so I can't screw up, right?"

"Richard, my boy, breathe deep and relax, let the crisp beauty of the morning open your heart."

"Thank you, Betts, you already have. I love you. Come on, Howdy, let's go. I have a Christmas Eve cake to bake."

"Maggie, I can smell the magic already."

"I know, Auntie Betts. I get so much good energy just thinking about all the people that have and are doing exactly what we're doing right now. I love thinking about the different customs and special traditions. And today we get to share some of them with folks that may never have known them before. Speaking of that, I do believe I hear the sound of laughter, a sound that we'll be sharing for the rest of the day."

"Indeed we shall, Maggie."

"Good morning, everyone. I trust you slept well."

"Oh, Maggie, we did. It was so funny. We were all so excited about our accomplishments. One minute we were all talking and then there was complete silence."

"That's pretty much the way it was here, Mary Beth."

"However, we all look very much awake now. How can we help?"

"Richard has the plan of action for you, folks. Very soon, we will be ready to start celebrating the Festival of Nations."

"What does that mean, Aunt Maggie?"

"On Xmas Eve and Xmas Day, we honor many customs. This morning, we will be serving favorite recipes from our Amish friends, Italian, and German. Your Uncle Richard is making a Moravian Sugar Cake from a recipe dated in 1740. I promise there will be something for everyone. Aunt Betts and I will give you a very brief comment on the dish and where it originated. We believe you are all adventurous people, willing to try new things, although understandably missing some of your usual traditional foods. Are you all willing to embrace this adventure? Trust me, it will be so much more than a meal. It's a journey."

"It sounds so exciting to me. I've never thought about food as an experience or a journey. Have you, Jamie?"

"Nope but the smells in here have sold me. I can't wait to get started."

"Maggie, I keep thinking I am going to wake up, however I don't want to. Kev and I are so happy that we chose to spend the holidays here. We are so grateful for sharing all of this with you folks."

"Thank you. We have just begun, my sweet sister. And speaking of beginning, let's do just that. Let us gather around the table. Our custom is to hold hands as we have a moment of silence, and then I will say the blessing this morning. I am so blessed.

"I begin in quiet contemplation and gratitude, as I relinquish control and surrender to the spirit. In the silence, my open heart and mind reap the rewards of God's living, loving spirit. I experience deep peace and well-being. Every moment brings an opportunity to experience life anew. As I connect with the spirit within I know I am supported in every way. I am confident and excited as I venture into new territory and embrace this turning point in my life. According to Ecclesiastes 3:1, 'For everything there is a season, and a time for every matter under heaven.' And so it is. Thank you, Margaret my love. Now let's enjoy the beauty of this table. Thank you, guys, for being so creative. I have the honor of serving this morning. We will start with the fruit cups, and from there, Jamie and I will bring everything to the service table, and you're on your own."

"I am so hungry I want to eat everything all at one time."

"It's probably a good thing to pace you, Kara. We will be eating pretty much the rest of the day and evening."

"Now, Maggie, that's not exactly true. Sure, those wonderful smells from the oven will certainly be served. However, in between, we celebrate with song and dance. We always do the Mambo because Auntie Betts loves it, and several folk dances, again to celebrate the customs and cultures that have taught us so much. We usually end with a spiritual Native American dance. They are all easy to learn and fun to do, and we work up a great appetite for eating some more."

"Mom, Dad, do you think this is a little bit of paradise?"

"Kara, it just may be. I know that these are the best pancakes I have ever eaten. No offense, Mom, yours are great, but there's something so different about these."

"Well, Jamie, it just could be that the buckwheat flour is made at the mill, the maple syrup is from our own trees, and of course Maggie's magnificent gift of cooking with magic."

"Whatever. I want some more please."

"With all of the singing, dancing, and feasting, when do we get to decorate the tree and open a present and play games?"

"Darling girl, one moment at a time. Everything will happen in its time. Live and love this moment."

"I really do, Uncle Richard. My mouth just kind of gets a mind of its own sometimes."

"I know, Kara. Mine does too. Are you having a good time now?"

"Oh yes. Would you rather be anywhere else, doing anything else?"

"No! No! Well, as Maggie tells me and it works, take a deep breath, and be where you are."

"Right. And I would like some more pancakes also, please."

Richard, I am so happy. I love my new family so very much, and I have missed this kind of energy in the house for so long."

"Darling, may I give you my Xmas gift tonight? I'm a little like Kara, but I can wait if you have something else in mind."

"I would love to get my gift from you tonight, Richard."

"I loved every one of the dances, but the last one felt special to me. Could you tell me just a little bit about why you do it and how did you learn to do the storytelling with the dance?"

"Jamie, sorry, I'm not the one to ask. I have the same questions. Aunt Betts, Maggie, care to share?"

"I would be very happy to explain the spirit dance, but first, there is something I would like for you and Kara to do, Jamie. The day after Xmas is our quiet time. We have no schedule. There are plenty of leftovers. We eat what we want and when we want it. Your cottage will be well-supplied. Now I don't mean you are banned from the house. It's just a day that we use for rest and reflection. Typically, we read, think, meditate, and go for a short hike in the afternoon. You may have noticed the bookshelves in the cottage are full. Have either of you read Henry Wordsworth Longfellow's poem 'Hiawatha'?"

"No, I haven't. Have you, Jamie?"

"I'm familiar with Longfellow's name, but no, I haven't. Well then, you have an assignment. One of you can read Walt Whitman's 'Leaves of Grass,' while the other one reads 'Hiawatha,' which, by the way, you take your time reading. It is quite long, but you will definitely understand the spirit dance better after you have read the poem. Also just a bit of background. Longfellow was born in Portland, Maine. It was actually Massachusetts then. He personally witnessed a delegation from the Sauk and Fox tribes, which included Chief Blackhawk. Longfellow weaves together many aspects of American Indian Mythology concerning life, nature, and ritual. Well, enough about that, but I do hope you will find it interesting. At least give it a try, OK?"

"Sure, I'm looking forward to it."

"Me too. I love to read, and Jamie, we can take turns between reading in front of the fireplace and the reading nook. They are both great places to be and really just eat."

"Richard, I think we're all ready for the cake. Is it ready for us?"

"Oh yes. And if it tastes as good as it smells, then I am a master cook."

"What kind of cake is it, Uncle Richard?"

"Maggie, my dear, your turn."

"It is a Moravian Sugar Cake and the recipe origin is Pennsylvania Dutch. For Christmas, Moravians festooned the tree with fancy home-baked cookies, which Auntie Betts has prepared for your tree, by the way, and then they would joyfully indulge in the sugar cake, which is exactly what we are going to do right now. We also have the special Galapagos coffee, hot chocolate, cider, tea, or milk, your choice."

"Uncle Richard, you did a very good job. This is so good. It's still warm and moist and smells so good."

"It is great, Richard. Thank you for being willing to bake a cake that you had to boil potatoes for. I know you were surprised. This cake has potatoes in it?"

"Yes, it does, Jamie, and yes, I did have my moment of doubt, Maggie, but only a moment. I knew this wasn't your first Moravian Sugar Cake. It is great, and no, we have never tried it before."

"Maggie, this is indeed an adventure."

"Kevin, the week is young. We have so much more to enjoy. But for now, let's finish the cake and move on to the living room, where Auntie Betts has the lead. We will sing carols, and make music. Yeah!"

"I didn't know I could sing so well, Mom."

"Well, I didn't know I could either, Kara. I think there was something in that special cake that gave all of us angel voices. What do you think?"

"I think you're probably right. At least, I wouldn't doubt it."

"Well, Kara and Jamie, are you two ready to go down to the cottage and trim a tree?"

"Yes, yes, let's go. Can Howdy come with us, Aunt Maggie?"

"Sure. He has rested well today. I think he would like to help with the tree. What do you think, Howdy?"

"He's already at the door, Maggie. So let's do it. We'll come back later and get the chicken potpies. We definitely won't need them for a while."

"Maggie, would you consider sharing some of those family recipes? I will understand if you are not comfortable doing it."

"Mary Beth, first of all, you are family, and the recipes are for sharing, just like everything else. I am always so glad when someone asks. It's an honor. I will keep a list of the ones you want and put them together with a short summary of the cultural aspect."

"Thank you, Maggie. We will always remember this holiday."

"It is the first of many, Mary Beth. Now, let's decorate this tree. Who wants to string cranberries? Mary Beth and Kara, good team. Jamie, I see you're busy already creating the treetop. Who wants to help Auntie Betts with the cookie project? Ah yes, Kevin and Richard. Remember we have some extra to eat tonight so these can actually go on the tree. Would you be willing to put the candleholders on first, please? Are we going to have real burning candles, Aunt Maggie?"

"Yes, my dear, but only burning when we are here and not nodding off, if you know what I mean."

"We have never seen real candles on a tree. I wondered how they used to do that, and now I know. Those are really cool candleholders. Are they really old?"

"I'm sure they would seem very old to you, Kara. Actually, I don't really know how old they are. Do you, Auntie Betts?"

"I know we haven't used them for a long time. They are probably twenty-five to hundred years or more. I know they were used when I was a child, and that was a long time ago. It's a treat to decorate this tree."

"Yeah, especially the cookies."

"Yes, Jamie, they are really good. Mom and I have the first string of cranberries finished."

"Well, I'm not going so fast with the popcorn strings. I didn't remember it taking so long."

"Well, child, that's because time speeds up as we slow down. That's for sure. I love the smells, and chattering, and just look what we have accomplished."

"Aunt Maggie, we all love this cottage so much. It is absolutely perfect. And now with our very own Christmas tree, it's totally complete. Except for the presents, of course. Are we ready to do presents now?"

"I think we need to decide something. Do we want all of the presents brought to the cottage and have Christmas breakfast here, or do we want just the exchange ones for tonight and leave the rest under the big tree? Richard, what do you think?"

"We're having a casserole and muffins for breakfast, and we have everything else here. Kevin, Jamie, and I could bring the gifts down here very easily. We really don't have that much. I would love to hear the ocean and watch the waves while I'm drinking that exquisite Galapagos coffee."

"What a great pitch salesman!"

"Auntie Betts, you're the elder here, therefore the center of wisdom. What are your comments?"

"I think it would be absolutely perfect to be here at the cottage together, and of course, after breakfast and gift exchanges, we're going to play games and use that wonderful versatile game table that Richard designed. Then we will go up to the big house for dinner. Everyone OK with that?"

"Yes! I can't believe we all spontaneously said yes together. That's wonderful."

"Mary Beth, would you be willing to go up to the house with me to get the chicken potpies? They should be just about ready, and we'll bring the sugar cake down also. Just in case someone may want some later."

"Oh yeah, you can bet on it. Mom, please get that recipe."

"I won't let you leave without it, Jamie."

"Thank you, Aunt Maggie. You, guys, can work out transporting the presents, and we'll take care of the food. Fair enough?"

"Yes, my darling Maggie, and remember you promised to open the gift from me tonight."

"Indeed I did, and I am catching Kara's excitement about the gift exchange."

"Maggie, every time I open this door, the most tantalizing rich mysterious aromas of food awaken all of my sensory systems. I'm not kidding. I'm salivating. This cannot simply be chicken potpie."

"Well, Mary Beth, it really is pretty simple, and it definitely is chicken pot pie. I think the primary secret is the saffron spice, and yes it is quite different from what I have tasted in other places. I do hope expecting something familiar won't disappoint folks."

"Oh no, I can tell you that for sure. If they smell what I smell, this is going to be another recipe request for sure. This is actually more like a stew than a potpie."

"It's another Pennsylvania Dutch recipe."

"Enough chatter about the food. I think we had better get it down to the cottage. We have a full night ahead. I'll bring the cake. Can you manage the stew, Maggie?"

"Yes, I'm fine, Mary Beth. Thank you. Let's do it. We have had a wonderful Xmas Eve. The food was wonderful, the tree is beautiful, and so are all of you. Although the three of you are the champions of the board games played tonight, however, you do know that we have more game time on the schedule for tomorrow. So, Mary Beth, Kevin, Richard and I are challenging you three for the next round."

"Sure, Aunt Maggie, but I think you guys had better invite Howdy to help you because we are the mighty three."

"Right, Jamie, and with Auntie Betts on our team, we're hot. We'll see. We just needed a warm-up session."

"The gift exchange was wonderful. I am so glad we chose to open your gifts to each of us, Auntie Betts."

"Yes, I am intrigued by the pattern. It is so unusual, an amazing flounced hood which can be used as a face mask, scarf, hood, hat, or close the drawstring on one end or use it as a carrying bag. I can't wait to share it with my home economics students. I love the colors, especially because mine is red, and that's my favorite color. I'm looking forward to wearing it on our next ski trip. Everyone is going to want one of these, but I swear, Auntie Betts, I won't give them your phone number."

"Thank you, Kara. I loved making them for all of you, but six is quite enough. I'm so glad you like them."

"We'll feel your love every time we wear them, Auntie Betts, and we will wear them often."

"Thank you again, Kara. There is one more gift, remember, Margaret. I have a very special gift for Margaret, and Mary Beth I want to thank you for bringing it with you."

"Aunt Betts, would you be willing to come here and sit by Maggie, please?"

"My goodness, Richard, this is quite a production. Why are you on the floor?"

"Margaret Anne Scott, would you do me the great honor, to accept this ring and to become my beloved wife?"

"Oh, Richard, my dear Richard. I will wear this ring forever. So I guess that's a yes? Oh yes, that is a yes. What a beautiful ring, Richard. I had no idea. I mean we went to see Matt the jewelry design guy in town for our wedding rings. How and when did you get this one? My you are the nosy one, aren't you?"

"Maggie, this was my grandmother's ring and Mary Beth brought it with her for me."

"I love it. Look, everyone, it fits perfectly, like Cinderella's."

"Maggie, child, I am so happy for both for you. What a perfect way to welcome Xmas. It is almost midnight."

"Aunt Maggie, I am so glad you're our family now. I mean, really, I'm so glad we are all family."

"That we are, Kara. Family is a precious gift."

"Now that everyone has blessed the engagement. It's time to circle around the piano and sing a couple of your favorite carols, and then we'll end with 'Silent Night'. After 'Silent Night,' it truly is."

"Yes, Auntie Betts, and what a night it has been."

"Jamie, thank you for being the photographer tonight."

"Well, you're welcome, Aunt Maggie."

"However, I thought I was being very sly and no one would notice."

"We will all still be very surprised, Jamie, because we were far too focused on fun to notice very much."

"I must have been because I was totally unaware."

"Richard, I do believe you may have had something else on your mind."

"You are right as usual, Aunt Betts. I surely did have. Now let's sing Xmas in."

"Good night, all. We will see you about ten or so, and we will get to eat again. Sleep well."

"I know we shall, Maggie, and welcome to our family. My grandmother would be so proud to have you wear her ring. I'll tell you more about her later. She was quite a lady."

"Thank you, Mary Beth. I'll look forward to it."

"Merry Xmas, love. It feels so good to be here with you, Richard. You are much better than a hot water bottle for my feet. I used to let Howdy warm my feet."

"Margaret!"

"Well, not very often, and your body warmth is much better."

"Well, thank you. I'm glad I have something to offer."

"Seriously, Richard, I am so happy. I feel so complete now. I love my ring, and it was quite a surprise. Now I have a surprise gift for you."

"Really, now! Yes, my darling, right now. Give me your hand."

"Oh, good. It's warm. Put your hand on my stomach."

"Gladly, but what are we doing, really?"

"Richard, my surprise gift for you is that we are going to have a baby."

"A what? How . . . how long . . . when are . . . you sure?"

"Yes, I am very sure. I think I know when it happened. Are you happy?"

"Oh, Maggie, my darling Maggie, I am very happy. Just a bit overwhelmed for the moment. What a surprise gift!"

"Wait until we tell everyone tomorrow."

"Darling, let's not."

"But why, Maggie? This is perfect, and everyone's here to share it. Why do you not want to, darling?"

"Rich, I have had more time to think about this than you, and that's a little unfair. I understand wanting to tell everyone, but I also think it is something we need to share together for a while. There's plenty of time for everyone to know, but for now, darling, let's think about Christmas and our wedding, which is very soon now."

"I do agree, Maggie. Live in the moment, and there is so much going on. I do want this precious gift to have its very own moment. Do we know when or approximately when?"

"Probably in late July or so, which is so perfect. Mary Beth and family will be here for the summer, and that's perfect timing, kind of like it was planned."

"We both know of course it is, and I am so happy with our gift, darling. Thank you, Maggie, and Merry Xmas."

∗

"Good morning, sleeping beauty, and I mean that."

"Good morning, Richard, and Merry Christmas to you. You brought me coffee and I'm still in bed. I could get used to this. How long have you been up bustling about?"

"Howdy and I took a short walk. There is a little snow, which is beautiful."

"Everything seems so quiet when it's snowing. Have you noticed that?"

"As a matter of fact, one of my poetry books was pretty much about snow, and yes, I love the quiet, especially of a morning snow."

"I'm glad you and Howdy shared some Christmas time alone. How is Howdy, Richard?"

"He is very tired, Maggie, but that indomitable spirit is still there. I don't think he has any discomfort. He's just very tired."

"Yes, he is. However, when Kara and Jamie are around, I swear he has an energy surge, but of course, so do I."

"They are great young people, aren't they? I am so proud of them. I probably shouldn't say this, but Maggie when you see what Kara and Jamie made for you—Wow!"

"Richard, that's kind of cruel, teasing me like that."

"I'm sorry. It just kind of slipped out. Anyhow, everything will be revealed very soon. This is Christmas, you know."

"Yes, and I am awake and ready to go. I think I just heard Aunt Betts go downstairs. She probably smelled the magic coffee."

"I'll go down and turn the oven on. I know caramel French toast is ready. The Christmas Morning brunch casserole is ready except for the eggs and milk, and they both cook at 350 degrees."

"I will be down to help in just a few minutes. Although I'm sure Auntie Betts has a head start."

"Great, because I'm getting hungry. Last night, I thought I would never say that again."

"Like that's ever going to happen, Richard."

"Really, Maggie, you're right, and it's Christmas. We have snow, family, each other, and I love you. I'll see you downstairs, but take your time, darling. Betts and I will get everything going."

"Good morning, Richard, you seem to be the official coffee maker, and may I add, you have perfected the art. This taste as good as it smells."

"That is quite a compliment. Thank you very much. I see you already have the oven on and everything going."

"Well, maybe not everything."

"Good, because I'm in the mood to help create a masterpiece, I mean food."

"Yes, I know you mean food, Richard, however I believe you are an artist as well as a writer. I've seen some of your sketches, and they are very good."

"Thank you, Betts, I have been taking some classes and I have surprised myself. It's still kind of a secret, but Maggie and I have worked together on our Christmas project. I won't say any more about that. It is so hard for me to keep secrets. I'm just not used to it."

"We don't have very long now, Richard."

"Santa's about here. Thank goodness and yet I'm not sure I want it to end, you know?"

"The most important part will never end, Richard. That is the joy, the precious memory moments, and they kind of get into our DNA, I think, and that's a good thing. I hear Lady Margaret approaching."

"So you do, Aunt Betts. I have arrived and I think I smell brunch in the oven. There's really nothing for us to do right now but pour a cup of coffee and revel in the magic of the moment. I know I can do that, how about you, Richard?"

"Count me in. I love reveling and especially with two beautiful ladies. Yes, and you, Howdy. He really likes to have company while he eats. Has he always been like that, Margaret?"

"Yes, however, I have always thought that was totally natural. I think most of us enjoy sharing, being together, as much, or almost as much as what we're eating. What do you think, Aunt Betts?"

"I think Howdy is a very intuitive being, and yes, I think good company enhances the flavor of food and life in general."

"OK, Howdy, it looks like you will keep having company, especially at breakfast. We have kind of created a system."

"Yes, and I'm so glad."

"Richard, he used to nudge me out of bed on weekend mornings, when he was hungry and I was sleepy. Now he has you, and we are both grateful. By the way, everyone, Merry Christmas."

"I wondered how long I would have to stand under the mistletoe before someone noticed. Well, Auntie Betts has lost her opportunity. I love mistletoe. I think I will put it everywhere."

"Richard, my love, I believe you have."

"It's almost ten o'clock. I'll bet the family is up. Kara and Jamie are probably peeking out the window. Sometimes the time goes so slowly, as I imagine it is for them right now. I must admit I am really curious to see what amazing creations will emerge. I know a lot of work, fun, and love will be wrapped up in every gift. That was the oven timer."

"Breakfast is ready. They can smell us before they see us. Let's go. I am famished."

"Of course you are, Richard. It's been literally hours since we've eaten."

"Absolutely, and it's definitely time again, right, Betts?"

"Amen, Richard."

"OK, OK, let's go."

"Merry Christmas—ho-ho-ho."

"Uncle Richard, you don't even have a beard or a red suit, but Good morning and Merry Christmas to all of you. We thought you would never get here."

"Now, Kara, maybe not we, but you and Jamie, yes. Everything is ready here and whatever you have in there smells so good."

"Thank you, Mary Beth. The table looks beautiful. Let's gather around it, and who would like to say the blessing this morning?"

"I kind of think I would, Aunt Maggie, but I may not be very good at it."

"Kara, my dear one, we would love for you to do the blessing, and you cannot be anything but perfect because that's what you are. So please do."

"Yes, Kara, we're hungry, so just do it, OK?"

"All right, Jamie, you hold my hand please, and Auntie Betts, would you take my other hand? Then I know I will be fine. I celebrate Christmas with joy, peace, love, and thanks to God for his gift. Every gift I offer and receive is with love. I am grateful for all of the wonderful food we share and the adventure of being with family in this wonderful cottage, and so it is."

"Thank you, Kara."

"Yeah, Kara, thank you for not taking forever. I'm hungry, really."

"Kara, good job."

"Thank you, Jamie."

"Mom—"

"Yes, I know, Jamie. More recipes, right?"

"Especially the French toast."

"Yes, it's very good. I want in on this recipe request thing. I also want the egg bake added."

"Maggie, what all is in this? It is very good."

"Very easy to make, Kevin. Potatoes, onions, peppers, ham layer, all of that with shredded cheese on top. Stick it in the refrigerator and then mix the eggs and milk when you bake it and eat it. There are a few other ingredients but those are the basics."

"Mary Beth, it looks like you're going to get a cook book. We still have days to go and lots of food to eat."

"Sounds great to me, Maggie. I am always looking for new ways to do old things, and I know when I make any of these recipes, we will all have such wonderful memories, which will make the food taste better."

"Auntie Betts, Mary Beth and I are going to go up to the house and do some food stuff. I know we just got up from the table. However, this is Christmas, and Mary Beth really wants to help me with some preparations. If you don't mind getting Jamie and Kara started with games, oh yes, Kevin and Richard also, you are a great game master. We will be back very soon. I don't want to miss anything either."

"Maggie, you know I love doing this. However, I don't know how long any of us are going to be willing to wait to open the presents."

"I know, but just think the longer we wait, curiosity grows."

"Sure, my dear. Just get back as soon as you can, OK?"

"You bet. Have fun."

*

"Maggie, do you have time to tell me what we are having for dinner?"

"Sure, I can talk and work at the same time. I'll get you going, and then I'll tell you what the plan is, and thank you so much for offering to help."

"This way, Maggie, I'll get some inside scoop on the recipes that I know my family is going to put on your list."

"I certainly hope so, Mary Beth. I chose to stick with turkey although it's wild turkey, so it will be different. If you would be willing to finish the dressing, I'll prepare the bird. The recipe is right by the red mixing bowl, and I have everything in it except the pumpernickel bread and apples."

"What is that smell, Maggie?"

"Which one, Beth? I imagine there are many, cinnamon, spice and stuff. Oh yes. That is the *Texas Stollen*. It's a German recipe contrary to its name-long story. Usually we have it for Christmas morning, but I chose to save it for after dinner. It is really good. I think I'd better put that one on the recipe list for you.

"The rest of dinner is really pretty simple—mashed sweet potatoes with maple syrup and cinnamon, a variety of roasted winter vegetables, and Auntie Betts famous angel biscuits. They are so good. Anyhow the bird is ready and the stuffing's ready for the bird, so in it goes, and we can get back to the cottage before Kara and Jamie sends out a hunting party to find us."

"This was fun, Maggie. Thank you. Things seem to flow so easily. Do you ever get ruffled about anything?"

"Mary Beth, darling, I'm very human, therefore, my answer would be yes. However, I generally don't have very much to get ruffled about."

"I was right. Jamie is on his way to meet us. Boy, was our timing good. They have been very patient about the gifts."

"Everyone is ready to open presents, you know."

"Yes, Jamie, we are also, so let's go inside and do it."

"Yeah, they are here. Jamie brought them."

"Honestly, Kara, they were on their way down here, so my job was way too easy. So here's the Santa cap. Who wants to be Santa first?"

"What do you mean, Aunt Maggie?"

"We take turns being Santa, which means Santa gives everyone a gift, and we take turns opening them. Then another Santa does the same thing until all of the presents are open."

"Since I am the elder, I will be the first Santa. So here we go."

"Betts, you do look good with that Santa cap. It really fits."

"Thank you, Richard, and you get to wear it next."

"Great. I'll practice my 'ho ho hos'."

∗

"Richard, what are you doing out here all alone? I missed you."

"Oh, Maggie, I am so happy. I love watching and listening to the ocean sounds. This is a perfect moment in time. All the gifts were kind of like each of us sharing and exchanging little parts of ourselves to one another. I don't remember anyone creating anything for me at Christmas before. Lot's of gifts and good times, but not like this. And all day, while enjoying every moment, underneath everything, a part of me was thinking about our baby."

"Me too, Richard. How could we not. It's such a profound gift."

"I love you, Maggie."

"And I love you. I really don't like being the one to break this magic moment, but as soon as the group finishes this game, they are ready to eat. So would you be willing to go with me, and we'll have dinner ready very soon."

"We are a great team, Maggie."

"Yes, my dear, let's sneak away, except I'll tell Aunt Betts what we are doing, and she can bring the gang up in thirty to forty-five minutes."

"Good idea, and you know what, I am hungry again."

"Richard, that is hard to believe."

"Margaret, what did you and Mary Beth do? This place smells like heaven must feel."

"Thank you, sir. It was really nothing. Just a few herbs, spices, and such. We are doing dinner buffet-style this evening, Richard."

"Sounds like a great idea. I know how to set up for that, so shall I do that now?"

"Yes, darling, and then if you would make the punch, I will get the rest of dinner in the oven."

"What a team! We really are, you know."

"Yes, Richard, I do know."

"I think tomorrow will be very good for us, Maggie, with no routine and no cooking, just a day to kind of absorb everything."

"That is a great tradition by the way. I have always enjoyed the day after Christmas. Usually just Howdy and I, but I am so glad everyone is here this year, and yes, Richard, I think tomorrow will be a very special day for us. However, being in the moment now, let's enjoy the rest of this glorious day, shall we?"

"Yes, Maggie, every moment of it. Shall I go down to the cottage and tell them we're ready?"

"No need, Richard. I'm sure Aunt Betts has everything under control, and they will be here momentarily. No hurry. You might want to check the fire. I think we'll be eating in the living room since that's where our tree is. Do you know where the stackable trays are, Richard?"

"Yes, ma'am, as a matter of fact I do. I'll be right back."

"Thank you. The trays fit very nicely around the fireplace, and Howdy has his special spot that he loves, and he will really enjoy being surrounded by so much love and laughter, and so will I. This is a dream I have had for a long time, Richard. Thank you for having such a wonderful family."

"They are great, Maggie, and I thank you for just being you. I love everything about you."

"Even my inability to track or relate very well to time?"

"You do everything that ever needs to be done, and it all works out perfectly."

"So I guess that is a yes?"

"Yes, Maggie, my love. Speaking of time, I hear the Christmas carolers making their way to the door. They sound really good, Maggie, even without us."

"Remember, Rich, they have Auntie Betts."

"Oh yes, what a lady and what a voice!"

"Come in out of the cold, Christmas dinner awaits that is if anyone is hungry?"

"Uncle Richard, I, for one, am famished."

"Oh no, another new word for Kara watch out!"

"Jamie, it is not a new word. I only use it on special occasions. Merry Christmas, everyone. We have had so much fun today."

"Yes, Kara, and the evening has just begun."

"Maggie, this buffet is beautiful and everything smells so good. You two have been slaving while we were playing."

"Oh no, Mary Beth, really it was nothing."

"Sure, how can I help?"

"How can we help, Aunt Maggie?"

"Honestly, there is nothing to do except to gather around the tree and have a few minutes of silence. So each of us, in our own way can think about what we are grateful for. I know it could take forever, and hopefully it will, but for this moment, we'll just enjoy the feeling of gratitude."

"Now we reverse the order of the elders being first served. Kara and Jamie, you are first to start the buffet line. So I suppose that means I am last."

"Yes, Auntie Betts, unless you want me to serve you, which I would be glad to do."

"Oh no, Maggie. I know exactly what and how much I want. I am going to start with dessert first."

"Betts, are you really?"

"I have wanted to do that so many times. No time like the present, Richard."

"You two are not setting a very good example. However, it is Christmas, so enjoy."

"Uncle Richard, do we have a special place to sit?"

"No, Jamie, just grab a place with a tray. There's not a bad seat in the room."

"I think you're right. I'm going to sit here by Howdy. He looks so comfortable."

"I'm going to sit on the other side of Howdy. We have front row seats to the fireplace and the tree."

"Isn't this a beautiful room, Jamie?"

"Yes, and this is a beautiful plate of food I have. I'm not sure what everything is, but boy, is it good. I'm so glad that we all decided to leave one gift to open tonight. Although, Kara, you were the one that voted no."

"I didn't really mean it. You know I didn't, Jamie."

"Oh no, you meant it at that moment, Kara."

"Yes, but we all agreed, including Kara. That's called compromise."

"Yes, I did agree, and I'm glad."

"So are we, Kara. It is wonderful to have that last gift to anticipate, kind of like dessert. I do hope we have pumpkin pie for dessert, or cheesecake, or perhaps both and maybe even other choices."

"Now, Richard, just how much dessert can one eat?"

"I'm not sure, Maggie. We're getting ready to find out."

"Sounds like it's time for the dessert menu, so here goes. Now remember we do not have to eat everything tonight. Everything will taste even better tomorrow. We have a Spanish flan, which is a delicate but hearty custard, Armenian Bverek, which is cheese-filled flaky pastries, a variety of dried fruits and roasted walnuts, a tray of assorted choices—baklava, chocolate walnut cokes with cherries and whipped cream, and pumpkin pie with whipped cream, and remember it's still early in the evening. So you may want to pace yourself, especially if you are going to stay up until midnight."

"Oh yes, let's all agree to do that."

"Yes, that was a clear response. We don't need to waste any time on compromise."

"Kara, I am glad we are all in agreement, however compromise is a good thing and sometimes very necessary. Now let's check out the dessert buffet, and guess what? I forgot one of my favorite desserts, Christmas Stollen."

"This is a beautiful buffet, Maggie. I love all of the candles everywhere and the fireplace. The beautiful smells and sights of Christmas. Thank you again."

"Mary Beth, without you and everyone, it just simply would not be the same. You folks have added so much joy and love, the greatest gifts of Christmas. So we thank you and yours. That's my toast to you. Merry Christmas everyone. Enjoy!"

"Will the desserts be out all evening, Aunt Maggie?"

"More or less, Jamie. Most of them will be. A few will be in the refrigerator but totally accessible whenever you have the urge."

"I really like Christmas."

"So do I, Jamie, and tomorrow sounds pretty cool too."

"Yeah, I'm pretty interested in that Hiawatha story, at least the way Auntie Betts talked about it, and I'm also interested in the walk tomorrow, whenever that is."

"Wait a minute. You two are getting to far ahead. Look around this beautiful room. What do you see?"

"I see Christmas everywhere. I smell the tree and other stuff and I see happy faces, and Howdy's face is probably the happiest."

"Well, Kara, if you looked in a mirror right now, you may see one that's full of light and love."

"Thank you, Aunt Betts."

"I do believe it's time to open the remaining gifts. What do you think?"

"Oh yes, I think there was agreement on that, so, Jamie, would you like to give Margaret her gift from you?"

"You bet I would, but would you help me, Uncle Richard?"

"Yes, Jamie, I think this is going to be a really big surprise, and when I say big, that's exactly what I mean. We will be right back. This is one that's not under the tree."

"Well, I'm certainly intrigued. Hurry back, guys. I'm waiting."

"That is a really big present, Jamie, and you did a great job of wrapping it. I'm not sure where to start."

"I'll help you, Aunt Maggie."

"Thank you, Kara. It's looking like a dollhouse or something like that. Hurry up, you guys, I want to see it."

"So do I, Auntie Betts."

"Jamie, is this a chicken coop?"

"I'm glad you could recognize it. I was beginning to wonder. Uncle Richard said you really wanted a few chickens. What do you think?"

"I think it is one of the most fascinating chicken coops I have ever seen. It's like a chicken condo."

"Yes, it really is, and you can roll around as you wish. The bottom just slides out, and the chickens can forage for worms and insects and fertilize your soil at the same time."

"Jamie I love it, and you did such a great job of building it. It is beautiful, and it looks like the top does something special. What's that?"

"You can actually have a mini garden there or flowers, or whatever you'd like."

"Where did you get the design for this, Jamie? It is perfect, and your Uncle Richard was right. I really miss not having my chickens. I used to, and I loved it, and now I will have them again and soon. But really, did you build this yourself?"

"I did, Aunt Maggie. Mr. Fitzgerald was building one, and he showed me a lot, but I actually did all the work myself. Kara helped with the painting and decorations. I'm pretty proud of it."

"As well you should be. Thank you so much, Jamie. And, Kara, I love it!"

"It is a beautiful piece of work, Son. We are all so proud of you."

"Thanks, Dad."

"Now I think it's time for the remaining gifts, and they are from Maggie and Richard. I understand that they did a project together."

"That's right, Aunt Betts, we did, and we will give you yours first."

"Richard, the unveiling please!"

"Richard, I am almost speechless. You are truly an artist. You captured this house, the cottage, and everything. I love it. Thank you so much, and every time I look at it, all of this I will be right there as well!"

"Thank you, Auntie Betts. I loved working on it for you, and also Margaret was working with me and has created something to go with the painting. We have really had fun with this project."

"I have a short poetry book that I put together while Richard was painting. You can read it later if you'd like."

"I love your poetry always, Maggie, and this I know will be especially appreciated. Thank you both so much."

"Uncle Richard, I didn't know you were an artist. That is beautiful."

"I'm really glad you like it, Kara, because there's more to come."

"Great, let's see the next one—who gets the next present?"

"Maggie, you get to unveil the next one."

"How about two, Kara's and Jamie's? They are smaller, and we can mail them to you if you'd like—the first one is for Kara."

"Uncle Richard, I love it. A picture of the cottage. It's perfect. Thank you so much."

"You are so welcome, my dear one."

"What about my poems, Auntie Margaret?"

"Oh yes, here is your book, Kara."

"What a beautiful cover. Did you autograph it for me?"

"Yes, as a matter of fact I did, my dear."

"Good. I've already told my friends that you are a number one poetry writer. Now I can show them. Thank you, Aunt Maggie. I love you."

"I love you too, Kara. You are so welcome. Next is for Jamie."

"Wow! That's the ocean view from my favorite spot in the cottage. Uncle Richard, you really are an artist. It's very cool. Thank you."

"You are so welcome, Jamie. It's also one of my favorite views."

"Here's your book of poetry to go with the painting."

"This is such a great Christmas. Thank you, Aunt Maggie."

"Now let's see. We have Kevin and Mary Beth. Did we get around to doing something for them, Rich?"

"I do believe we did—Mary Beth."

"Oh, Richard, a still life of my favorite things—bread and jam, grapes, wine and flowers, and that beautiful table. Richard, I love it!"

"Your very own recipe book put together with some poetry that I think you will find amusing. Actually, Kevin, this gift is for both of you."

"I am sure I will enjoy every recipe in there and the still life. Richard, you definitely have another career. You are a very good artist."

"Thank you, both of you. I am so glad we are going to be here for your wedding."

"Oh yes, Maggie. We are all so happy for you and Richard and for all of us. We feel like family and have since we first arrived."

"I know, Mary Beth. I feel the same way."

"Well, I think it's time for us to circle around the tree and sing a few songs after we get our eggnog. What do you folks think?"

"A great idea, Auntie Betts. Let's do it."

"Kara and Jamie, there's some hot cider, hot chocolate, and eggnog. Help yourselves. Richard, you made special eggnog for us, didn't you?"

"That I did, Betts."

"Good, and oh yes, it is good!"

"What a perfect day and evening, Maggie"

"Merry Christmas, darling. I love you, Richard, and you really are a fine artist. I know I love going to my art lessons, and the whole process of creating, and I really enjoy having you interpret my painting with poetry. It was a fun project. We'll have to do it again."

"So we shall. Now let's go sing. I hear the piano. Betts has begun."

"My goodness, the clock says it is midnight. This day and evening has had wings. I can't believe Christmas Day has come and gone. Auntie Betts, I think I will keep this Christmas in my treasure chest of memories forever."

"Very well, Kara, and so shall I."

"Uncle Richard, are you going with us tomorrow when we go on our exploration walk?"

"Actually, Jamie, I haven't thought about it, and I didn't know it was an exploration walk. That sounds intriguing. It also sounds like Auntie Betts."

"Right you are, Uncle Richard. I think you might be up to the challenge."

"Yes, Jamie, I definitely want to be included in the adventure, thank you. How about you, Kevin? Would you like to join our adventure?"

"I really would, Rich. I think I just may learn a few things. We will have the best guide there is, so I'm sure it will be very interesting."

"So, Maggie, you and Mary Beth are very quiet. Are you going to join us?"

"No, Rich. We have decided to hibernate tomorrow. You folks can tell us all about it. I'm sure you will have a lot to share."

"It appears as though we have a plan, and now my plan is to bid you all a Merry Xmas good night. I am ready to nod off, so I had better get to bed."

"Good night, Aunt Betts. Actually it's a good night from all of us, also Maggie. We probably won't see you folks until after lunch tomorrow. Good night all!"

"Sleep well, and Jamie, say good night to the ocean for me."

"I sure will, Aunt Maggie. Good night, Uncle Richard. See you tomorrow, and for the last time this year, Merry Xmas to all and to all a good night."

"What a wonderful day and night!"

"Yes, Richard, it was perfect. I am so glad that Jamie and Kara assumed the role of host and hostess. They left the house spotless, not a thing out of place. All I had to do was show them where to put the trays. I protested weakly, but I am so glad they ignored my feeble attempt to stop them. They really seemed to be having fun. There was a lot of laughter and so much energy. Richard, listen what do you hear?"

"Silence?"

"Yes, except for Howdy's snoring, and we're so used to that. We don't really hear it. Just a few moments ago, the house was full of laughter, talking, activity, and now it is very quiet."

"Yes, it is. I wonder, Maggie, if that's a little bit like life. We're busy, full of energy and projects, work, play, and then gradually things just become a little slower and a little quieter."

"Yes, Richard, I think that's true, and what I know is true for me right now is that I am going to bed, where I will be very quiet very soon. How about you?"

"I think I'd like to just watch the fire, and meditate with Howdy for a while. Good night, darling. Sleep well."

∗

"Good morning, my love."

"Richard, coffee in bed again? What a delightful way to awaken! Did you sleep downstairs last night?"

"No, Maggie. I slept in my place right beside you."

"Well, I certainly didn't know it. We both slept very well. Where's Howdy?"

"He did sleep downstairs. I just didn't have the heart to awaken him, but he is up and has been out already, and I'm sure he's waiting for me to come back down so he can have breakfast."

"If you don't mind, Rich. I think I will stay here for a while and just do nothing."

"I think that's a great idea, and I will bring you a warm muffin and some jam."

"That sounds perfect."

"I'll be right back, Maggie."

"I will be right here, Rich, and I plan to take this quiet day very seriously."

"Maggie, are you awake?"

"Semi-awake, Richard. Just dozing a bit, however, that muffin smells very enticing. I may even sit up to eat it."

"As a matter of fact, yes, my dear, that's part of the deal. I haven't practiced my life-saving skills for a very long time, and I don't want to practice today. Also I brought fresh coffee as a bonus."

"You are such a genuinely sweet person, Richard. Auntie Betts is right, as usual. You definitely are a keeper."

"That's a good thing since I never plan on leaving. Except I really do need to feed Howdy and keep him company while he eats, so I guess you are on your own, my dear."

"Thank you, darling. I'll be down in a bit."

"Take your time, Maggie. Remember this is our quiet day."

"Good morning, Aunt Betts, you look like you're ready and raring to go, so I'm thinking you had a restful night?"

"I did indeed, Richard. I always sleep so good here. There's just something so healthy and healing about this place. I always know I'll get my batteries recharged here."

"You bring a lot of it with you, Betts."

"Thank you, Richard. The coffee master has done it again. This is wonderful. I think part of the magic for me is the great honey. Margaret always has the best honey in the entire world, and that is my scientific pronouncement. I may even do a research paper on it. It's that good."

"So it is, Betts. You know you really may be on to something with that research theme. We, at least I, don't know enough about or respect bees nearly as much as I know I should. They are vitally important parts of nature, I know that, but really now I'm curious. I will add bees to my list of questions."

"Well, let's not do that today, Richard. Today is R&R time. Although I am really looking forward to our walk this afternoon. Right now, however, I am looking forward to one of those delicious muffins that I could smell upstairs, and they lured me out of bed. By the way, where's Margaret?"

"I took her coffee and a muffin upstairs, and she's very content to stay right there. I could have brought the same to you Betts. Room service at no extra charge."

"I'll keep that in mind, Richard. Could I have a little bell?"

"Sure, I'll get right on that."

"So what are you up to this morning, Richard?"

"I am going to arrange pillows around the fireplace where Howdy and I will read and probably nod off. In other words, nothing, just be."

"We certainly don't have to cook today. This refrigerator is packed."

"Yes, Betts, and that's a good thing."

"Yes, it is, Richard. I'm going to go get into the soaking tub, play some beautiful music, and just be. I'll see you two later. Howdy has certainly found his spot, Richard."

"Yes, we fit together pretty well, Betts. He is a love."

"So are you, Richard. I'll see you two later."

"We'll probably be right here."

✳

"Good afternoon, Margaret. You look perky."

"I feel brand new, Auntie Betts, and ready to eat whatever."

"Great! That's what brought me out of my cocoon, and I'll just bet Richard will be joining us any minute. I thought at least the young ones would be showing up by now."

"You did give them quite a reading assignment, Betts."

"I also told them we would have an adventure today. So I hope they get here soon, or I'll be forced to go get them. I'm just about ready to go."

"They will be here, I am sure of that. They don't want to miss anything."

"Richard, I thought you'd smell the food. Come joint us. We are sampling a little of everything."

"Great! I'm ready. OK, Howdy, we'll go out first. Be right back."

"He certainly is attached to Howdy. Both of you seem to know what Howdy wants before he even knows. Quite a nice team, I'm happy to say."

"I think you are absolutely right, Aunt Betts. Howdy actually seems to be stronger recently. I thought maybe all of the activity would be too much for him, but it seems to have given him a boost."

"Yes, darling, but after everything goes back to normal routine, don't be surprised if he slows down. I think he is kind of going on fumes, and that's fine. He is having a great time, so let's just enjoy these moments."

"Absolutely, thank you, Aunt Betts. You always seem to know the right things to say, and the right time."

"Well, maybe not always, just most of the time. I do believe I hear the sound of youth approaching. Thank goodness because I am raring to go. How about you, Maggie?"

"No, Mary Beth and I decided yesterday that we were going to spend some time together this afternoon. Just tea, something tasty, the fireplace, and talk. She wants to share some childhood stories, a little history of herself and Richard. Of course if she has questions, I'll be happy to share also."

"Sounds like fun, Maggie. It looks like you finally have your sister."

"We do really enjoy a lot of the same things, and I do feel like I've know her forever. Actually the whole family."

"Maggie, perhaps I shouldn't mention it, but don't you feel that way about every one?"

"Pretty much, Auntie Betts, something I inherited, I think."

"Well, it's a good thing, and here they are. Good morning, fellow adventurers."

"Good morning, Auntie Betts. We are ready to go, but where?"

"Well, I know I'm going on a treasure hunt. Who wants to join me?"

"Where are you going, Auntie Betts?"

"James, my lad, treasure is hidden. I just follow my instincts. Where that may take us I can only imagine. However, we dress warmly, take food and drink, and only one rule. We will all solemnly promise to lose all track of time. No watches and no electronic devices. They keep us from discovery of the mystical and magic."

"When do we go?"

"Well, I see I have two. Will there be more?"

"Yes, there will be three, says Richard and a fourth says Kevin."

"Margaret, do you have matches for us?"

"There are no matches for you, Aunt Betts. However, if you might be wanting to start a fire, here you are."

"Thank you, darling. We shall return. You two have fun and keep the fire going. We may need to thaw out when we return."

"Somehow I think there will be enough hot air surrounding all of you that you will keep quite warm, and we will keep the home fires burning. Have a fun adventure. We'll see you later, and it looks like Howdy has also chosen the fireplace for his adventure. Have fun, Rich, and I am sure you will. How could you not."

"Maggie, I'm so glad you and Mary Beth will have some time together. Although I hope she doesn't tell you too much about me. There will be no mystery left."

"That, my dear Richard, is not possible, and I am sure of that. Go now, your fellow adventurers are leaving you behind."

"Mary Beth, bless your heart, you have made my favorite tea. I can smell it."

"Honestly, Maggie, I didn't think I could go wrong."

"I know that's something you have in common with Richard and me. Our taste for tea continues to expand. I haven't tried this one yet, so therefore a little adventure for me."

"It is all good, Margaret. This is such a crazy spot. I love your house, but this fireplace has such a comforting warmth that fills the room."

"It definitely is my favorite spot, and of course Howdy's presence adds to the ambiance. Howdy and I have spent many special times together in this room, and you are right, Mary Beth, this is everyone's favorite gathering place in the house. As I think back through my childhood, that has always been true. My parents had 'open house' almost continually. I think I just took it for granted. Now I realize what a special childhood I had. I was totally accepted and included, and I learned so much. I am so blessed to have been born into this amazing community. Now I believe you are going to share some history of you and Richard. I am so looking forward to learning everything I can about both of you."

✳

"Boy, I had a great time, Aunt Betts. You are a really great storyteller and teacher."

"Thank you, Kara."

"I had a great time, but what about the treasure hunt?"

"Jamie, the real treasures in life often can't be seen. It's inside of us, that is, the source of wisdom. We found that. Strength, boy, did we find that, right?"

"Oh yes, we did, Uncle Richard. What else, Auntie Betts?"

"Joy. The spirit's presence brings treasures of love, life, and besides all that, we found glorious seashells, rocks, driftwood, made friends with many trees, and listened to the quiet."

"Yeah, that was very cool. I had definitely never listened to quiet before. Pretty amazing adventure, Auntie Betts."

"Thank you for sharing so much knowledge with us. I had a great time."

"So did I, Kev, and you know what? It's not over yet. I heard Aunt Betts say that we were going to do an art project using the bounty from our treasure hunt."

"Yes, what are we going to do, Auntie Betts?"

"We are going to make something for the cottage, maybe stepping stones. We'll let the ideas flow this evening and decide it tomorrow. Each time you return, the memories of all of this will flood your soul. Or actually any time you wish to recall, just picture the piece or pieces and all the feelings will return. That's part of the magic. Keep the joy stored and delete anything else, that's the mystery. I want to thank all of you for being such great fellow adventurers. I had a very good time, and Kevin, thank you for getting our fire started. I think we really needed that, and it created a great singing circle."

"Yeah, except the smoke seemed to follow me every time, I moved."

"Funny thing about smoke, Jamie, is that it seems to choose someone it especially likes, and then it just stays with them. So you were chased."

"Well, that's great. However, I hope it will choose someone else next time, but I really did have a great time, and it was an adventure."

"I see smoke coming from the chimney, so the fireplace is where I'm heading. I think I can already smell hot chocolate, soup, and other stuff."

"Sure, Kara. I smell your imagination."

"Very soon, I don't think it will be imagination. Remember the refrigerator is full of the food of your choice. Let's go check it out."

"We are with you, Rich. I think we're going to have another treasure hunt."

"You're right, Kevin, and I, for one, am very ready to help clean out that refrigerator."

"No, Aunt Betts, remember it's a treasure chest."

"Right you are, Kara. Thanks for the reminder."

"What a picture you three make, a regular Norman Rockwell moment."

"Thank you, darling. However, I'm not quite sure what kind of picture you folks make. I do believe you are all very hungry people."

"That we are. We are hungry, happy, soon to be warm, full, and contented."

"Boy, this refrigerator is full of everything."

"Not everything, Jamie. I have found some pretty wonderful stuff already out here on the buffet."

"Yes, fortunately, Mary Beth and I have grazed all afternoon. Between our tea and talking time, we managed to forage pretty well. So we can just stay out of your way."

"So, Mom, we can just have anything and everything we want and even dessert first?"

"Yes, Kara, remember today we are all on our own. Eat what you want, when you want it, and just clean up when you're through. Also remember, we have food in the cottage, so you are not going to starve."

"Auntie Betts, you look very hale and hearty."

"Yes, Maggie, it was so exciting to be out with such genuinely inquisitive minds, and I'm not just talking about the young ones. Rich and Kevin have so much energy, and I was really put to the test with the questions asked. I am actually going to have to do a little research and get back to them."

"I know you love that, Auntie Betts. I remember that gleam in your eyes when we would get a good discussion going."

"How was your discussion time with Mary Beth?"

"Wonderful! We covered a lot of ground, and we have a lot in common. She and Kevin are very serious about coming back for the summer. They want to know so much about this community."

"You can't blame them, can you? We have quite a rare jewel here, Maggie. We don't ever want to take it for granted. It's far too valuable, and I really am aware of how special it is because I spend so much of my time lecturing across the country, and I am always so happy. Every time I come back, I find everything is as good or better than the last time I was here."

"I know I treasure your time here, Aunt Betts. Maybe someday, you'll be ready to stay."

"Maybe, darling, but I still have a lot to do. We'll see."

"Maggie, Kevin, and I are going down to the cottage if you don't mind. Jamie and Kara are still foraging. I'm sure they will be through soon. They are both really looking forward to getting back to their books tonight. Actually, that's what we're all going to do this evening—absolutely nothing."

"Sounds great, Mary Beth, and that's our plan as well. Do you want to have breakfast here in the morning?"

"No, we have plenty of food at the cottage, and I think we'll just be lazy, and I should say I'm going to be, but how about lunch? Then we can plan the rest of the day."

"Sounds great, Mary Beth, I really enjoyed our time together today."

"So did I, Maggie, although we really never got to the wedding-plan part. So tomorrow, OK?"

"Good idea. Good night, group. Rest well."

✳

"Richard, my boy, you are quite the outdoors man. I am impressed by your never-ending skills and talents. You truly are a renaissance man."

"Thank you, Betts. I truly had forgotten how much time I used to spend examining trees, insects, and nature in general. I really was an Eagle Scout. I wasn't just trying to impress Jamie and Kara. Although I really did appreciate their obvious pride. It was very helpful to me to remember that part of my life, and how hard I worked to accomplish that goal. I enjoyed the day, Betts. Thank you for sharing so much with us and making everything fun."

"I'm glad, Richard, and I truly do believe that every moment is a precious gift, and we certainly shared a lot of them this afternoon. Maggie girl, we missed you and Mary Beth today, but I was also just a little bit envious thinking about you three sitting by the fire, sharing life stories, and probably talking about the next very big event."

"We did indeed do most of that. However, we really never got to the wedding plans. We three will have some time together tomorrow. Rich and Kev can hang out with Jamie and Kara. I heard them talking about a project for the cottage. I know they think they need you, but I'll just bet they can figure it out, and I really do need and want you. We only have a few days before New Year's Eve and the wedding. Auntie Betts, I am so excited about it. I wasn't until after X-Mas but today, right now, I am goose bumpy."

"Just as long as you don't have cold feet, my dear."

"Oh no, I can assure you I have never been more sure of anything in my life as I am about Richard and his family join ours. I think it's time this family grows a bit, if you know what I mean."

"Yes, ma'am, and didn't I hear you say you were on your way to bed?"

"Yes, Maggie, my dear, I am. We'll have fun tomorrow. I love you, Maggie girl."

"I know you do, Auntie Betts. I've always known it."

"Good night, love. Rest well."

"Howdy, my friend, I see you are keeping Richard warm and happy."

"He really is. I was pretty cold. I didn't notice it until I came in. Boy, I love this spot and I love it even more when you are here with us."

"You know, it's kind of funny we have a big formal dining room and an even larger living room or parlor as it used to be called, and yet all of my life we have spent most of the time in this room. Everyone may start out in the living room, then to the dining room, and conversation was always lively. Somehow we would always end up in here, and everything or perhaps I should say everyone became so much more open and relaxed. I think it is a magic room."

"Well, I would agree, Maggie. However, I have had so many magical adventures today. I probably don't want to think about another one right now, yet as I say that, I can feel the magic of you and your body fitting into mine so perfectly. Your very essence and blending that with Howdy on the other side looking at me with those eyes that seem to know everything there is to know in the universe. I agree this is a magic room filled with love, warmth, and just a feeling of completion."

"Richard, I love you so much. Oh yes, Howdy, you too. Richard, perhaps you had better rest well tonight because tomorrow it would be so helpful if you and Kevin did the cottage project with Jamie and Kara. Whatever that turns out to be. Mary Beth, Aunt Betts, and I have a full day tomorrow, discussing our wedding, and I have a final fitting of my gown, and I must say, I'm feeling a bit giddy with pleasure, not anxiety. Mary is preparing lunch for us, and we will probably be back by dinnertime. So what do you think?"

"About the project, I'm sure we can do it. I'm not sure how the wedding will be. I trust if there's anything I need to do, you or someone will tell me. I am totally ready as far as I know. I absolutely love all of the traditions you have shared with me. So yes, and yes, my lady, I am at your service. I am sure you three will find a way to have a lot of fun, and I am equally as sure that we will have a very creative day, and there's lots of food, so we will be fine."

"Things always work out so well with us, Richard. I really do believe we are soul mates."

"I think so also, Maggie. Life flows."

"Howdy has obviously gone to sleep, and I don't think I'm far behind, so I'll go on upstairs before you have to carry me."

"Oh thank you, Maggie. That is a great idea, and I'll be right up. I think Howdy may want or need to go outside for a moment. Keep the bed warm for me. It's really cold outside."

"Thank you, Rich, and Howdy, thank you."

"Good morning, sleeping beauty, I think you may have been asleep before you knew you were in bed. I came right upstairs maybe five minutes after you, and you were soundly asleep."

"Good morning, darling. Yes, I slept soundly and I feel so rejuvenated this morning. I am ready to jump out of bed, go downstairs, and make coffee for a change."

"Sorry, darling. It's waiting for us, unless you want me to bring yours upstairs."

"Thank you, Rich, but I truly am ready to get this glorious day started. I have had my meditation time along with Howdy, and I feel so focused and so hungry!"

"Maggie, that's my line."

"Sorry, beat you to it. Let's go surprise Auntie Betts and make her favorite breakfast."

"Which favorite is that, Maggie?"

"Dutch babies with maple syrup, lemon wedges, and a 'little' bit of powdered sugar on top."

"I think you just described another one of my favorites."

"I love that morning coffee smell. Thank you, Rich. Auntie Betts, what are you doing up so early?"

"Obviously, my dear one, you, as usual, have not looked at a clock. Trust me, it is not that early."

"It is nine o'clock. No wonder I feel so rested. I am. Rich and I were going to surprise you with a favorite breakfast, Auntie Betts. However, I can smell something cooking already."

"Yes, my dear, we are going to have Dutch babies."

"That is so funny. We were going to make them for you. Oh well, great minds and all."

"I really don't care who makes them. I just know that I am ready to eat them."

"Rich, what a surprise! You are ready to eat?"

"Yes, Maggie, I am ravenous."

"How can we help, Betts?"

"Rich, you can warm that fantastic maple syrup and cut some lemon wedges, and Maggie, I think some of those canned apples in cinnamon and nutmeg would be great."

"Yes, and I'll heat them up a bit."

"Well, we have a great team going here. I don't remember, Maggie, is the rest of the family going to joint us? I believe they said they would have breakfast at the cottage."

"Yes, they did, and I remember Kevin and Mary Beth talking about watching the waves while they had their breakfast."

"I'm glad someone was listening. I think I was sleep walking before I got up the stairs."

"That's funny, Aunt Betts, so was I, and now just look at us, up and ready to go."

"Now we are ready to eat, and I made a lot. Let's start the day with a blessing, shall we?"

"Wait just a second. Someone is at the door. Good morning, Kara. You're just in time for breakfast. Where is everyone else?"

"Good morning, Aunt Maggie. It's only me, or I, or whatever. The rest of the family are still in their PJs and munching on stuff."

"I certainly understand that. Join the circle, Kara. Aunt Betts was just going to do a gratitude blessing."

"These are new to me, but I really like them. They taste kind of like a pancake, or a crepe, or I don't know. I give up. What are they?"

"They are Dutch babies, Kara. We like them with a squeeze of lemon and a slight dusting of confectionary sugar."

"Don't forget the maple syrup."

"Oh yes, Uncle Richard, I saw that, and the apples are really good. I'm so glad I got here in time for breakfast, and Uncle Richard, I asked Dad, and he said to ask you. When are we going to start on our project?"

"Kara, you are a bundle of energy, and that's good because we can always use a little energy. I think we should be able to start around one o'clock this afternoon? Yes, my dear, I have a few things to do, and we're going to have lunch together, and then we'll dive right in. The plan came to me last night. I think I probably dreamed it, but whatever, it is brilliant and something we can complete this afternoon."

"Great, thanks, Uncle Richard. Now I'll help clean up and then go read some more of my book."

"Kara, darling, thank you for offering to clean up, but I think we're probably going to linger here for a while. So, if you would just put the juice away, and take care of your plate. We'll be fine, and we'll see you before we take off for the afternoon, and you are all probably going to have to forage for dinner. It may be late when we return."

"Good, that will surely give us time to finish our project, right, Uncle Richard?"

"Yes, Kara, we'll have a great time."

"Bye now. See you guys, later."

"Bye, Kara."

"So you ladies are really going to make an evening out of it, aye?"

"Richard, my darling, we only have a few days until our wedding. I've shared a lot of our traditional wedding activities with you, and today Aunt Betts and I will share with Mary Beth, and she can let the rest of the family know about the process. I'm quite sure none of them, including you have experienced a wedding celebration like this community creates."

"I'm sure you four will have a very full day, and so will we. We will all be very creative today. Tomorrow, we will tour the community. I haven't forgotten my promise. Aunt Betts and I will take turns as historians. I'm going to arrange to have the horse and carriage reserved for us."

"I love that, Margaret, and so will they. I do hope we get one with the top on it, just in case."

"I'll do my best. Let's get this kitchen in order, and then I'm going to have a niece meditation bath."

"You, ladies, go on upstairs, and do what you need to do. Howdy and I can take care of the kitchen. I think he has actually decided to eat a bit."

"Thank you, Richard. You are a jewel, and I won't protest. I'll just be grateful. Let's go, Aunt Betts."

"I am ahead of you, Maggie."

✳

"Mary Beth, thank you so much for that delightful lunch."

"Actually, Maggie, thank you. I used leftovers, and they just turned into a casserole."

"Hey, Mom!"

"Yes, Jamie, this is another one for the recipe book."

"Really, it was great."

"Yes, Mom, I think I should start my own recipe book."

"Good idea, Kara, and your father and I have decided that you and Jamie will have at least one night to prepare and serve dinner, and as often as schedules allow, a breakfast preparation."

"But, Mom, you love to cook. You're always saying that, and you do such a great job, doesn't she, Kara?"

"Oh, absolutely, Mom."

"Good try, guys. Actually, I think you'll love it. You've both helped me often enough. Anyhow, that's the way it is. Now let's get this kitchen in order so you can be about your project and we can get about the wedding plans."

"Aunt Maggie, I am so excited about you and Uncle Rich getting married, and so very glad that we are going to be here for it."

"I am too, Kara. It will be a memorable time for all of us."

"Sorry to break this up, however, it's project time, guys, so let's get busy."

"Bet, I can great you to the cottage."

"Oh no, not me. I am on the track team, Uncle Richard."

"OK, Jamie, give me a handicap. I'll start before you."

"OK, old man, get a move on."

"Away they go, and away we go. We have appointments all afternoon. I will be the self-appointed timekeeper."

"Are you sure, Aunt Betts? That's a lot of pressure."

"Not for me, my dear. Ready, set, let's go."

"I think this is going to be a very interesting day."

"I believe we can guarantee that much, Mary Beth. First stop is the spiritual center, and it may also possibly be the only stop. Mary and Eleanor have assembled everyone, and everything is scheduled. So hang onto your hat, Maggie, you are going to be fitted, and we will review everything. Mary Beth, please ask questions as we go through the process. Although we have a schedule, we always have time to give information. Actually, it would be very helpful to have new eyes and energy. So please don't hesitate."

"Maggie, I am so curious and excited to be a part of this party."

"Mary Beth, I think you are right. This is pretty much a party. I love our wedding book, Auntie Bets. Who did this book? It's beautiful."

"John and his wife Elsie. John works with leather, Mary Beth, so he did the leather work and binding, and Elsie created the rest."

"He did the cover design, I'm sure."

"Yes, he did, Maggie. Mary Beth, this is the first chance to share. We don't bring gifts or cards to weddings, not the kind generally thought of for a traditional wedding. This book is presented to the bride and groom from the community. Everyone signs the book and a pledge of their gift which is to be given any time within the first year of the marriage. It's things like preparing a special dinner for the couple or giving a pig, it's anything and everything. The idea is to give the new couple a lot of support for that first year especially. So you can see why this book is so special to me. It will be filled with love, support, and a message of good will from everyone. This is something that gets passed down as part of the family legacy. I think this will be our sixth one. Is that right, Auntie Betts?"

"I believe so, if you'd like, Mary Beth, I can get them out for you."

"I would love that, Aunt Betts. What a grand tradition! I love it. Thank you for taking the time to share, Maggie."

"It's helpful to me, Mary Beth. Sharing always makes things even more precious. So where do we start, Aunt Betts?"

"We start with Mary. She has the schedule, and Eleanor has the gown and headpiece, and of course, we can always find Mary by following the aroma of something cooking, and here we are."

"Good afternoon, Mary, my love. We can always smell you before we see you."

"That is a compliment. And a very good day to the three of you, and what a beautiful sight you are. When we are ready for our tea break, I have just the thing to go with it."

"Mary, thank you for the hug. You are one of the bet huggers ever."

"Maggie, love, I miss you, and I am so honored that you chose me to be your coordinator, and Eleanor, of course. We are a great team, much like a Clydesdale, I would imagine."

"Great analogy, my friend. You are indeed strong, courageous, beautiful, proud, and accomplish whatever you decide to do."

"Thank you, Betts. I'll accept that. Now, on that note, let's get to it. Do we want tea and blueberry-walnut muffins as we talk?"

"Oh yes, and that was unanimous. I love it when we have consensus."

"Yes, you do, Maggie. Find a chair with a big table. Actually, I have everything on the table so just gather around. Eat, drink, and be merry."

"Mary, that is your motto, and wherever you go that will always follow, and thank you for everything."

"Maggie love, have a muffin, and there is blueberry jam and butter. Cooking to me is like saying a prayer constantly. I guess it's my passion. I love watching all of you now as you're showing me just how much you appreciate the food.

"Now to the activity list. Maggie, Eleanor is ready for you so that will be the first priority—the fitting of the gown and headpiece. Everyone be prepared for the sight of an angel appearing before us. Then we will discuss the rest, although let me warn you, this is not going to take very long because as usual everyone knows their part very well and we know that, so let the fun begin. Are you ready for Eleanor, Maggie?"

"Oh yes, I am so ready."

"Eleanor, Maggie is here and ready for action."

"What an exciting time this is, Maggie. I am so honored to design and create your gown. Of course, actually, you did most of the design."

"It was a team effort, Eleanor. We even let Auntie Betts give a couple of suggestions."

"So we did, and how are you, Betts?"

"Grateful for the opportunity to be here for this beautiful event, Eleanor."

"Mary Beth, I'm so glad you and your family are able to stay for the wedding."

"We would not miss it for anything, Eleanor."

"Well, Maggie. Step into the fitting room, and let's see the vision of perfection that you are, and we have the headpiece completed as well."

"Eleanor, it is spectacular. Every sequin, pearl, and whatever else you have created. I haven't even dreamed of anything so perfect. Thank you, all of you, for this creation."

"Maggie, you are so welcome, and you are so beautiful. The gown and the headpiece were truly made for you. Now let's go let them see what I see."

"Maggie, you are breathtakingly beautiful."

"Thank you, Mary Beth."

"Auntie Betts, what do you think?"

"I can't think right now, child. I can only feel, and what I feel, I can't find words for. You are making me think of things past and things to come. In other words, I think this moment is perfect."

"Eleanor, there is not one thing to change. I love it, and it fits perfectly, and I will not gain a pound or an inch until the wedding. Of course, that's only three days from now, so I think I'm safe. We are definitely off to a good start, Aunt Betts. What's next?"

"Back to Mary. She and her team are in charge of the *cake*, food, and drink, so we know that will go well. She has coordinated enough weddings, I can't even imagine how I could possibly make a suggestion or have a question."

"Maggie, Mary really wants you to be involved. Maybe you can find a way to contribute some suggestions."

"Well, Aunt Betts, I usually can. I know what you mean. This is a very special occasion for her. I think she was about to give up on me. Bless her heart. She tried playing cupid for me several times. I'm sure now she's very happy that I was not in a hurry and for very good reason."

"That reason is of course, my brother, right?"

"Absolutely, Mary Beth, and both of us knew it almost immediately."

"I am so glad, Maggie. Just being around you two makes everyone happy."

"What's this about? Happy? How could anyone be happy about a wedding? How was the fit, darling?"

"Mary, it was literally like a glove—perfect and except I can't gain any weight or inches."

"So we shall discuss food, drinks and especially the cake?"

"Only if you promise my gown will still fit after muffins and tea."

"That I will, Maggie, my dear. I made calorie-free blueberry, walnut, and spice muffins."

"I have been getting the aroma for the last thirty minutes, and I don't have a gown to worry about, so I'll have two."

"Good girl, Betts. I just may join you, and how about you, Mary Beth?"

"I'll start with one and go from there."

"Here's a basketful. Have what you will. Tea for everyone?"

"Oh yes, tea it is. Now we can get down to business, Maggie. Let's create the cake first. What is your dream, Maggie?"

"What a great question. I assumed you would have a design for me to choose. Now I have to come up with my dream?"

"That's the way it works, Maggie. The cake is an expression of love, and sharing that love with everyone."

"Yes, I know you're right, Mary. I think I had better have a few moments to really focus on creating a vision."

"Take your time, darling. We're not going anywhere."

"Mary, thank you, I can see, smell, and taste that cake. So this is what I want. It has apples—they remind me of the apple harvest with Richard. Carrots because they remind me of my mother. She used carrots in everything. I especially loved the juice. Cranberries and raisins. Am I getting too crazy, Mary?"

"No, Maggie, keep going."

"I know you can do the rest, Mary."

"What about the design?"

"Oh yes, it will look like our center, and I know you can do that also. I have seen you create castles, butterflies, and I do believe I remember someone else choosing the spiritual living center design."

"Yes, I'm sure you do, and I create it a little different for everyone. I have had that request several times, and I love the challenge."

"Also, Maggie, there was one you didn't see that was your mother's. She chose the same design."

"Betts, you are right. I had forgotten that."

"No wonder, Mary, I wouldn't begin to guess how many cakes you have made, and I suggest you don't even think about it. Good idea, Betts."

"Thank you for sharing that, Aunt Betts. That is, as they say, the icing on the cake. I really do feel my mother's presence, her spirit of joy. It's a good thing. Mary Beth let's go outside and really look at the center. By the way, Mary, why didn't I bring Richard with me today? The men have Richard and Kevin all afternoon and evening tomorrow. They have their plan for him. It's kind of like a bachelors' event."

"You can share your day with him, and he can do the same with you."

"Thank you, Mary. This is my first wedding, you know."

"Yes, my love, I do indeed know."

"Let's go, Mary Beth."

"This is so enthralling, Maggie. I'm glad Kev is going to be involved."

"Mary Beth, everyone is involved. When we have a wedding, it's a community wedding. Richard and I will have our own special part. We make our pledge to one another and with the community, and then the community makes their pledge of support and love to us."

"Maggie, this place never stops surprising me in a very good way."

"I'm glad, Mary Beth. Can you imagine a cake shaped like this beautiful building?"

"Yes, I can, Maggie. It will be awesome. Well, let's go find out what's next. This is fun."

"So you have a vision of the cake, Maggie?"

"I do, Mary. Thank you. I really assumed that you just created it, and whatever it was, I would love it, but this is so meaningful. Every bite will be full of memories. Thank you, and what is next?"

"I do have several menus prepared. You may mix, match, change things around to your liking. I'm going to leave you there to work on this, and I'll go find Flo. She's in charge of the decorating group."

"Well, that didn't take long. Mary really knows what she's doing. That's very obvious."

"Mary Beth, I think Mary was born with a recipe in one hand and a baking pan in the other. When we were children, Mary was always the cook. She never wanted to have any other pretend role."

"So, Aunt Betts, you were raised in this community?"

"Off and on. My parents were like me, or perhaps I should say, I am like them. They were happy wherever they were, and they were a lot of places. They always had one more place to explore, so off we would go. I had a marvelous childhood, and most of the time, I was what they now call homeschooled. Except most of my education, before the university, was hands on and lively discussions about everything."

"Good afternoon, Flo. How very nice to see you."

"Betts, I am just so very grateful that I get the great pleasure of contributing in some small way to this long-awaited event."

"She did take her time, didn't she? And it was obviously the right thing to do. Richard is a fine addition to our family and community. Flo, have you met Mary Beth, Richard's sister?"

"Yes, I have had the pleasure. Nice to see you again, Mary Beth. I enjoyed working with you and Maggie at the Christmas workshop."

"Yes, and you were very helpful. That was an evening to remember."

"So, Maggie, are we ready to talk about the decorating?"

"Honestly, Flo, this place is perfect just the way it is. I don't want to disappoint you, but this is one reason Richard and I chose New Year's Eve and here for our wedding. I love the trees, wreaths, lights, everything. I can't imagine how it could be improved. However, if you have suggestions, I certainly will listen."

"Maggie, that's just about what I thought you would say, and I totally agree. We only really need to talk about a few minor additions. I understand you and Richard want to exchange vows at around 11:00 p.m. Is that correct?"

"Yes, it is, Flo. We want to welcome the New Year married to one another and exchange vows with the community before midnight."

"Well, we have the three large candles for the vow exchange. So what do you think about everyone having a candle for the community exchange. You and Richard could start the lighting, then everyone could light the candle of the next person, and Betts has the selection of songs that you and Richard have chosen. She could be singing while the lighting happens. What do you think?"

"Flo, I love it, and I know Richard will. We will finish just before midnight, and then we can ring the New Year in with cake and champagne."

"Well, my job was certainly easy, Maggie."

"That's the way it's supposed to be, Flo. Thank you for adding the candles. I can't image anything more perfect."

"Maggie, I am in awe. This is flowing so gently. I don't feel any anxiety or pressure from anyone, including you and Richard, actually especially you and Richard."

"I am so glad, Mary Beth. We as a community are just like an extended family which is quite functional. So events like ours are easy, really kind of like a play. We all know our parts very well, so we can relax and enjoy the moment."

"I must tell you, Maggie, to an observer it looks a bit like magic, and I love magic, so I am prepared to relax and enjoy. I have been wondering when all the preparation pressure was going to start, as has been my experience with weddings. Now I know there really isn't going to be any. I realize how I have created my own anxiety from past experiences. What a relief to let that go."

"Great job, Mary Beth, release-relax-let it go. It's wonderful. Now I want to check in with Mary and see if she has any questions. Actually, I really just want to get my hug. That's my magic."

"May I come with you, Maggie? I want my hug too. Mary's hugs are like comfort food, maybe that's why she is such a good cook."

"I think you're right, Mary Beth. Let's go, and here comes Auntie Betts, which means Mary has completed her list for the day."

"My goodness, ladies, we have had a very productive, delightful day and evening. At least I know I have. Maggie my love, I am walking on clouds. I am so delighted to be here with all of you for this very happy occasion. I had no idea when I got this very strong urge to spend the holidays with you and Richard and what a blessing I would receive. I should say blessings. Mary Beth, you, Kevin, and of course, the young ones have increased my bounty of pleasure, and this community always fills my soul with joy. Maggie, you and Richard are a fine fit, and I am so grateful that I can be a witness to your vows."

"Auntie Betts, you would just have to be here. It would not be the same without you. Your beautiful voice, your calm easy manner, and your presence is like having my mother close by. Do you know what I mean?"

"Yes, I do, child. Your Mother's and Father's presence is very strong. I wonder what the guys have been up to all day. Is Richard having a bachelor party, Maggie?"

"I suppose we could call it that, although it is really more about traditions, and I guess kind of like a boot camp. Questions and answers about becoming a full-fledged member of this community."

"That sounds kind of scary, Maggie. I wonder how Kevin is doing. He's used to a very different kind of bachelor party."

"Nothing to worry about, Mary Beth. Believe me, there will be a lot of fun, food, and laughter, along with the process of information sharing. Right, Aunt Betts?"

"Yes, indeed. We have never lost a groom. We only gain another member of the family. I've been watching Kevin. He is very sincere in his quest for information. So I think he is probably soaking it up."

"You are right about that, Aunt Betts, he is. We are seriously considering relocation, and we know that we are coming back for the summer. I think the information gathering time is great, and I think the timing is right for me to go to the cottage. I am ready for a cup of tea, my book, and that magnificent ocean view. Thank you again, both of you, for sharing so much with me today. I don't mean just the food, although that was great also."

"It is a very special day. Of course, every day is precious, however, I don't get married every day. So thank you, both of you, for your support and love. Rest well, Mary Beth, we have another glorious excursion tomorrow, and then it's New Year's Eve. Good night, all. See you in the morning."

*

"Maggie, darling, are you up to sharing a cup of tea or hot chocolate before we drift off?"

"I'd love that, Aunt Betts. I'd like hot chocolate please. You make it like no one else."

"Thank you, child, and flattery will get you a cookie to go with it. Go on in by the fire, Maggie, I'll join you in a minute. Howdy wants to be with you right now, and he's not shy about letting us know that."

"Come on, Howdy. Let's snuggle by the fireplace."

"This is so nice, Maggie. I have loved every minute of this visit."

"I'm glad, Auntie Betts, but you make it sound like your visit is over."

"No, not really. We have tomorrow, and I will truly enjoy sharing community history and trying to answer the many questions the two young ones will have. I think it will take the three of us to keep up with them. Richard has learned a lot during the short time he has been here. You are an excellent guide, Maggie. We will have a fun and full day tomorrow. It would be nice if Richard was here now. I will be leaving shortly after the family leaves, and I have something I would like to share with both of you."

"Auntie Betts, are you sure you can't stay just a little longer? You know we have decided not to go on our honeymoon right now."

"Yes, I know that, Maggie, but I have a commitment, and I'll be meeting the team on the fifth, so I have some traveling to do. Oh great, I hear Richard now. His timing is perfect. Welcome, Richard. I was just talking about you."

"Well, coming from you, Betts, I know it was something very nice, and yes, I would love a cup of hot chocolate, Betts."

"You are a mind reader, Richard."

"Hello, darling, I've missed you."

"Me too, Rich, although I'm sure we have both had an unforgettable day and evening."

"You are right about that, Maggie. I have learned so much and had a great time doing it, so did Kevin. What I wasn't asking he was. It was amazing."

"Now that I have you two alone for a change, I have something I want to talk to you about."

"Rich, Auntie Betts is leaving shortly after our wedding."

"Betts, I am really sad to think about you not being here. I love you, you know."

"Yes, Rich, I do know, it's just time for me to get back to work. However, I do have a gift that I would like to give you two tonight. Yes, I know we don't give wedding gifts, but you're not married tonight. I really hope that you will be able to accept my gift, but I do understand if you would rather not."

"I'm intrigued, Aunt Betts, so let's unwrap it or whatever we're doing."

"I am giving you travel and full accommodations, whenever you choose. I only need a few days' notice for a trip to Galapagos. You may stay in the bed-and-breakfast, or the cottages. Either way, your meals will be prepared to perfection. You can actually try both places if you'd like. I may not be able to be there with you, very much, or at all. But you will have family waiting for you—they are the best. They will be available when you want them and gone when you don't. They have a way about them to understand how that works. I can't figure it out, but it works. What do you say?"

"Rich, we have talked about doing this sometime in the future, and the future is now. What do you think?"

"Maggie, I think it's a miracle. Betts, we would love to accept your generous gift. Thank you for nudging us in the right direction, and I do sincerely believe it will be an adventure beyond our comprehension."

"Rich, shall we share our gift with Auntie Betts?"

"I would love for us to, Maggie."

"Please do. You have my curiosity glowing. What is it?"

"We are going to have a baby."

"I knew it. I just knew it. I am so happy for all of us. This is the greatest gift of all and at Christmastime. How perfect is that?"

"We're not actually having the baby right now, Betts."

"I know, Rich, however we do have that little spirit with us right now. At least, that's the way I see it. When will the little one join us?"

"Late July or early August."

"Maggie, Richard, I am so happy for both of you. Does anyone else know?"

"Oh no, we plan to keep it just between the three of us. Rich and I want to just share it together for a while."

"Great idea, Maggie, and I certainly won't tell anyone, but thank you so much for sharing with me. It's such a special time. I will bid you two good night. I am sure I shall have lovely dreams. I love you both very much. Oh my, actually it's now you three, no four. Howdy is certainly a part of the circle. I'll see you in the morning, loves."

"Good night, Auntie Betts, and thank you again for our special honeymoon gift. I think we'll not share that right now either."

"You are so welcome. I know you are both going to fall in love with Galapagos. The creatures, people, everything. Just come prepared to be pampered and awed."

"That we shall, Betts. I may even write a piece about it. I am feeling very productive these days. However, not at this very moment. I think we will be following you upstairs very soon. Those guys wore me out, in a good way. See you in the morning, Betts."

"Maggie, darling, I love you."

"You too, Richard, and I am looking forward to our carriage ride tomorrow and showing the family what a gem we have here in Port Haven."

"I love watching those youngsters especially. Soaking up everything and wanting more. I'm very glad there are three of us, and I know it will be a grand day, and Maggie no wedding decisions. Isn't it wonderful to know that everything is as it should be, and all we have to do is show up? So tomorrow, no wedding talk, at least that is my suggestion."

"Yes, Aunt Betts, I totally agree. We will be completely present for our adventures and discoveries."

"Well, I think you know you can count me in, ladies. Rest well, Betts. We'll see you in the morning."

"Good night, all. Yes, you too, Howdy."

*

"Maggie, my darling, I am ready to go upstairs, how about you?"

"In a few minutes, darling. Howdy and I have some things to talk about. Get the bed warm for me, I'll be up shortly."

"Then I'm going to kiss you good night love, because I will be asleep before I know I'm in bed."

"Good night, Richard, my love."

"We haven't had alone time for a while, Howdy. There is so much that I want to tell you. I know you are very tired, although you still have that bright light of love in your eyes. You and I have cuddled in front of this fireplace, in this very spot, for so many years, sometimes in meditative silence, other times when you were the world's best listener. Always my beloved friend and companion. Thank you, Howdy, for the gift of unconditional love. I treasure our shared memories which will live in my heart forever. I am so grateful to have had you as my friend, mentor, and teacher. Although you shared your love with everyone you met, I have always felt blessed to have you as a special companion. I want you to know that when you are ready to move on to your next adventure, I will be fine. Yes, I will mourn my loss and celebrate your freedom. I will rejoice in the lessons I have learned from you. Especially as I remember the absolute joy of living in the moment. You are such a great teacher. You and I, Howdy, have no regrets. We never shared a moment of distress in our relationship. What a blessing! I can only remember love, joy, your

324

patience, and your love in my times of grief. Your complete acceptance of everything I am. Not one negative memory. What a rich legacy, my dear friend. Yes, Howdy, I treasure these precious moments. Thank you."

∗

"Good morning, Maggie, my love."

"Good morning, Richard. It looks like I never made it upstairs."

"No. I checked on you sometime in the night when I missed you. You and Howdy were so content. I checked the fire and put a blanket over both of you."

"Thank you, darling. Yes, we were exactly where we were supposed to be. We had a lot to talk about."

"Good morning, Howdy, my friend. Yes, I will take you out. I'm sure that won't take long. It's really cold out there."

"I'll start the coffee, Richard. Well, good morning, Auntie Betts. Did you sleep well?"

"Good morning to you, Maggie, my girl. I swear that coffee you make is pure magic. The aroma makes its way into my bedroom, and I simply couldn't resist. Here I am wide awake and hungry as a bear in the spring time."

"That's great, Auntie Betts, because we are all eating breakfast together this morning and I would love it if you would make the angel biscuits that you are famous for."

"As long as I can have my juice and coffee, I am ready for anything. What is the plan, Maggie?"

"Richard makes an amazing omelet, so that's his part. I'm doing an apple and blueberry bake dish, and with your biscuits, who could ask for anything more? So, let's do it!"

"When are the troops arriving, Maggie?"

"I believe we settled on a 9:00 a.m. target time. We were all a little tired last night, so we'll see."

"A little tired, Maggie! I don't even remember the last few steps upstairs. I truly was asleep before I consciously got into my bed. How about you and Richard?"

"Rich went to bed right away. Howdy and I snuggled up together by the fire in our special spot and had some very good quality time. I began to realize that time was going so fast and we haven't kept to our routines during the holidays, which is fine. However, I also know that Howdy is slowing down a lot, and his appetite is declining. There is so much I want to tell him. Although I know he doesn't need for me to do it. It's something I need and want to do."

"Maggie, I'm so glad, even with so much going on, that you and Howdy are making the best of this opportunity. It would be so easy not to."

"Our time together last night was very healing for me. I do want him to know that he has taught me well. I know that I can be a much better partner for Richard because I have learned so much from Howdy about life in general, and the special gift of life in the moment. Like right now, Aunt Betts. How special to smell your biscuits and see you with flour on your face. And that great big hug from you even before you got your morning coffee."

"Maggie, child. I love every minute of my life, and I know that you do also. And Richard and the young ones are in for such an adventure."

"Speaking of Richard, here they are. Howdy, you look frozen. Yes, go for the fireplace. Richard, the biscuits are cooking. I'm getting ready to put my dish in the oven. I think we are ready for your omelet magic, and let me know if I can help."

"I'll tell you for sure. This kitchen is exactly where I want to be right now. It is really cold out there. Howdy decided to take his time looking at and smelling everything. He was not in any hurry. Now that my hands are functional again, and I thank you for the coffee, Maggie, my love, I will get the omelets going. I saw a lot of activity down at the cottage. So I am sure they will be here soon. This promises to be a very full and wonderful day. Maggie, Betts, are you up for the adventure?"

"Oh yes, Richard, we are indeed."

"Good morning, everyone. Your timing is perfect. Everything is ready."

"So are we, Aunt Maggie. I don't think I slept last night, or maybe I did, because I kept seeing us in the carriage or whatever it is, and the sun just came out and, and . . ."

"Whoa, Kara. Slow down. Remember, we are going to stay in the moment today. It was even your suggestion."

"OK, Mom. You're right. And when we opened the door, all of these luscious smells came out and my appetite awakened."

"So did your mouth, Kara. Give it a break."

"Yes, Jamie. Really, I will. I am starved."

"Sure you are, Kara. I suggest we have a moment of quiet and gratitude, while we all settle in to this moment. Thank you, Maggie, and thank you all for this bountiful breakfast."

"You are welcome, Mary Beth. It truly was a pleasure to prepare. And, as you know, we are quite a team."

"That was wonderful, especially my favorite biscuits and gravy and, well, everything. When are we going, Aunt Maggie?"

"Very soon, Kara. Aunt Betts and I have to excuse ourselves and go upstairs for a few minutes."

"You two do what you need to do. We are going to do kitchen duty. Right, guys?"

"Sure, Mom. Let's do it!"

"Thank you, Mary Beth. We'll be back shortly."

"What a great job you did, Aunt Betts. The kitchen literally sparkles."

"Maggie, I think it's the bright energy that's making the house shine."

"I believe you're right, Aunt Betts. Anyhow, thank you all."

∗

"Now, I do believe we are all set for our excursion. Just a few hints that might be helpful. I know that you have been downtown a few times. Rich has kept me updated on what you have seen. So Auntie Betts and I have planned a route that we think you probably haven't seen yet or that you may have questions about. We have tried to anticipate your questions. However, I am quite sure that you will surprise us with others. The carriage is covered, but otherwise pretty open. Blankets are available, and we have hot chocolate prepared. Howdy is going with us today. Also, I think your bright energy has revitalized him. So if everybody is ready, let's be off."

"I'm so glad you are going with us, Howdy. I love you so much."

"Yes, Kara. He can sit between you and Jamie."

"Aunt Maggie, you really did it! You anticipated my question. How cool!"

"Maggie, Ken, and I have looked forward to this opportunity. We love this community. Truly, all of us have become so attached so quickly. We are not even thinking about going home because this feels so much like being home."

"Auntie Betts, I think our job today is going to be very easy."

"It always is, Maggie girl, and the sun is shining. We have so much to be grateful for."

"That we do."

"Wow, these carriages are beautiful. Aren't they, Jamie?"

"They are pretty cool, Kara, and actually look very comfortable. What are the horses' names, Aunt Maggie?"

"Albert and Maude. They know their job very well. They have been doing this for several years, and they still seem to love it. They will let us know when they want to retire. Everyone comfortable and ready to roll?"

"Let's all take a deep breath, close your eyes, and just focus on your breathing for a moment. Thank you. Now I'm ready to be the first tour guide."

"You folks are in for a treat. When Auntie Betts shares information, well, you know it's going to be full of surprises and excitement. Thank you, Margaret. Let's have fun."

"Folks, I think it's time for a break and some good, warm food."

"Yes, everyone is in agreement with that suggestion, Auntie Betts."

"I want to tell you, Betts, how grateful I am for this excursion. You have managed to make it fun, informational, and so personal, like living history. You brought everyone and everything to life. Mary Beth, I don't know about you, but I know I have literally fallen in love with this community, and I hope you have."

"Kev, I couldn't have said it better. Yes, I am totally sold."

"Does that mean we are really going to move here, Mom?"

"Yes, Kara. It does mean just that."

"I really like the idea folks, but I have a couple of school commitments coming up."

"Whoa, Jamie! We are not going to move next week. It's not an urgent thing. We will finish the school year and work out a transition plan."

"That's so exciting, Mary Beth, all of you. I know Rich and I are kind of like Kara, thinking the sooner the better."

"However, folks, being the elder here, I think a transition plan is a very wise decision. Port Haven has been here for a very long time and will continue being here for a lot longer. Thank you, folks, for enduring my endless chatter. However, there is a lot to say, and a short amount of time to say it. So now let's go inside, thaw out, and fill up. Shall we?"

"This is the best soup and bread I have ever eaten in my entire life. I don't know what it is, but wow!"

"Kara, you may be surprised to know what it is. It is called 'back to our Roots soup'. I think the secret is in the seasoning. I haven't been able to get the recipe yet, but when I do, I will send it to your, Mom."

"Oh, yes, Aunt Maggie. Let's make that recipe book as big as the Bible."

"Good idea, Kara."

"Maggie, you take the reins from here. It's your turn to be the tour guide."

"You are a hard act to follow, Aunt Betts, but somebody has to do it. No, really I am so proud of our town. I love sharing the stories. Everything."

"After all, Aunt Maggie, you are the librarian. So you're supposed to know everything. Right?"

"Absolutely not, Kara. I'm so happy to say I learn something new every day. Sometimes several things. Those are the really special days."

"Well, I can tell you, Maggie, that we are all having a special day today, thanks to you three and Rich. I am impressed that you have learned so much about this community already."

"Thanks, Kev. And quite honestly, I agree. I have felt loved and supported from my first moment here. And now that you folks are joining us, it is really complete."

"Let's go folks. There's more to see and do"

"Aunt Maggie, can we go by that medical place, you know, the one that has the baby birthing center?"

"Sure, Kara. It's only about two blocks away."

"May I tell about it, Aunt Maggie?"

"Sure, Kara. Be my guest. I'll be your backup if you need me."

"Thank you, Aunt Maggie."

"You did a great job, Kara. You remembered everything about the clinic and made it very interesting as well as informative. Thank you."

"You are most welcome, Aunt Maggie. It was fun."

"We will finish our tour back at the town square where Howdy's statue is. And of course, it's one of my favorite spots."

"Is that where the checker players are, Aunt Maggie?

"There are usually some checker players and some folks just enjoying the day and one another. It's a very popular gathering place for all ages, Jamie. Fortunately, we have gathering places all over town. However, if we had to vote, this is, of course, the one I would vote for."

"I think Howdy should be our tour guide for this one, Maggie."

"Yes, Rich, I am quite sure he will be very happy to oblige. And there he goes."

"He can move sometimes, can't he, Jamie?"

"Yes, Kara. Let's see if we can keep up with him."

"He is so proud of that sculpture. As soon as he gets there, he will pose just like it does."

"Do you think he knows it's of him, Maggie?"

"Oh yes, Mary Beth, I wish you folks could have been here for the dedication. It was wonderful. The entire town was here, and Howdy was majestic."

"Look at him now, Maggie. He's pretty regal. Kevin, isn't he beautiful?"

"He is the most genuine, loving spirit I have ever met, Mary Beth, and yes, he is beautiful."

"Maggie, it is really cold now that the sun is going down, and yet there are people out everywhere, seemingly oblivious to that fact."

"I think that's just it, Mary Beth. It does get cold in the winter. We all know how to dress for it. Be grateful and enjoy it. So yes, people still play checkers and card games, talk, laugh, sing, and live. The biggest difference between winter and summer is that during the summer, we stay out longer and have more picnics."

"Speaking of food, I for one am ready to head for home and have some of the magnificent chicken noodle soup. Auntie Betts, do you have soup waiting for us at home, really?"

"Almost, Kara. The chicken has been simmering in the crock pot, and we'll have it ready to eat before you know it. So do we have a consensus on taking the carriage back and heading for home?"

"Oh yes, let's do it. That is if we can persuade Howdy."

"You just did, Jamie. He's going to be there before us."

"What a wonderful day. Mary Beth, I feel like we are already a member of this special community. Thank you all for the adventure. We have had a great time. Actually every day and minute since we arrived has been filled with sheer joy. We know your wedding is the total focus for tomorrow, and we leave the next morning. So we all really want to share our gratitude for you and with you."

"Thank you, Kev, all of you, for being here with us during this very special chapter of our lives. This holiday season will certainly go down in our collective memory boxes. Personally, my memory box has already turned into a steamer trunk, Rich, and I just think the best is yet to come."

"Maggie, I swear you have a special glow tonight."

"Yes, Aunt Maggie, we may not even need those dinner candles!"

"All right you two, I get it, you are right. It is time to get the food on the table and wouldn't you know it, while we have been talking. Aunt Betts has been working her kitchen magic, and it smells heavenly."

"Thank you, Maggie. I've been cooking, but I'll tell you I can cook and listen at the same time, and I just want to add an amen to everything that was said. We all have a great deal to be grateful for and especially for one another. Now I don't think we need to say a blessing before we eat because we have already. Let's just hold hands for a minute and enjoy the smells, warmth, and energy. And so it is."

"Aunt Maggie, are you really excited about tomorrow?"

"I am, Kara. I suppose excited is one way to describe it. I have so many emotions jumping around, a bit like a roller coaster, and that's certainly exciting. However, I also feel very content. I think it's a bit complicated, but more than anything else, I feel happy, I love having all of you here, and I am so gland that you are my family now, and on the other hand, you are all going to be leaving very soon, and you will leave a lot of space. Fortunately, we have our extended family, and of course each other and we have our treasure chest of memories. So yes, tomorrow is a very special day for all of us. You folks are in for another really big party. It is New Year's Eve you know. We won't have fireworks, I'll bet, since it is also a wedding."

"Jamie, my boy, you are wrong. We will indeed have fireworks. We will say our vows, have candle lighting, toast one another the New Year's birth, and the fireworks begin. Wow, Jamie, I think we are really going to like this wedding."

"Kara, you like every wedding, but yes, this one sounds like a blast!"

"Good one, Jamie. My goodness, I'm sorry to say it, but I must be rude and leave you folks to fend for yourselves. I love your company, but my body yearns for a warm bath and some soft music. I would love to have a hug from you two, young ones, and I want to give you a few words of wisdom, or at least good advice."

"Oh yes, Auntie Betts, are you going to tell us a story?"

"No, darlings, just a simple way to remember our community and why it is so special. I call it the three Ps. The first P is for presence. You can think of it as spirit, God, whatever feels right to you. The main thing is to feel that presence within you and to be grateful. The second P is for practice, which means to practice love as a way of life. As an example, every time a thought occurs, that is less than loving, change it. It's a lifetime process, so don't be surprised if you forget from time to time, it happens. The important part is to keep on practicing. The third P is for power. The more you practice living love, the more power you have for your mission. Now, I know mission can sound like a big deal, and actually it is. It creates happiness. We are all unique beings and where one may become a brain surgeon and another, a farmer, and they are both doing the same thing, which is sharing this gift of life in their own unique way. So remember the three Ps, and when we are together again, we'll have a talk about them."

"Thank you, Auntie Betts. We will all miss you so much, but we are also so much more for having you in our lives."

"Thank you, Auntie Betts, and likewise."

"Yes, Auntie Betts, you are my special angle. Now get yourself upstairs and take your bath."

"Yes, Madam Maggie, I will do that very thing. Good night all of you. See you tomorrow."

"Good night, Auntie Betts. We love you!"

✳

"My, it is so quiet, Richard, but I can still feel the energy, which is a very good thing."

"Maggie, my love, thank you again for being such an amazing person. I just keep learning. I thought I knew so much about our town, and I didn't know as much about our health clinic and birthing center as Kara, and that is a really important piece of information for us. I am so relieved, excited, and anxious to learn more. Maggie, I don't mean tonight. You have done more than enough talking today."

"Well! Richard, do you mean I talk too much?"

"Oh no, my love, never. You were a superb guide."

"I'm joking, Richard. I know what you mean, and I thank you, darling. I had so much fun hearing the excitement in everyone's voice as they asked questions. Kevin and Mary Beth were as curious as Kara and

Jamie. It was another great day of awe and wonder. We are really going to miss them, Richard."

"Yes, we will, however, we have a wonderful way of filling empty spaces with opportunities."

"Rich, are you still OK about not telling them about our baby?"

"Absolutely. I am really glad that we told Betts, and I am more than OK about not telling the family. It's just not the right time. However, I do think it is the right time for bed, how about you?"

"I will be up shortly, Rich. Howdy and I have a little catching up to do."

"All right, you two. I'll see you later, love."

"Can you believe that tomorrow is our wedding day, Rich?"

"Yes, I can, Maggie. As a matter of fact, I have imagined it several times. So in a way, I guess I've had a rehearsal."

"I am so ready to be Mrs. Richard King."

"You will also always be Margaret Scott. Actually, Maggie, think about keeping the Scott name or having both. You have a history and some responsibility for maintaining it. So seriously think about it. I know the right answer will emerge."

"Richard, thank you. I do really want to give that some consideration, and honestly, I hadn't, but, I will now. I love you so much."

"Now I am going to bed, Maggie my love."

∗

"Good morning, Howdy, although I really don't remember doing it, apparently we made it upstairs last night. You probably had to carry me up those stairs. Ah, I smell that strong robust aroma that tells me Rich has made his special blend of coffee. I think he knows how to get me out of bed, or did he send you? Either way it worked. Howdy, you look so bright this morning. You certainly are more energetic the past few days, and I am so glad my friend."

"Well, what a fine pair you are."

"My coffee! Thank you, Rich. I was just getting ready to come downstairs, but Howdy wouldn't let me."

"Sure, blame poor old Howdy. Good morning, darling Maggie, I will bring your coffee any time. Especially on New Year's Eve."

"Thank you, Rich, and I will let you do that for me. Right, Howdy? Is Auntie Betts up yet?"

"No, not yet, I want to get her Dutch baby in the oven before she does it herself."

"I agree. I'll be right down to help."

"Take your time, darling."

"Good morning, Betts, you look fresh as a daisy. You look like you bathed in the fountain of youth."

"Thank you, Richard. Honestly, I kind of feel like I did really. However, the magic that you create with your coffee awakens all of my senses, but most of all, it teases my imagination. Each cup creates a new story that unfolds with each sip."

"Betts, we are going to miss you, you are such a joy. Thank you for spending this time with us."

"Richard, I am so happy for you, Maggie and the family to come. You truly are soul mates, and that is such a blessing. Speaking of blessings, I hear one approaching. Good morning, Maggie, my love. You look exactly like a bride to be should look. Radiant, full of energy and vitality, ready for life to unfold."

"Thank you, Aunt Betts, and you are looking rather chipper yourself."

"You two lovely ladies have a seat, and I will be most happy to serve."

"Richard you did everything, what a beautiful breakfast, and yes, darling, more coffee. I assume the rest of the family is not joining us for breakfast."

"Correct assumption. They are on their own this morning. By the way, Maggie, what time are we expected at the center today?"

"We really don't have a definite time, Rich. There will be folks there all day cooking, playing games and such, but it's pretty informal until dinner, which is at 7:30 p.m. After dinner will be music, dancing, singing, and then at around 10:30 or so, there will be a quiet time, a meditation and time for giving thanks for blessings of this year, and gratitude for all of the blessing to come in the new year. After that is when we dress and start the wedding event."

"It sounds so easy, Maggie, I've always heard that weddings were very stressful, and I certainly haven't felt any stress yet."

"Oh no, Rich, our weddings are beautiful, relaxed, full of joy, good food, surrounded by love. I have attended more weddings than I can count, and trust me, they have been anything but stressful, right, Auntie Betts? You certainly have attended more than I."

"Yes, just relax, breathe, and enjoy the moment, darlings."

"You two are very convincing. I wasn't really concerned, but now I'm looking forward to it. I mean food, champagne, and I know I am the most fortunate guy alive to have found you, Maggie, my love."

"You are both the perfect blend. Now when do we rouse the rest of the family?"

"Any time, I told them, we would probably be down to the cottage by about noon. How does that sound?"

"Perfect Richard. I think we should take up where we left off on those games that Jamie and Kara were gloating over."

"Absolutely, Betts, let's do it. Maggie, is there anything we need to do for the dinner tonight?"

"No, Rich, we are only to arrive and be totally supported in every way by everyone."

"So really, we don't have anything to do at our own wedding."

"Yes, darling, we get to say 'I do' together at the same time, and those other words that we have prepared. That's pretty much it. Except of course to eat, drink, and be merry!"

"Well, Happy New Year's Eve to each and every one."

*

"Maggie! Rich! Oh, there you are, of course, in your fireside cocoon. Howdy, I swear you're smiling. He has really been rejuvenated. I don't know what happened, but whatever it was, I am grateful. Betts, did you mix up one of your elixirs for him? And if you did, may I have some? Rich, you don't need any more energy, you are just fine."

"No, I didn't give Howdy anything, except of course love, which he gets from everyone. Maybe that's it, Auntie Betts."

"Could be, Maggie. We don't need to know why, just be grateful for the moment. Speaking of the moment, are you three ready to go down to the cottage?"

"We are ready, Betts, just waiting for you to show us the way."

"What I will show you is how to play that dice game."

"That sounds like a challenge, and on my wedding day, I may let you win one time."

"We'll see."

"It's about time you guys got here. I wanted to come up and get you, but Mom and Dad wouldn't let me."

"Sure, Kara, that was all of five minutes ago."

"Oh no, Mom, it was way longer than that."

"Mary Beth, you have a major banquet ready. Are you expecting company? It does look like a lot, doesn't it? Kev and I cleaned out the refrigerator and cupboards. I didn't realize how much we had, and since we're leaving tomorrow, well, this is what we have, and it's going to be an 'eat what you want, when you want it'. Maggie, do you think it would be appropriate to take leftovers to the center this evening?"

"Oh yes, Mary Beth, you know Mary. She lets nothing go to waste. By the way, when are we going to the center? I plan to go home around 4:30 p.m., and I'll only need about thirty minutes to make sure I check off everything on my list for tonight. So shall we kind of loosely say between 5:00 p.m. and 5:30 p.m.?"

"Sounds good to me."

"We have been saying good-bye to everything all morning. Jamie and I went down to the beach and for a little walk on the trail. We have had such a very good time here. Thank you so much, Uncle Richard and Aunt Maggie."

"You are so welcome, however, now, we are here to challenge you and Jamie to a hot dice game, or are you two too tired?"

"Nope, it's all set up and ready to go. I was sure we would get to play again."

"I won the bet, Jamie.

"OK, but now let's win the fame, come on, Auntie Betts, let's do it."

"That was fun, and I think it is great that we had a tie. We are, of course, all winners, and when you folks return in the summer, we will resume our positions!"

"So, Aunt Maggie, that must mean that Auntie Betts is coming back this summer also?"

"I think we had better ask Auntie Betts about that."

"How about it, Betts? You know we really need you on our team."

"I really can't make a commitment because I have already made a commitment to this project in India. I'm part of a team there also. There is a slight chance that we may finish by then, and I could do my written work here."

"Auntie Betts, I would love for you to be back this summer. So let's all keep that thought alive and focused, shall we?"

"Absolutely."

"Betts, that was unanimous. So I believe we shall all be here, together again this summer. Now it's time for me to get going. I have a few things to check off my list."

"So do we, Maggie. By the time we leave for the center, we expect to be packed and ready to go. Fortunately, we don't have an early flight. However, there are always those last-minute things."

"We will see you folks up at the house around five?"

"Sounds perfect, Maggie. We will be there. See you then."

"Before I forget, Mary Beth, will you folks have time for a New Year's day brunch in the morning?"

"Maggie, are you sure? You will be a new bride, you know. However, if you guys really want us to be there, we certainly can arrange it."

"Spoken like a true connoisseur, Kevin, and a great brother. Maggie and I really want to do this. We've already started it actually, so I think that's settled. Brunch tomorrow morning at ten o'clock. That will give us plenty of time to get to the airport."

*

"Margaret Scott, you are so beautiful. Did you talk to Betts about your name decision? It's getting very close to that time!"

"Yes, Rich, I did. However, I think I had already made my decision."

"And what is that decision?"

"I truly love both names—Scott and King, so that's my decision. Margaret Scott-King. Sometimes, I will be Scott, other times King, and occasionally Scott-King."

"Well, that should be very clear to everyone."

"Really, it will not be a problem. I know who I am and so does everyone in the community. So it will be a very natural easy transition."

"I am sure of that, Maggie. Is there anything I can do to help you with preparations?"

"Thanks, darling. The check-off list is complete. Really, all there is to do now is simply enjoy the experience. I suggest that you and I and Betts have a cup of tea and join Howdy by the fireplace and just be."

"Richard, that sounds perfect. Let's go downstairs and see if Betts needs some help!"

"Apparently not. I hear her singing, and I smell the tea brewing."

"Betts, we were just coming down to make you a cup of tea, but you beat us to it, and it smells divine."

"Maggie, my girl, you look like you have taken a cloud from the sky and wrapped yourself in it. You are floating on air."

"As a matter of fact, that is exactly what I feel like. Oh, Auntie Betts, I love you so much. Thank you for being here with us for everything."

"Thank you, Betts. I understand you are placing this young lady into my care tonight."

"Yes, Mr. King, I do have that honor, I am pleased to say, and I do consider it an honor, Richard."

"Auntie Betts, this tea is very good, strong, and yet gentle. What is it?"

"It is very special, Maggie. I saved it for tonight. It comes from India, and it represents the living history of your ancestors. This teapot belonged to your great grandmother. The cup that your tea is in was your mother's, given to her by your grandmother, and she drank tea from it on her wedding day. So savor the warmth, drama, taste, and feel the presence of those that love you so very much."

"Auntie Betts, thank you."

"I hear the sound of youth approaching. Perfect timing. I think we are all ready to go to the center and get this party going, right, Richard?"

"Anything you say, Betts, your wish is my command."

"Come on in, folks, your timing is right on. We are ready to go."

"So are we, Auntie Betts. We have been ready for a long time, but Mom and Dad said we had more stuff to do."

"Yes, it seems there is often more stuff to do, however, you are here now and we are ready to go, so let's do it."

"I'll go warm up the van, guys. It's pretty cold out there."

"Thank you, Richard, that's a good thing. These bones of mine are yelling for the sun."

"Well, Betts, a nice warm heater will have to suffice for now."

"I am so glad all of the lights are still up. The building is so beautiful. I know it's warm and cozy in there, Aunt Betts."

"Yes, my dear, we can always be sure of that."

"I suggest we actually go inside and join the party."

"You and Aunt Maggie are the party, Uncle Richard."

"Oh no, we aren't officially at a wedding celebration until dinner at 7:30 p.m. Until then, it's fun and games.

"See, Jamie. I told you this would be a fun wedding."

"Mary, it smells so good in here and how wonderful it is to see you."

"Let Don take your coats and stuff. Maggie, you look radiant, and it's not just the cold air."

"Welcome, everyone. Now the party can really start. You all know where the food is, however, I must warn you, the dinner menu is rather spectacular if I do say so myself."

"Mary, everything is so beautiful. I love the bayberry mixed with pine. It's such a clean smell. Especially when it's mixed in with whatever those herbs and spices you are cooking with, Mary."

"I can tell you I am really going to miss all of this. I feel quite pampered, and it's not me that's getting married."

"Well, Betts, I wouldn't be surprised if you were the next one to surprise us with such good tidings."

"Mary, you are the funny one. I am truly like the rolling stone. I gather no moss. Well, that's not entirely true. I do gather moss occasionally, but only for a very good reason. Anyhow, one wedding in this family is enough for some time. Now, Kara, Jamie, shall we find the best gamers and joint them?"

"Yes, let's do, Auntie Betts. However, since we are the best gamers, we won't have to look far, right?"

"Yes, Kara, my dear, you are right on."

"Whatever, anyhow, let's go play and have fun."

"That's right, Jamie, and that's really what it's all about."

"Maggie, my love, the dinner gong will sound in minutes. Kevin is gathering the others. He has given me my instructions. We are to wait for ten minutes after the gong. Mary was very specific about the timing. We have a family table in the front, and we are to be the last ones in. You and I are in the middle or sort of. Auntie Betts sits to your right with Kara and Jamie on the end and Mary Beth to my left and Kevin beside her. Howdy will choose his own spot as usual. It was also my responsibility to keep you out of the dining room until dinnertime. Fortunately you made that very easy. Mary and her crew want this to be the special event that it is destined to be."

"Richard I love all of these folks so much. I feel like I am in a cocoon of love. I know I have said that before, but I don't know how to express it better. Everything is absolutely perfect, and I am so grateful."

"There is the gong, and what a beautiful sound it makes, I don't know about you, Maggie, but I am suddenly very hungry."

"So am I, Rich, however, my gown fits quite well, so if I eat too much, we will have to dance until ceremony time."

"Then, so we shall, my darling, soon-to-be wife. Eat, drink, and be merry. Kevin, I see your task is done. Everyone is here and ready to proceed. Maggie, my love, prepare to be impressed."

"Richard, I am impressed. This room is enchanting. The table looks like it is set for the royal family. Crystal, silver, china, holly and holly berries, candles, the food and music. I do feel like a princess, Richard, or perhaps a queen, as I am escorted by a king."

"That you are, my lady, and your throne."

"Everyone is still standing, Rich."

"When you sit, then everyone else will."

"I have the distinct honor of presenting the first toast to this wonderful couple that needs no introduction. Margaret and Richard, may you travel gracefully together, supporting, strengthening, honoring, and loving one another. May your journey be joyful and filled with the harmonizing power of the universe. To Maggie and Richard!"

"Thank you, Auntie Betts, and to all of you, my dear community family, and a very special thank you to Mary and everyone that prepared this elegant presentation of food and beauty."

"You are most welcome, my dears, and I truly mean it when I say it was a pleasure, and now I strongly suggest that we stop admiring it and start eating it. Enjoy."

"Richard, I am so happy for you and Maggie. Honestly, when you told me you were getting married, Kevin and I were concerned about you. It had happened so fast, and well, you had some pretty dark times, you know. However, once we arrived, almost immediately all concerns vanished. Now we, as a family, have fallen under the spell of contentment and love. We are so grateful that you are sharing all of this with us. We love you so very much, my brother."

"Thank you, Sis, it never occurred to me that you would relocate, honestly. I did not have an ulterior motive other than I longed to be with all of you and feel the love that we have always shared, and Maggie wanted a sister, so in a way, you are a wedding gift. Really, I believe the move will be a great change for all of you, and I know it will be for us, and thank you so much for being here tonight."

"Rich, I think I know why Kevin and I decided to move here. We were in town, and the kids wanted to go explore by themselves, and without any hesitation, Kev and I both said fine, meet you back here in an hour. There was no fear. The love in this community has replaced fear. We live in a nice community, as you know, but fear has replaced so much that we used to take for granted. We have vandalism and speeding even on our quiet little street. At school, I see the number of angry youth and parents increasing every year. Coming here and experiencing an absence of anger is so refreshing. I want to return as soon as possible, and so do Jamie and Kara. I apologize for dominating you for so long. This evening belongs to you and Maggie. However, this may be the only opportunity to share these thoughts with you. We will be leaving tomorrow, but it does not seem like we are going home. It's more like we're leaving home."

"Thank you, Mary Beth, and I do truly understand what you're saying. As a matter of fact, I looked for the police department during my first few days here. I honestly haven't thought about it since. We are indeed blessed."

✳

"Maggie, you smell so good."

"Rich, I do believe you are smelling dessert, however, I will take credit for it. Thank you, darling. I feel quite lazy, so relaxed, that's a better description. The food tastes as good as it looks. Mary and her crew make everything look so easy. The serving folks were always anticipating everyone's next request. Now I think we are all about ready to nod off. Richard, people may sleep through our wedding!"

"Oh no, Maggie. Aunt Betts has a plan to liven things up in just a few minutes. Actually, when you and I have finished our dessert and coffee, that will be her cue, and she will get folks up and moving about. No one is going to sleep through our ceremony, Maggie, after we created our masterpiece to share with everyone."

"What's next, Uncle Richard? I feel like we are in a castle, and maybe there will be a court jester or something like that."

"I like the way you think, Kara. You have a great imagination, and I think you are going to be a writer or an actress, or perhaps both, and more."

"Thanks, Uncle Richard, but I think your imagination may be working over time. Anyhow, you didn't answer my question."

"Quite right and possibly because I don't know the answer, Kara. I am just here as a groom. Aunt Betts is really the coordinator, so you know that whatever it is will be fantastic, and I believe we are going to find out right now. She is standing, so I think we had better be quite and listen."

"What a glorious way to spend a New Year's Eve. A royal feast and gathering place warmed by the presence of every one of you. We are so grateful for all of the beauty that surrounds us. I want to share with you a general program for the evening. I believe everyone will be ready to get up and move around for a few minutes so that will be the next thing to do. Then Maggie and Richard have requested a few songs that I am so happy to share with all of you. So please return to your places here in about fifteen to twenty minutes. Mary has assured me that it will not take longer than that for the room to be transformed into a parlor, or sort of a parlor. After the music, and giving the food time to digest a bit, we will gather in the great room for dancing. Then Maggie and Richard's wedding ceremony will be in this room. I am told that the room will be ready at 11:15 p.m. Again, Mary and the mighty crew will create yet another transformation. Following this ceremony will be another major event. Midnight with champagne, cider, and fireworks. After that, you're on your own. Oh yes, the cake-cutting, we mustn't forget that. I haven't seen it yet, but I hear that it is spectacular. So get up, move around, but return in twenty minutes."

"Thank you, Betts, you look fresh as a daisy. We are looking forward to your music. It means a lot to us."

"Thank you, Rich and Maggie. I do sincerely mean it when I say it is my great pleasure, and the music you have chosen also happens to be favorites of mine. Now we had best move out of the way, the carts are on the way. Clean up has begun."

"Maggie, we are being photographed. Shall we do something?"

"Yes, Rich, exactly what we are doing, holding hands, and looking at Howdy sleeping so peacefully in his bed by the fireplace. We don't typically do staged photography. It's all candid. However, I don't think we even discussed photography, Rich. Would you like some formal photos?"

"No, Maggie. I love the idea of candid photography. It sounds like a lot of fun."

"Good. I'm glad you approve. There are three photographers, although they are so good they're seldom noticed. The three of them get together and create a combination of photo-video-music DVD, and we have a movie preview here. We chose the date and time."

"Maggie, that is fantastic, and I'm betting there's a potluck that goes with the evening."

"You are absolutely right Rich."

✳

"I am looking forward to Betts's performance. She is an amazing lady with such diverse talent. All of that, and she is so much fun to just be around."

"Speaking of her performance, I hear piano music, Rich. I think we have somewhere to be."

"Yes, and I was responsible for getting us there, so let's do it."

"Maggie, again we have assigned seating and this time, the rest of the family arrived before us."

"Which makes it very easy to see where we are going to sit."

"Yes, in those two very lovely comfortable chairs with all of the cushions. I'm not familiar with this piano piece, but it is lovely."

"It's an original piece that Auntie Betts composed, and she knows how much I love it, Rich."

"Auntie Betts, thank you so much. That was lovely."

"Yes, Betts, you are indeed a very talented lady, and I am sure I honestly have no idea just now talented you really are. However, I am hopeful that you will be in Galapagos while we are there, and we can explore more treasure hunting."

"Rich, I can promise you I will try to arrange my commitments to accommodate the time."

"Auntie Betts, you tell us what time will work for you, and we will arrange to be there during that time. I want to share the island with you. It has been a part of your life for so long, and I've heard you and mom talk about it so often that it feels very familiar to me. Thank you again for this opportunity. Rich and I will be ready the minute you say the word."

"Wonderful plan, Maggie, and I can tell you it will be approximately three weeks from now, and I should be able to call you next week and make a definite date. Now, you two are going to be the first to dance, and

I have the band warming up, so I suggest we go in there and liven things up a bit."

"Maggie and Rich, don't be concerned about time. Mary Beth is going to let you know when it's time for you to turn into Cinderella, and Kevin is in charge of you, Rich, so go out there and show us what you've got."

"Richard, you really are a good dancer. You make me feel like I am Ginger Rogers or something like that."

"Maggie, you are like a feather flowing with the air. Except in this case, it's the music. This really is fun I can feel the music. I mean literally. You and I will be married very soon, Maggie, and this evening has already been so spectacular. I should not have written a prescription this great."

"I know, Rich. I am relaxed, elated, and, in general, I feel so complete and content."

"Maggie, may I have this dance please?"

"Yes, Kevin, I would be honored."

"Well, Sis, I guess you get me. Lucky you."

"Actually, yes, Rich, it is lucky for me to have a brother like you. You are a pretty nice guy and a very good dancer."

"Thank you, my dear. We haven't danced together since high school, have we?"

"I don't think so, and that was a disaster. Do you remember my then boyfriend actually dumped me almost literally at the dance? His old girlfriend cut in and away they went. Thank you, my dear brother, you made sure I danced with almost every boy there. Thank you again."

"Mary Beth, I was so angry with him that I wanted to punch him out, but somehow I didn't think that would work out well for either one of us, and here we are in paradise. Here comes Kevin. I think it is time for Maggie and me to go turn into pumpkins or princes or something like that. I can hardly wait to see her in the gown, and stuff, you know what I mean."

"Yes, Rich. I know what you mean, and I get the honor of assisting my new sister with all of the mysteries of preparation. So I will see you later, Bro."

*

"Auntie Betts, your voice is fantastic and the way you play the piano. I practice a lot actually, but I know I could never be that good."

"Now, Kara. Never say never, and I would suggest that you don't compare yourself to anyone else. Play the piano for the joy that it brings to you, and that will be your reward."

"Thank you, Auntie Betts, I am going to miss you a lot, and you know what else I am going to miss a lot?"

"What would that be, Kara?"

"The chimes in the morning and evening. They are so beautiful. Why do they ring, Auntie Betts?

"Kara, they have been doing that for about a hundred and forty years, and do you know what? I never take them for granted, and I am so glad that you have noticed. The chimes sound at daybreak and sunset and they do that to remind us to greet the day with gratitude, and to end the day the same way. Really what it does for me, even if I'm kind of asleep in the morning, it still puts me in touch with the oneness of everything. I am so happy that you responded to the chimes, and yes, they are lovely, and so are you my young lady. You look like you are going to a wedding or something. You are beautiful, Kara, inside and out."

"Thank you, Auntie Betts. Is it about time for the wedding?"

"Just about, another ten to fifteen minutes. I think it's time for us to go hand out the candles, Kara, and Jamie is going to help us do that, I believe?"

"Yes, he is, and here he comes. Jamie, my lad, just on time and so handsome."

"Actually, I don't mind wearing this tie. It's comfortable and easy to put on. It snaps on, Kara, and you have several choices of snapping. I really like it."

"That is a first, Jamie. All I have ever heard was can I take this thing off now!"

"This is really different. I like it."

"OK, young ones, let's hand out the candles. Actually you two are going to do that. I will be playing the piano, until it's time for me to escort Maggie down the aisle, and you know after the ceremony, Richard and Maggie will light their candles from the big candle, that's when you Jamie light your candle from Richard's, and Kara the same thing from Maggie's, then all you do is light the first candle of the aisle, each aisle. Everyone will light their neighbor's candle. As soon as all candles are glowing, Richard and Maggie will join the group and then will officially be married. We'll have a moment of quiet, blow out the candles, and then you grab the baskets and quickly pick up all of the candles and return as soon as you can because Mary will have trays of cider and champagne passed out and the bride and groom will cut the cake."

"Is that when the fireworks start, Auntie Betts?"

"Pretty close, Jamie. It is all going to be so beautiful, and a new year will be born."

"Maggie, you truly do look like an angel, and whoever did your headpiece created a piece of art. The holly berries and the baby's breath with the greenery is perfect. Your gown is beautiful and so are you."

"Thank you, Mary Beth. We are going to enjoy so many wonderful adventures together, and I am sincere when I say I have always wanted a sister."

"Well, so have I, Maggie. It took a while, but here we are. I hear Auntie Betts playing the piano. That's our cue. It almost seems like a dream. Everything is so perfect. Maggie, everyone is seated, and we are ready for the bride, and you are positively glowing."

"Thank you, Auntie Betts, and the bride is ready to greet the groom. Let's go. Oh, but where is Howdy?"

"He is already out there, Maggie. He is right beside Richard. It's like he knows he is the best man. Kevin is there also, but Howdy is alert and ready to participate."

"I am so glad, Auntie Betts. Now let's go."

"The choir is singing 'Ave Maria a capella'. It is so beautiful. I can imagine we are in a very sacred beautiful cathedral."

"Well, then, my dear Maggie, that is exactly where we are."

"Richard is so handsome, Auntie Betts, and he is even a better person than he is handsome."

"Maybe for right now stick with the handsome part, Maggie. This is your wedding night, you know."

"Oh yes, I know."

"I welcome you and yours into our family, Richard, from this day forward."

Richard takes Maggie's hand and the ceremony beings with Maggie sharing the vows that she has written first, then Richard. The community elder and licensed minister, and Maggie's godfather proclaims the merging of their lives together with few words. Mary Beth and Kevin light the large center candle symbolizing the family borne of their new marriage. Auntie Betts sings while all of the candles are being lit by Jamie and Kara. There is circle after circle formed, with Rich and Maggie and Howdy in the middle of the inner circle, being supported and loved by the energy surrounding them. Mary and helpers had champagne and cider served to everyone, and as if by magic, the clock struck twelve. The candles were extinguished, and Aunt Betts started 'Auld Lang Syne' as the fireworks began.

"Maggie, you are so beautiful. I am so honored to have you as my wife, my friend, mentor, and the mother of my child. I love you."

"Rich, I still feel like I'm in a fairy tale. Everything is so beautiful and has been so effortless. Perhaps I should say everything has been flawless. I know so many people did so much to achieve such perfection. Rich, I am humbled by the great privilege of carrying our child. What a magnificent way to start out our new year. Now, I do believe Mary will be bringing out the cake. I see the trays of drinks prepared. It will be so beautiful, Rich, and I know it will be as good to eat as it is beautiful to look at."

"Are we supposed to cut it, Maggie?"

"Only the first two pieces—mine and yours—then Mary Beth, Kevin, Kara, and Jamie are in charge. They were so sincere and serious about the candle-lighting, and it was so beautiful. Yes, Rich, here it comes, and Auntie Betts just did a drumroll."

"That lady has enough energy to fill a mountain."

"Rich, you should have known her twenty years ago."

"I wouldn't have been ready then, Maggie, and you are right again, that is the best cake creation I have ever seen."

"Uncle Rich, Aunt Maggie, this was the best wedding. It is like a storybook fantasy."

"Yes, and the fireworks were the best ever."

"Yes, Jamie, they were beautiful, but everything else was so grand. I will never ever forget it, and I don't think my friends will ever believe me. How could they?"

"Well, darlin girl, some things just belong to us individually. It's wonderful to share, and I encourage you to do so. However, I am quite sure when I see a rainbow I would not be able to share what I felt or probably not even what I saw. We all see and feel things that belong only to us, so savor those moments, Kara. Remember the treasure chest of memories."

"Yes, Auntie Betts, and you will always be right on top, so I can pull you out all of the time."

"Thank you, Kara, by the way, you two did a splendid job of candle-lighting, cake serving, and making sure Howdy was not neglected, and you both look very spry. It's another year already. Actually, it's the next day. The more I think about it, the more I realize that I am really tired."

"We heard that, Auntie Betts, and you know what? So are we. As a matter of fact, we were looking for all of you to see if maybe we could go home. We don't really need to stay, do we, Aunt Betts?"

"No, you two are expected to disappear. I mean this was your wedding and the bride and groom are expected to have better things to do than hang around here."

"Wonderful because we really are ready to go home. Jamie, do you know where your mom and dad are?"

"I think so. Anyhow, I know I can find them. We'll be right back."

"Thank you. We will be right here."

✳

"Thank you, all of you, for sharing such a special time with us."

"Maggie, I know I can speak for all of us. The entire evening was truly magical. This day will be alive in our memories forever. Thank you, we love you so much, but now we are going to say good night or rather good morning. We will see you folks at about 10:00 a.m., and fortunately, we are all packed and ready to go except for the last-minute stuff, so until then Mr. and Mrs. Scott-King, we will be on our way."

"Well, Auntie Betts, you can sleep in this morning. Goodness knows you deserve it. You were everywhere, doing everything seemingly at the same time. Bless you."

"Maggie and I have this brunch thing already prepared at least for the most part, and I would be honored to bring you your morning coffee."

"Rich, I am definitely ready for bed, however, I think I recover by morning. We'll see, and thank you for the suggestion. And now, my dear ones, I am off to bed, and Howdy, bless his heart, has already passed out."

"Good night, Auntie Betts. We love you."

"My dear wife, Maggie, shall I carry you up the stairs, since I didn't carry you over the threshold, wherever that is?"

"Thank you, darling, but no, thank you, darling. Although I am definitely ready to go up these stairs, shall we, Mr. Scott-King?"

"Am I really Mr. Scott-King, Maggie?"

"I don't know, darling, but I do know that we are the same people tonight that we were this morning, and I know that when you kiss me like that, I feel like I am transported to another dimension. And that's a good thing."

"Then maybe, I should do it again."

"Oh yes, Rich, but first, please help me out of this dress. I love it, but it's definitely time for it to come off. Thank you, darling, now I can take a deep breath, and we can pick up where you left off."

"Maggie, I love you."

"I know you do, Rich, and I am so happy. My wonderful husband come to bed. I promise your place here beside me is quite warm."

"Oh, Maggie—."

∗

"Good morning, Howdy. We certainly had a very full day and evening, didn't we? Did Richard send you up here to get me out of bed? I really do think you are just going to have to learn how to bring my coffee up here with you. I love you, Howdy."

"Good morning, sunshine, did I hear you complaining about not having your coffee?"

"Good morning, darling, and thank you so very much for bringing my coffee up to me."

"It is my pleasure, especially this morning. Everything seems special. Good job, Howdy. You almost got her going."

"Richard, what time is it?"

"It's a little after nine, darling. We are fine. I have started everything that needed to be cooked, so take your time, enjoy your coffee, and I'll see you downstairs when you're ready."

"Rich, is Auntie Betts up yet?"

"Nope. I haven't heard her stirring about, but I'm sure she'll be down soon."

"I'm so glad, she's going to be with us this evening, and she doesn't leave until early afternoon tomorrow, and we will have no commitments.

Just catch our breath, deep breaths. Relax and enjoy. No fancy dinners or anything. Is that all right with you, Rich?"

"Better than all right. She promised me at least a little information on Galapagos. I do hope we will have time for that."

"Oh yes, that will be wonderful, but for now, brunch and family time, off with you and I will be down in a jiffy."

"Good morning, Richard."

"And a good morning to you, Betts. I trust you slept well because you look totally resurrected to me."

"I'm not quite sure if I like the resurrected part, Rich, but thank you anyhow, and actually you could say anything to me, and I would like it as long as you followed up with a cup of your most delightful coffee."

"Thank you, sir, and I'm really serious about the coffee. I know I brought it with me, but I don't mind telling you that it never tasted this good before. I do hope I have the formula down."

"I'm sure you do, Betts. You've made it several times, and Maggie thought I had made it, so obviously, you've got it."

"Well, I know I will miss you folks and my wonderful extended community family. However, from past experiences, I also know that I will be so immersed in the project and living in the moment, that I will be doing just that."

"That is wonderful, Betts, and I am getting better at it all the time. You are a great inspiration. Thank you. I love you very much."

"Thank you, Richard. You have made the circle complete."

"Good morning, Maggie, my love, you look radiant."

"Morning, Auntie Betts, thank you, and I can honestly return the compliment."

"Yes, I am surrounded by brilliant rays of sunshine. Good morning again, darling. It smells wonderful, Richard, whatever you have prepared it is delicious, and how can we help?"

"Well, since it is 9:45 a.m. and I expect a lot of energy to come through that door any moment, if you would be willing to get the tableware and napkins out and sent the juice and fruit on the buffet, I think everything else is pretty much ready."

"Everything looks and smells heavenly, Rich. Thank you. Oh and do you want me to go to the airport with you?"

"No, darling, well that didn't come out right. I am always delighted to have you with me, and you are absolutely welcome. However, I think it would be fine if you chose to stay here and have some teatime with Betts."

"Thank you, Rich, and yes, I will do just that."

"And there they are just as the clock strikes ten. Good morning, everyone."

"We are so hungry, and I think I could smell food all the way down to the cottage. Mom and Dad couldn't, but I think Jamie could. Anyhow, we are here and hungry."

"Welcome, one and all, I think you know your way around here. It's buffet-style again. Your chairs and serving tables are all set up by the fireplace, and Howdy has, of course, claimed his spot already."

"Thank you, Uncle Richard. I, for one, will not mind being first, unless this is an elders' first time."

"Speaking as the senior elder, Kara, I say each person is on their own, so go for it."

"Mary Beth, you look rested and ready. Isn't it wonderful what a good night's sleep can do?

"Yes, Maggie, and I can certainly return the compliment. You are still glowing. What an indescribably wonderful wedding. I know I can never share the essence of the evening with anyone that wasn't there to share it, but that's fine. I know I will always feel that bond. Truly, I really do feel as though the ceremony was for all of us. That sounds a bit presumptuous, doesn't it?"

"No! Mary Beth, you are absolutely right, and I am so glad that you felt included because you were. The part about the community acceptance and support, that is such a vital part of the vows and so important to both Rich and I."

"Kevin and I have an anniversary next fall, and we have decided we want to have an anniversary recommitment of our vows."

"Sis, that is beautiful and what a great way to embrace and be embraced by the community."

"Thank you, Richard, and also thank you again for this beautiful brunch masterpiece. It truly is as good as it looks."

"Yes, Kevin, this is a new breakfast casserole, and Maggie has the recipe card ready for your book."

"Man, I am too predictable, and yes, you are right on, Brother Rich. We have all obviously enjoyed each and every moment of our time here with you, and this community that has embraced us so warmly, and well, that's enough. You all know what I mean."

"Yes, we do, Kev. Now, Jamie, would you be willing to refill the coffee cups for us please?"

"You bet, Uncle Richard."

✳

"My goodness, it is quiet in here, Maggie, and this room seems so large with only the three of us here."

"Yes, it really does, Betts, and yet, Howdy and I have lived here for so long, and somehow, it just seems to expand when folks are here, and then it's just right for the two of us."

"Oh, Maggie, love, it's not just the two of you anymore, and soon, it won't even be just the three of you. This house has a lot of adjusting to do."

"Yes, and you are absolutely right, Aunt Betts. It's not just the house that will be adjusting. I am not feeling like a mother, Aunt Betts. I'm a little confused. I certainly am happy that we are having a child, but I guess I don't know what I'm supposed to feel like. Yes, I'm a bit confused."

"Maggie, child, you will get back into your routine, and as you do your meditation, everything will become clear and calm. Give yourself time to develop and enjoy your new partnership. Just focus on a moment at a time, remember."

"Auntie Betts, you always say exactly what I am ready to hear. Thank you. I know you are right. I am really going to miss you, you know that, don't you?"

"I do know that, Maggie because it's reciprocal. However, I also know us, and we will turn the next page of life and embrace it fully and so it is. Now, now my dear girl, I am going to fix us a special pot of tea, and we will join Howdy by the fireplace and just watch the logs burn. How does that sound? Exciting enough for you?"

"You know, Auntie Betts, it really is."

"There truly is something golden about silence. In its own way, it's like taking a shower from the inside out. That may not make any sense at all, Aunt Betts."

"It does to me, Maggie. When I'm quiet is when I feel the presence of the spirit, and I become so focused. I think that's why I enjoy Galapagos so much. It's really very quiet. You can hear the birds and other nature sounds, but it's really very quiet, and you know what, I need to be very quiet about Galapagos right now. I promised Richard we would discuss it tonight."

"Yes, he is really excited about our trip and so am I, Aunt Betts. I don't miss work at all. I am somewhat confused about it. Mom was always so exuberant about the library, as I have been until recently. I love the work and people. I just don't feel motivated."

"Maggie, my darling, we have just come through a Christmas season, lots of stimulation, company, celebrations, a new pregnancy, and husband. And oh yes, by the way, your mom took a six-month leave after you were born, and she wasn't at all sure that she would ever return. As the time passed and it was decision time, she was ready to return a couple of days a week. Your dad took care of you, and he loved it. So gradually, she returned to three, then four days a week, which is how she continued. So what I am saying again is, give yourself some space and let life flow, as there are no wrong directions. You are fine, Maggie. Just be."

"I love you so much, Auntie Betts, and I hope you don't mind, but I always feel so close to my mother when you are around, and that's a good thing."

"I take that as a real compliment, Maggie, and Richard is back. My, the time has flown, as time will."

*

"Welcome back, darling. Apparently, the plane was on schedule."

"Yes, the roads were clear, and the flight was on time. We had time to have a cup of hot chocolate and visit for a while. They are definitely committed to returning. Kev and Mary Beth said to tell you how grateful they are for the cottage offer, and they forgot to discuss buying land from you for them to build on. It was mentioned, but fortunately, I could honestly say I really didn't know anything about the land."

"There really is not much to discuss. There are no restrictions on building, as long as you have ample water supply, which we do, and a waste-management system. As a courtesy, we will go to the council and present our plan. If they have suggestions, they would be very good ones, and as far as buying, there is no land for sale. This acreage has been in the family for five generations, and they are family. I will write a letter clarifying questions."

"Thank you, darling. Betts, did you create a magic potion in the kitchen?"

"Maybe I did, Rich. Why do you think Aunt Betts has slaved over a hot stove?"

"Honestly, Maggie, it just smells like Betts."

"Richard, I heard that and I'm not sure I'm flattered because I threw a wide variety of leftovers in the pot and just let them simmer. Now that I think about it, you are absolutely right. I am flattered that you think I am so versatile and spicy."

"He is right, Auntie Betts. The smell is pungent, sweet, and some indefinable subtle aromas, and I never even really noticed you doing it. I must have dozed while you were busy cooking."

"Trust me, Maggie, it is a bunch of leftovers in a tomato sauce with a few spices thrown in."

"I don't intend to rush you, Betts, but I can tell you, I am ready to eat anytime you are. How about you Maggie?"

"Just tell us when and what we can do to help, and yes, Rich, I'm ready anytime."

"Dinner was as good as it smelled, Betts. Thank you."

"You are very welcome, Rich. After a bit, I thought we would have our dessert and hot drink in by the fireplace, and perhaps you'll have some questions about Galapagos, Richard."

"No, perhaps about it. I want to know so much, and our time is so short."

"Then we had best get on with it, so everyone get comfortable."

"Rich and I will bring the dessert and drinks, but you get comfortable, Auntie Betts. Just look at Howdy. He is the epitome of comfort."

"That he is. He is a fine model of relaxation."

"Thank you, Rich. Now tell me what's on your mind?"

"Betts, I am in love with the idea. I have created a fantasy about Galapagos, but few facts. I am interested in your impression. I don't expect you to give me a scientific profile, although I'm sure you could."

"Maggie, do you have any specific questions?"

"Not really, Aunt Betts, I just remember you and mom talking about the birds and beauty. Richard and I have always had a longing to go there, probably because of the way you look when you talk about it. I just know it is very special. So we are a couple of sponges, Auntie Betts, and yet, I know you will only give us a teaser because you like people to do their own discoveries. So share with us what you will, and soon we will be creating our own adventures there."

"Maggie, my love, you do know me quite well. I am pleased to say. My first suggestion is to encourage you not to set a definite return date. We can always do that once you are there. You must be aware, however, of a potential hazard. I fell under the spell of the Galapagos immediately. I could feel the presence of Darwin, and understood at least in part the basis for his theory. It is totally captivating, you become part of nature. Surrounding the islands is a melting pot of marine species, marine Iguanas are found only on the Galapagos Islands. Snorkeling is a must. However, someone needs to be your monitor. I know I was completely absorbed by the absolute acceptance of the marine life. Sea turtles, schools of fish that are indescribable, dolphins, whales and so forth. Anyhow the first time I went snorkeling, I completely lost all sense of time and place. My watcher had to practically drag me out of the water. I'm not much better now. There are also the giant tortoises on land. Everything has innocence about it, even the birds, and there are so many of them. One of my favorites are the salmon-pink flamingos. They do this beautiful ballet. I can hear the music, which is created by the winds."

"Are there a lot of tourists, Betts?"

"Truly one is too many. I realize that is hypocritical, since I am one, but yes, people are a threat. Fortunately, there are efforts to protect the islands. In 1986, there was a law passed to control fishing and over-exploitation of Galapagos marine resources, and in 1998, that law was strengthened to include conservation and sustainable development. Tourism is regulated, however, approximately 170,000 tourists visit the islands each year. Thirty thousand of us live on the islands. So yes, there is a lot of damage done by humans. The place is a living museum, so ideally we should not be there.

"Richard and Maggie, you are the first people I have ever invited to the islands. Other than the research teams, I actually don't invite them. I believe both of you will make a positive difference to the islands. Richard, I am sure that you will write something of significance, and Maggie, I am equally sure that you will create an amazing book of poetry, and who knows what else? I am very pleased that we will share this experience, and oh yes, we will have an adventure."

"Betts, thank you so much. I am humbled and grateful for the opportunity, not only to experience the islands but to share those times with you and Maggie. It is such an honor."

"Thank you, Richard."

"Auntie Betts, thank you for sharing so much with us tonight. You are appreciated."

"I know, Maggie. This community, you, and Richard are my Galapagos on this side of the world."

"That, my dear lady, is a real compliment. May I get you something more to eat or drink?"

"No, thank you, Richard. I have a few things to do tonight. One of which is to get into that wonderful soaking tub, so, Maggie, when you go to bed, you might just check to see if my head is still above water. Just joking, Richard. I'll see you two in the morning. Sorry, Howdy, you're right, you three. Good night, all."

"Thank you, Auntie Betts. We are in love with Galapagos for sure."

"Richard, the silence is deafening. I have often heard that said and truly never understood it until tonight with only the noise from the fire burning and Howdy's breathing. So much has happened in such a short time. I am so excited about our trip to Galapagos, and at the same time, I am looking forward to getting back to work and our routine beautiful life."

"Maggie, my love, I am living 'in the moment' more often each day because each moment is so full of love and wonder. I think I know what you mean about routine and the beauty and security of it, and I love that part of life as well, and then there are the unexplored parts of life, such as Galapagos, which I trust will enlarge our lives, and make us even better parents, because we will just naturally have more to offer our child, or children. So as a very wise woman (once or twice) told me, take a deep breath. Breathe in life and exhale, love one moment at a time, fully engage in life and love."

"Richard, I love you, and now I am ready for that comfortable warm cozy bed that seems to be calling my name. Would you like to join me in that adventure?"

"Funny, you should ask, I am hearing that same call."

$$*$$

"Good morning, Maggie, my love."

"Good morning, Richard. I have been thinking about getting up, but then I guess I just went back to sleep. However, now that I smell the coffee, I am for sure wide awake, and I really don't want to miss another moment of Auntie Betts's time with us. So thank you, my love for the delightful awakening. Is Aunt Betts up yet?"

"Not yet, darling, but I have the Dutch babies in the oven, along with those wonderful spiced apples you canned. The aromas should be making their way up the stairs any moment now, and I know that will create action."

"It already has with me, darling. I'll be right down. See you in a few minutes."

"Great timing, Maggie, I just heard Betts's door open. See you downstairs."

"Good morning, Betts. I see you found the coffee."

"Oh yes, no challenge at all."

"Did you rest well?"

"Always do, Richard. I swear I think I go to sleep, before I go to bed."

"I want to thank you again, Betts, for sharing Galapagos with Maggie and me. We do hold it sacred. I actually always have, however, last night, listening to you, and the depth of your passion, I will absolutely tread lightly through the territory."

"Thank you, Richard. I made a call this morning, and confirmed the project's schedule, and it is perfect. I can return to Galapagos in three weeks, and then I intend to be there for at least two months. So Maggie can check her schedule and let me know what works for you, folks, and we will have a firm time set. Richard, I am so happy that you two are coming to my island.

Good morning to you Maggie, your timing is perfect. Richard is just taking the Dutch baby out of the oven. Doesn't it smell heavenly?"

"Yes, it does, Auntie Betts and good morning to you. Richard, you are amazing, you have prepared everything, and what a beautiful centerpiece."

"Please be seated, ladies. I am at your service."

"That was delightful, Richard. Thank you again."

"Betts, you are indeed a joy to know. You will be missed, and yet your presence will linger in so many ways. Thank you so much for, well, honestly, just being you with my family. Especially Kara and Jamie, they are absolutely full of questions."

"Their questions were great, Richard. They truly are open to learning and listening. A lot of folks, not just youth either, ask questions because they can't think of anything else to say, and then when you answer them, they don't hear what you're saying because they are busy trying to think of another question. That kind of behavior makes me very tired. When Kara and Jamie are questioning, they really want to learn. They are open at the top, and ready to receive. They are a source of joy and positive energy much like their uncle."

"Thank you, Betts, would you like some more coffee or anything?"

"No, thank you, Richard, I am completely satisfied in every way. Maggie, my dear girl, this entire trip has been a blessing to me. I am so grateful that I listened to that small but strong voice that is always there to guide me, and this time, I listened and called you. I know as soon as we started to talk that this is where I was to spend the holidays, and of course be a part of the wedding, which by the way was absolutely perfect."

"Auntie Betts, believe me when I say it would not have been complete without you."

"Do you need help with anything, Betts, suitcases or boxes?"

"I will, Richard. Thank you. I have some more gathering to do, and then I will definitely accept your offer. Those stairs grow more every day, it seems."

"What is your schedule today, Aunt Betts, and is there anything I can do to help?"

"I would like to leave by two o'clock, Maggie. I plan to drive until about eight o'clock this evening, and no, thank you, darling, I really don't have much to do. I would like to go to the pharmacy in town for lunch before I leave. Could I talk you two into joining me?"

"Absolutely, Betts, we would be delighted. Just give me a yell when you're ready for the luggage to be moved."

"Will do, Rich, and now, I am going to go do what I need to do. I will see you two shortly. Oh yes, Howdy, you too, and you may come upstairs with me, if you'd like. I know I would certainly like your company."

"Howdy really bounded up those stairs, Rich. He is rejuvenated, it's amazing."

"I think some of it is adrenaline, Maggie. We shouldn't be too surprised if he needs to rest a lot for the next few days."

"No kidding, Rich, and you shouldn't be surprised if I am right there beside him."

"You have a point, Maggie. All three of us will just hibernate for a while."

"That sounds really good to me. We have leftovers enough for several days, and lots of great tea, and wood for the fireplace. I think we have a plan."

"I like it, Maggie."

"Everything has found its place in your car, Betts, and there's plenty of room left. So you can pick up treasures as you find them along the way."

"Thank you, Richard, and I am sure, with five hundred miles ahead of me, I shall find many treasures, although plane travel has forced me to adjust my needs. So therefore, I shall also distribute treasures along the way and that's the joy of it. Shall we meet at the pharmacy? I have a couple of very short stops to make, so I will be there in about thirty minutes. Will that work for you two?"

"Perfect, Auntie Betts, we will see you there then."

"Auntie Betts had a grand send off from the folks at the pharmacy, so much love from so many."

"Yes, and the food was good too. What a delightful lady Betts is, Maggie. I would have loved your mother. I can imagine both of them and how dynamic they were together. Betts shared a few of the family gems as she called them, and I am absolutely sure that's exactly what they were. I think we are probably two of the most fortunate people in the world to have one another, to share Howdy, this unique community, and to have such wonderful family members supporting us. Wow!"

"Yes, Richard, I believe you are right again, and I think Howdy is suggesting that it may be time to go home, Rich, and you know what, as usual, I think he is right."

"I agree, Maggie."

"Although you know, it is going to be very quiet there."

"Not for long, my dear one. There are actually four of us, and yes, one is rather quiet right now, but its presence is profound. We are a family, Maggie, ready to write a new page in our book of life every day."

"So we shall, Richard."